AF166360

Communications
in Computer and Information Science 2331

Series Editors

Gang Li ⓘ, *School of Information Technology, Deakin University, Burwood, VIC, Australia*
Joaquim Filipe ⓘ, *Polytechnic Institute of Setúbal, Setúbal, Portugal*
Zhiwei Xu, *Chinese Academy of Sciences, Beijing, China*

Rationale

The CCIS series is devoted to the publication of proceedings of computer science conferences. Its aim is to efficiently disseminate original research results in informatics in printed and electronic form. While the focus is on publication of peer-reviewed full papers presenting mature work, inclusion of reviewed short papers reporting on work in progress is welcome, too. Besides globally relevant meetings with internationally representative program committees guaranteeing a strict peer-reviewing and paper selection process, conferences run by societies or of high regional or national relevance are also considered for publication.

Topics

The topical scope of CCIS spans the entire spectrum of informatics ranging from foundational topics in the theory of computing to information and communications science and technology and a broad variety of interdisciplinary application fields.

Information for Volume Editors and Authors

Publication in CCIS is free of charge. No royalties are paid, however, we offer registered conference participants temporary free access to the online version of the conference proceedings on SpringerLink (http://link.springer.com) by means of an http referrer from the conference website and/or a number of complimentary printed copies, as specified in the official acceptance email of the event.

CCIS proceedings can be published in time for distribution at conferences or as post-proceedings, and delivered in the form of printed books and/or electronically as USBs and/or e-content licenses for accessing proceedings at SpringerLink. Furthermore, CCIS proceedings are included in the CCIS electronic book series hosted in the SpringerLink digital library at http://link.springer.com/bookseries/7899. Conferences publishing in CCIS are allowed to use Online Conference Service (OCS) for managing the whole proceedings lifecycle (from submission and reviewing to preparing for publication) free of charge.

Publication process

The language of publication is exclusively English. Authors publishing in CCIS have to sign the Springer CCIS copyright transfer form, however, they are free to use their material published in CCIS for substantially changed, more elaborate subsequent publications elsewhere. For the preparation of the camera-ready papers/files, authors have to strictly adhere to the Springer CCIS Authors' Instructions and are strongly encouraged to use the CCIS LaTeX style files or templates.

Abstracting/Indexing

CCIS is abstracted/indexed in DBLP, Google Scholar, EI-Compendex, Mathematical Reviews, SCImago, Scopus. CCIS volumes are also submitted for the inclusion in ISI Proceedings.

How to start

To start the evaluation of your proposal for inclusion in the CCIS series, please send an e-mail to ccis@springer.com.

Michalis Sfakakis · Emmanouel Garoufallou ·
Matthew Damigos · Athena Salaba ·
Christos Papatheodorou
Editors

Metadata and Semantic Research

18th Research Conference, MTSR 2024
Athens, Greece, November 19–22, 2024
Revised Selected Papers

 Springer

Editors
Michalis Sfakakis (iD)
Ionian University
Corfu, Greece

Matthew Damigos (iD)
Ionian University
Corfu, Greece

Christos Papatheodorou (iD)
National and Kapodistrian University
of Athens
Athens, Greece

Emmanouel Garoufallou (iD)
International Hellenic University
Thessaloniki, Greece

Athena Salaba (iD)
Kent State University
Kent, OH, USA

ISSN 1865-0929   ISSN 1865-0937 (electronic)
Communications in Computer and Information Science
ISBN 978-3-031-81973-5   ISBN 978-3-031-81974-2 (eBook)
https://doi.org/10.1007/978-3-031-81974-2

This Springer imprint is published by the registered company Springer Nature Switzerland AG
The registered company address is: Gewerbestrasse 11, 6330 Cham, Switzerland

If disposing of this product, please recycle the paper.

Preface

Metadata and semantics are integral to any information system and important to the sphere of Web of Data, Semantic Web, and Linked Data. Research and development addressing metadata and semantics is crucial to advancing how we effectively discover, use, archive, and repurpose information. The institution of Open Science policies and in particular of Open Access routes proved an accelerator for the development of repositories and information services that are based on the principles of FAIR digital resources. In response to this need, researchers are actively examining methods for generating, reusing, and interchanging metadata. Integrated with these developments is research on the application of computational methods, linked data, and data analytics. A growing body of literature also targets conceptual and theoretical designs providing foundational frameworks for metadata, knowledge organization, and semantic applications. There is no doubt that metadata weaves its way through nearly every aspect of our information ecosystem, and there is great motivation to advance the current state of understanding in the fields of metadata and semantics. To this end, it is vital that scholars and practitioners convene and share their work and research findings.

Since 2005, the International Metadata and Semantics Research Conference (MTSR) has served as a significant venue for the dissemination and sharing of metadata and semantic-driven research and practices. This year marked the 18th edition of MTSR, drawing scholars, researchers, and practitioners who are investigating and advancing our knowledge on a wide range of metadata and semantic-driven topics. The 18th International Conference on Metadata and Semantics Research (MTSR 2024) was organized by the Department of History and Philosophy of Science of the National and Kapodistrian University of Athens (NKUA) in Athens, Greece and the Department of Archives, Library Science and Museology of the Ionian University in Corfu, Greece, and took place in the Main Building of the National and Kapodistrian University of Athens between November 20th and 22nd, 2024. The MTSR 2024 Organizing Committee decided to organize the conference as a hybrid event and to allow a small number of papers to be presented online to accommodate the diverse requirements of delegates.

The MTSR conference series has grown in terms of the number of participants and paper submission rate over the past decade, marking it as a leading international research conference. Continuing the successful legacy of previous MTSR conferences, MTSR 2024 brought together scholars and practitioners who share a common interest in the interdisciplinary field of metadata, Linked Data, Ontologies, and the Semantic Web. The program included 29 research papers, two posters and a workshop covering a broad spectrum of topics from metadata and semantically focused tools and technologies to linked data, knowledge graphs, cross-language semantics and language models, metadata integration, and domain ontologies, exhibiting a rich diversity of research methods and practices. Moreover, the need to develop data management plans for research data based on the FAIR principles as well as the benefits and challenges of making data findable, accessible, interoperable, and reusable (FAIR) across domains and disciplines was recognized by the presented papers. Additionally, opportunities for reuse, repurpose, and redeployment of data using semantic technologies were verified. Last but not least, recent advances in neural networks, natural language processing, and knowledge graphs were presented, promoting innovations and methods for topic modelling, semantic annotation, and automatic metadata generation and enrichment.

Regarding the structure of the conference, it consisted of a General Track oriented thematically to Metadata Management topics, such as Foundations, Frameworks for Metadata Management, Technological Issues, and Case Studies, supported by a set of tracks on the topics: Digital Libraries, Information Retrieval, Big, Linked, Social, and Open Data; Agriculture, Food, and Environment; Open Repositories, Research Information Systems, and Data Infrastructures; Digital Humanities and Digital Curation; Cultural Collections and Applications, and a track hosting demonstrations and papers from European and National Projects. Each of these tracks had a rich selection of short and full research papers, giving broader diversity to MTSR that spans across health records, cultural heritage collections, environmental data, and manufacturing, enabling deeper exploration of significant topics. Also, MTSR 2024 organised a very successful workshop about "Metadata and Ontologies in Musicology: Advancing Heritage Preservation and Research in Digital Humanities".

In general, MTSR 2024 brought together researchers, scholars, practitioners, educators, and information professionals coming from libraries, archives, museums, cultural heritage institutions, and organizations from the educational sector and industry. All 59 submitted papers underwent a thorough and rigorous double-blind peer-review process, with two to four reviewers assigned to each paper. The review and selection for this year was highly competitive, and only papers containing significant research results, innovative methods, or novel and best practices were accepted for publication. The number of accepted papers was 29, and the acceptance rate of all research papers for both the general session and tracks was 49.1% of the total number of submissions. From the 29 papers 23 were full research papers with an acceptance rate of 46% of the total number of full research submissions. The conference also accepted two posters.

MTSR 2024 was pleased to host a remarkable keynote presentation by Timos Sellis, one of the most well-known and significant researchers in Data Science. His speech "Data curation for Intelligent, Reliable and Responsible decision-making systems" focused on how data management practices need to be re-configured in order to support Intelligent, Reliable, and Responsible decision-making systems. Currently Data Management faces complex socio-technical challenges associated with balancing the diverse demands of regulatory compliance and data privacy, social expectations and ethical use, business process agility and value creation, and scarcity of data science talent. Timos Sellis highlighted these interconnected challenges and introduced Information Resilience, as a scaffold within which the competing requirements of responsible and agile approaches to information use can be positioned. The aim is to develop and present a manifesto for Information Resilience that can serve as a reference for future research and development in relevant areas of Responsible Data Management.

We conclude this preface by thanking the many people who contributed their time and efforts to MTSR 2024 and made this year's conference possible. We also thank all the organizations that supported this conference. We thank all the institutions and universities that co-organized MTSR 2024. We extend our sincere gratitude to the members of the Program Committees (both main and special tracks), the Steering Committee, and the Organizing Committees (both general and local), to all the special track chairs, and to the conference reviewers who generously invested their time to ensure the timely review of the submitted manuscripts. Also, a special thank you goes to Esmeralda Dudushi, Vasiliki Georgiadi, Aliki Soultani, Iasonas Spanopoulos, and Konstantinos Myroforidis for supporting us on social media platforms, in the organization and communication tasks, as well as in the technical support of the website throughout the year for this event. Esmeralda also assisted us with the preparation of these proceedings and the Book of Abstracts. Our thanks go to our best paper and best student paper awards sponsor euroCRIS. Finally, our deepest thanks go to the MTSR community, and all the authors and participants of MTSR 2024 for making the event a great success.

October 2024   Emmanouel Garoufallou
                                                              Michalis Sfakakis
                                                             Matthew Damigos
                                                                 Athena Salaba
                                                    Christos Papatheodorou

Organization

General Chairs

Emmanouel Garoufallou	International Hellenic University, Greece
Michalis Sfakakis	Ionian University, Greece
Christos Papatheodorou	National and Kapodistrian University of Athens, Greece

Chair for MTSR 2024

Matthew Damigos	Ionian University, Greece

Program Chair

Athena Salaba	Kent State University, USA

Special Track Chairs

Miguel-Ángel Sicilia	University of Alcalá, Spain
Francesca Fallucchi	Guglielmo Marconi University, Italy
Riem Spielhaus	Georg Eckert Institute for International Textbook Research, Germany
Ernesto William De Luca	Georg Eckert-Institute – Leibniz Institute for International Textbook Research, Germany
Armando Stellato	University of Rome Tor Vergata, Italy
Nikos Houssos	Sentio Solutions, Greece
Michalis Sfakakis	Ionian University, Greece
Lina Bountouri	EU Publications Office, Luxembourg
Emmanouel Garoufallou	International Hellenic University, Greece
Jane Greenberg	Drexel University, USA
Richard J. Hartley	Manchester Metropolitan University, UK
Stavroula Antonopoulou	Perrotis College, American Farm School, Greece
Rob Davies	Cyprus University of Technology, Cyprus
Fabio Sartori	University of Milano-Bicocca, Italy
Angela Locoro	Università Carlo Cattaneo - LIUC, Italy

| Arlindo Flavio da Conceição | Federal University of São Paulo, Brazil |
| Rania Siatri | International Hellenic University, Greece |

Steering Committee

Juan Manuel Dodero	University of Cádiz, Spain
Emmanouel Garoufallou	International Hellenic University, Greece
Nikos Manouselis	AgroKnow, Greece
Fabio Santori	Università degli Studi di Milano-Bicocca, Italy
Miguel-Ángel Sicilia	University of Alcalá, Spain

Local Organizing Committee

Argyro Frantzi	National and Kapodistrian University of Athens, Greece
Vassilis Siochos	National and Kapodistrian University of Athens, Greece
Vassiliki Strakantouna	National and Kapodistrian University of Athens, Greece
Costas Viglas	National and Kapodistrian University of Athens, Greece
Kyriaki Zoutsou	National and Kapodistrian University of Athens, Greece

Organizing Committee

Esmeralda Dudushi (Coordinator)	International Hellenic University, Greece
Anxhela Dani	LIBER Europe, The Netherlands
Chrysanthi Chatzopoulou	Frontiers Media, Switzerland
Vasiliki Georgiadi	International Hellenic University, Greece
Chrysanthi Theodoridou	International Hellenic University, Greece
Aliki Soultani	International Hellenic University, Greece
Niki Maria Chatziefstratiou	International Hellenic University, Greece
Konstantinos Miroforidis	International Hellenic University, Greece
Pavlos Siskos	International Hellenic University, Greece
Iasonas Spanopoulos	International Hellenic University, Greece

Technical Support Staff

Ilias Nitsos   International Hellenic University, Greece

Program Committee Members

Trond Aalberg   Norwegian University of Science and Technology
                                   (NTNU), Norway
Rajendra Akerkar   Western Norway Research Institute, Norway
Getaneh Alemu   Southampton Solent University, UK
Arif Altun   Hacettepe University, Turkey
Stavroula Antonopoulou   Perrotis College, American Farm School, Greece
Ioannis N. Athanasiadis   Wageningen University, The Netherlands
David Bainbridge   University of Waikato, New Zealand
Panos Balatsoukas   King's College London, UK
Wolf-Tilo Balke   TU Braunschweig, Germany
Tomaz Bartol   University of Ljubljana, Slovenia
Dionysios Benetos   National and Kapodistrian University of Athens,
                                   Greece
José Alberto Benítez   University of León, Spain
Ina Bluemel   German National Library of Science and
                                   Technology TIBm, Germany
Lina Bountouri   Publications Office of the European Union,
                                   Luxembourg
Derek Bousfield   Manchester Metropolitan University, UK
Karin Bredenberg   National Archives of Sweden, Sweden
Patrice Buche   Institut National de la Recherche Agronomique,
                                   France
Özgü Can   Ege University, Turkey
Caterina Caracciolo   Food and Agriculture Organization of the United
                                   Nations, Italy
Christian Cechinel   Federal University of Santa Catarina, Brazil
Artem Chebotko   DataStax, USA
Philip Cimiano   Bielefeld University, Germany
Sissi Closs   Karlsruhe University of Applied Sciences,
                                   Germany
Ricardo Colomo-Palacios   Universidad Carlos III, Spain
Panos Constantopoulos   Athens University of Economics and Business,
                                   Greece
Mike Conway   University of North Carolina at Chapel Hill, USA
Constantina Costopoulou   Agricultural University of Athens, Greece

Phil Couch	University of Manchester, UK
Arlindo Flavio da Conceição	Federal University of São Paulo, Brazil
Ernesto William De Luca	Georg Eckert-Institute – Leibniz Institute for International Textbook Research, Germany
Mihnea Dobre	University of Bucharest, Romania
Milena Dobreva	Sofia University St. Kliment Ohridski, Bulgaria
Juan Manuel Dodero	University of Cádiz, Spain
Erdogan Dogdu	Çankaya University, Turkey
Anastasia Doxanaki	National and Kapodistrian University of Athens, Greece
Manuel Palomo-Duarte	Universidad de Cádiz, Spain
Gordon Dunshire	University of Strathclyde, UK
Biswanath Dutta	Indian Statistical Institute, India
Jan Dvořák	Charles University, Czech Republic
Ali Emrouznejad	Aston University, UK
Juan José Escribano Otero	Universidad Europea de Madrid, Spain
Francesca Fallucchi	Guglielmo Marconi University, Italy
María-Teresa Fernández-Bajón	Complutense University of Madrid, Spain
Manuel Fiorelli	University of Rome Tor Vergata, Italy
Muriel Foulonneau	Direction générale des Finances publiques, France
Enrico Fransesconi	EU Publications Office, Luxembourg
Panorea Gaitanou	Hellenic National Defence College, Greece
Ana Garcia-Serrano	UNED, Spain
María Teresa García	University of León, Spain
Emmanouel Garoufallou	International Hellenic University, Greece
Manolis Gergatsoulis	Ionian University, Greece
Elena González-Blanco	Universidad Nacional de Educación a Distancia, Spain
Jorge Gracia	University of Zaragoza, Spain
Jane Greenberg	Drexel University, USA
Jill Griffiths	Manchester Metropolitan University, UK
Siddeswara Guru	University of Queensland, Australia
Richard J. Hartley	Manchester Metropolitan University, UK
Steffen Hennicke	Georg Eckert Institute – Leibniz Institute for International Textbook Research, Germany
Nikos Houssos	Sentio Solutions, Greece
Carlos A. Iglesias	Universidad Politécnica de Madrid, Spain
Antoine Isaac	Vrije Universiteit Amsterdam, The Netherlands
Keith Jeffery	Keith G. Jeffery Consultants, UK
Frances Johnson	Manchester Metropolitan University, UK
Dimitris Kanellopoulos	University of Patras, Greece
Pinar Karagöz	Middle East Technical University, Turkey

Cristina Ribeiro	INESC TEC, University of Porto, Portugal
Eva Méndez Rodríguez	Universidad Carlos III of Madrid, Spain
Dimitris Rousidis	International Hellenic University, Greece
Athena Salaba	Kent State University, USA
Salvador Sánchez-Alonso	University of Alcalá, Spain
Ricardo Santos-Muñoz	Spanish National Library, Spain
Fabio Sartori	University of Milano-Bicocca, Italy
Noemi Scarpato	San Raffaele Roma Open University, Italy
Christian Scheel	Georg Eckert Institute – Leibniz Institute for International Textbook Research, Germany
Jochen Schirrwagen	University of Bielefeld, Germany
Birgit Schmidt	University of Göttingen, Germany
Joachim Schöpfel	University of Lille, France
Michalis Sfakakis	Ionian University, Greece
Cleo Sgouropoulou	University of West Attica, Greece
Kathleen Shearer	Confederation of Open Access Repositories, Germany
Rania Siatri	International Hellenic University, Greece
Miguel-Ángel Sicilia	University of Alcalá, Spain
Flávio Soares Corrêa da Silva	University of São Paulo, Brazil
Ahmet Soylu	Norwegian University of Science and Technology, Norway
Riem Spielhaus	Georg Eckert Institute – Leibniz Institute for International Textbook Research, Germany
Lena-Luise Stahn	Freie Universität Berlin, Germany
Armando Stellato	University of Rome Tor Vergata, Italy
Imma Subirats	Food and Agriculture Organization of the United Nations, Italy
Shigeo Sugimoto	University of Tsukuba, Japan
Hussein Suleman	University of Cape Town, South Africa
Maguelonne Teisseire	Irstea Montpellier, France
Jan Top	Wageningen Food & Biobased Research, The Netherlands
Robert Trypuz	John Paul II Catholic University of Lublin, Poland
Giannis Tsakonas	University of Patras, Greece
Chrisa Tsinaraki	Technical University of Crete, Greece
Andrea Turbati	University of Rome Tor Vergata, Italy
Maria Tzamtzi	National and Kapodistrian University of Athens, Greece
Yannis Tzitzikas	University of Crete and ICS-FORTH, Greece
Christine Urquhart	Aberystwyth University, UK
Evgenia Vassilakaki	EIOPA, Germany
Sirje Virkus	Tallinn University, Estonia

Andreas Vlachidis	University College London, UK
Zhong Wang	Sun Yat-sen University, China
Katherine Wisser	Simmons College, USA
Georgia Zafeiriou	University of Macedonia, Greece
Cecilia Zanni-Merk	INSA Rouen Normandie, France
Fabio Massimo Zanzotto	University of Rome Tor Vergata, Italy
Sofia Zapounidou	National Library of Greece, Greece
Marcia Zeng	Kent State University, USA
Marios Zervas	Cyprus University of Technology, Cyprus
Thomas Zschocke	World Agroforestry Centre (ICRAF), Kenya
Maja Žumer	University of Ljubljana, Slovenia

Special Track on Metadata and Semantics for Agriculture, Food & Environment (AgroSEM 2024)

Special Track Chair

Miguel-Ángel Sicilia	University of Alcalá, Spain

Program Committee

Ioannis Athanasiadis	Wageningen University, The Netherlands
Patrice Buche	Institut National de la Recherche Agronomique, France
Caterina Caracciolo	Food and Agriculture Organization of the United Nations, Italy
Stasinos Konstantopoulos	NCSR Demokritos, Greece
Claire Nédellec	INRAE, France
Ivo Pierozzi	Embrapa Agricultural Informatics, Brazil
Armando Stellato	University of Rome Tor Vergata, Italy
Maguelonne Teisseire	Irstea Montpellier, France
Jan Top	Wageningen Food & Biobased Research, The Netherlands
Robert Trypuz	John Paul II Catholic University of Lublin, Poland

Track on Metadata and Semantics for Cultural Collections and Applications

Special Track Chairs

Michalis Sfakakis	Ionian University, Greece
Lina Bountouri	Publications Office of the European Union, Luxembourg

Program Committee

Trond Aalberg	Oslo Metropolitan University, Norway
Enrico Francesconi	EU Publications Office, Luxembourg and Consiglio Nazionale delle Recerche, Italy
Manolis Gergatsoulis	Ionian University, Greece
Antoine Isaac	Vrije Universiteit Amsterdam, The Netherlands
Sarantos Kapidakis	University of West Attica, Greece
Christos Papatheodorou	National and Kapodistrian University of Athens and Athena RC, Greece
Andreas Vlachidis	University College London, UK
Maja Žumer	University of Ljubljana, Slovenia

Track on Metadata and Semantics for Digital Libraries, Information Retrieval, Big, Linked, Social and Open Data

Special Track Chairs

Emmanouel Garoufallou	International Hellenic University, Greece
Jane Greenberg	Drexel University, USA
Rania Siatri	International Hellenic University, Greece

Program Committee

Panos Balatsoukas	King's College London, UK
Özgü Can	Ege University, Turkey
Sissi Closs	Karlsruhe University of Applied Sciences, Germany
Mike Conway	University of North Carolina at Chapel Hill, USA
Phil Couch	University of Manchester, UK
Milena Dobreva	Sofia University St. Kliment Ohridski, Bulgaria

Ali Emrouznejad   Aston University, UK
Panorea Gaitanou   Hellenic National Defence College, Greece
Jane Greenberg   Drexel University, USA
Richard. J. Hartley   Manchester Metropolitan University, UK
Nikos Korfiatis   University of East Anglia, UK
Rebecca Koskela   Research Data Alliance, USA
Dimitris Rousidis   International Hellenic University, Greece
Athena Salaba   Kent State University, USA
Miguel-Ángel Sicilia   University of Alcalá, Spain
Christine Urquhart   Aberystwyth University, UK
Evgenia Vassilakaki   EIOPA, Germany
Sirje Virkus   Tallinn University, Estonia
Georgia Zafeiriou   University of Macedonia, Greece
Marios Zervas   Cyprus University of Technology, Cyprus

Track on Metadata and Semantics for European and National Projects

Special Track Chairs

Richard J. Hartley   Manchester Metropolitan University, UK
Stavroula Antonopoulou   Perrotis College, American Farm School, Greece
Robert Davies   Cyprus University of Technology, Cyprus

Program Committee

Panos Balatsoukas   King's College London, UK
Mike Conway   University of North Carolina at Chapel Hill, USA
Emmanouel Garoufallou   International Hellenic University, Greece
Jane Greenberg   Drexel University, USA
Nikos Houssos   Sentio Solutions, Greece
Nikos Korfiatis   University of East Anglia, UK
Damiana Koutsomiha   American Farm School, Greece
Paolo Manghi   Institute of Information Science and Technologies
                               (ISTI), National Research Council, Italy
Dimitris Rousidis   International Hellenic University, Greece
Rania Siatri   International Hellenic University, Greece
Miguel-Ángel Sicilia   University of Alcalá, Spain
Armando Stellato   University of Rome Tor Vergata, Italy
Sirje Virkus   Tallinn University, Estonia

Track on Metadata and Semantics for Open Repositories, Research Information Systems and Data Infrastructures

Special Track Chairs

Armando Stellato	University of Rome Tor Vergata, Italy
Manuel Fiorelli	University of Rome Tor Vergata, Italy
Nikos Houssos	Sentio Solutions, Greece

Honorary Track Chairs

Imma Subirats	Food and Agriculture Organization of the United Nations, Italy

Program Committee

Gordon Dunshire	University of Strathclyde, UK
Jan Dvorak	Charles University, Czech Republic
Jane Greenberg	Drexel University, USA
Siddeswara Guru	University of Queensland, Australia
Keith Jeffery	Keith G. Jeffery Consultants, UK
Nikolaos Konstantinou	University of Manchester, UK
Rebecca Koskela	University of New Mexico, USA
Jessica Lindholm	Malmö University, Sweden
Paolo Manghi	Institute of Information Science and Technologies - Italian National Research Council (ISTI-CNR), Italy
Brian Matthews	Science and Technology Facilities Council, UK
Eva Mendez Rodriguez	University Carlos III of Madrid, Spain
Joachim Schöpfel	University of Lille, France
Kathleen Shearer	Confederation of Open Access Repositories, Germany
Jochen Schirrwagen	University of Bielefeld, Germany
Birgit Schmidt	University of Göttingen, Germany
Chrisa Tsinaraki	European Commission, Joint Research Centre, Italy
Yannis Tzitzikas	University of Crete and ICS-FORTH, Greece
Zhong Wang	Sun Yat-sen University, China
Marcia Zeng	Kent State University, USA
Manuel Fiorelli	University of Rome Tor Vergata, Italy

Track on Metadata and Semantics for Digital Humanities and Digital Curation

Special Track Chairs

Ernesto William De Luca	Georg Eckert Institute – Leibniz Institute for International Textbook Research, Germany
Francesca Fallucchi	Guglielmo Marconi University, Italy
Riem Spielhaus	Georg Eckert Institute – Leibniz Institute for International Textbook Research, Germany

Program Committee

Maret Nieländer	Georg Eckert Institute – Leibniz Institute for International Textbook Research, Germany
Elena González-Blanco	Universidad Nacional de Educación a Distancia, Spain
Steffen Hennicke	Georg Eckert Institute – Leibniz Institute for International Textbook Research, Germany
Ana Garcia-Serrano	UNED, Spain
Philipp Mayr	GESIS, Germany
Noemi Scarpato	San Raffaele Roma Open University, Italy
Andrea Turbati	University of Rome Tor Vergata, Italy
Christian Scheel	Georg Eckert Institute – Leibniz Institute for International Textbook Research, Germany
Armando Stellato	University of Rome Tor Vergata, Italy
Wolf-Tilo Balke	TU Braunschweig, Germany
Andreas Lommatzsch	TU Berlin, Germany
Ivo Keller	TH Brandenburg, Germany
Gabriela Ossenbach	UNED, Spain
Francesca Fallucchi	Guglielmo Marconi University, Italy

Special Track on Metadata, Identifiers and Semantics in Decentralized Applications, Blockchains and P2P Systems

Special Track Chair

Miguel-Ángel Sicilia	University of Alcalá, Spain

Program Committee

Sissi Closs	Karlsruhe University of Applied Sciences, Germany
Ernesto William De Luca	Georg Eckert Institute – Leibniz Institute for International Textbook Research, Germany
Juan Manuel Dodero	University of Cádiz, Spain
Francesca Fallucchi	Guglielmo Marconi University, Italy
Jane Greenberg	Drexel University, USA
Nikos Houssos	Sentio Solutions, Greece
Nikos Korfiatis	University of East Anglia, UK
Dimitris Rousidis	International Hellenic University, Greece
Salvador Sánchez-Alonso	University of Alcalá, Spain
Michalis Sfakakis	Ionian University, Greece
Rania Siatri	International Hellenic University, Greece
Armando Stellato	University of Rome Tor Vergata, Italy
Robert Trypuz	John Paul II Catholic University of Lublin, Poland
Sirje Virkus	Tallinn University, Estonia

Contents

Track on Digital Libraries, Information Retrieval, Big, Linked, Social and Open Data

Track on Cultural Collections and Application

Track on European and National Projects; and 8th DOAbLE - Papers for Libraries, Archives, Museums

Track on Agriculture, Food and Environment (AgroSEM'24)

Track on Digital Humanities and Digital Curation

Track on Metadata, Linked Data, Semantics and Ontologies - General Session

Towards MatCore: A Unified Metadata Standard for Materials Science

Jane Greenberg[1](✉), Pámela Bóveda-Aguirre[2], John Allison[3], Pietro Asinari[4], Maria Chan[5], Anand Chandrasekaran[6], Elif Ertekin[7], Emmanouel Garoufallou[8], Giulia Galli[9], Paolo Giannozzi[10], Feliciano Giustino[11], Gerhard Goldbeck[12], Hendrik Heinz[13], Arthi Jayaraman[14], Vincenzo Lordi[15], Kristin A. Persson[16], Gian-Marco Rignanese[17], Aidan Thompson[18], Eric Toberer[19], Scott McClellan[1], and Ellad B. Tadmor[2]

[1] Metadata Research Center, Drexel University, Philadelphia, USA
jg3243@drexel.edu
[2] University of Minnesota, Minneapolis, USA
tadmor@umn.edu
[3] University of Michigan, Ann Arbor, USA
[4] Politecnico di Torino, Italian National Institute of Metrological Research, Turin, Italy
[5] Argonne National Laboratory, Lemont, USA
[6] Schrödinger, Inc., New York, USA
[7] University of Illinois, Urbana-Champaign, Champaign, USA
[8] MetaDATA LAB, International Hellenic University, Thermi, Greece
[9] University of Chicago, Chicago, USA
[10] DMIF, Università di Udine, CNR - IOM, Udine, Italy
[11] University of Texas, Austin, USA
[12] Goldbeck Consulting, EMMC, Cambridge, UK
[13] University of Colorado, Boulder, USA
[14] University of Delaware, Newark, USA
[15] Lawrence Livermore National Laboratory, Livermore, USA
[16] University of California, Berkeley, USA
[17] UCLouvain, OPTIMADE, Ottignies-Louvain-la-Neuve, Belgium
[18] Sandia National Laboratory, Albuquerque, USA
[19] Colorado School of Mines, Golden, USA

Abstract. The materials science community seeks to support the FAIR principles for computational simulation research. The MatCore Project was recently launched to address this need, with the goal of developing an overall metadata framework and accompanying guidelines. This paper reports on the MatCore goals and overall progress. Historical background context is provided, including a review of the principles underlying successful core metadata standards. The paper also presents selected MatCore examples and discusses future plans.

Keywords: Materials Science · Metadata · Open Data · Data Sharing · FAIR Data

M. Sfakakis et al. (Eds.): MTSR 2024, CCIS 2331, pp. 3–14, 2025.
https://doi.org/10.1007/978-3-031-81974-2_1

1   Introduction

Materials science is an interdisciplinary field that draws from physics, engineering, biology, mathematics, and other intersecting disciplines [1–3]. Materials scientists study matter, specifically the relationship between the atomic or molecular level of a material's structure and its associated properties. The overall goal is to design and develop new materials, or improve the performance of existing materials. For example, a process for producing metal alloys may be modified to improve corrosion resistance.

Materials scientists use a range of research techniques spanning experimental, in-the-lab activities to modeling and simulation. These approaches along with technical and computational advances have radically increased the amount of materials science research data that is generated on a daily basis. This growth has further introduced unprecedented challenges and opportunities as researchers seek to effectively manage their research data, support the FAIR (Findable, Accessible, Interoperable, and Reusable) data principles [4], and apply machine learning (ML) and artificial intelligence (AI) techniques.

Metadata has taken on a an increasingly significant role in concert with these changes, as small-scale university research groups to large-scale industry laboratories mandate the use of metadata standards. As a result, materials scientists have adopted and modified existing metadata standards, and formed groups to develop new standards. Although these activities have advanced metadata practices and various research infrastructures, they lack a cohesive framework. Consequently, materials scientists seeking to work with metadata standards are challenged on where to begin. The materials science community needs a scaffolding that provides a base-level entry point and which also contains core components to facilitate connectedness across the field. Development of a framework containing core standards supporting discovery and other metadata functions is particularly important for those engaged in computational simulation given unprecedented opportunities occurring in the field of AI [5].

This need underlies the *Materials Core Metadata* (MatCore) project, which was launched in early 2024. MatCore includes seven working groups organized across a unified framework. The aim is to develop a set of core metadata standards and implementation guidelines supporting key area of computational materials science research. This paper reports on the MatCore work. First, by way of background the paper describes historical metadata developments, identifies several important materials science metadata approaches, and reviews a number of core metadata standards. Next, the paper identifies MatCore's goals and objectives and describes the standard structure. This is followed by the initial process of establishing the effort (Phase 0) and the development of the initial standard (Phase 1) including some examples. The last section summarizes MatCore progress and identifies next steps.

2   Background Context

2.1   Materials Science Metadata

Metadata, while primarily viewed as a digital asset, may exist as a physical artifact, or a digital record of a physical object. Consider the Greek astronomer Hipparchus of Nicaea, who compiled the first known stellar catalog in the second century BCE [6]. He recorded positions of stars and their celestial coordinates, essentially capturing both data and metadata about stars observed in our stellar environs. Throughout history materials science researchers have shared their "recipes" for material synthesis, first through oral tradition and then the written word. For example, the Kaogong Ji, a technical encyclopedia, written in western China between the 3rd and 5th centuries BCE, contains recipes for bronze casting [7]. Another example is the Leyden Papyrus found in Thebes, Egypt, and written in the 4th century CE [8]. This metallurgical handbook includes recipes for gilding silver, formulating base metal alloys, and soldering gold, some of which are drawn from older works.

The exact starting point for digital, structured materials science metadata is difficult to determine, although such activities began in the early 1960's with database development establishing key–value pairs in relational databases, and the transition to hypertextual environments [9, 10]. Data interoperability presented a significant challenge [11] and underscored the need for solutions. The American Society for Testing Materials (ASTM) committee E49, "Computerization of Material Property Data" [12] recommendations present another metadata milestone. The recommendations, released in 1985, advocated for researchers to include standard descriptors, identifiers, characterization data, and other features in materials databases. Roughly a decade later we see the adoption of standardized markup languages, such as the eXtensible Markup Language (XML), which underlies the materials markup language (MatML) developed by NIST [13] and ontology design, supported by RDF/XML. Additionally, the Crystallographic Information Framework (CIF) format for crystallographic data was introduced in 1991 [14], and serves as an exemplary metadata standard adapting to disciplinary change. Indeed, the CIF format is a well-established standard, although views vary on if it is a metadata standard or a data standard.

Today, materials scientists can further draw from repositories, such as the Digital Curation Center's Disciplinary Metadata Directory (DCC/DMD), which provides access to an array of metadata standards. The DCC/DMD categorizes disciplinary metadata standards, profiles, tools, and use cases [15] under the following five categories: *general research*, *physics*, *biology*, *earth science*, and *social science & humanities*, and many of the schemes registered are relevant to various areas of materials science. Materials science researchers also have access to ontologies and other semantic systems through resources, such as the Industrial Ontology Foundry [16], MatPortal [17], and NOMAD [18]. Collectively, these metadata developments have advanced materials science metadata practices. Despite this progress, the dispersed standards environment presents boundaries [9] that impede materials scientists' full embrace and use of metadata. A look at core standards within longer-standing cohesive metadata environments can provide guidance for addressing this challenge and better situating MatCore activities.

2.2   Core Metadata Standards: Motivation and Success

The course of metadata history has included a series of core standards developed by disciplinary community members. The most successful of these efforts embody the spirit of *open science, transparency,* and *community ownership*. These factors are grounded in the *open-source movement*, which many metadata developers also traversed.

One of the earliest core metadata standards is the Internet Anonymous FTP Archives (IAFA), developed by the Internet Engineering Task Force (IETF) and released in 1995 [19,20]. IAFA offered a suite of metadata templates for publishing and exchanging of anonymous FTP information via Gopher, such as text indices, Linux Software Maps (LSMs), and other objects. Members of the IAFA community were instrumental in developing the Dublin Core, which is arguably one of the best known, interdisciplinary core metadata standards [21–23]. Initiated in March 1995 at a workshop co-hosted by the National Center for Super Computing Applications (NCSA), the Dublin Core principles aim to support metadata *simplicity, interoperability, modularity,* and *extensibility*. Dublin Core has had a global impact, and many of today's frequently used metadata standards map their core properties to the this standard.

Additional core standards include the VRA Core [24] for describing images of art and artifacts, the Darwin Core [25] for scientific, primarily biological specimens and samples, and the minimum information standards spearheaded by the Minimum Information for Biological and Biomedical Investigations (MIBBI) project [26]. Darwin Core has a series of extensions, such as the Audiovisual Core (formerly Audubon Core) [27] for describing multimedia collections related to biodiversity. The MIBBI guidelines also includes a suite of standards (e.g., Minimum Information About a Plant Phenotyping Experiment (MIAPPE) [28], Minimum Information About a Microarray Experiment (MIAME)[29], etc.) to guide reporting. All core standards noted here have been developed in open, community-driven environments and support the FAIR principles, even prior to their publication. Indeed, reviewing the full spectrum of core metadata standards supporting community connections is beyond the scope of this paper. What is important is to recognize that the success of core metadata standards hinges on open, community-driven approaches. The examples here have presented RFC (request for comment) documents, a requirement for formal standard endorsement. Additionally, many of these standards adhere to the ISO 11179, Metadata registries (MDR) standard [30]. Overall, lessons learned from these examples both inform and motivate the work being pursued with the MatCore project.

3 MatCore: Goals and Objectives

MatCore's overriding goal is to support the FAIR principles for computational materials science research. In order for the data generated by computer simulations of materials to be useful, they must be accompanied by information that fully characterizes the nature of the computation performed and the material being modeled. Further, to enable researchers to reproduce generated results, the specific parameters and settings input to the simulation program must be provided. Interoperability is also critical, given the goal to publish simulation data and information in open repositories for the purpose of collaboration. An additional, unifying MatCore goal is to build and sustain a metadata framework that facilitates a more cohesive, community-driven metadata approach.

Specific objectives being addressed in the Phase 1 working groups (WGs) include the development of core metadata standards covering the following five computational materials science methods:

1. Density Functional theory (DFT): First-principles computational methods based on quantum mechanics for predicting the ground state structure and properties of materials.
2. Classical Molecular Dynamics (MD): Methods for integrating the equations of motion of atoms using approximate fitted models for atomic interactions to predict classical static and dynamics properties of materials.
3. Many-Body Perturbation Theory (MBPT): First-principles computational methods based on quantum mechanics (such as GW and BSE) for computing properties of materials involving excited states.
4. Machine Learning (ML): Data-driven approaches that employ ML techniques to predict material structure and properties.
5. Derivative Methods: Hybrid calculations involving mixtures of other computational methods to predict material properties.

Additionally, there is Minimal Metadata WG that is working on defining a core set of common metadata properties required for every computational method. Finally, there is also a Metadata Implementation WG focused on identifying best practice recommendations to assure metadata quality.

4 MatCore Standard

MatCore defines required and optional metadata to accompany datasets generated through computational materials science techniques that will allow researchers to understand, use, and, if desired, reproduce the data. The structure of the MatCore standard is based on a two-tier hierarchy (see Fig. 1). The top level comprises the *Minimal MatCore Metadata*, and the second level consists of templates of specialized metadata for key computational materials science methods.

1. Minimal MatCore Metadata
   The core component of the standard is the "Minimal Matcore Metadata."
   Capturing this information is required for all datasets to specify the basic
   characteristics of the material being modeled and the performed computation.
   These general metadata properties apply to all computational methods.
2. Method-Specific Metadata
   In addition to the core component, each dataset may optionally be accompanied by method-specific metadata. This secondary level provides detailed
   information in the form of method-specific parameters and settings to allow
   experts to better understand the nature of the computation.

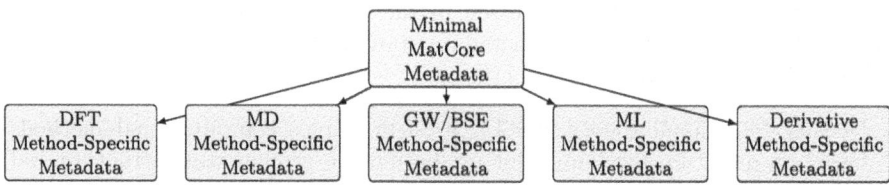

Fig. 1. Schematic of the MatCore structure.

While the above presents the current structure for the MatCore standard,
it may evolve over time. In particular, it is anticipated that additional method-
specific WGs will form for existing and new computational method.

5   The MatCore Standard Development Process

Establishment of a metadata standard for computational materials science
requires careful planning and building community support. This will be achieved
through a series of phases:

- Phase 0: Establishment of the MatCore Standards Committee and Funding
  Recruitment
- Phase 1: Development of the Draft MatCore Standard
- Phase 2: Community Request for Comment
- Phase 3: MatCore Committee Hearings and definition of the Final MatCore
  Standard
- Phase 4: Reporting and Planning for Ongoing MatCore Standard Support

At the time of writing, Phase 0 has been completed, and Phase 1 is underway,
as described below.

5.1 Phase 0: Establishment of the MatCore Standards Committee and Funding Recruitment

Phase 0 of the MatCore standard began in January 2023. The development of MatCore standard requires the collective expertise of leading researchers in the computational materials science methods discussed in Sect. 3. To this end, over a period of about a year, a committee comprised of the authors of this paper was established and engaged in discussions to establish a preliminary standard design.

A key consideration in establishment in the MatCore Committee was to assemble a group of researchers with expertise that spans that topics to be covered by the standard as well as in metadata standard development. Although, the focus of the current effort is on computational methods for solid-state materials, it was considered important to include both experimentalists as well as researchers working on soft matter on the Committee to benefit from their experience. With this broad input, it is hoped that a more robust standard will be developed that can be expanded to support computational materials science for both hard and soft matter, and ultimately experimental materials science, which is a far more difficult problem.

Following the established of the MatCore Committee and the completion of a preliminary standard design, a proposal was submitted to the U.S. National Science Foundation (NSF) by authors Tadmor, Persson and Giustino to support the development of the MatCore Standard. NSF funding was received from the Division of Materials Research (DMR), and work on Phase 1 has been initiated.

5.2 Phase 1: Development of the Draft MatCore Standard

Phase 1 of MatCore Standard development began in June 2024 and involves a series of steps that are currently underway. Figure 2 presents the development process in Phase 1. Step 1, involves a historical review that is being performed in parallel to steps 2, 3, and 4 that are focused on the definition of the metadata structure:

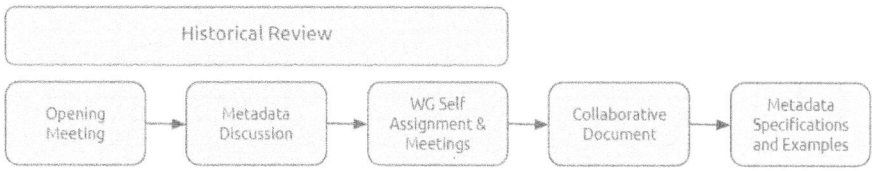

Fig. 2. Phase 1 of the MatCore standard development Process.

1. *Historical Review:* A historical review is being conducted to identify and study previous efforts, frameworks, standards, and projects aimed at providing FAIR access to data in materials science.

2. *Kickoff:* A series of kickoff meetings were held for the MatCore WGs to provide an overview to new MatCore Commitee members and discuss next steps.
3. *Metadata Primer:* A talk by an expert on metadata theory, followed by an open discussion, was held for the MatCore Committee. The talk presented metadata definitions, outlined the standards development process, reviewed the FAIR principles, and shared recommendations for the MatCore project.
4. *Working Group Self-Assignment and Meetings:* MatCore Committee Members selected which general and method-specific WGs to participate in (see Sect. 3) based on their expertise, experience and preference. Regular meetings were arranged for each WG. The minimal metadata and method-specific WGs discussed which metadata needed to be included, and the implementation WG focused on metadata best practices for the MatCore standard.
5. *Collaborative Development of MatCore Metadata Standard:* A collaborative document was shared with all participants, which allows members to view and contribute to each others activities. As a result, each WG benefited from both its own members' expertise, as well as that of the other WGs.

Key	Description
creator*	The author(s) who generated the data and institutional affiliation.
title*	Title of the dataset.
date*	Date(s) of dataset creation
description*	Brief description of the dataset.
disclaimer	A statement of applicability provided by the author informing users of the intended use and/or limitations of this dataset, if available.
material*	The material that the data pertains to, including the elemental composition and range of chemistry covered, the structure (amorphous, cluster, crystal, molecule, quasicrystal), and microstructure.
calculation-type*	The type of calculation (static, dynamic, sampling)
simulation-conditions*	The environmental and boundary conditions imposed in the calculations, such as the ensemble (e.g. NPT) along with the required values (e.g. pressure and temperature), with support for custom nonstandard conditions.
method*	The CMS method(s) used in the calculation (DFT, GW, BSE, MD, DER, ML).
software-code*	Name and version of the software used to generate the data, along with a DOI if available.
software-files	Complete input file (runscript) used to generate the data, and description, as well as sample data files if available or not exceeding a certain file size.
Source-citation	Citation to source(s) that describe the data including a DOI, if available and/or publication.
doi	Additional dataset DOI, if available and separate from the publication. And Data Repository (e.g. FigShare)
funding	Funding source(s) for the project denoted using Crossref designations, if available.
matcore-version*	Version of the MatCore standard for this document.
matcore-id*	MatCore ID for this dataset.
matcore-date*	The date that this MatCore document was created.
license*	License under which the dataset is provided following the SPDX standard.

Fig. 3. Preliminary draft of the Minimal MatCore Metadata specification. Starred keys are required.

Over the last few months since the beginning of Phase 0, the MatCore WG's have been holding virtual meeting on an ad hoc to collaborate on their assignments. These meetings are difficult to arrange due to the range of time zones

Key	Description
creator	Bob @ CUBoulder
title*	Platinum-nickel alloy
description*	Two hundred different nanoparticles of Pt-Ni with 2-4 nm size calculated with DFT to correlate with catalytic activity in various reactions.
disclaimer	The DFT D2 functional has limited reliability for surface energies.
material*	Pt99Ni1 alloy with 2000 atoms in a spherical nanoparticle of radius 1.5 nm. Ni are randomly decorating a fcc crystal structure.
calculation-type*	Static DFT calculation PBE D2 functional
Simulation-conditions	Structure determined from electron tomography without relaxation; energy minimization at 0K.
Model type	3D atomistic model to determine electronic structure
method*	DFT
software-code*	VASP version 6.3.1
software-files	<insert 3D coordinate file and run script here>
Source-citation	Nature Catalysis 5,3,332 (2024), DOI: XXX
doi	DOI: YYY on FigShare.com and backed up on Materials Data Facility
funding	NSF DMREF XXXXXXXX
matcore-version*	MMC 0.0.0
matcore-id*	00000000000001
matcore-date*	31/7/2024
license*	CC-BY-NC

Fig. 4. Preliminary example of a Minimal MatCore Metadata specification for a dataset generated through DFT computations for a platinum-nickel alloy.

Key	Description
xc-functional*	The exchange correlation functional (LDA, GGA, hybrid). Additional parameters, as needed (e.g., mixing parameters for hybrid, when relevant, etc.)
potential*	Potential type and details (all-electron, pseudopotential, PAW). If not all-electron, number of electrons in the valence. For pseudopotentials, name and identifying information for the pseudopotential used and its type (norm-conserving, ultrasoft).
calculation-physics	Physics functionality employed in the calculation (spin polarization, relativistic effects, noncollinear spin, …)
basis-set*	Type of basis (LAPW, plane waves, localized orbitals). Depending on which basis type (or combination of types) is used, additional information is provided. For plane wave codes, the energy cutoff specified. For local orbital codes, the number and type of basis functions is specified. Some codes require both.
k-points	The k-point mesh description and type (gamma-centered, Monkhorst-Pack) for periodic systems.
k-smearing	Smearing function and integration algorithm used for reciprocal space integrals for periodic systems
Self-consistent-field-convergence	The self-consistent field mixing scheme and tolerance.
state-occupations	Any special occupation of states, e.g., for finite-T calculations or DeltaSCF, etc. (may be somewhat duplicative with k-smearing, but is separate, and covers probably the intent of the earlier fermi-smearing tag)
relaxation-convergence	If the dataset is a result of a relaxation, convergence criteria used

Fig. 5. Preliminary draft of the Method-Specific MatCore Metadata specification for DFT. Starred keys are required.

with participants across the United States and in Europe, and are also challenging due to the range of backgrounds of the participants (engineers, physicists, chemists, computer scientists, data science, metadata, etc.).

The Draft MatCore Standard, which is the end goal of Phase 1, is still under development, however significant progress has been made to date. Each WG has produced an initial draft of their metadata specification and the Implementation WG has identified several best practice recommendations. Additionally, several of the WG's have documented examples for their computational methods. Some of these are presented below. Figure 3 presents the Minimal MatCore Metadata specification, and Fig. 4 provides an example of its application to a dataset generated by a DFT computation. Finally, Fig. 5 presents the DFT Method-Specific Metadata specification. Note that all of these specifications are preliminary and subject to change.

6   Conclusion

MatCore has been able to progress due to an engaged, open community of experts. The open approach and the shared MatCore development document has allowed for collaboration within and across all of the WGs. This is important as the materials researchers participating in MatCore may work more frequently with some methods, but they are knowledgeable across all methods. Additionally, MatCore includes those with expertise in standards development. This collaborative approach helps MatCore support the FAIR principles and ensures that computational materials science outputs are:

- Findable, by providing clear identifiers and making them easily located.
- Accessible, by providing details about the methods, underlying code, and tools use.
- Interoperable, by using standardized formats, definitions and units.
- Reusable, by offering details for accurate replication of the resource.

Another important aspect of the MatCore project is the open, transparent, community-driven approach. This will allow for continued development and improvement over time. The work being conducted in Phase 1 will form a draft standard, which will be published online, and open for public comment in Phase 2. Feedback received will be evaluated at a MatCore Committee hearing in which selected community members will be invited to appear, and integrated into a revised version. The long-term goal is to establish the MatCore standard so that the materials science community can continue contributing to MatCore development and sustainability.

Acknowledgements. The authors acknowledge partial support by the National Science Foundation (NSF) under grants DMR-2404283, OAC-2118201, and OAC-2320600. GG acknowledges funding from the European Union's Horizon 2020 research and innovation programme under grant agreement No. 953167 (OpenModel). PG acknowledges support from the European Union through the MaX Centre of Excellence for Supercomputing applications (project No. 101093374).

References

1. Bensaude-Vincent, B.: The construction of a discipline: materials science in the united states. Hist. Stud. Phys. Biol. Sci. **31**(2), 223–248 (2001)
2. Callister Jr, W.D., Rethwisch, D.G.: Fundamentals of materials science and engineering: an integrated approach. Wiley (2020)
3. National Research Council: Materials Science and Engineering for the 1990s: Maintaining Competitiveness in the Age of Materials. The National Academies Press (1989)
4. Wilkinson, M.D., et al.: The FAIR guiding principles for scientific data management and stewardship. Sci. Data **3**(1), 1–9 (2016)
5. Pyzer-Knapp, E.O., et al.: Accelerating materials discovery using artificial intelligence, high performance computing and robotics. NPJ Comput. Mater. **8**(1), 84 (2022)
6. Goldstein, B.R., Bowen, A.C.: The introduction of dated observations and precise measurement in Greek astronomy. Arch. Hist. Exact Sci. **43**, 93–132 (1991). https://doi.org/10.1007/BF00375347
7. Luo, W., Song, G., Yongqing, H., Chen, D.: Tentative determination of a special bronze material by multiple technological test on a Xuan-Liu dagger-axe from the Xujialing site, the Eastern Zhou period, Henan Province China. J. Cult. Heritage **46**, 304–312 (2020)
8. Hunt, L.B.: The oldest metallurgical handbook. Gold Bull. **9**(1), 24–31 (1976)
9. Ghiringhelli, L.M., et al.: Shared metadata for data-centric materials science. Sci. Data **10**(1), 626 (2023)
10. Westbrook, J.H., Grattidge, W.: The role of metadata in the design and operation of a materials database. Second Volume. ASTM International, In: Computerization and Networking of Materials Databases (1991)
11. Stanton, E.L.: Computerization of polymer matrix composite materials data and metadata. Mater. Des. **12**(2), 92–96 (1991)
12. Rumble, J.: Standards for materials databases: ASTM Committee E49. Second Volume. ASTM International, In Computerization and Networking of Materials Databases (1991)
13. Varde, A.S., Begley, E.F., Fahrenholz-Mann, S.: MatML: XML for information exchange with materials property data. In: Proceedings of the 4th International Workshop on Data Mining Standards, Services and Platforms, pp. 47–54 (2006)
14. Hall, S.R., Allen, F.H., Brown, I.D.: The crystallographic information file (CIF): a new standard archive file for crystallography. Found. Crystallogr. **47**(6), 655–685 (1991)
15. Ball, A.: Metadata standards directory (2016). In: RDA Europe Webinar
16. Open Applications Group: Industrial Ontology Foundry (2023). https://www.industrialontologies.org/
17. BAM Fraunhofer Materials. MatPortal (2024). https://matportal.org/ontologies
18. Scheffler, M., et al.: et al. FAIR data enabling new horizons for materials research. Nature **604**(7907), 635–642 (2022)
19. Beckett, D.: IAFA templates in use as internet metadata. In: Proceedings of the Fourth International Conference on World Wide Web, pp. 135–143 (1995)
20. Deutsch, P.: Publishing information on the internet with anonymous FTP (1995). http://www.nlc-bnc.ca/ifla/documents/libraries/cataloging/metadata/iafa.txt
21. Weibel, S.L., Koch, T.: The Dublin core metadata initiative. D-lib Mag. **6**(12), 1082–9873 (2000)

22. Weibel, S.L., Lagoze, C.: An element set to support resource discovery: the state of the Dublin core: January 1997. Int. J. Digit. Libr. **1**, 176–186 (1997)
23. Arakaki, F.A., Alves, R.C.V., Amorim, P.L.V., da Costa, D., et al.: Core: state of art to 2015. Informação & Sociedade **28**(2), 2018 (1995)
24. VRA Core. https://www.loc.gov/standards/vracore/schemas.html
25. Wieczorek, J., et al.: Darwin core: an evolving community-developed biodiversity data standard. PLoS ONE **7**(1), e29715 (2012)
26. Taylor, C.F., et al.: Promoting coherent minimum reporting guidelines for biological and biomedical investigations: the MIBBI project. Nat. Biotechnol. **26**(8), 889–896 (2008)
27. Morris, R.A., et al.: Discovery and publishing of primary biodiversity data associated with multimedia resources: the Audubon Core strategies and approaches. Biodiver. Inf. **8**(2), 185–197 (2013)
28. Pommier, C., Le Floch, E., Arend, D., Anna, F.D.: Long term plant phenomic data sharing in generic data repositories (Zenodo, Dataverse, e! Dale) using MIAPPE. In: Plant and Animal Genome (PAG) (2024)
29. Brazma, A., et al.: Minimum information about a microarray experiment (MIAME)-toward standards for microarray data. Nat. Genet. **29**(4), 365–371 (2001)
30. ISO/IEC JTC1 SC32. ISO/IEC 11179-1:2023, Information Technology — Metadata registries (MDR) (2023). https://www.iso.org/standard/78914.html

DATA-FW: An Ontology Network for Annotating Open Datasets

Antoine Dupuy[1]([✉])[ID], Nathalie Aussenac-Gilles[1][ID], Christophe Baehr[2][ID], and Cassia Trojahn[1][ID]

[1] IRIT, Université de Toulouse, UT2, CNRS, Toulouse, France
{antoine.dupuy,nathalie.aussenac-gilles,cassia.trojahn}@irit.fr
[2] CNRM UMR-3589, Université de Toulouse, Météo-France, CNRS, Toulouse, France
christophe.baehr@meteo.fr

Abstract. Open datasets are often exposed with insufficient metadata, making difficult to end users the task of identifying those that better fit their needs. One way to overcome this weaknesses is to guarantee compliance of data to the FAIR principles, in particular where the use of ontologies is a key aspect for proving richer metadata schemes. This paper proposes an ontology network, DATA-FW, that aims at representing rich metadata to assist in dataset usage. It exploits different features that are required to meet the user's needs, which have been divided into four distinct components: Core Metadata Component, Structure Component, Usage Component, and Quality Component. Each Component reuses existing and known vocabularies and serves a specific purpose.

Keywords: FAIR data · metadata · structure · ontology network · data quality · data usage

1 Introduction

Bridging the gap between the data needs of end users and the data shared by producers, who generate it primarily for their own purposes, is a major challenge in many domains. Consider the example of meteorological data: the producer Météo France uses its own data to forecast the weather, study climate change, analyze the environment, and create products for various sectors such as agriculture, aviation, rail and health. However, end users may have specific needs and data understanding, such as a company using cranes in Toulouse, wishing to know the number of days in the year when wind speed is too high to maneuver the cranes. This divergence between the producers' and users' needs raises a key issue: how to effectively map the data needs of end users into data information from the producer vocabulary?

Data produced by such producers are in general exposed as large volumes of open data on the web. They can be accessed under open licenses from different portals, such as governmental portals for public data (e.g., data.gouv in France[1] or data.gov[2] in the

---

[1] https://www.data.gouv.fr/fr/.
[2] https://www.data.gov/.

M. Sfakakis et al. (Eds.): MTSR 2024, CCIS 2331, pp. 15–27, 2025.
https://doi.org/10.1007/978-3-031-81974-2_2

US, European portals like the European Data Portal[3]), portals of public services (e.g., the French National Library[4]), or portals of scientific data like Copernicus[5] portals for Earth Sciences. However, it is often exposed with insufficient metadata, making difficult the task of identifying suitable datasets that better fit the needs of users [1].

To address these issues, it is crucial to ensure that data aligns with the FAIR principles (Findability, Accessibility, Interoperability, and Reusability) [12]. These principles consist of 15 recommendations aimed at simplifying data sharing and reuse for both humans and machines. The first step in implementing the FAIR principles is to establish metadata schemes, as 12 out of the 15 FAIR principles are directly related to metadata. Numerous researchers have advocated for metadata schemes based on semantic models (i.e., ontologies), which offer a richer and more detailed representation of metadata [6]. Ontologies are essential for making data types explicit in a format that machines can process, thereby facilitating data FAIRification [7]. While many efforts to enhance data FAIRification focus on specific metadata types, primarily those describing general dataset features and data catalogues, such approach does not fully address the FAIR principles [8]. In addition to the dataset description, it is important to understand the user's context, to translate the language they use to express their needs into the terminology used to describe the data, and to clearly define their requirements to provide relevant data. All this should improve dataset usage. A first step in this process is to identify relevant metadata schemes for describing the datasets.

To serve to this purpose, we propose to design a system that is composed of a conversational agent linked to a large language model and an ontology serving as a knowledge base for representing dataset metadata and open portals information, as illustrated in Fig. 1. A key element in this architecture is the dataset metadata schemes, which we address in this paper. This work is a follow-up to the Semantics4FAIR project[6] and the DMO-Core [2, 11] ontology proposed to represent the structure of tabular open datasets. The DMO-Core ontology is a metadata schema which includes DCAT 2, QB (RDF Data Cube) and CSVW (CSV vocabulary) to describe structured and tabular datasets and their distributions. DMO-Core, however, is not suited to represent information about data usage, data users and data quality. Other complementary ontologies or vocabularies are required to represent such metadata and to meet the user's needs. Moreover, DCAT evolved toward DCAT 3 which includes additional features to describe version history and dataset series. This is why we propose a new and richer model based on an ontology network, that we call DATA-FW. DATA-FW keeps the metadata categories described by DMO-Core: (i) descriptive metadata, provenance metadata, access rights and license metadata and (ii) structure metadata. It extends this representation to (iii) usage and (iv) quality metadata. DATA-FW is organized into four distinct components: Core Metadata Component, Structure Component, Usage Component and Quality Component. Each component reuses existing and known vocabularies and serves a specific purpose. DATA-FW is available on[7].

---

[3] https://ec.europa.eu/info/statistics/eu-open-data-portal_en.

[4] https://data.bnf.fr/.

[5] https://www.copernicus.eu/en/access-data.

[6] https://www.irit.fr/semantics4fair/, accessed on 08th September 2024.

[7] https://w3id.org/data-fw.

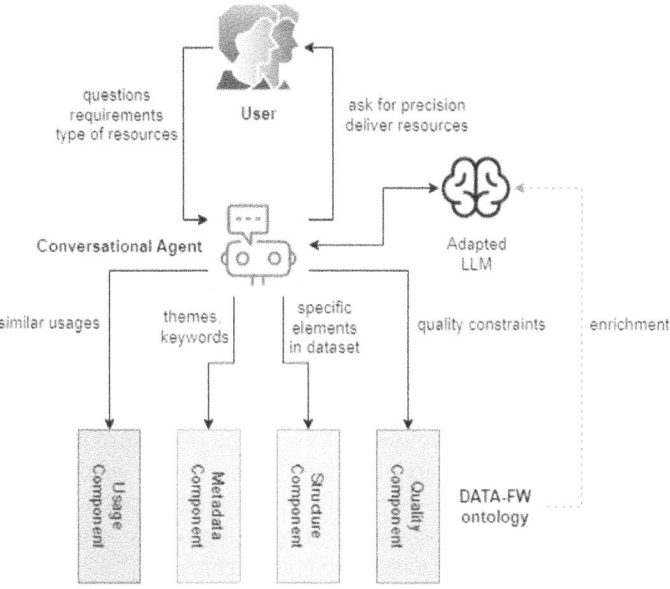

Fig. 1. Data-search system composed of a conversational agent and DATA-FW.

The rest of the paper is organized as follows. Section 2 introduces an illustrative example of data search, with the specific use case of a building company using cranes for their activities. Section 3 specifies the ontology requirements and presents the DATA-FW ontology and its components. Section 4 illustrates the example presented in Sect. 2 and instantiates the ontology. Finally, Sect. 5 summarizes the contributions of the paper and discusses directions for future work.

2   Illustrating Example

2.1   Usage Scenario

The use case is based on the activity of a construction company in the Toulouse metropolitan area. The building company is looking for meteorological data concerning real wind speed measurements and the number of days in the year when crane activity may be disrupted. This estimation requires high-quality data for the entire Toulouse metropolitan area. Two data producers are present in the area and offer wind speed data: Toulouse Métropole and Météo France, the public establishment responsible for weather and climate forecasting in France and leading producer of reference meteorological data, respectively. In our use case, we consider that the user searching for wind speed data is a beginner in the field of meteorology. He will conduct a research to find datasets referenced on three platforms: the Toulouse Métropole platform[8], the

---

[8] https://data.toulouse-metropole.fr, accessed on 08th September 2024.

meteorological data platform of the French government[9] and Météo France historical platform[10]. We will then propose an implementation of the user's research with our solution, focusing on the role of the DATA-FW ontology.

2.2   Querying Toulouse Métropole Data Platform

Toulouse Métropole's open data platform (Data Toulouse Métropole) is part of the Open Data movement, which aims at making the raw data produced by local authorities in their day-to-day activities available to citizens, scientists, associations, businesses and other public services. The building company is looking for meteorological data on this platform. The user enters the keyword 'wind' on the platform. Several datasets contain wind information. However, only three of these are found in the search results. This is due to the fact that the keyword 'wind' is not present in the datasets descriptive metadata. However, we can find two similar terms in the columns of the dataset schema: 'wind' and 'max_gust_wind' (which describes the maximum wind speed for several hours in a single day). In fact, the user can access this information by visualizing the dataset content. With a more precise search, using the keywords 'wind speed', the filter is even more selective. Only one dataset is returned to the user.

2.3   Querying Météo France Data Platforms

Météo France publishes data on two platforms: the recent government data platform[11] and the historical Météo France platform[12]. Basic climatological data, climatological data for climate change and numerical weather prediction (NWP) data are published on the recent government platform. Météo France's historical platform offers a more extensive catalog of in situ observations, radar observations, climatological data, forecast models and data, and climate forecast data. When data has been exported to the new platform, a link was added to the old one, redirecting users to the government platform.

There are several types of information to search for data on the Météo France historical platform. Prior knowledge on the way data is organised in Météo France catalogs (including domain expertise) is rather required to navigate this platform. In the case of a text search with the keyword 'wind' or the keywords 'wind speed', we obtain several datasets, comprising several datasets from several of the catalogs mentioned above. The wind speed measurement data for the Toulouse metropolitan area can be found in the in situ observations category. The information corresponding to the user's needs requires an additional filter, to facilitate the discovery of station data, which corresponds to real wind measurements, necessary for the user. For example, it would be interesting to identify data that has been used for a purpose similar to the one of the user (usage).

The new government data platform also allows users to find data with the keyword 'wind'. Four results are returned to the user, but three of them provide wave model data, which is far from the user's needs. The fourth result is the one obtained when entering

---

[9] https://meteo.data.gouv.fr, accessed on 08th September 2024.

[10] https://donneespubliques.meteofrance.fr, accessed on September 8, 2024.

[11] https://meteo.data.gouv.fr, accessed on 08th September 2024.

[12] https://donneespubliques.meteofrance.fr, accessed on the 8th of September 2024.

the keywords 'wind speed' and contains datasets by French department and periods: 1852–1949, 1950–2022, and 2023–2024. It is not possible to filter out by location and period; all results are displayed, and the user must choose the file(s) of interest. Once the file is selected, the user obtains the available metadata, the data structure, and a data preview. They can then filter the data to find the information they are interested in. The field names are encoded using a nomenclature specific to Météo France. This nomenclature is explained in an accompanying file that describes the codes and data. However, the meteorological vocabulary can be complex for non expert user.

2.4 Target Scenario

Our target scenario involves the user and its interaction with the conversational agent to express their needs. The conversational agent will perform queries on the DATA-FW ontology, which contains datasets metadata from the Toulouse Metropole and Météo France platforms. The conversational agent, with the help of the DATA-FW ontology, automates part of the dataset search. A requirement is that existing datasets are fully described with the DATA-FW ontology (this process could also be automated with the help of an agent).

The user will use the same keywords as before: 'wind' and 'wind speed.' The purpose of the conversational agent in this system is to ask for additional information to refine the user's request. The user is guided in their search to specify the location, the target period of the data, and the intended use of these data, until obtaining daily maximum wind speed data focused on the years 2022 and 2023.

The DATA-FW ontology lists several key pieces of information from the datasets that will serve as filters for the user's queries. By providing additional information regarding usage and quality, it is possible to suggest datasets that have been used in contexts similar to that of the user and take quality constraints into account. For example, in the case of Météo France, the stations are certified by the Weather Meteorological Organization (WMO) and provide standardized data, whereas there is no specified certification for the stations of Toulouse Métropole.

We present the ontology specification in the following section and illustrate this example in Sect. 4.

3 DATA-FW: Dataset Description Ontology Network

The development of the ontology proposed in this paper is based on several steps: specification, conceptualization, formalization, and implementation. These steps are defined in most ontology construction methodologies [4,5,13]. In particular, the NeOn methodology [10] further proposes ontology construction scenarios that enable ontology developers to reuse existing ontological resources, like the Scenario 3 "Reusing ontological resources" promoting the reuse of existing vocabularies and ontologies as a way to improve interoperability.

3.1 Ontology Specification

This specification is organised into four dimensions answering the following four questions: (i) how is the dataset described (Core Metadata), (ii) how is the dataset structured (Structure), (iii) what is the quality information represented in the dataset description (Quality), (iv) who is the final user and how did he use the dataset (Usage). The concept of "dataset", a key element in our ontology, is rather abstract and can vary depending on the community [3]. In this paper, we use the DCAT (Data Catalog Vocabulary)[13] definition of dataset: "A collection of data, published or curated by a single agent, and available for access or download in one or more formats".

3.2 Ontology Reuse

The NeOn methodology includes a set of activities related to the reuse of existing ontologies within the conceptualization step. In order to structure the knowledge about datasets, we need to represent the dimensions defined above: Core Metadata, Structure, Quality and Usage. According to these dimensions, we searched for ontologies into the following repositories: Linked Open Vocabularies (LOV)[14], vocab.org[15], ontologi.es[16] and OntoHub[17]. We also searched for ontologies under development, in the current and past work of the W3C working groups. The selected ontologies were then evaluated regarding their relevance to the ontology specification and FAIRness criteria. Five vocabularies were selected to cover the dimensions of the dataset description: (1) DCAT 3 (Data Catalog Vocabulary, prefix: dcat)[18] to describe dataset core metadata (descriptive, provenance, access right, license, distributions); DCAT 3 is under development but proposing dataset versioning and dataset series, which are collections of datasets sharing common features; (2) RDF Data Cube (QB, prefix: qb)[19] to represent the structure of a dataset thanks to the "component" concept, including their dimensions, measures, and indicators; (3) Friend Of A Friend (FOAF, prefix: foaf)[20] for describing people and their relationships to represent individuals involved in the dataset publishing, discovery and usage processes like the dataset producer and the users; (4) Dataset Usage Vocabulary (DUV, prefix: duv)[21], which is dedicated to describing users and the usage of datasets; (5) Data Quality Vocabulary (DQV, prefix: dqv)[22], to describe quality certificates, quality metadata, quality policies, quality measurements and quality feedbacks.

These five vocabularies are organized into the four components of the DATA-FW ontology presented below.

---

[13] https://www.w3.org/TR/vocab-dcat.

[14] https://lov.linkeddata.es/dataset/lov/, accessed on 08th September 2024.

[15] http://purl.org/vocab/, accessed on 08th September 2024.

[16] http://ontologi.es, accessed on 08th September 2024.

[17] https://ontohub.org/, accessed on 08th September 2024.

[18] https://www.w3.org/TR/vocab-dcat-3/, accessed on 08th September 2024.

[19] https://www.w3.org/TR/vocab-data-cube/, accessed on 08th September 2024.

[20] https://xmlns.com/foaf/spec/, accessed on 08th September 2024.

[21] https://www.w3.org/TR/vocab-duv/, accessed on 08th September 2024.

[22] https://www.w3.org/TR/vocab-dqv/, accessed on 08th September 2024.

3.3   Core Metadata Component

The Core Metadata Component, based on the DCAT-3 Vocabulary (Data Catalog, version3) and inspired from DMO-Core, is dedicated to describing and representing the following types of dataset metadata: (i) descriptive metadata for data indexing and discovery (title, keywords, etc.), (ii) metadata about data provenance and (iii) metadata about access rights and usage licenses. DCAT 3 provides a standardized way to describe datasets and data catalogs, including metadata such as title, description, keywords, and distribution details, dataset series and dataset version. The Core Metadata component is illustrated in Fig. 2. The major difference between this component and the DMO-Core ontology relies on the use of DCAT 3 instead of DCAT 2. DCAT 3 includes the representation of version history and series of datasets. Furthermore, in DMO-Core, the distribution is linked to the tabular structure of the dataset through the CSVW vocabulary[23], whereas in DATA-FW the distribution is independent of the dataset structure.

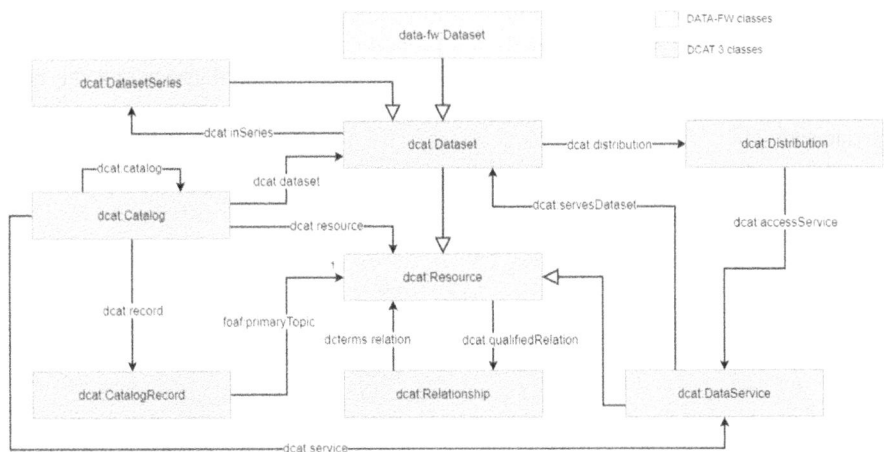

Fig. 2. DATA-FW Core Metadata Component based on DCAT 3.

Figure 2 shows the DCAT-3 vocabulary classes used in the Core Metadata component. The classes `dcat:Dataset`, `dcat:Distribution` and `dcat:DataService` are used to define datasets and their distribution (Excel, JSON, CSV files), and data access (through API, download). The `dcat:Resource` class defines creators, publishers, title, keywords, license and version. The `dcat:Catalog` and `dcat:CatalogRecord` classes are used to define the catalogs in which the datasets are stored, and the metadata linked to these catalogs. The `dcat:DatasetSeries` class enables the creation of collections of datasets with common characteristics (theme, location, period). The Core Metadata Component is linked to other components through the `data-fw:Dataset` class, which is a subclass of `qb:DataSet` and `dcat:Dataset`.

---

[23] https://www.w3.org/ns/csvw/, accessed on 08th September 2024.

Specifically, `data-fw:Dataset` serves as a central class that connects the Core Metadata Component to other components. `data-fw:Dataset` combines the properties of `dcat:Dataset` and `qb:DataSet`.

3.4   Structure Component

The Structure Component, grounded in the RDF Data Cube vocabulary, was primary designed to represent the structure of a dataset defining it in components, including their dimensions, measures, and indicators. RDF Data Cube enables the representation of statistical data in RDF format, allowing for the description of multi-dimensional datasets and their structure. The user's query can thus focus on specific structural elements of the datasets. Additionally, the user may only need a portion of the data contained in the dataset; the RDF Data Cube vocabulary can return only the part of the dataset that matches the user's needs. The Structure Component is illustrated in Fig. 3. The classes `qb:DataStructureDefinition` defines the structure of the dataset and the `qb:DimensionProperty`, `qb:AttributeProperty` and `qb:MeasureProperty` classes specify the properties of the dataset components. The `qb:DataSet` and `qb:Observation` classes are used to define datasets and the data they contain. The `qb:Slice` class, on the other hand, is used to represent portions of the dataset.

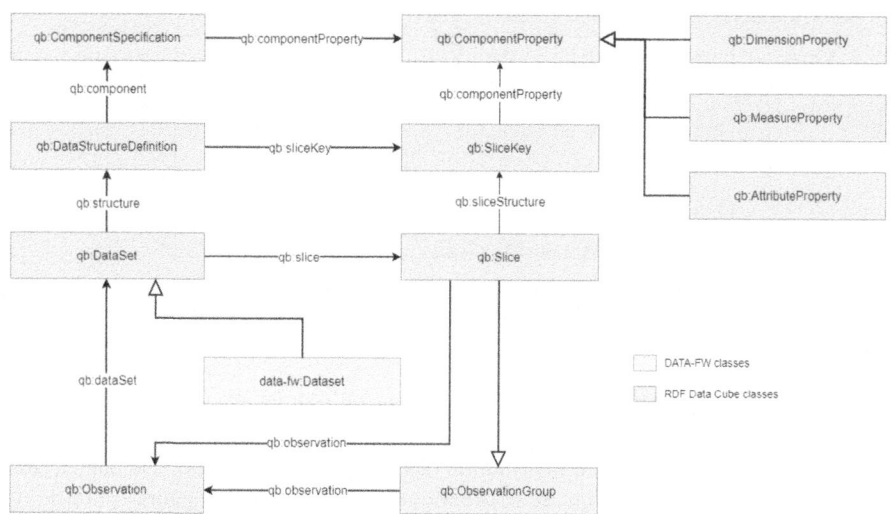

Fig. 3. DATA-FW Structure Component based on RDF Data Cube

As for the Core Metadata Component, the Structure Component is connected to other components through the class `data-fw:Dataset`, as explained in Sect. 3.3.

3.5   Usage Component

The Usage Component, combining the Friend of a Friend Vocabulary (FOAF) and the Data Usage Vocabulary (DUV), is dedicated to describing the datset users and usage. FOAF provides a vocabulary for describing people and their relationships, allowing for the representation of users involved in the dataset publishing, discovery and usage processes. For example, the professional social network LinkedIn uses FOAF to model user profiles and professional relationships [9]. DUV focuses on describing data usage and user's feedbacks, enabling users to specify how data can be used, reused, and attributed. Figure 4 presents the classes of the Dataset Usage Vocabulary (DUV) and Friend of A Friend (FOAF), with the class foaf:Agent and its subclasses foaf:Person, foaf:Organization and foaf:Group. The duv:Usage represents usages that can be associated to a given dataset or distribution. The duv:UsageTool class represents tools for using datasets. The duv:UserFeedback and duv:RatingFeedback classes represent user feedback. The dqv:QualityFeedback class will be covered in the following section on the Quality Component.

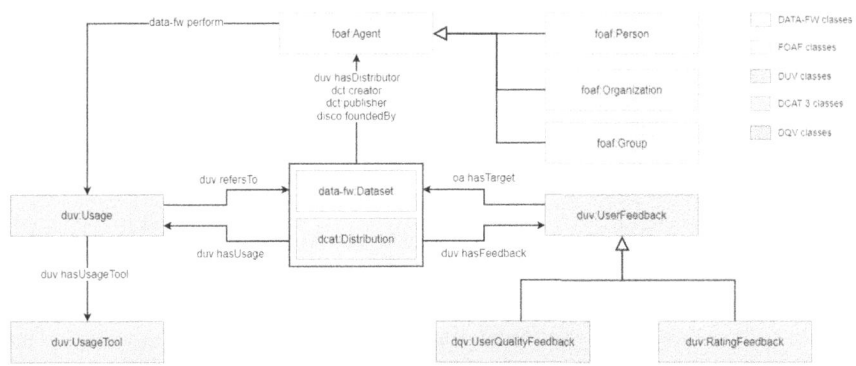

Fig. 4. DATA-FW Usage Component based on the DUV vocabulary

The Usage Component is linked to the Core Metadata Component through various properties and relationships. Specifically, the duv:hasUsage and duv:refersTo properties establish connections between the duv:Usage class and the data-fw:Dataset and dcat:Distribution classes, facilitating the association of dataset usage with relevant metadata. Additionally, the oa:hasTarget (from the Web Annotation Ontology, http://www.w3.org/ns/oa#) and duv:hasFeedback properties link the duv:User Feedback class to the data-fw:Dataset and dcat:Distribution classes, enabling the capture of feedback related to dataset usage. Furthermore, the duv:hasDistributor, dct:creator, dct:publisher, and disco:foundedBy properties establish connections between the foaf:Agent class and the data-fw:Dataset and dcat:Distribution classes, indicating the involvement of agents in dataset distribution and publication activities. In addition, a data-fw:perform property has been introduced between the foaf:Agent and duv:Usage classes to describe users who use one or more datasets, linking the FOAF and DUV vocabularies.

3.6   Quality Component

The Quality Component of DATA-FW, built upon the Data Quality Vocabulary (DQV),
aims to describe the quality of datasets. DQV allows for the description of data quality
aspects. It enables users to assess the quality of datasets and make informed decisions
about their suitability for specific tasks or analyses.

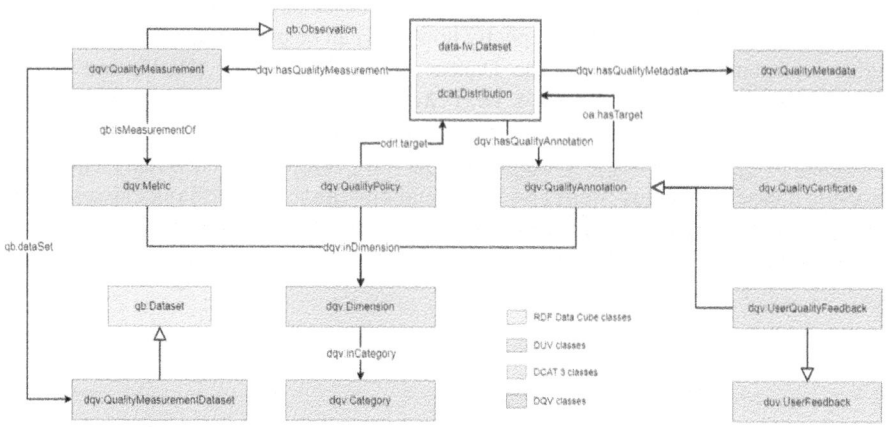

Fig. 5. DATA-FW Quality Component based on the DQV vocabulary

Figure 5 illustrates the Data Quality Vocabulary (DQV) classes used in the
DATA-FW ontology. The classes dqv:QualityPolicy, dqv:QualityMetadata,
dqv:QualityAnnotation and its subclasses dqv:QualityCertificate and
dqv:QualityUserFeedback represent information about dataset quality. The
dqv:QualityMeasurement class is used to collect measurable quality information. This information can then be collected in a dataset represented by the
dqv:QualityMeasurementDataset class, itself a subclass of the RDF Data
Cube qb:DataSet class. The Quality Component is connected to the Core
Metadata Component through various properties and relationships. Firstly, the
dqv:hasQualityAnnotation property establishes connections between quality annotations and data-fw:Dataset and dcat:Distribution classes. This property
allows for the inclusion of quality-related annotations, providing additional context about their quality attributes given by users feedback or certificates. The
odrl:target property links the class dqv:QualityPolicy to data-fw:Dataset
and dcat:Distribution classes, allowing the specification of a quality policy
applied to a dataset or a distribution. Furthermore, the dqv:hasQualityMetadata
property linking the dqv:QualityMetadata class with the data-fw:Dataset
and dcat:Distribution classes allows the incorporation of structured metadata describing quality-related aspects of datasets and distribution entities.
Finally, the dqv:hasQualityMeasurement property establishes connections between
dqv:QualityMeasurement and the data-fw:Dataset and dcat:Distribution
classes, which enables the representation of quality-related metrics and indicators.

Additionally, the Quality Component is linked to the Structure Component through the extension of two classes from the Data Cube ontology: `dqv:QualityMeasurement` inherits from `qb:Observation` and `dqv:QualityMeasurementDataset` inheritants from `qb:DataSet`. The Quality Component is also linked to the Usage Component by extending the `dqv:UserQualityFeedback` class from the `duv:UserFeedback` class. This link captures user feedback on the quality of datasets, providing information on the perceived quality of `data-fw:Dataset` and `dcat:Distribution` and their impact on user interactions.

4   Use Case

This section looks backs at the construction company user presented in Sect. 2.1, who uses our conversational agent to search for datasets related to wind speed in order to calculate the number of days in the year when their cranes will not be able to operate. We focus on the role of the ontology in this dataset search. First, the user asks a question containing the keywords 'wind' and 'wind speed' to retrieve the corresponding datasets. The role of the conversational agent is then to refine the user's request. For example, it may ask the user to specify the location or the intended use of the data. The metadata associated with the datasets are fetched through the platforms APIs and stored in the DATA-FW ontology, enabling a comparison of the four metadata dimensions (core, structure, usage, and quality). The step of instantiating the ontology with the metadata from the platforms can also be performed by the agent. Listing 1.1 presents the instantiated ontology according to the Sect. 2 use case.

```
1   ex:MeteoFrance a foaf:Organization .
2
3   ex:QUOT_departement_31_periode_2023-2024_RR-T-Vent a data-fw:Dataset ;
4       dct:title "QUOT_departement_31_periode_2023-2024_RR-T-Vent"@fr ;
5       dct:creator ex:MeteoFrance ;
6       dcat:distribution ex:QUOT_departement_31_periode_2023-2024_RR-T-Vent-CSV ;
7       qb:structure ex:QUOT_departement_31_periode_2023-2024_RR-T-Vent-structure ;
8       dqv:hasQualityAnnotation ex:WMOCertification ;
9       duv:hasUsage ex:PreviousUsage ;
10      duv:hasFeedback ex:feedback-1, ex:feedback-2 .
11
12  ex:WMOCertification a dqv:QualityCertificate .
13
14  ex:QUOT_departement_31_periode_2023-2024_RR-T-Vent-CSV a dcat:Distribution ;
15      dcat:downloadURL ex:QUOT_departement_31_periode_2023-2024_RR-T-Vent-CSV-URL .
16
17  ex:QUOT_departement_31_periode_2023-2024_RR-T-Vent-structure
18      a qb:DataStructureDefinition ;
19      qb:component [
20          a qb:ComponentSpecification ;
21          qb:measure ex:FXY] .
22
23  ex:FXY a qb:MeasureProperty ;
24      rdfs:label "FXY" ;
25      skos:definition """Daily maximum of the hourly maximum wind force averaged
26          over 10 minutes at 10 meters (in m/s and 1/10)."""@en .
27
28  ex:feedback-1 a duv:UserFeedback ;
29      data-fw:content "CSV distribution file not properly encrypted"@en .
30
31  ex:feedback-2 a duv:UserFeedback ;
32      data-fw:content "A lot of information is missing from the dataset."@en .
33
34  ex:user-1 a foaf:Agent ;
35      data-fw:performs ex:CalculationDaysCranesActivityOff .
36
37  ex:PreviousUsage a duv:Usage ;
38      dct:description "Statistical calculations."@en .
39
40  ex:CalculationDaysCranesActivityOff a duv:Usage ;
41      dct:description """Calculate the number of days crane activity may be
42          disrupted with real wind speed measurements."""@en .
```

Listing 1.1. Building Company Search implemented in DATA-FW

The core metadata provides an initial filtering by retrieving dataset titles, descriptions, distributions, etc., to match the user's keywords 'wind' and 'wind speed'. The structural metadata representation helps to identify datasets where a component (e.g., a column description in a CSV distribution) corresponds to data related to 'wind' or 'wind speed', like the `ex:FXY` (l.37) measure property of the `ex:QUOT_departement_31_periode_2023-2024_RR-T-Vent` dataset (l.14 in Listing 1.1). The usage metadata allows for the discovery of datasets specifically used for statistical calculations, as described by `ex:PreviousUsage` (l.55). Finally, the quality metadata representation enables the system to offer the user either certified or non-certified data, depending on their requirements. In our use case, the `ex:QUOT_departement_31_periode_2023-2024_RR-T-Vent` dataset is certified by the `ex:WMOCertification` (l.24).

5   Conclusion

This paper has presented an ontology network to represent different kinds of metadata dimensions: dataset description, dataset structure, usage and users and dataset quality information. This model was used to illustrate a use case involving a user searching for wind force data in the Toulouse Metropole area. This work is part of an approach that aims to facilitate and improve the results of data research, by proposing a representation of complementary information about users and their data use.

In the future, we plan to implement several improvements. First, we will exploit the ontology to integrate datasets of various themes and check the completeness of the properties added to the ontology on more datasets. Indeed, it could be interesting to deepen the representation of user needs and dataset usage. Second, we will implement the conversational agent to test its proposed results. We will test cases with specialized and non-specialized conversational agents to compare results on datasets from specific domains, such as meteorology, which includes a specific vocabulary and nomenclature.

Acknowledgments. This work was funded by the Occitanie region in the context of the MOCK-UP project.

References

1. Ahmad, R.A., et al.: Toward fair semantic publishing of research dataset metadata in the open research knowledge graph (2024)
2. Annane, A., Kamel, M., Trojahn, C., Aussenac-Gilles, N., Comparot, C., Baehr, C.: Improving FAIRness of the SYNOP meteorological data set with semantic metadata. Int. J. Metadata Semant. Ontol. **16**(2), 118–137 (2023)
3. Chapman, A., et al.: Dataset search: a survey. VLDB J. **29**(1), 251–272 (2020)
4. Cuel, R., Cristiani, M.: Ontologies as intra-organizational coordination tools. In: Proceedings of I-KNOW 2005 (2005)
5. Grüninger, M., Fox, M.: Methodology for the design and evaluation of ontologies. In: Workshop on Basic Ontological Issues in Knowledge Sharing (1995)

6. Guizzardi, G.: Ontology, Ontologies and the "I" of FAIR. Data Intell. **2**(1–2), 181–191 (2020)
7. Jacobsen, A., et al.: FAIR principles: interpretations and implementation considerations. Data Intell. **2**(1–2), 10–29 (2020)
8. Koesten, L., Simperl, E., Blount, T., Kacprzak, E., Tennison, J.: Everything you always wanted to know about a dataset: studies in data summarisation. Int. J. Hum. Comput. Stud. **135**, 02367 (2020)
9. Sah, M., Li, J., Wade, V.: Developing knowledge models of social media: a case study on linkedin. Open J. Semant. Web **1**, 1–24 (2014)
10. Suárez-Figueroa, M.C., Gómez-Pérez, A., Fernández-López, M.: The NeOn Methodology for Ontology Engineering (2012)
11. Trojahn, C., Kamel, M., Annane, A., Aussenac-Gilles, N., Nguyen, B.L., Baehr, C.: Fairification of multidimensional and tabular data by instantiating a core semantic model with domain knowledge: case of meteorology. In: Garoufallou, E., Vlachidis, A. (eds.) Metadata and Semantic Research, pp. 163–174. Springer Nature Switzerland, Cham (2023). https://doi.org/10.1007/978-3-031-39141-5_14
12. Wilkinson, M., Dumontier, M., et al.: The FAIR guiding principles for scientific data management and stewardship. Sci. Data **3**(1), 1–9 (2016)
13. Zulkipli, Z.Z., Maskat, R., Teo, N.H.I.: A systematic literature review of automatic ontology construction. Indones. J. Electr. Eng. Comput. Sci **28**(2), 878 (2022)

A Proposed Methodology for Sub-Ontology Development in Comprehensive Scientific Investigation Methods and Tooling

Maria Ioanna Maratsi[1]([✉]) [iD], Nina Gialoussi[2] [iD], Charalampos Alexopoulos[1] [iD], and Yannis Charalabidis[1] [iD]

[1] University of the Aegean, University Hill, 81100 Mytilene, Greece
{ioanna.m,alexop,yannisx}@aegean.gr
[2] Greek Free and Open-Source Software Alliance, Iroon Polytechneiou 9, 15780 Athens, Greece
ninagial@eellak.gr

Abstract. The role of ontologies in facilitating search capabilities within large collections of data is critical; the integration and analysis of diverse data sources becomes feasible as ontologies frame the data conceptually and provide a common understanding of terms and their relationships- the lack of ontological and conceptual support entailing the opposite effect. Along with documents and data lost in the vast-ness of available yet disparate data sources, numerous scientific papers and published research remain undiscovered due to poor linking to their respective scientific domain and investigation method(s) described in them. Within the scope of this study is to retrieve existing Wikidata method codes for 3 disciplines: psychology, neuroscience and cultural heritage, and analyse them, with the purpose of identifying gaps in the usage of hierarchical levels or codes, and examining whether they are currently capable of sufficiently describing the methodological domains in question, while also pertaining to a suitable level of specificity in order for the related data to be efficiently and effectively queried and retrieved. The findings revealed several issues regarding the discoverability and semantic search capabilities to retrieve scientific literature papers on research (or investigation) methods and tooling for the in-word disciplines. In this light, a proposed methodology to alleviate the current situation is drafted, introducing the utilisation of technological means, such as LLMs, to assist in identifying orphan categories of methods or tools and, by benchmarking against basic existing ontologies (e.g., FrameNet or other related Linked Open Vocabularies), to enrich the hierarchical structure of current representation practices in this regard.

Keywords: Linked data · linked open data · semantic interoperability · wikidata · semantic search · knowledge graph · scientific method · wikidata codes · LLMs · linked open vocabularies · LOV · ontology mapping · scientific tools

M. Sfakakis et al. (Eds.): MTSR 2024, CCIS 2331, pp. 28–43, 2025.
https://doi.org/10.1007/978-3-031-81974-2_3

1   Introduction

The role of ontologies in facilitating search capabilities within large collections of data is critical, allowing for better management and organisation of information in data lakes or warehousing cases. Ontology mapping and reuse can improve data discover-ability and findability across vast data sources, while at the same time enabling a semantic search which is not limited to keyword matching. The integration and analysis of diverse data sources also become feasible as ontologies frame the data conceptually and provide a common understanding and structurisation of terms and their relationships, therefore the lack of ontological and conceptual support entails an adverse effect. Along with documents and data lost in the vastness of available yet disparate data sources, numerous scientific papers and published research remain undiscovered due to the poor linking of the articles to their respective scientific do-main and method(s) used. If a researcher tries to fetch "Concepts/Methods in X Discipline", there is no structured, uniform, or predictable way to retrieve content. Re-search articles can often be retrieved by keyword searches of the respective scientific domain one wishes to explore, however, the case is not that trivial when the in-word domain is not explicitly mentioned in the article's metadata (e.g., title, keywords, description etc.), when the research falls into multidisciplinarity, or when it uses shared scientific methodological tools which belong to more than one domain, thus making it difficult to retrieve relevant and efficient results. In this light, the present study focuses on identifying existing challenges in scientific papers discovery and looking into the status of a known repository (e.g., Wikidata) in order to pro-pose a method to alleviate this issue by introducing more efficient and relevant search capabilities. The methodology proposed relies on the ability of ontological structures to capture complex relationships between concepts, which can be used to infer new knowledge, for instance allowing a user (e.g., researcher) to identify new relationships or hypotheses regarding a specific scientific experiment they are interested in.

In this context, the first phase of the present study is to analyse existing Wikidata codes referring to scientific evaluation metrics and methods of three chosen disciplines (Psychology, Neuroscience, and Cultural Heritage) in order to assess the status for each domain and provide an overview of needs and inadequacies currently pre-sent. More specifically, the research question posed in this small-scale study is: "Is there currently a sufficient system of codes to describe the disciplines chosen, the methods and lab techniques for each, in a clear and efficient manner? Are they following a semantically sound hierarchical structure to allow for scientific literature discovery?" In graph theory terms: "do the existing relevant codes on Wikidata have the betweenness centrality one would expect?". In addition, the goal is to examine whether it is possible to retrieve scientific papers by method and not by discipline, in other words, whether a domain-agnostic search approach can bring forth relevant results for the user. Within the scope of this study is to retrieve existing Wikidata method codes for the disciplines/domains of psychology, neuroscience and cultural heritage, and analyse the existing hierarchical structure that these codes follow, with the purpose of identifying semantic gaps in the usage of hierarchical levels or codes, and examining whether they are currently capable of sufficiently describing the methodological domains in question, while also pertaining to a suitable level of specificity in order for the related data to be efficiently and effectively queried and retrieved. Afterwards, a methodology based on the results of this study and involving automation and technological means, such as the use of Large Language Models (LLMs) is proposed in this direction.

The rest of the paper is structured as follows: a brief reference to closely related background literature is included in Sect. 2, while the methodological steps and results, along with the proposed methodology for future research built upon the findings, are presented in Sects. 3 and 4 respectively. Lastly, Sect. 5 includes the insights gained through the conducted research but also some limitations and future directions.

2 Background

Reusable ontologies may provide the ground for standardisation, help reduce ambiguity, and improve data consistency across different research disciplines, making it feasible to integrate findings from various resources. Especially in the case of studies where inter-disciplinary methods and approaches take place, the role of a common framework to describe concepts and their relationships becomes pivotal, enabling the combination and analysis of data, but also allowing for advanced search capabilities, such as searching for all studies that used a specific research method or experimental tool or setup, regard-less of the domain-specific terms used to describe them in the initial scientific study. Furthermore, the use and reuse of well-established ontologies may facilitate metadata annotation, allowing for the enrichment of a given dataset or document file with infor-mation about the methods used to collect or analyse the data in it. General knowledge organisation ontologies and schemas such as Dublin Core, or the Simple Knowledge Organisation System (skos) allow for a high-level structural description, yet in targeted disciplines, domain-specific schemas might be preferred or developed. The emphasis on domain-specific vocabularies and their reuse to establish standardization for knowledge representation as one of the cornerstones of Linked Data principles was pinpointed by Maratsi et al. (2024) [1] who analysed the potential of Linked Open Vocabularies (LOV) in identifying suitable vocabularies as bases for reuse in domain-specific context. In the context of the present study, the aim is to also involve relevant ontologies/vocabularies of the chosen analysed domains in order to use them as additional ontological basis for experimentation.

Kume and Kozaki (2022) [2] proposed a method to extract relevant concepts from linked open data (LOD) using Wikidata as the main knowledge graph to extract class hierarchies for a given domain (in their case polymer materials and physical properties) and then construct a domain-specific ontology based on those structures. Wikidata, one of the most prominent open knowledge graphs (KGs), has several times been studied to analyse relations of cross-domain data. Haller et al. (2022) [3] investigated the potential of Wikidata's ontological expressiveness and discovered that while a great number of entities (classes, individuals, properties) are sufficiently described, the links among them are not sufficiently established. The rationale behind the present study is also to initially examine the status of Wikidata's existing codes for scientific methods and tools referred to in available scientific literature and papers in order to check whether they are sufficient to describe the respective knowledge disciplines' research. As far as science maps to visualise the landscape of scientific activity and domains is concerned, Bollen et al. (2009) [4] used large-scale (approx. 1 billion) clickstream data to track user behaviour on Web of Science search and showcased their results in their own derived science map, presented in Fig. 1.

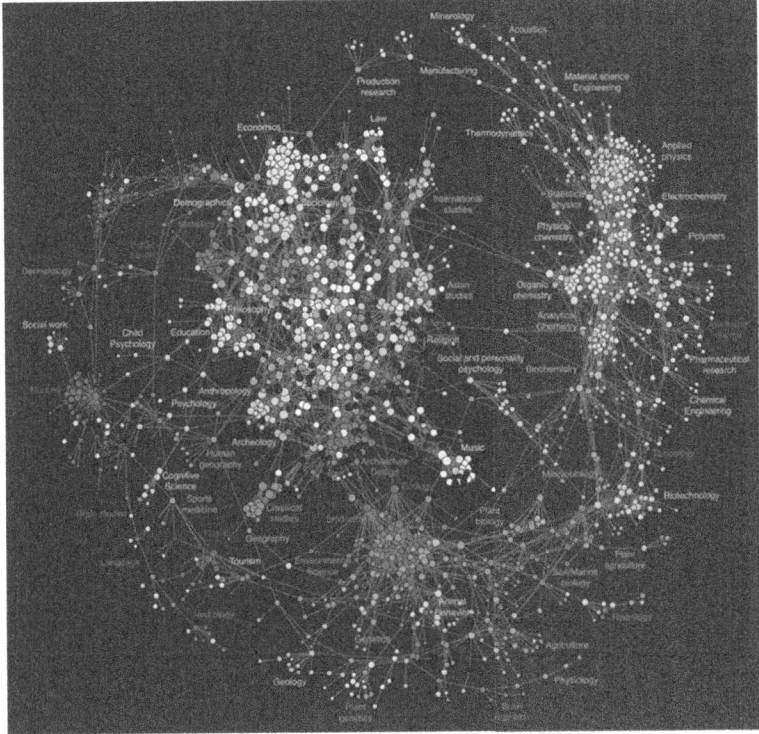

Fig. 1. The map of science derived from clickstream data by Bollen et al. (2009)

Figure 1 shows user behavior from link following over the Web of Science (Fig. 1). The figure shows that social sciences and humanities are lumped together in a big pile. It is noticeable that some scientific domains would expectedly lie closer to each other due to their proximal concepts and areas of study, however, this is not the case here. Furthermore, the different fields of science are fragmented, and more quantitative fields in humanities like behavioral economics, psychology, cognitive science show a "tendency towards fragmentation". No matter how distinct the "hard" sciences are to the "soft" ones, whenever the scientists and engineers meddle in topics as education, politics, or social issues, they usually resort to more or less the same techniques as the "target fields" and, instead of "savoring" those via the scientific method, they might adopt bad practices from another era, e.g., the things that might use to seem as a good idea to the education/political science/sociology expert in the past.

On another note, Wikidata has been used as the basic knowledge graph to create more coherent, structured and readable data and metadata, such as the case of Agarwal and Mamidi (2023) [5] who developed a method to generate articles about scientists in Hindi, Schmidt et al. (2022) [6] who aimed to address data publishing practices in

Archaeology by presenting the current challenges and potential of linked open data in this domain, and Thornton et al. (2017) [7] who used Wikidata as the knowledge base to investigate the perspective of cultural heritage description and metadata generation as linked open data.

3 Methodology

In this study, the first step has been to analyse available Wikidata codes representing and describing relevant to the chosen domains' scientific methodological tools. The analysis includes three chosen domains/disciplines: Psychology, Neuroscience, and Cultural Heritage. In this small-scale experiment the search is limited to these example disciplines and respective publicly available ontologies/vocabularies (e.g., in LOV) for each of them. Initially, the authors retrieved methods, tests, experiments, and practical approaches used for the 3 chosen domains using Wikidata's SPARQL Query Service. To facilitate the search and refine the queries to return as many results as possible, the basic methodological and experimental tool categories for each domain, apart from the authors' prior knowledge, were informed by ChatGPT in the form of the question: "Which are the main categories of scientific methods and experiments in the X domain?", where X is the given domain each time. The reason for this step is that the conventional SPARQL queries initially used to retrieve experiments and method tools for each domain returned either too few or plenty of irrelevant or too generic results, so eventually the queries which returned the highest number of relevant results (they are shown in Table 1) were constructed using the UNION operator for the most basic categories of methods and tools for each. The queries return the UNION of all instances (P31) of any subclass (P279) of the chosen categories in the English language annotated by the respective Wikidata code. For instance, wd:Q873512 is the code for "psychological test", wd:Q2116008 for "psychological experiments", and wd:Q60784892 for "psychological methodology".

The fact that the results of the initial queries were too few or too generic raised suspicions about the structure of the respective codes, so further analysis was performed. The overall methodological steps followed for the initial Wikidata code analysis are shown in Fig. 2.

The analysis on Wikidata was centred on the hierarchical structure of basic, domain-specific retrieved codes, for each domain, having the class "method" in focus. Then, having the desired method categories for each domain on the other end, the hierarchical distance between them and the "method" code is recursively followed as a path in the form of "Subclass of" (annotated as P279 on Wikidata) until they meet. In Table 2, some examples of codes for each domain are presented, including both cases of codes which could trace back to "method" and others which do not belong in the same path (tree branch) as "method", tracing back to other parent nodes (code).

Table 1. The SPARQL queries used for code retrieval and the number of returned results

	Psychology	Neuroscience	Cultural Heritage

Index of Queries	SELECT ?item ?itemLabel ?itemDescription WHERE {
	
	{
	
	?item wdt:P31/wdt:P279* wd:Q873512.
	
	}
	
	UNION
	
	{
	
	?item wdt:P31/wdt:P279* wd:Q2116008.
	
	}
	
	SERVICE wikibase:label {
	bd:serviceParam wikibase:language
	"[AUTO_LANGUAGE],en". }
	
	}
		SELECT ?item ?itemLabel ?itemDescription WHERE {
		
		{
		
		?item wdt:P31/wdt:P279*
		wd:Q551875.
		
		}
		
		UNION
		
		{
		
		?item wdt:P31/wdt:P279*
		wd:Q4914995.
		
		}
		
		UNION
		
		{
		
		?item wdt:P31/wdt:P279*
		wd:Q901663.
		
		}
		
		SERVICE wikibase:label {
		bd:serviceParam wiki-
		base:language
		"[AUTO_LANGUAGE],en". }
		
		}
			SELECT ?item ?itemLabel WHERE
			{
			
			{
			
			?item wdt:P31/wdt:P279*
			wd:Q959782.
			
			}
			
			UNION
			
			{
			
			?item wdt:P31/wdt:P279*
			wd:Q2667413.
			
			}
			
			UNION
			
			{
			
			?item wdt:P31/wdt:P279*
			wd:Q780909.
			
			}
			
			UNION
			
			{
			
			?item wdt:P31/wdt:P279*
			wd:Q1196545.
			
			}
			
			UNION
			
			{
			
			?item wdt:P31/wdt:P279*
			wd:Q1074953.
			
			}
			
			SERVICE wikibase:label {
			bd:serviceParam wikibase:language
			"[AUTO_LANGUAGE],en". }
			
			}

# Number of retrieved codes	320	48	1541

As can be noticed, the depths for each path can differ significantly, ranging from depth 1 (1 intermediate code between "method" and the desired domain-specific code) to depth 7 (7 intermediate codes/hierarchical levels between them) and not following a clear bifurcation in uniform depth hierarchical levels. In addition, many domain-specific methodologies and tooling fall under the structure of other codes, such as "science", "class", "entity", or none, indicating a lack of sufficient intermediate nodes to capture the desired specificity of tools and methods found, but also their clear link and relationship

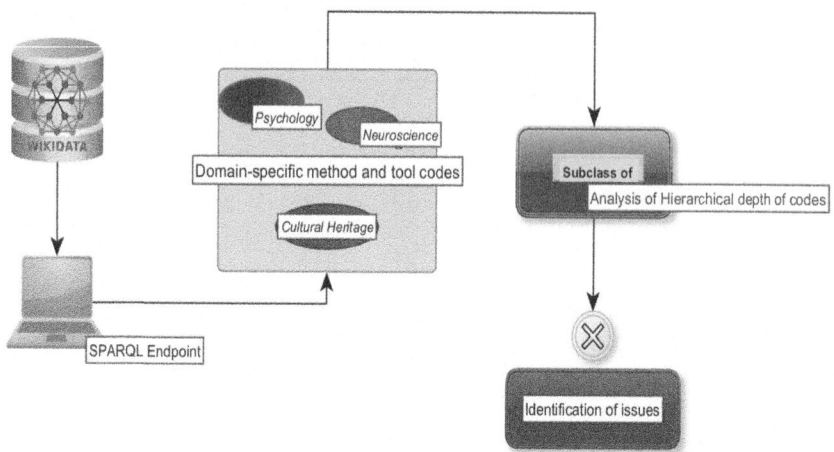

Fig. 2. The methodological steps followed for the analysis of Wikidata codes

with similar methods and tools of the other domains, something which bears semantic significance.

Table 3 shows the distribution of retrieved codes, the average number of hierarchical levels of the results (distance from "method") and the number of results per hierarchical path (the hierarchical paths refer to the included codes in the queries of Table 1, showing how many results were returned for each part in the query, separated by commas). The indicative average number in this Table is calculated based on the presented examples of Table 2 and focuses on the "method" code as starting node.

The third parameter of Table 3 shows a tendency for an imbalanced return of results per category, although practically it should not be so, considering that, for example, the last category of Neuroscience (wd:Q901663 - molecular dynamics simulation) only returns 1 result, or the Cultural Heritage category wd:Q2667413 - characterization returns only 2 results, while the Cultural Heritage category wd:Q959782 - archaeological excavation returns 1527-most of the query results.

Table 2. Examples of hierarchical depth between domain-specific method-related codes on Wikidata.

Psychology
method/test/experiment/**psychological experiment**
method/procedure/medical procedure/medical test/**psychological test**
method/scholarly method/analysis/methodology /**psychological methodology**
method/procedure /medical procedure/medical treatment/psychotherapy/behavior/therapy/**cognitive behavioral therapy**
biological phenomenon/biological process/psychological process/mental process/**emotional process**
science/natural science/life sciences/health sciences/psychology/**experimental psychology**

Neuroscience
method/procedure /medical procedure/medical diagnosis/radiology/roentgenology /neuroimaging
method/technique/visualization/biological imaging
method/scholarly method/analysis /data analysis/behavior analysis
method/technique/visualization/biomedical imaging
entity/observable entity/phenomenon/natural phenomenon/biological phenomenon/neural coding
science/natural science/biology/computational biology
science/natural science/biology/physiology/electrophysiology
science/natural science/biology/histology
science/natural science/life sciences/health sciences/pharmacology

Cultural Heritage
method/scholarly method/analysis/methodology/field research/archaeological excavation
method/test/materials testing/characterization
method/quality control method/monitoring and evaluation/monitoring/environmental monitoring/ecological assessment
method/scholarly method/scientific method/dating method/chronological dating/dating method in archaeology
method/technique/ artistic technique/storytelling/digital storytelling
method/scholarly method/analysis/microscopy
science/natural science/materials science/characterization
entity/converter/means/conservation technique
class/series/process/research/Archival research
class/series/activity/process/activity/use/modeling and simulation/scientific modeling/3D modeling
class/series/process/activity/preservation/conservation
class/series/process/activity/preservation/conservation/collections care
none/Imaging of cultural heritage

Table 3. Level path measurements for the retrieved codes.

	Psychology	Neuroscience	Cultural Heritage
# of retrieved codes	320	48	1541
indicative average # of hierarchical levels of the results	4.5	4.666	4.5
# of results per domain method category	260, 60	2, 45, 1	1527, 2, 5, 2, 5

3.1 Directed Graph Construction

The results of Table 2 were used to create the directed graph depicting all the nodes and their hierarchical relationships. The directed graph is presented in Fig. 3.

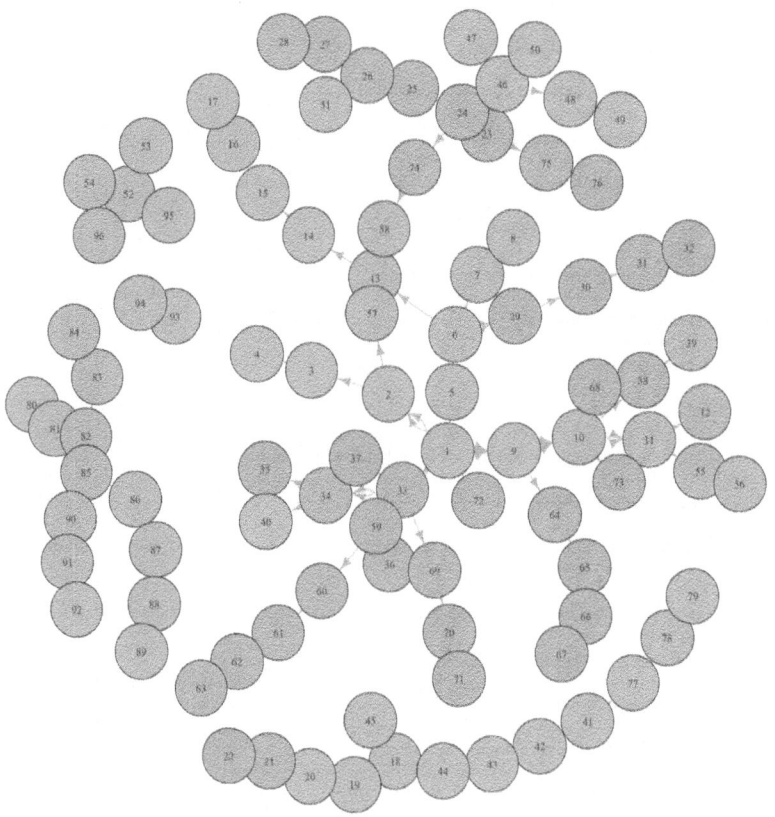

Fig. 3. The directed graph of codes and their hierarchical relationships

The colours used reflect the respective domains. Pink: Psychology, Purple: Neuro-science, Green: Cultural Heritage.

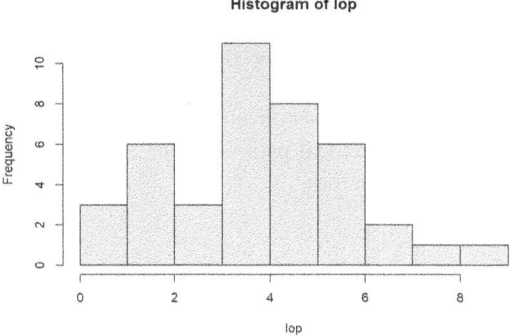

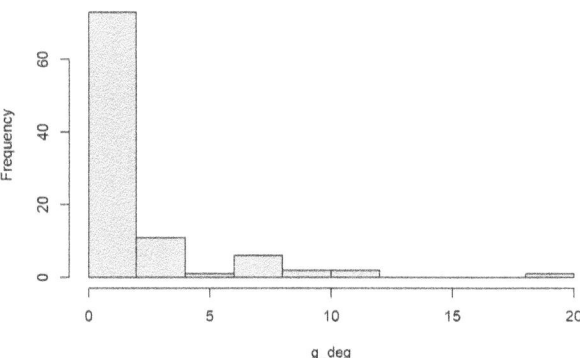

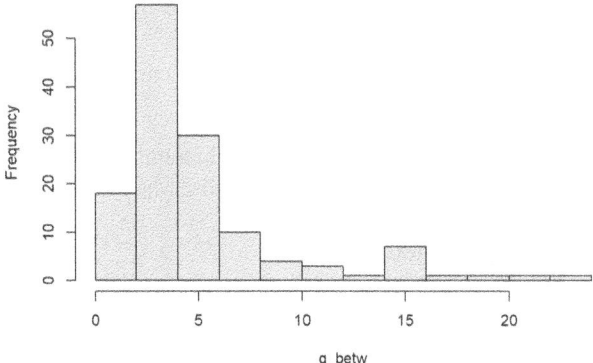

Fig. 4. Graph statistics

Figure 4 shows some statistics and metrics about the constructed graph. For instance, plot length of paths (lop): mean: 4.2, min: 0, max: 9, Graph degree (g_deg): mean: 2.79, min: 1, max: 19, and Graph betweenness (g_betw): mean: 5.45, min: 1, max: 24, range: 23.

The directed graph of Fig. 3 can easily be converted and represented as a tree, where each branch corresponds to one hierarchical path of Table 2. The tree is presented in Fig. 5, using the same colour code as before.

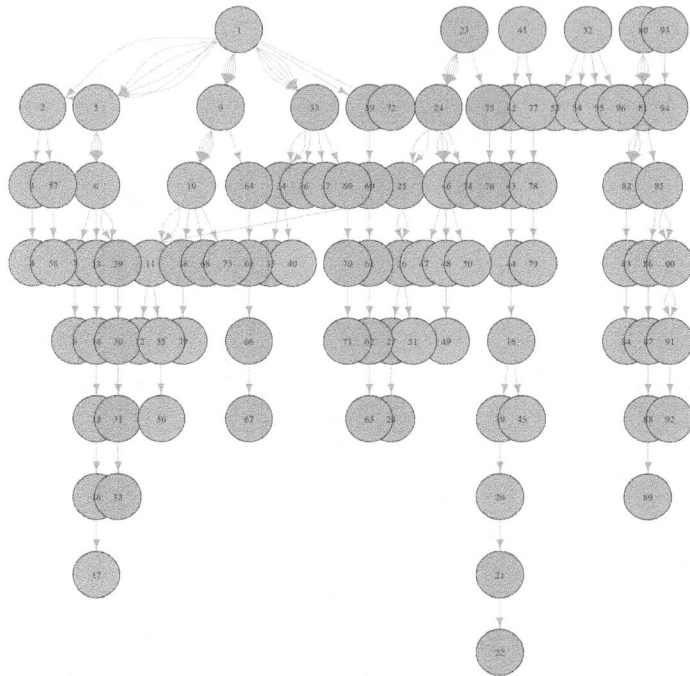

Fig. 5. The tree representation of codes and their hierarchical relationships

The tree structure allows for a clearer view of the hierarchical paths followed by the different nodes. Looking at the paths, the following observations are made:

Nodes With the Most Betweenness
[20] "psychological process", [19] "biological process", [53] "Neural modeling fields", [54] "chemogenetics".

Main Branches of [1] "Method"
[2] "test", [5] "procedure", [9] "scholarly method", [33] "technique", [59] "quality control method", [72] "historical method".

Nodes NOT Present Under "Method"

[24] "natural science", [75] "applied science", [42] "observable entity", [77] "converter", [53] "Neural modeling fields", [54] "chemogenetics", [95] "Imaging of cultural heritage", [96] "Direct historical approach", [81] "series", [94] "Category: Dating methodologies in archaeology". Instead, they derive from [23] "science", [41] "entity", [80] "class", [93] "Wikimedia category", or [52] none.

Of specific interest is also to see where different disciplines "meet". For instance, it is observable that the interface of Science to Cultural Heritage is via [74] materials science and [76] conservation science.

4   Results

4.1   Identified Issues

The applied method described in the previous Section revealed several insights but also issues emerging from the Wikidata codes analysis and the presented graph. Some of them concern all three domains (Psychology, Neuroscience, Cultural Heritage), while others are more oriented towards one specific domain. The common issues identified are the following:

i) Inability to retrieve all (or the majority of) relevant results using only one query.

The SPARQL queries used to retrieve the scientific method codes for each domain had to be manually adapted in order to return more results, otherwise the result sample was either poor in relevance/too generic or very small. This implies an insufficiency of intermediate codes which would enable a targeted search for one (or more but not too many) specific branch of hierarchically sound structure to retrieve all the relevant results. As a consequence, to retrieve all of the desired results one should manipulate the query towards including (with the help of logical operators) several "sibling" nodes which are currently considered as "orphans" and could otherwise be organised semantically under intermediate parent nodes to facilitate a more efficient semantic search.

ii) Scholarly publications contain knowledge not captured sufficiently by the existing Wikidata codes.

A lot of knowledge on Wikidata belongs to scientific/scholarly publications which are not easy to include in the querying service yet include a lot of information that is not always captured in the current hierarchical structure. Many of them include plenty of basic information about the methodological concepts, techniques, experiments and other tools used, however, they are not sufficiently linked to the respective domain(s) they refer to. Especially in cases of multidisciplinary research where various methods mentioned might concern more than one knowledge domain, in the current situation, should one search in a domain-agnostic way (e.g., specifying the method or tool instead of scientific domain), they would not retrieve so many relevant results, leaving plenty of research undiscovered.

iii) Many code groups of average hierarchical depth level (up to 3 or 4) are empty, not returning any results.

On many occasions, the search was made more difficult due to the lack of codes on certain levels. For instance, while backtracking from a specific method or tool towards its parent node, there were many times either no intermediate nodes (codes) at all, jumping from a general one such as "Wikimedia category" directly to the specific method, or following a very long (deep) and domain-specific path, not allowing for bifurcations or semantically important links to other, proximal concepts and domains.

Some identified issues which were more domain-prominent include the following:

- For **Psychology**, some methodological concepts overlap with other scientific domains (e.g., neuroscience, biology, social science) so the more one expands the search query the more remotely relevant results they get. Similarly, for Neuroscience, there is big overlap with other scientific domains (e.g., medicine, biology, psychology) so the same issue exists. For Psychology, some levels that were identified but not involved "method" in their path structure include the concepts of "biological phenomenon", or "science".

- For **Neuroscience**, as a hard science domain, many relevant branches in the tree structure start from the level of "science", or others, and do not include in the path the level of "method" at all. So many methodological approaches, tools, or measurement techniques of shared domains (e.g., with Psychology or Social Science) are not going to be retrieved as relevant results. The same goes for scholarly publications referring to those methods, so they will remain undiscovered by researchers who conduct interdisciplinary analysis or wish to find methods and mixed techniques used in both disciplines. For Neuroscience, some levels that were identified but not involved "method" in their path structure include the concepts of "science", "entity", or none.

- For **Cultural Heritage**, the results retrieved are a lot more in number because they represent bigger, more generic groups of codes on Wikidata, some of which might not be solely dedicated to cultural heritage, so this is an issue. In addition, there was a big imbalance in the retrieved results: as mentioned earlier, the first code group of "archaeological excavation" is very rich in number while the others are very limited. For Cultural Heritage, some levels that were identified but not involved "method" in their path structure include the concepts of "science", "class", "wikimedia category", "entity", or none.

4.2 The Proposed Methodology

Considering the identified problematic areas and insufficiencies regarding the currently offered Wikidata codes with respect to scientific investigation and tooling for the chosen domains, a methodological approach to alleviate these issues is proposed for development. The general proposed methodology is presented in Fig. 6.

The proposed methodology will also conduct the steps described in Sect. 3 in an automated way, in order to return comprehensive results instead of manually extracted examples. So, the recursive scraping of "P279 Subclass of" will be conducted in a systematic way, for the levels up to and including "method".

The steps of the proposed methodology include the following:

1) Data Collection and Preprocessing. The experiment will be initiated by collecting a diverse corpus of scientific/scholarly papers (but related to the same chosen 3 scientific domains for a start) for analysis. The textual data will be processed including cleaning, tokenizing, and standardizing it for further analysis.

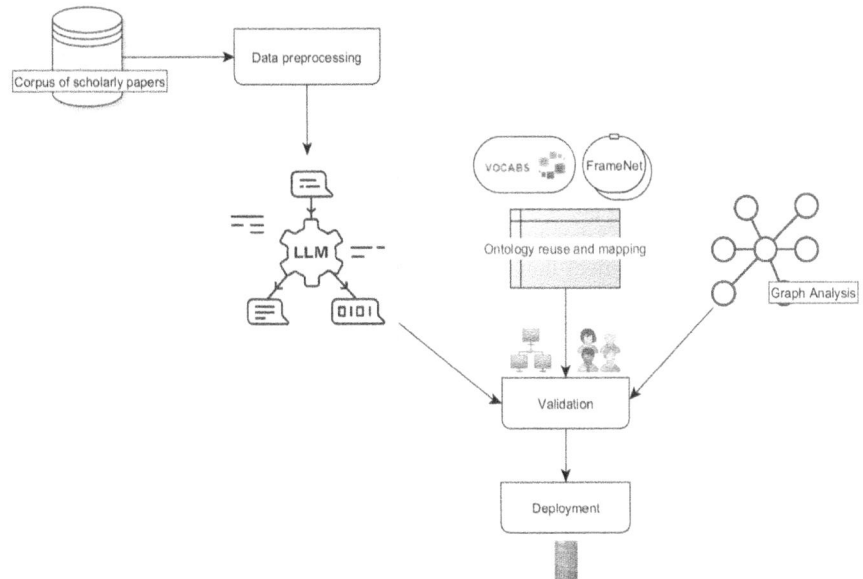

Fig. 6. The proposed methodology

2) Utilisation of a Large Language Model (LLM). Utilise an LLM such as GPT-4 to identify the "orphan" categories/methods and either add them or assign them under the respective hierarchical depth for whichever domain needs structural enrichment. The LLM will identify relevant entities (e.g., Named Entity Recognition - NER) related to scientific investigation tooling within the research papers. This includes instruments, methodologies, techniques, materials, and other entities pertinent to the research process.

3) Ontology Reuse and Mapping. FrameNet [8] will be used as the basic ontology to incorporate other schemas (dbpedia, wikidata, schema.org, skos, etc.) and assess their status for this purpose and as a resource of the basic conceptual properties/attributes/roles that are important in scientific investigation. Additionally, FrameNet provides relevant vocabulary, and example sentences out of the box, which could be leveraged by language models, in either producing synthetic data, or guiding the discovery/retrieval of investigative techniques in unstructured text. Also, mappings between the entities identified by the LLM and concepts within these ontologies could help enrich the representation of scientific investigation tooling. Relevant ontologies and vocabularies from Linked Open Vocabularies (LOV) can also be included for this purpose. A SPIDER-like approach can also be adopted to sort and search through LOV, and possibly create a similar, tailored framework. For instance, the vocabularies could be chosen based on some selection criteria such as the vocabulary source (is it reliable and trusted?), purpose (what is its intended purpose? Is it relevant?), its interconnections and links (is it linked to other vocabularies, and does it include the relationships for your use case?), its level of detail (does it cover all the concepts and terms you need?), and evolution (is it updated and maintained?).

4) Graph Analysis. At this point, graph theory metrics for common ancestors (parent nodes) can be considered, as also supported by [4]. A directed graph where nodes represent entities identified in the research papers and edges represent relationships between them could be produced to explore the hierarchical structure and interconnectedness of entities within the graph.

5) Validation of Results. The results of the previous steps could be validated by domain experts and researchers via relevant workshops or seminars in order to receive feedback on the adequacy, relevance and precision of the produced results and decide whether they accurately reflect their respective domain. The utility and evaluation of the produced results can also include community engagement, such as feedback from users and other stakeholders, in an iterative process to integrate valuable feedback in the proposed methodological process.

6) Deployment. Finally, the developed results and associated tools could be made accessible to the broader research community through open repositories, ontology libraries, links to the open data cloud (LOD), etc.

5 Discussion and Future Directions

The present study was a small-scale experiment to showcase current issues on the representation of scientific tooling and methods for research. Wikidata codes were analysed in order to check whether the current system of codes is sufficient to de-scribe the three domains/disciplines chosen in this case (Psychology, Neuroscience, Cultural Heritage), and whether they follow a semantically sound hierarchical structure to allow for scientific literature (e.g., publications, papers, journals etc.) discovery by interested researchers and stakeholders who put emphasis not solely on domains but focusing on methods and tooling as search criteria to retrieve their desired results. Although the present study is limited in scope (the codes retrieved and their respective relationships are not exhaustive but indicative) and mostly aims to serve as motivation for the existing problem the authors intend to alleviate with the proposed methodology in future work, it allows for the elicitation of conclusions strong enough to support the claim its purpose. First off, the Wikidata category of "Method" is not as "coherent" as one would expect; it does not manifest the same centrality across different domains. Moreover, the aphorism that "each field dictates its own methods", like the user behavior (clickstream data) from link following over the Web of Science (as described earlier by [4]), shows that social sciences and humanities are lumped together in a big pile. The different fields of science are fragmented, and more quantitative fields in humanities like behavioral economics, psychology, cognitive science show a "tendency towards fragmentation".

The findings of this study revealed several issues regarding the discoverability and semantic search capabilities to retrieve scientific literature papers on research (or investigation) methods and tooling for various disciplines. The aim is to develop an ontology for the space between "specific techniques" that are used with very precise objectives in a laboratory or field setting up to the "method" code. In the authors' view, querying for "instance of method" should retrieve records across fields. It was shown, however, that this type of query on Wikidata, returns unbalanced results. In this light, the present study proposed a methodological process to improve the current situation by introducing the utilisation of technological means (e.g., LLMs), to assist in identifying orphan categories of methods or tools and, by benchmarking against existing ontological structures (e.g., FrameNet or other relevant LOV), to enrich the hierarchical structure of current representation in this regard. The most imminent future direction of this study is to develop the designed methodology, apply, and validate it to show its potential in improved results and retrievability of relevant information.

Acknowledgments. This project has received funding from the European Union's Horizon 2020 research and innovation programme under the Marie Skłodowska-Curie grant agreement No 955569.

Disclosure of Interests. The authors have no competing interests to declare that are relevant to the content of this article.

References

1. Maratsi, M., Alexopoulos, C., Charalabidis, Y.: A Structured Analysis of domain-specific linked open vocabularies (LOV): indicators for interoperability and reusability (2024). https://doi.org/10.1007/978-3-031-56478-9_10
2. Kume, S., Kozaki, K.: Extracting domain-specific concepts from large-scale linked open data. In: Proceedings of the 10th International Joint Conference on Knowledge Graphs (IJCKG 2021), pp. 28–37. Association for Computing Machinery, New York, NY, USA (2022). https://doi.org/10.1145/3502223.3502227
3. Haller, A., Polleres, A., Dobriy, D., Ferranti, N., Méndez, S.J.R.: An analysis of links in Wikidata. In: Groth, P., et al. (eds.) The Semantic Web: 19th International Conference, ESWC 2022, Hersonissos, Crete, Greece, May 29 – June 2, 2022, Proceedings. Springer, Berlin, Heidelberg, 21–38 (2022). https://doi.org/10.1007/978-3-031-06981-9_2
4. Bollen, J., et al.: Clickstream data yields high-resolution maps of science. PLoS ONE **4**, e4803 (2009). https://doi.org/10.1371/journal.pone.0004803
5. Agarwal, A., Mamidi, R.: Automatically generating hindi wikipedia pages using Wikidata as a knowledge graph: a domain-specific template sentences approach. In: Proceedings of the 14th International Conference on Recent Advances in Natural Language Processing, pp. 11–21, Varna, Bulgaria. INCOMA Ltd., Shoumen, Bulgaria (2023)
6. Schmidt, S., Thiery, F., Trognitz, M.: Practices of linked open data in archaeology and their realisation in Wikidata. Digital. **2**, 333–364 (2022). https://doi.org/10.3390/digital2030019
7. Thornton, K., Cochrane, E., Ledoux, T., Caron, B., Wilson, C.: Modeling the domain of digital preservation in Wikidata. In: iPRES (2017)
8. Schneider, N., Wooters, C.: The NLTK FrameNet API: designing for discoverability with a rich linguistic resource (2017)

Representation Learning on IoT Knowledge Graphs

Roderick van der Weerdt[1]([✉])(iD), Victor de Boer[1](iD), Laura Daniele[2](iD), Ronald Siebes[1](iD), and Frank van Harmelen[1](iD)

[1] Vrije Universiteit Amsterdam,Amsterdam, The Netherlands
`r.p.vander.weerdt@vu.nl`
[2] TNO - Netherlands Organization for Applied Scientific Research, The Hague, The Netherlands

Abstract. In order to make the large amounts of messages generated by IoT devices in Smart Buildings interoperable, ontologies are used to represent the data as knowledge graphs (KGs). Learning over these IoT KGs can be used for various tasks, such as prediction or classification. Existing methods for KG representation learning are often evaluated on benchmark KGs and it is not explored how such methods perform on IoT KGs. The specific structure of the IoT KGs is likely to influence the quality of the representations. In this study, we investigate how the structure of IoT KGs affects the effectiveness of representation learning methods. Additionally, we look at the effect on representation quality of enriched IoT KGs, with for example temporal sequences or measurement value similarity, and the effect of the size of the IoT KGs. We perform experiments on three IoT KGs, with two representation learning methods (RDF2Vec and GCN) and two evaluation tasks (classification and value prediction). The results show that models trained with representations from enriched KGs outperform models trained with representations from original KGs on the evaluation tasks.(This article is a revised and extended version of [24]. It constitutes a significant extension with regards to the number and scale of experiments, embedding methods and evaluation tasks.)

Keywords: Internet of Things · Smart Buildings · Knowledge Graphs · SAREF · ML

1 Introduction

With the widespread diffusion of IoT devices in homes and workplaces, common frameworks that enable IoT devices to interact with each other and their environment become increasingly important [1]. Some of these frameworks use ontologies as a means to create a common representation of the knowledge shared by IoT devices [26]. The resulting knowledge graph (KG) contains the information coming from IoT devices and, additionally, through the organisation of the ontology, the context of this information.

© The Author(s), under exclusive license to Springer Nature Switzerland AG 2025
M. Sfakakis et al. (Eds.): MTSR 2024, CCIS 2331, pp. 44–57, 2025.
https://doi.org/10.1007/978-3-031-81974-2_4

IoT KGs are typically used for various applications, such as interoperability [4], reasoning [18] or maintenance [7]. However, all this information combined in a single KG also provides the opportunity to learn over the shared knowledge. By using representation learning methods to create vector representations of the entities in a KG, they can be used to train Machine Learning (ML) models used as forecasters or classifiers. A classifier, for example, could be used to predict whether the outdoor temperature is expected to be warm or cold, which in turn can be used to turn a heater inside the building on, or off, in order to save energy.

Representation learning methods use the structure of the graph to learn patterns that provide information about the entities [9,19]. These methods are well-established and evaluated in general-purpose KGs, such as DBPedia [20]. However, IoT KGs differ in structure from these general-purpose KGs, since they include a large amount of measurement data [25]. Ontologies such as SAREF are designed for interoperability purposes rather than representation learning [4]. Therefore, explicitly adding information that is implicitly available in the ontology could potentially improve the quality of entity representations that are created with the representation learning methods [15]. In Sect. 2 we go deeper into the various existing methods to represent entities in a KG as a vector, and their limitations in the context of IoT KGs. In this paper, we investigate representation learning methods on IoT graphs and, specifically, how the addition of this explicit information affects learnability. This is tested by taking as input existing IoT KGs and creating new IoT KGs that are semantically enriched through the addition of explicit properties and entities for each measurement. Models are trained with the respective entity representations and the evaluation score of these models, depending on the kind of task, is used to determine the quality of the entity representations.

The paper is further structured as follows: Sect. 2 provides an overview of relevant research and defines some foundational concepts of this work. Section 3 describes the datasets we have used, the method we have applied and the experiments we have conducted. Section 4 outlines the results and finally, Sect. 5 presents our conclusions.

2 Related Work

In this section we give a short overview of existing work that is relevant to our research. The first part elaborates on the concept of IoT graphs, while the second part provides background for the two representation learning methods that we use in our experiments.

2.1 Knowledge Graphs for IoT

In this work, we define IoT graphs as KGs specifically created to represent measurement data from IoT devices. SAREF[1] [4,6] was created to enable interoperability among IoT devices, serving as a common "language" to share information at the semantic level, regardless of the specific data formats exchanged

---

[1] Throughout this paper, when we refer to SAREF, it concerns version 3.1.1 of SAREF.

by the underlying communication protocols. A central concept in SAREF is
the one of device (e.g., a temperature sensor), which makes a measurement of
a property (i.e., temperature) in a certain unit of measure (e.g., degree Celsius). The measurement can have a context, as it can be related to a certain feature of interest (e.g., the room in which the measurement is taken).
In Fig. 1, we show an example of a SAREF IoT graph. White boxes are entities,
grey boxes are literals and black arrows represent the original SAREF properties (the colored arrows are discussed in Sect. 3.2). Four of the six original
properties of a `saref:Measurement` entity[2] connect to an entity (depicted in
white) that connects to every measurement made by that device, connecting
to the same `saref:Device`, `saref:FeatureOfInterest`, `saref:Property` and
`saref:UnitOfMeasurement` entities, with the other two properties relating to
literals (depicted in grey). Therefore, when walking through this graph, every
measurement is reachable within two steps.

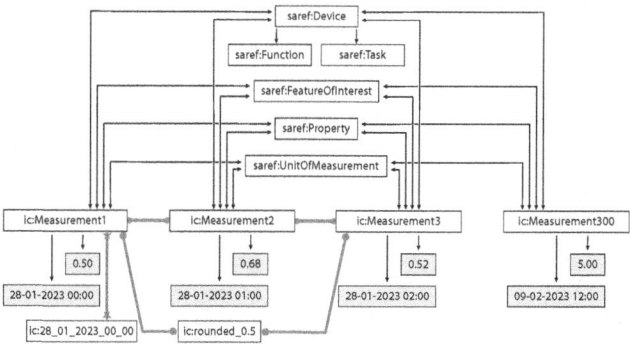

Fig. 1. Subset of four measurements from a SAREF IoT graph, white boxes are entities, grey boxes are literals. → represent the direction of the predicate. The grey →
(explained in Sect. 3.2) represent the semantic enrichments. Predicates names have
been left out for readability.

As further shown in Fig. 1, there are a few entities, such as `saref:Device`
or `saref:Property`, which are connected to a larger amount of measurement
entities. In other words, there are numerous measurements for the same device
or property. This imbalance between numerous measurement entities and other
entities, such as device or property entities, is what we consider to characterise
an IoT KG. As stated in [17], the New York entity in DBpedia is specifically
highly connected since from it half of all other entities can be reached within
two steps. This high connectivity is also characteristic for IoT graphs, however,
rather than being a specific characteristic of one entity, this holds for every entity
in the graph. Section 3.1 describes how the datasets we used follow this structure. When examining the Web of Things ontology a similar structure can be

---

[2] We refer to nodes in the KG as *entities*.

observed, with the `wot:property` entity acting as the `saref:Measurement` entity [22]. Similarly, the Semantic Sensor Network ontology uses `ssn:observation` [3]. Earlier research by Moreira et al. [12] has shown that, with minimal mappings, most properties of IoT data can be represented by both SSN and SAREF. In our experiments we focus on KGs that were modelled with SAREF, but based on similarities between all discussed ontologies we expect our results to be representative also for KGs modelled with other IoT ontologies, such as WoT and SSN.

2.2   Representation Learning Methods

RDF2Vec. The purpose of embedding models is to create a numerical representation for specific entities. Word2vec learns embeddings for words based on with which other words they co-occur in sentences [11]. RDF2vec uses random or directed walks to mimic sentences, working under the assumption that satisfactory representations for nodes can be learned based on with which other nodes they co-occur in random walks [19]. Research has shown that this assumption holds for several graphs, such as DBpedia or Wikidata [20].

In [17] the authors describe multiple variants of RDF2vec methods, which are all evaluated on different KGs. These graphs were generated based on specific characteristics that a KG can have, such as cardinality restrictions or relations to particular individuals. Similarly to their work, we research the effect of KG characteristics on the quality of RDF2vec embeddings. However, our characteristics are based on graphs that are used in practice, instead of highly specific logical definitions.

Adding new information to a graph based on implicit information can have an adverse effect, as shown by [8]. In their paper, experiments are performed to test the effect of adding implicit information explicitly, showing that the quality of the embeddings actually declines. They hypothesise that the initial absence of the implicit information was a signal in itself. Our semantic enrichment approach similarly utilises implicit knowledge, but in the case of IoT KGs the implicit information is used to create new relations, as the current relations are insufficiently connecting relevant entities.

Graph Convolutional Networks. Similarly to how RDF2Vec is an extension of Word2Vec, graph convolutional networks (GCNs) [9] can be considered an extension of convolutional neural networks (CNNs), that are often used for images. When using a CNN for an image, instead of using each individual pixel of an image as input, it uses a sliding window over the pixels. By including the surrounding pixels it includes the context for each pixel in the learning process. Translating this to a graph: GCNs learn a representation for a node by including the representations for the surrounding nodes.

GCNs are used with IoT data [10], since the relations between IoT devices are an important source of information, which can be accessed with GCNs. For example, the combination of GCNs with IoT data is used for emotion recognition in conversation [2], where the graph is populated with measurements from IoT devices related to emotion recognition, such as facial information. An additional example is provided by measurement data such as air quality [14]. Here the authors take as input the air quality of a city measured at different points in the city and predict what the air quality will be at a point in the future. Zhang et al. use a GCN model to forecast indoor air temperature changes based on different air-conditioning settings [27].

Whereas these efforts explore graph-learning methods, in this work we specifically address the learning over KGs that use an explicit ontology (in our case SAREF) and investigate the effect of different levels of explicit semantic structure.

3 Method

To investigate representation learning on IoT KGs we perform experiments that use three different datasets, two different representation learning methods and two different evaluation tasks. For each of these settings we compare the enriched and basic graph, and we test different sizes of the graph. In this section we describe the experiments, by distinguishing three phases: enrichment, representation and evaluation.

During the enrichment phase, the *enriched graph* is created by adding specific semantic enrichments to the original *basic graph*. This is followed by the representation phase, where a model is trained to learn representations for the timestamp entities. Finally, in the evaluation phase, the evaluation score of the model trained with the enriched graph entities is compared with the evaluation score of the model trained with the basic graph entities. These three phases are described from Sect. 3.2 to Sect. 3.4, while Sect. 3.1 provides a description of the datasets used in the experiments. To investigate whether the amount of devices affects the representations, the experiments were performed with different subsets of KGs. How these subgraphs are built for each specific dataset is also described in Sect. 3.1. All the code and hyperparameters used in these experiments are available in our github repository[3].

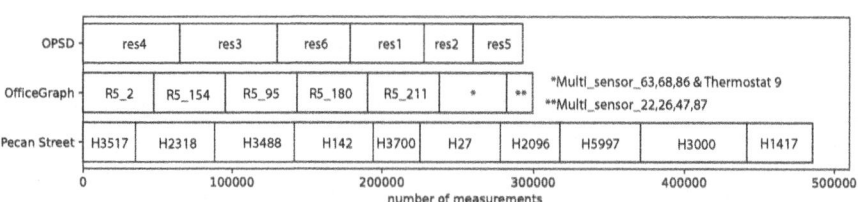

Fig. 2. Each block are the collected measurements of residences (for OPSD and Pecan Street) or devices (OfficeGraph) of each IoT KG. With the exception of the last two OfficeGraph blocks, which add multiple devices per block.

---

[3] https://github.com/RoderickvanderWeerdt/representation_learning_on_iot_graphs.

3.1   Datasets

For the experiments three different datasets are used, namely, two energy consumption datasets that we transformed to IoT KGs, and one heterogeneous sensor measurements KG. The mapping process to create the IoT KGs are detailed in [23,25]. Templates were created for each device in the dataset, mapping each measurement to the graph together with related properties. We perform the experiment on multiple datasets to get a better insight on which aspects of the IoT KGs affect the representation quality.

OPSD Household data. The OPSD Household 1hour dataset [13] consists of energy consumption measurements from devices in different types of buildings, of which we use only the six residential homes.[4] The dataset contains measurements taken over a five years duration, but not every device recorded measurements for the entire period. In order to have a complete dataset we chose to extract a subset of ten months where all devices had recorded measurements. We removed two devices (i.e., the freezer from residence 2, and the grid export from residence 6), as they included only two months of measurements, as opposed to the ten months period we considered. The final manipulation to the data was to transform the energy consumption measurement from its original value of accumulated consumption since start, to accumulated consumption over the last hour. This manipulation was performed to ensure that the measurement values in the graph would be recurring, which would not be the case for accumulated measurement values, because those would only increase. The final graph represents 8133 timestamp entities linking to a total of 292,788 measurements from 37 devices from ten device types, spread out over six residences. Figure 2 shows how the number of measurements compares to the other KGs and how it is distributed over the different residences. In order to examine the effect of adding more devices from other households, six graphs were created of increasing sizes, which we call the *subgraphs* of OPSD. Following the ordering presented in Fig. 2, the first subgraph only includes measurements from residence 4, the second subgraph combines the measurements from residence 4 and residence 3, continuing until all residences are collected in the final subgraph, when the subgraph entails the entire graph.

Pecan Street New York Residential Data. Similarly to the OPSD dataset, the complete Pecan Street NY 15-min dataset [16] contains energy consumption measurements from devices in 25 residences, with a total of 277 devices from 27 device types. Measurements were recorded over six months, from May 2019 through October 2019. From the 25 initial residences, we make a selection of ten residences to keep the dataset within the computational limitations of our setup. Additionally, this allows for a better comparison with the other datasets, keeping the number of residences similar. The selection of these ten residences is made by choosing the residences with the highest correlation between their measurements values and the outdoor temperature to be used in the evaluation. This selection

---

[4] OPSD   KG: https://github.com/RoderickvanderWeerdt/SAREFized-OPSD-household-graph.

method is chosen to keep the results reproducible, as opposed to using a random selection among the residences. For the remainder of this paper, when we refer to the dataset Pecan Street, we refer to this subset of ten residences. The initial dataset has measurements for every 15 min, but in order to keep the evaluation similar with the other datasets, and due to the limitation of hourly temperature measurements for the evaluation tasks, we combine the quarterly consumption measurements to create hourly measurements. This results in 4416 timestamp entities and 485,760 measurements. Similarly to OPSD, we create the subgraphs of Pecan Street following the ordering of the residences presented in Fig. 2.

Table 1. Distribution of the properties measured by each device in OfficeGraph.

measurement types	OfficeGraph (device ID)													total
	R5-2	R5-154	R5-95	R5-180	R5-211	Multi S-63	Multi S-68	Multi S-86	Thermos-9	Multi S-22	Multi S-26	Multi S-47	Multi S-87	
Battery level						1	1	1	1	1	1	1	1	8
CO_2 level	1	1	1	1	1									5
Contact										1	1	1	1	4
Device Status						1	1	1	1	1	1	1	1	8
Thermostat setpoint									1					1
Humidity	1	1	1	1	1									5
Temperature	1	1	1	1	1	1	1	1	1	1	1	1	1	13
total	3	3	3	3	3	3	3	3	4	4	4	4	4	44

OfficeGraph. OfficeGraph is a KG containing measurements from 444 sensors in a large office building [25]. The building contains seven floors and numerous rooms. Information about where the devices are located is available in the graph. The measurements relate to eleven different properties, with differing units of measure: battery level (percentage), CO_2 level (ppm), contact (binary), device status (binary), running time (seconds since start), thermostat heating setpoint (degrees Celsius), humidity (percentage), motion (binary), occupancy (number of people), power (watt) and temperature (degrees Celsius). OfficeGraph is a heterogeneous graph in the sense that there are different properties being measured. As opposed to the homogeneous nature of OPSD and PecanStreet, which only measure energy consumption. The measurements were recorded for eleven months, from March 2022 through January 2023. For these experiments, we only use the devices on the 7th floor, since the complete graph is too large to use on regular hardware. The 7th floor is chosen due to the number of sensors and measurements available on this floor, which is similar to the total number of measurements available in the OPSD dataset, making the datasets comparable. Throughout the remainder of the paper, whenever we refer to OfficeGraph, it will be the floor 7 subset. Table 1 shows the properties measured by the devices.

OfficeGraph contains 299,336 measurements, as shown in Fig. 2, and 7,913 timestamps. Instead of being separated according to residences, OfficeGraph is separated according to devices. Since each device makes multiple distinct measurements (for example, temperature, CO_2 levels and humidity), it can be considered similar with the residences in OPSD and Pecan Street, given that although a residence contains multiple devices, each device only makes one type of measurement. As with OPSD and Pecan Street, we created the subgraphs for OfficeGraph following the ordering in Fig. 2.

3.2   Enrichment of the Graphs

While in each of the KGs information about measurements is represented using SAREF, there is still implicit information, for example the chronological ordering of the measurements, that can be made explicit. Our assumption is that making this information explicit will benefit representation learning. When examining Fig. 1, without the grey arrows, it can be noticed that all measurements have similar neighbourhoods, with the exception of the literals. This means that, based only on this graph structure, each entity will be considered "similar" by representation methods. For example, with RDF2Vec, the random walks will be similar for each measurement entity. However, information that makes the neighbourhoods more representative is implicitly available, through the timestamps and the measurements values. Through semantic enrichment of the graphs we add entities that represent this implicit information and make it explicit. Below we describe each of these enrichments in more detail. *Rounded value* (•—• in Fig. 1): Each measurement entity has a measurement value. By taking this rounded value we create a new entity that will be connected with measurements with similar, but not necessarily equal, values. In this research the value was rounded to one decimal.

Sequence links ((▶—◀ in Fig. 1): For each measurement entity a property is added towards the "next" and "previous" measurement entities, making the chronological sequence of the measurements explicit.

Timestamp ((✳—✳ in Fig. 1): The literal timestamp value is used to create a new entity in the graph, which has a relation towards every measurement taken at that moment. Making the timestamp an URI allows us to create an representation for it with the representation methods and to add bi-directional properties between the measurements and timestamps. This entity will bring together measurements taken at the same time.

We applied these enrichments to the KGs, which we refer to as the enriched graphs.

3.3   Representation Learning Methods

To create representations for the entities in the graphs we used two different methods of graph representation learning in the experiments: RDF2Vec, which creates an embedding for each entity that is used to train a MLP for the evaluation task, and GCN, which is end-to-end trained with the evaluation task.

RDF2Vec. We use the pyRDF2vec implementation of RDF2vec [21]. This is an implementation of RDF2vec light, which only creates embeddings for specific entities in KGs, instead of creating them for all nodes. For our experiments, we selected timestamps as the entities to be embedded, since they correspond with the evaluation task, as described in the next section. This also provided the freedom to add and remove devices and measurements without having to adjust the pipeline, keeping it as similar as possible between experiments. All experiments used the reverse function of pyRDF2vec. The parameters were set to a walklength of 2 and 25 walks per retrieved entity. The model was trained for 20 epochs.

Both the classification and value prediction models are a Multilayer perceptron (MLP) implementation, consisting of two hidden layers with 512 ReLU activation nodes. These are used as the default hyperparameters. The input to the MLP are embeddings of the timestamp. The MLP is trained for 20 epochs. During the experiments we retrain the RDF2Vec embeddings three times and each time perform the evaluation step with the MLP an additional three times, in order to capture the variation of the results.

GCN. We created the GCN scripts using the PyTorch Geometric (PyG) library [5]. Similarly to the RDF2Vec implementation, timestamps were used as entities. However, as opposed to the RDF2Vec implementation which first creates the embeddings, and subsequently trains an MLP for the evaluation task, the GCNs are trained end-to-end. This means the representations are not only trained on the graphs, but also take into account what the representation will be used for, i.e. the evaluation tasks.

The GCN uses two layers, to remain comparable to the RDF2Vec implementation that uses walks of length 2. A learning rate of 0.01 is used for the classification task, and 0.1 for the classification task. The number of training epochs varies between 400 and 1000, depending on when the learning rate of each specific dataset plateaus. During the experiments we retrain the GCN three times, to capture the variation of the results.

3.4 Evaluation Tasks

The representations' quality is tested with two different evaluation tasks: a classification task and a value prediction task. Both use the outdoor temperature measured in the city to create the target class or value. We use a 80%/20% split for the training and test sets.

In order to create the entity files for the evaluation step the timestamps of a dataset are collected and used to connect with the outdoor temperature at that location at the specific time. From those temperatures the hot and cold labels are created. The outdoor temperature values are retrieved through https://www.worldweatheronline.com for OPSD and Pecan Street, and through https://www.knmi.nl for OfficeGraph.

Classification. The classification task classifies each timestamp as either hot or cold. The timestamps are labelled by dividing the dataset in two by sorting the timestamps based on the outdoor temperature of the city, from hot to cold. The first half is labelled *hot* and the second half is labelled *cold*. These labels are not included in the KGs. As evaluation metric we use the classification accuracy on the test set.

Value Prediction. In the second evaluation task we predict a numerical value: the outdoor temperature of the city in which the sensor is located. Just as with the labels in the classification, the outdoor temperature is not included in the KGs. The prediction is again based on the learned representation of the timestamp entity. Instead of accuracy we use the mean absolute error (MAE) as the evaluation metric. Because the evaluation score now represents the MAE, a lower score corresponds with a better prediction, as opposed to the accuracy, where a higher score represents a better prediction.

4 Results

The results of the experiments are visualized in Fig. 3. Each consecutive point along the x-axis is the result of the next subgraph (as described in Sect. 3.1) of each IoT KG. All enriched graphs consistently outperform the basic graphs in all experiments, regardless of the graph size. A Student t-test showed that for the RDF2Vec experiments, the difference between the basic setup and enriched setup are significantly different, with the exception of the first subgraph from OfficeGraph. For the GCN experiments it was not possible to perform a t-test, because we have too few evaluation scores.

Table 2. Maximum average deviation of the subgraphs, for each IoT KG.

Dataset	Evaluation task	PECAN Basic	Enriched	OPSD Basic	Enriched	OfficeGraph Basic	Enriched
RDF2Vec	Classification (accuracy)	1.8%	1.2%	1.5%	1.1%	1.3%	0.9%
GCN	Classification (accuracy)	6.2%	3.5%	8.4%	0.5%	3.4%	2.4%
RDF2Vec	Value prediction (MAE)	0.13	0.12	0.15	0.12	0.17	0.19
GCN	Value prediction (MAE)	0.13	0.15	0.09	0.06	0.08	0.02

Each data point in Fig. 3 is the average of 3-9 experiments. We calculated variance for these experiments. Table 2 shows the *maximum* deviation for a specific task-dataset combination (accuracy for classification and MAE for value prediction). In most cases, variance is higher for basic graph compared to enriched graph, showing that semantic enrichment leads to more consistent performance.

Within the classification results with basic graphs, experiments with Office-Graph reach accuracies closer to those of the experiments with the enriched graphs, compared to the experiments with the other datasets (which remain below 65%). A possible explanation for this is the heterogeneity of the Office-Graph (as described in Sect. 3.1). The argument for the semantic enrichment is to make clearer distinctions between the measurements (see Sect. 3.2). With OPSD and Pecan Street having only measurements related to energy consumption, the instances of the classes: saref:Property and saref:UnitOfMeasurement

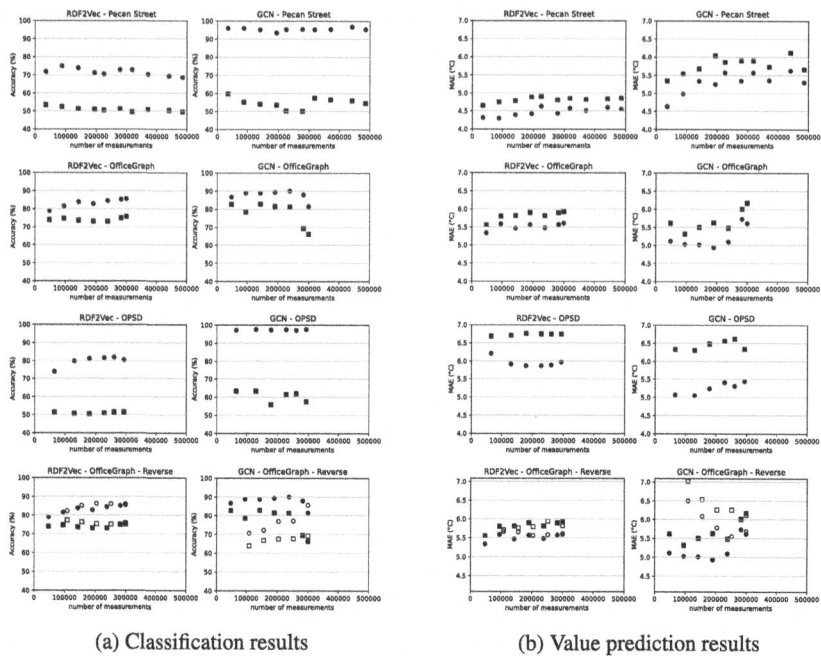

(a) Classification results   (b) Value prediction results

Fig. 3. Results of the experiments: ■ are trained on the basic subgraphs, ● are trained on the enriched subgraphs. ● and ■ represent the original OfficeGraph experiments results, ○ and □ show the results of the experiments with the "reverse" combined subgraphs, where the subgraphs are created in reverse order compared to OfficeGraph.

were all identical, since no distinctions are made due to the homogeneous nature of the data. With OfficeGraph, different `saref:Property` and `saref:UnitOfMeasurement` instances are used, since there are different kinds of measurements being made. Therefore, the measurements already have more distinct neighbourhoods for the representation learning methods to learn from.

Increasing the number of residences or devices in the IoT KGs does not show a consistent effect of the evaluation scores. The RDF2Vec implementations with OfficeGraph shows a slight increase on the classification task, but it is not significant. The other classification experiments seem similar for each subgraph, except the GCN implementation with OfficeGraph.

On the value prediction task all evaluation scores seem to slightly decrease while increasing the number of residences and devices, but it is again not significant, except the GCN implementation with OfficeGraph.

Using the GCN with OfficeGraph produces some notable results with the last two subgraphs on both evaluation tasks. There is a clear decline in the evaluation score, both for the classification and the value prediction task. One explanation for this is that due to the fact that the additional devices added in those last two subgraphs have irregular time intervals for the measurements, while all other subgraphs, for all datasets, only contain devices with measurements for each hour in the graph.

In order to investigate whether the addition of the irregular measurements indeed leads to these divergent results, we run all experiments with OfficeGraph again, but now we add the devices in the "reversed" order from Fig. 2. This means the first subgraphs only contains the measurements from Multisensor 22, 26, 47 and 87, the second subgraphs contains those, and Multisensor 63, 68, 86 and Thermostat 9, and so on. However, we can not perform the experiments with the first two subgraphs, because due to the irregular interval of the measurements these subgraphs do not contain all timestamps yet. Therefore, we start the experiments from the third subgraph. The bottom row of Fig. 3 shows the results of these experiments. When using RDF2Vec, there is again little noticeable difference, with the exception that the first two subgraphs in the reverse experiments do not produce significantly distinct scores for the value prediction experiments, between the basic and enriched graphs. However, with the GCN we now see that the predictions and classifications are impacted by the irregular measurements from the start, and never reach the same scores as the original experiments, until the biggest subgraph is used, since this is the entire graph and therefore includes all the same measurements in both experiments.

5 Conclusion

In this research we examined the effectiveness of representation learning methods on IoT KGs. We performed experiments with three IoT KGs, two representation learning methods and two evaluation tasks. For these settings, we investigated the effect of making implicit information explicit in enriched graphs, for various graph sizes.

The information added in this semantic enrichment for each measurement is threefold: 1) rounded values to group similar numerical values; 2) triples to make sequential relations explicit and 3) timestamps as URIs to allow for more effective random walks. When we consider the evaluation scores an indicator of the quality of the entity representations, the results of our experiments show that semantic enrichment has a positive effect on the entity representation quality. The semantically enriched IoT KGs outperformed their corresponding basic IoT KGs in every instance, regardless of graph size, dataset, evaluation task and KG representation learning method.

The effect of the graph size was tested by performing the experiments with subgraphs, containing increasing amounts of residences or devices from the IoT KGs. Increasing the graphs size did not cause a significant effect on the evaluation scores.

Results of the experiments show that the specific characteristics of IoT KGs affect representation learning methods. We found that semantic enrichment of the IoT KG can mitigate some of these effects. However, when an IoT KG is heterogeneous, in terms of different kinds of measurements and different kinds of devices, it already diminishes the IoT KGs characteristics that affect representation learning methods.

Acknowledgements. This work is part of the InterConnect project which has received funding from the European Union's Horizon 2020 research and innovation program under grant agreement No 857237.Additionally, this work is also part of HEDGE-IoT (https://hedgeiot.eu) which has received funding from the European Union's Horizon Europe research and innovation program under grant agreement No 101136216.

References

1. Akasiadis, C., Pitsilis, V., Spyropoulos, C.D.: A multi-protocol IoT platform based on open-source frameworks. Sensors **19**(19), 4217 (2019)
2. Choi, Y.J., Lee, Y.W., Kim, B.G.: Residual-based graph convolutional network for emotion recognition in conversation for smart internet of things. Big Data **9**(4), 279–288 (2021)
3. Compton, M., Barnaghi, P., Bermudez, L., et al.: The SSN ontology of the W3C semantic sensor network incubator group. J. Web Semant. **17**, 25–32 (2012)
4. Daniele, L., den Hartog, F., Roes, J.: Created in close interaction with the industry: the smart appliances REFerence (SAREF) ontology. In: Cuel, R., Young, R. (eds.) FOMI 2015. LNBIP, vol. 225, pp. 100–112. Springer, Cham (2015). https://doi.org/10.1007/978-3-319-21545-7_9
5. Fey, M., Lenssen, J.E.: Fast graph representation learning with PyTorch Geometric. In: ICLR Workshop on Representation Learning on Graphs and Manifolds (2019)
6. García-Castro, R., Lefrançois, M., Poveda-Villalón, M., Daniele, L.: The ETSI SAREF ontology for smart applications: a long path of development and evolution. ESAAMC (2023)
7. Gouda Mohamed, A., Abdallah, M.R., Marzouk, M.: BIM and semantic web-based maintenance information for existing buildings. Autom. Constr. **116**, 103209 (2020)
8. Iana, A., Paulheim, H.: More is not always better: the negative impact of a-box materialization on RDF2Vec knowledge graph embeddings. In: CEUR WP, vol. 2699, pp. Paper–5 (2020)
9. Kipf, T.N., Welling, M.: Semi-supervised classification with graph convolutional networks. In: International Conference on Learning Representations (2016)
10. Li, Y., Xie, S., Wan, Z., Lv, H., Song, H., Lv, Z.: Graph-powered learning methods in the internet of things: a survey. Mach. Learn. Appl. **11**, 100441 (2023)
11. Mikolov, T., Chen, K., Corrado, G., Dean, J.: Efficient estimation of word representations in vector space (2013). arXiv
12. Moreira, J., Daniele, L., Pires, L.F., et al.: Towards IoT platforms' integration semantic translations between W3C SSN and ETSI SAREF. In: SEMANTICS workshops (2017)
13. Open power system data: data package household data. Version 2020-04-15. (2020) https://data.open-power-system-data.org/household_data/2020-04-15/
14. Ouyang, X., Yang, Y., Zhang, Y., Zhou, W.: Spatial-temporal dynamic graph convolution neural network for air quality prediction. In: IJCNN, pp. 1–8 (2021)
15. Özcan, F., Lei, C., Quamar, A., Efthymiou, V.: Semantic enrichment of data for AI applications. In: Proceedings of the Fifth Workshop on DEEM, pp. 1–7 (2021)

16. Pecan street research institute: Dataport from pecan street. https://dataport. pecanstreet.org/academic. Accessed 16 Jan 2023

17. Portisch, J., Paulheim, H.: The RDF2Vec family of knowledge graph embedding methods. In: Semantic Web (2024)

18. Reda, R., et al.: Supporting smart home scenarios using owl and SWRL rules. Sensors **22**(11), 4131 (2022)

19. Ristoski, P., Paulheim, H.: RDF2Vec: RDF graph embeddings for data mining. In: Groth, P., et al. (eds.) ISWC 2016. LNCS, vol. 9981, pp. 498–514. Springer, Cham (2016). https://doi.org/10.1007/978-3-319-46523-4_30

20. Ristoski, P., Rosati, J., Di Noia, T., De Leone, R., Paulheim, H.: RDF2Vec: RDF graph embeddings and their applications. Semant. Web **10**(4), 721–752 (2019)

21. Steenwinckel, B., Vandewiele, G., Agozzino, T., Ongenae, F.: pyRDF2Vec: a python implementation and extension of rdf2vec. In: Pesquita, C., et al (eds.) ESWC, pp. 471–483. Springer, Cham (2023). https://doi.org/10.1007/978-3-031-33455-9_28

22. W3C: Web of Things (WoT) thing description (2020). https://www.w3.org/TR/2020/REC-wot-thing-description-20200409/

23. van der Weerdt, R., de Boer, V., Daniele, L., Nouwt, B., Siebes, R.: Making heterogeneous smart home data interoperable with the SAREF ontology. IJMSO **15**(4), 280–293 (2021)

24. van der Weerdt, R., de Boer, V., Daniele, L., Siebes, R., van Harmelen, F.: Evaluating the effect of semantic enrichment on entity embeddings of IoT knowledge graphs. In: Proceedings of the 1st International Workshop on SWoCoT at ESWC 2023, vol. 3412 (2023)

25. van der Weerdt, R., de Boer, V., Siebes, R., Groenewold, R., van Harmelen, F.: OfficeGraph: a knowledge graph of office building IoT measurements. In: ESWC, pp. 94–109 (2024)

26. Xie, C., Yu, B., Zeng, Z., Yang, Y., Liu, Q.: Multilayer internet-of-things middleware based on knowledge graph. IEEE Internet Things J. **8**(4), 2635–2648 (2020)

27. Zhang, J., Xiao, F., Li, A., et al.: Graph neural network-based spatio-temporal indoor environment prediction and optimal control for central air-conditioning systems. BE **242**, 110600 (2023)

The Use-Case of Enhanced AEON in Education

Cornelia Veja(✉) and Christoph Schindler

DIPF | Leibniz Institute for Research and Information in Education, Rostocker Street 6,
60323 Frankfurt am Main, Germany
{c.veja,c.schindler}@dipf.de

Abstract. The ontology presented in this paper completes and extends the Academic Events Ontology (AEON), which reuses several ontologies from the OBO foundry, especially the information artifact ontology (IAO). The present work formally represents the education-related event domain. The challenge is to describe the knowledge underlying the organization of educational meetings, academic and professional, and model it using semantic technologies. To capture and exchange structured knowledge in this domain, an ontology should address the organization of educational meetings in all steps, along with the associated scientific evidence base. It describes event formats, venues, calls for papers, the audience, information on submission, and fees. In addition, it addresses organizations and people involved in the process. The ontology was created using the NeOn methodology and OBO foundry guidelines for ontology development. Several domain experts also provided their expertise. The ontology is available on GitHub and licensed via an open-source license.

Keywords: Event Calendar · Educational Meetings · Ontology · Basic Formal Ontology · Knowledge Graph

1 Introduction

Events refer to happenings, planned occasions, or activities in social settings. They serve as a natural paradigm for explaining complex relations between people, locations, actions, objects, and actions' consequences.

Academic conferences and professional meetings, as crucial planned events in the educational domain, play a significant role in promoting quality scholarship. These events, in the form of meetings, work sessions, and academic conferences, are organized and attended by those dedicated to enhancing the educational landscape.

In contrast to academic conferences, professional meetings have a broader reach and aim to disseminate new information or knowledge from research and practice. They serve as a platform to promote new ideas and facilitate information exchange, keeping professionals abreast of the latest practices and trends [12].

A knowledge base for an event calendar must conform to event-centered modeling that effectively captures a domain's dynamic characteristics and follows the meeting organizing steps. We propose that an event-oriented semantic web knowledge representation technique is the key.

© The Author(s), under exclusive license to Springer Nature Switzerland AG 2025
M. Sfakakis et al. (Eds.): MTSR 2024, CCIS 2331, pp. 58–69, 2025.
https://doi.org/10.1007/978-3-031-81974-2_5

Several ontologies have been proposed and published in recent years to represent events using semantic web technologies [1, 11]. These ontologies vary in scope, domain specialization, size, and degree of formalization [15]. Only a few of them concern planned events, like conferences. There is no academic event ontology that also models professional meetings ready for use in an Event Calendar Knowledge Graph. Integrating professional events is crucial for research, which addresses transfer aspects and aims for practical applicability.

We propose to extend the Academic Events Ontology (AEON) [17], the sole academic event ontology covering most of our competency questions for academic meetings, to model professional meetings. We use these events from the research and practice communities as a case study to model the event calendar knowledge graph in education. This is a crucial step in our research, emphasizing the importance of the transfer work.

This paper presents the extension of the AEON ontology concerning professional meetings. We use these events of the research and practice communities in education as a case to model the event calendar knowledge graph in education.

This work is part of our "Literature Information Systems" (LIS) team at the "DIPF I Leibniz Institute for Research and Information in Education" effort to develop an educational knowledge graph (KG) based on a variety of existing data points which will be further enriched in the future. We have started the KG by modeling educational events: we are upgrading the current in-house LAMP architecture event database (the Event Calendar database) by switching to the Semantic Web approach. The data it contains will also be integrated into the Knowledge Graph [11].

An essential step in achieving our goal is creating an ontology for the Event Calendar by reusing other ontologies as much as possible. The heavy reuse of ontologies is part of the original conception of the Semantic Web field.

Ontologies play a relevant role in supporting interoperability. As research outputs, ontologies are research artifacts, such as data and software. They should follow the same principles to make them findable, accessible, interoperable, and reusable (FAIR) to others [14]. Therefore, our approach to the Event Calendar ontology follows the FAIR principles, emphasizing interoperability and reusability. Our concept of reusability is twofold: first, we reuse other ontologies in the design of the Event Calendar ontology, and second, we make this ontology reusable.

The articles' structure is as follows: In Sect. 2, we present several theoretical aspects of ontologies as knowledge artifacts. Then, in Sect. 3, we present the ontology engineering methodology and the selection of the AEON for reuse. Section 4 outlines the reengineering of AEON to fulfill our use case. Section 5 discusses the implementation of the Enhanced AEON. Section 6 presents the evaluations of Enhanced AEON. Finally, we outline several directions for future work and conclude in Sect. 7.

2 Ontologies

2.1 Ontology as Knowledge Artifact

According to Gruber [6], ontology is "an explicit specification of a conceptualization." Arp et al. [2] view ontology as a knowledge artifact that captures and represents reality by defining classes and their relations formalized using definitions, axioms, rules, and constraints. Usually, a taxonomy is the backbone of a good ontology, representing the class-subclass relationship between two entities ('is_a' relation). An ontology extends the taxonomy by adding other kinds of relations between classes.

The primary purpose of ontology work is to create common computable semantics for concepts and to foster knowledge sharing [8]. Depending on the level of abstraction and generalization of the real world, there are three ontology types [7].

1. Upper or core ontologies (top-level ontology, upper model, foundational ontology, reference ontologies) are crucial for providing a well-founded reference model that can be shared across domains, solving interoperability issues among ontologies.
2. Domain ontology is an explicit and formal description of the corresponding portion of specific reality regarding concrete artifacts.
3. Application ontologies are tied to local data, mission, and element. They are prone to errors due to the discrepancies between the intended semantics of the initial domain of foundational ontologies and the misusage in applications.

2.2   BFO Top-Level Ontology

The Basic Formal Ontology (BFO) framework that Barry Smith and his associates developed consists of a series of sub-ontologies [2], extending the core. The BFO core and sub-ontologies can be conceived as a window on a certain portion of reality at a given level of granularity [10].

BFO is a well-documented, heavyweight foundational ontology with an interesting horizontal stratification [2, 3]. The ontologies are divided into two varieties: relating to continuant entities such as three-dimensional enduring objects and occurrent entities (primarily) processes conceived as unfolding in successive phases through time [3].

A *continuant* domain ontology descending from BFO can be conceived as an inventory of entities existing at a time. Each *occurrent* domain ontology can be conceived as an inventory of processes unfolding through a given interval of time.

BFO was initially developed to support the integration of scientific data obtained through research. Since 2005, it has been used in over 300 ontology initiatives [4].

The OBO Foundry was created around the BFO framework to promote best practices and community resources. Its 20th principles promote openness, common format, versioning, textual definitions, naming conventions, documentation, commitment to collaboration, maintenance, and responsiveness of ontologies. OBO Foundry created tools to support ontology development based on BFO (ROBOT [9], an open-source library and command-line tool, and the Ontology Development Kit (ODK)).

3   Ontology Engineering

For ontology development, we followed the scenarios and guidelines of the NeON methodology [18] and the OBO Foundry's recommendations for a good ontology [2].

The NeOn methodology is scenario-based and emphasizes the development of ontology networks and the reuse of existing ontological and non-ontological resources to develop an ontology. It also considers the collaborative development of ontologies and the reuse and re-engineering of knowledge. NeOn has been based on analyzing a set of

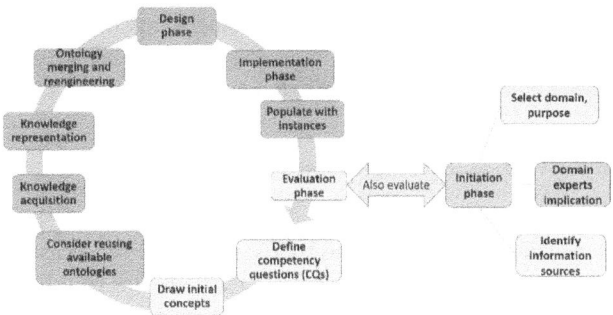

Fig. 1. The ontology development life-cycle.

nine ontology development scenarios, from which we consider scenarios 3 and 4 [18]. Combining with OBO Foundry guidelines results in a stepwise, hybrid methodology (see Fig. 1). This is an incremental and iterative process, presented in the following subsections.

3.1 Initiation Phase

We initiated the ontology development process by gathering competency questions from stakeholder interviews, workshops among colleagues working on the Event database in DIPF, and literature on event organization.

CQ1. What are the event topics and targeted audience for professional (practical) meetings in a period?

CQ2. What are the meetings interesting for a certain group of interest?

CQ3. What is the geographical coverage for professional meetings for a certain audience?

CQ4. What professional meeting is available in my region, such as an exhibition or a learning session?

CQ5. When and where is the meeting scheduled?

CQ6. Who were the local organizers?

CQ7. Was an event part of a series?

CQ8. Who is responsible for the series?

CQ9. Is the event affordable, and does one have to travel and where?

CQ10. When is the deadline for the call for papers?

CQ11. Who is on the organizing committee?

Several competency questions concern only professional meetings (CQ1 to CQ4), while others concern academic and professional meetings (CQ5 to CQ9). Finally, competency questions concern only academic meetings (CQ10 to CQ11).

The initial concepts were derived from the competency questions and discussions with the domain experts. This phase resulted in a list of terms and properties. Each entity is described in natural language with examples of usage. In this step, several challenges in reaching a consensus must be overcome. The goal is for the consensus to allow a wider community of users that implicitly adopt the ontology as a shared reference point. This list, after consensus agreement, is available in [19].

While this step was carried out mainly by domain experts and users, the technical team searched for available ontologies for reuse. The candidate list contains general event ontologies, domain ontologies, and reference ontologies.

3.2 Select and Evaluate Meeting-Related Ontologies

The general event ontologies don't specifically address the subject of the meeting, as they are mostly interested in events related to sports, news, and broadcasting. The reference ontologies have some event-related classes (BFO *'occurrent'*, DOLCE *'perdurant'*) and properties, but they are not specific enough, as they are mainly taxonomies.

Selecting domain and domain-related ontologies results in a list containing several ontologies. For the domain ontology's evaluation, we consider the following criteria:

1. Meetings as a main entity.
2. The degree of coverability of our term list;
3. The expressivity of the implementation language;
4. The interoperability, vertical (reference ontology usage);
5. The interoperability, horizontal (terms from vocabularies);
6. The amount of envisaged work for customization.

In conformity with the literature of ontology reusing [13, 16], to understand and evaluate these ontologies, we used multimodal tools to visualize and query the content of the selected ontologies. We also consulted the documentation and the definitions of terms in natural language (if available). In the following sections, we discuss the evaluation of domain ontologies.

The evaluation result is summarized in Table 1. The table header contains the number of evaluation criteria above.

The Conference-Ontology[1]. From scholarlydata.org introduces the organized event class and categorizes events as academic and non-academic. Non-academic events are only social events, and professional events are neglected.

Semantic WEB for Research Communities Ontology[2]. Consider Events as secondary entities modeled in relation to the Person. The ontology doesn't consider the event series but models an event-subevent relationship.

The Scientific Event Ontology (SEO)[3]. This ontology reuses part of **the conference ontology** and **Semantic Web for Research Communities Ontology.** SEO is more horizontally interoperable with similar approaches in the new re-engineered version than in the previous version [5].

schema.org/Event and schema.org/Eventseries[4]. These ontologies have two main disadvantages: they are not expressive enough to represent academic conferences and educational meetings accurately, and they have limited interoperability.

---

[1] http://www.scholarlydata.org/ontology/conference-ontology.owl.

[2] Https://lov.linkeddata.es/dataset/lov/vocabs/swrc

[3] Https://saidfathalla.github.io/seoontology/documentation/seo.html

[4] Https://schema.org/event

The Bibliographic Ontologies. (GND Ontology[5], BIBO[6], FRAPO[7], FaBiO[8]) consider meetings as second-class entities.

Table 1. Meeting ontologies evaluation.

Ontology	1	2	3	4	5	6
conference-ontology	yes	Partial, moderate	$ALCHIQ(D)$	no	no	moderate
SWRC	yes	Partial, low	$SHI(D)$	no	DC	high
SEO	yes	Partial, moderate	$ALCHIQ(D)$	no	yes	moderate
Schema.org/event	yes	Partial, moderate	AL	By itself	no	moderate
bibliographic ontologies	no	Partial, low	$SHOI(D)$	no	DC, foaf	high
conference supporting tools	yes	Partial, moderate	Only one $SROIQ(D)$	no	no	high
AEON	yes	Partial, high	$SROIQ(D)$	yes	Wikidata	moderate

Ontologies for Conference Supporting Tools. The OntoFarm Project[9] was developing a collection of 16 ontologies, modeling the domain of conference organizing based on conference support tools, the experience of people who participated in conference organizing, and conference series web pages [20]. Currently, only 11 of these ontologies' web pages are still reachable.

The Academic Event Ontology (AEON)[10] is a BFO-based ontology representing information regarding academic events. Its development fully adheres to the BFO principles enunciated by Arp and Smith [2]. AEON also represents valuable information in assessing an event's research impact [17].

- Meetings, specific academic meetings, are the primary entities. The ontology models meeting series.

[5] https://d-nb.info/standards/elementset/gnd.
[6] https://github.com/structureddynamics/Bibliographic-Ontology-BIBO.
[7] Https://sparontologies.github.io/frapo/current/frapo.html.
[8] Https://sparontologies.github.io/fabio/current/fabio.html.
[9] Https://owl.vse.cz/ontofarm/.
[10] Https://github.com/tibonto/aeon.

64   C. Veja and C. Schindler

- AEON recognizes roles, processes, and process outputs.
- An event defined by this ontology produces outputs that are information artifacts.
- Authorship and outputs, such as proceedings, can be referenced from AEON but are outside the scope of AEON ontology.

After analyzing the results from Table 1, we concluded that AEON is the best candidate for reusing. We prioritized term coverage (up to 70%) and interoperability (vertical and horizontal) over the work necessary for customization, as we worked close to AEON's initial developers.

3.3 Selecting AEON

AEON supports the identification, development, management, evaluation, and impact assessment of events, their components, and event series and the identification and reuse of works presented or developed at events.

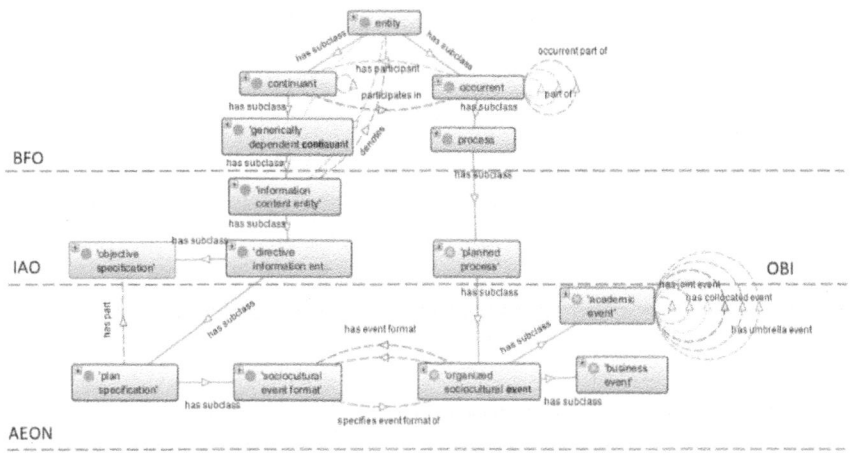

Fig. 2. BFO, IAO, OBI, and original AEON overview.

The ontology is independent of knowledge, creative domain, or other events-related topics. AEON is focused on planned events and assumes the representation of many entities associated with events, such as attendees, locations, academic works, date-times, and related processes defined in other compatible ontologies [17].

Figure 2 shows how AEON extends the BFO taxonomy. Meetings are modeled as subclasses of '*occurrent*' and '*process*.' The OBI module extends BFO by defining planned processes, which is the parent class of '*organized socio-cultural events*' defined in AEON. All kinds of meetings can be modeled as subclasses of '*organized socio-cultural events*' like '*academic meeting*' or '*business meeting*'.

On the other hand, the BFO's '*generically dependent continuant*' is extended by subsumption by the IAO module, which models all the information artifacts. The class '*plan specifications*' allows AEON to specify all meeting-related artifacts, like identifiers, descriptors, formats, deadlines, fees, etc.

4   AEON Reengineering

4.1   Identifying AEON Limitations

However, the AEON ontology has some limitations. One is the possibility of easily generalizing several terms' definitions and labels without changing the semantics of the terms. For instance, the '*academic field descriptor*' definition could be generalized and used in other contexts, such as professional or business meetings. Professional meetings are not considered at all, and here is the chance to extend the AEON ontology. AEON can successfully answer the competency questions CQ5 to CQ11 but cannot answer CQ1 to CQ4.

4.2   Extending AEON

Traditional conferences are primarily designed to deliver content rather than support delegates' learning. However, it is possible to design conferences that engage their delegates in powerful learning experiences that support their professional development, as in an educational context. The event calendar ontology should capture this desideratum.

This is the main reason we proposed extending AEON: to make the ontology usable in the extended context of a meeting (academic or non-academic) that promotes learning and exchanging experiences. The '*target audience*' is very important for these kinds of meetings. In professional meetings, actions like '*Call for papers*' and '*Camera Ready*', which are important in academic conferences, become optional in learning meetings.

4.3   Enhanced AEON with Professional Meetings

Enhancing AEON was a step-wise process. In the first step, we carefully checked the possibility of changing several entities' labels and definitions in the annotations, keeping the initial semantics unaltered. Second, we added missing entities to the ontology. In the last step, we added new axioms and constraints to the AEON ontology.

Changing Labels and Definitions in AEON. In AEON, several classes and object properties can be used to model the rest of the meetings, such as professional or business meetings. The aim is not to add unnecessary classes and object properties when the existing entities can be used. All the modified labels of entities are in GitHub. The initial AEON definitions and the enhanced AEON definitions are documented in GitHub. For example, the initial definition of '*academic field descriptor*' changed to "*A data item that contextualizes an obi:'planned process' or an iao:'information content entity' by providing a reference to a controlled vocabulary that codifies the subdivisions of knowledge taught and researched at the college or university level*" in Enhanced AEON. The label changed from '*academic field descriptor*' to '*event field descriptor*'. These modifications did not affect the consistency of the ontology, as we evaluated its validity at every step. The reason was to make the entities as reusable as possible.

For instance, the property '*has academic field descriptor*' has the domain '*information content entity*' or '*planned process*' and the range '*event field descriptor*'. Changing the label to '*has event field descriptor*' and definition makes this property more general. It can express the relations between any '*planned process*' and '*event field descriptor*', not only academic.

Table 2. List of extensions.

	Entities	Several axioms
Classes classes	*event audience*	- *event audience* is_a *objective specification* - *event audience* is_part_of *professional event format*
	professional event	- *professional event* is_a *organized sociocultural event* - *professional event* has_event_format *professional event format* - *professional event* has_event_series *professional event series*
	professional event format	- *professional event format* is_a *sociocultural event format* - *professional event format* has_part *event field descriptor* - *professional event format* has_part *event audience*
	professional event series	-*professional event series* is_a *professional event* -*professional event series* has_event_format *event series format*
Data *Properties*	*event keywords*	-*event keywords* subproperty_of *has representation* - *domain: organized sociocultural event*
	event relevance	- *domain: organized sociocultural event*
	event group of interest	- *domain: organized sociocultural event*

Additional Classes and Properties. Table 2 describes the AEON extensions with definitions required by OBO Foundry. The additional 4 classes and 3 data properties contribute to describing professional meetings in AEON. The enhanced AEON uses only the existing properties in RE or defined by AEON as object properties.

Figure 3 illustrates how the extended classes harmonize with the original AEON. For readability purposes, the picture shows only a few object properties.

A complete list of modifications and extensions is on GitHub.

Semantic Enrichment with Enhanced AEON. Table 3 highlights further differences between AEON and Enhanced AEON.

Table 3. Comparison between original and enhanced AEON.

Metrics	AEON including BFO	Enhanced AEON, including BFO
Class count	213	217
Class definition Count	434	518
SubClassOf axioms	316	326
Logical axioms count	754	1.054
Axioms total	3.727	4.318

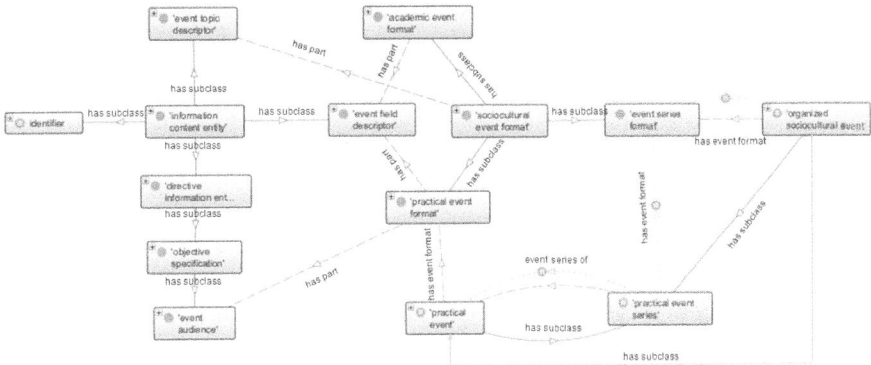

Fig. 3. Enhanced AEON overview.

5   Implementation

The AEON ontology was uploaded and extended using the Protégé[11] ontology editor. The language used was Web Ontology Language 2.0, Semantic Web Rule Language (SWRL), and SPARQL 1.1 Query Language. The DL expressivity is SROIQ(D) obtained by the Pellet reasoner. It is available on GitHub and licensed as open source. The GitHub project includes a corresponding SPARQL query file that answers the competency questions defined as part of the ontology development methodology. (https://github.com/liaveja/AEON-extended).

6   Evaluation of the Enhanced AEON Ontology

Two techniques were used to evaluate Enhanced AEON. First, the ontology was checked for consistency. Second, the enhanced ontology was queried to establish whether the results conformed with our pre-ontological knowledge of the meetings domain.

6.1   Ontology Consistency Checking

The ontology evaluation was conducted with the Hermit Reasoner in Protégé. The logic validation consisted of verifying the Enhanced AEON ontology's completeness and correctness. For each inconsistency found by the Hermit reasoner, the "Inconsistent ontology explanation" window popped up to indicate an error message. The ontology was rechecked, and the Hermit Reasoner was used to identify inconsistencies. The process was iterated until no error message was found or generated in the "Inconsistent ontology explanation" window. Once this was achieved, the ontology was judged to be consistent.

---

[11] Https://protege.stanford.edu/.

6.2 Querying the Enhanced AEON Ontology

This section describes practical examples of how to use AEON extended ontology for the event calendar project. For the testing, we created around 100 instances of events using data from the event calendar database existing in the house. The ontology and instances have been uploaded in a local GraphDB[12] RDF database running instance.

The SPARQL queries are written following competency questions outlined in Sect. 3. The following code gives an example of a SPARQL query corresponding to the competency question CQ1.

```
PREFIX obo: <http://purl.obolibrary.org/obo/>
PREFIX rdf: <http://www.w3.org/1999/02/22-rdf-syntax-ns#>
PREFIX skos: <http://www.w3.org/2004/02/skos/core#>
select ?s ?label ?audience_text ?startdate where {
  ?s rdf:type obo:AEON_0000802 ;
                    obo:AEON_0000142 ?startdate;
                    obo:AEON_0000041 ?topic.
     ?topic obo:OBI_0002815 ?label.
          ?s obo:AEON_0000032 ?format.
     ?format obo:BFO_0000051 ?audience.
     ?audience rdf:type obo:AEON_0000801;
               obo:OBI_0002815 ?audience_text.
  FILTER("2023-01-01"^^xsd:dateTimeStamp <= ?startdate
        && ?startdate < "2023-07-01"^^xsd:dateTimeStamp)
} limit 100
```

7 Conclusion

Reusing ontologies for new purposes or adapting them to new use cases is frequently reported to be difficult. This process requires learning time, established reuse strategies, and a collaborative environment.

In this paper, we introduced the extension of the AEON ontology to better model professional meetings. By incorporating the possibility of representing professional (practical) meetings, the enhanced AEON ontology is ready to be the knowledge base for the Event Calendar in Education. The main contribution of this research is making the AEON ontology more general and fostering the coverage of other use cases in various settings.

The Enhanced AEON promotes interoperability and collaboration with other domains that need to model professional meetings and can use the ontology. By leveraging ontological modeling for semantic interoperability, this extended AEON enhances data understanding among the stakeholders, ultimately leading to improved operations. The successful implementation of this Enhanced AEON underscores the importance of the AEON ontology's adaptability, reassuring us that it can meet the evolving needs in educational practices.

---

[12] Https://www.ontotext.com/products/graphdb/?ref=menu.

The next challenge in this respect is successfully working with AEON developers and promoting the ontology to be accepted as part of the OBO Foundry pool of ontologies. Also, the endeavor is to align Enhanced AEON to other connected ontologies in the research domain.

References

1. Ali, A., Noah, S.A.M., Zakaria, L.Q.: Event-based ontologies: a comparison review. IJCSNS **23**(5), 147–156 (2023)
2. Arp, R., Smith, B., Spear, A.D.: Building ontologies with basic formal ontology. MIT Press, Cambridge, Massachusetts, US (2015)
3. BFO Homepage. http://basic-formal-ontology.org/. Accessed 25 May 2024
4. BFO Users. http://basic-formal-ontology.org/users.html. Accessed 25 May 2024
5. Fathalla, S., Vahdati, S., Lange, C., Auer, S.: SEO: a scientific events data model. In: Ghidini, C., et al. (eds.) The Semantic Web – ISWC 2019, ISWC 2019. LNCS, vol. 11779. Springer, Cham (2019). https://doi.org/10.1007/978-3-030-30796-7_6
6. Gruber, T.R.: A translation approach to portable ontology specifications. Knowl. Acquis. **5**(2), 199–220 (1993)
7. Guarino, N.: Formal ontology in information systems. In: Proceedings of the 1st International; Conference. IOS Press, 1st edn. (1998)
8. Hogan, A., et al.: Knowledge graphs. ACM Comput. Surv. **54**(4), Article 71 (2021)
9. Jackson, R.C., Balhoff, J.P., Douglass, E., Harris, N.L., Mungall, C.J., Overton, J.A.: ROBOT: a tool for automating ontology workflows. BMC Bioinform. **20** (2019)
10. Kotis, K.I., Vouros, G.A., Spiliotopoulos, D.: Ontology engineering methodologies for the evolution of living and reused ontologies: status, trends, findings and recommendations. Knowl. Eng. Rev. **35**(4) (2020)
11. Kowalczuk, E., Lawrynowicz, A.: The reporting event ontology design pattern and its extension to report news events. Adv. Ontol. Des. Patterns **32**, 105–117 (2017)
12. Mundry, S., Britton, E., Raizen, S., Loucks-Horsley, S.: Designing successful professional meetings and conferences in education. Sage Publications, Thousand Oaks, California (2000)
13. Pâslaru-Bontas, E.: A contextual approach to ontology reuse: methodology, methods and tools for the Semantic Web, pp. 1–270. Free University of Berlin, Dahlem, Germany (2007)
14. Poveda-Villalón, M., Espinoza-Arias, P., Garijo, D., Corcho, O.: Coming to terms with FAIR ontologies. In: Keet, C.M., Dumontier, M. (eds.) Knowledge Engineering and Knowledge Management. EKAW 2020. LNCS, vol. 12387. Springer, Cham (2020). https://doi.org/10.1007/978-3-030-61244-3_18
15. Rodrigues, F., Abel, M.: What to consider about events: a survey on the ontology of occurrents. Appl. Ontol. **14**(11), 1–36 (2019)
16. Simperl, E.: Reusing ontologies on the Semantic Web: a feasibility study. Data Knowl. Eng. **68**(10), 905–925 (2009)
17. Strömert, P.: AEON - die academic event ontology. Zenodo (2021). https://doi.org/10.5281/zenodo.4629629
18. Suárez-Figueroa, M. C., Gómez-Pérez, A., Fernández-López, M.: The NeOn Methodology framework: a scenario-based methodology for ontology development. Appl. Ontol. **10**(2), 107–145 (2015)
19. Veja, C., Schindler, C.: The event calendar ontology. The approaches and mappings. Technical Report, v2.0. (2024) https://doi.org/10.5281/zenodo.10423581
20. Zamazal, O., Svátek, V.: The ten-year OntoFarm and its fertilization within the Onto-Sphere. In: Web Semantics: Science, Services and Agents on the World Wide Web, vol. 43, pp. 46–53 (2017)

A RAG Approach for Generating Competency Questions in Ontology Engineering

Xueli Pan$^{(\boxtimes)}$(iD), Jacco van Ossenbruggen(iD), Victor de Boer(iD),
and Zhisheng Huang(iD)

Vrije Universiteit Amsterdam, De Boelelaan 1105, 1081 HV, Amsterdam, Netherlands
{x.pan2,jacco.van.ossenbruggen,v.de.boer,z.huang}@vu.nl

Abstract. Competency question (CQ) formulation is central to several ontology development and evaluation methodologies. Traditionally, the task of crafting these competency questions heavily relies on the effort of domain experts and knowledge engineers which is often time-consuming and labor-intensive. With the emergence of Large Language Models (LLMs), there arises the possibility to automate and enhance this process. Unlike other similar works which use existing ontologies or knowledge graphs as input to LLMs, we present a retrieval-augmented generation (RAG) approach that uses LLMs for the automatic generation of CQs given a set of scientific papers considered to be a domain knowledge base. We investigate its performance and specifically, we study the impact of different number of papers to the RAG and different temperature setting of the LLM. We conduct experiments using GPT-4 on two domain ontology engineering tasks and compare results against ground-truth CQs constructed by domain experts. Empirical assessments on the results, utilizing evaluation metrics (precision and consistency), reveal that compared to zero-shot prompting, adding relevant domain knowledge to the RAG improves the performance of LLMs on generating CQs for concrete ontology engineering tasks.

Keywords: Ontology Engineering · LLMs · Competency Questions

1 Introduction

An ontology is a formal, explicit specification of a shared conceptualization of domain knowledge that can be communicated between humans and computers [14]. In recent years, significant progress has been achieved in the field of knowledge and ontology engineering due to the surge of data-intensive applications and the growing need for structured knowledge representation. Central to many methodologies for the development and evaluation of ontologies are competency questions (CQs), a set of queries in the form of questions that outlining and constraining the scope of knowledge represented in an ontology which an ontology must be able to answer [17]. Informal CQs are expressed in natural languages, whereas formal CQs are expressed in the formal language of the ontology [6]. In this paper, we focus on informal CQs.

Traditionally, the task of crafting CQs has relied heavily on manual effort of domain experts and knowledge engineers, which is often difficult and time-consuming. However, with the emergence of Large Language Models (LLMs), such as OpenAI's GPT-4 and Google's Gemini 1.5, there arises an opportunity to automate and enhance this process. LLMs are trained on vast amounts of text data and excel at generating human-like text in response to prompts, making them promising tools for aiding the formulation and refinement of CQs.

Recent work has investigated the use of different prompt templates in LLMs for the automatic generation of CQs given an existing ontology [11]. However, these methods which generate CQs from existing ontologies or knowledge graphs (KGs) are based on the premise that there is already an ontology or a KG, which is not often the case. Furthermore, CQs generated from existing ontology might be answerable for the same ontology, which makes these CQs not suitable for ontology evaluation. In addition, LLMs face the problem of hallucination and low ability to access and manipulate up-to-date knowledge [4].

Retrieval-augmented generation (RAG) [10] has been introduced to address the above mentioned limitation of LLMs and provide access to domain knowledge, which leads us to investigate to what extent we can use RAG with LLMs to generate competency questions.

Our contributions are shaped by addressing the following research questions.

RQ1: How well does the RAG-based LLM work in the task of generating CQs given a domain knowledge base, compared to zero-shot prompting?

RQ2: How do different parameter settings in a RAG pipeline affect the performance of the task?

To address RQ1, we applied a RAG-based approach to generate CQs for two domain ontology engineering tasks and compared the results to zero-shot prompting. For RQ2, we investigated the effects of adjusting two hyperparameters: the number of papers (N_{paper}) in the knowledge base and the temperature ($temp$) of the LLMs, on the performance of the tasks. Experimental results revealed that our RAG approach works well in the task of generating CQs for concrete ontologies/KGs that required more domain knowledge. Moreover, increasing N_{paper} in the RAG pipeline generally improves the performance of the tasks.

2   Related Work

2.1   Competency Questions Formalisation

Traditionally, ontology engineering relies on manual efforts of domain experts and knowledge engineers, especially for the formalisation of CQs. Different works have been investigated in identifying CQ patterns to improve the automation of CQ formalisation. Wiśniewski et al. [17] identified 106 CQ patterns by analysing a dataset of 234 CQs and their SPARQL-OWL queries for several ontologies in different domains. In their follow-up work [16], they released BigCQ, the largest dataset of CQ templates with their formalisation into SPARQL-OWL query templates for ontology engineers to use for particular needs. Based on this work [17], C. Maria Keet et al. [9] designed a template-based controlled natural language (CNL) to author CQs. In our RAG approach with LLMs, we employ zero-shot prompting and no CQ templates or CQ examples are required for the prompt.

2.2   Automation of Generating CQs

Several efforts have been investigated on leveraging natural language processing (NLP) or LLMs to generate CQs. The authors of [3] proposed AgOCQs, a method that took advantage of the combination of NLP techniques and a text corpus with CQ templates to generate CQs, whereas no CQ templates are required for our approach. Rebboud et al. [11] investigated the suitability of LLMs to automatically generate CQs given an existing ontology, and experiments were conducted with six LLMs and five ontologies. Alharbi et al. [1] proposed RETROFIT-CQs, a method to generate CQs using LLMs by extracting triples from existing ontologies and feeding them to three prompt templates of an LLM. These two approaches are based on the premise that there is already an ontology or a KG, which is not often the case. Our approach addresses this limitation by using the domain literature as input to our RAG pipeline to provide LLMs with accessible and up-to-date domain knowledge.

3   Methodology

The primary objective of this paper is to investigate the effectiveness of RAG with LLMs to generate CQs in ontology engineering. Our RAG approach consists of two components, a RAG pipeline and a prompt engineering.

3.1   RAG Pipeline

Figure 1 illustrates the main steps in the RAG pipeline: domain knowledge indexing, relevant data retrieval, and response generation.

In Step 1, the knowledge base consists of a set of documents that serve as external sources of knowledge to augment the generative ability of LLMs for specific tasks. During the data indexing process, each selected document is first split into small chunks according to the chunk size defined by different LLMs. The chunks are then converted to embedding vectors using an embedding model. The original chunks and their respective vectors would be indexed and stored in a vector database for retrieval.

In Step 2, a user query or a user prompt expressed in natural language is converted to an embedding vector to retrieve relevant chunks from the knowledge base. Top-k similar chunks are retrieved using a similarity method such as cosine similarity.

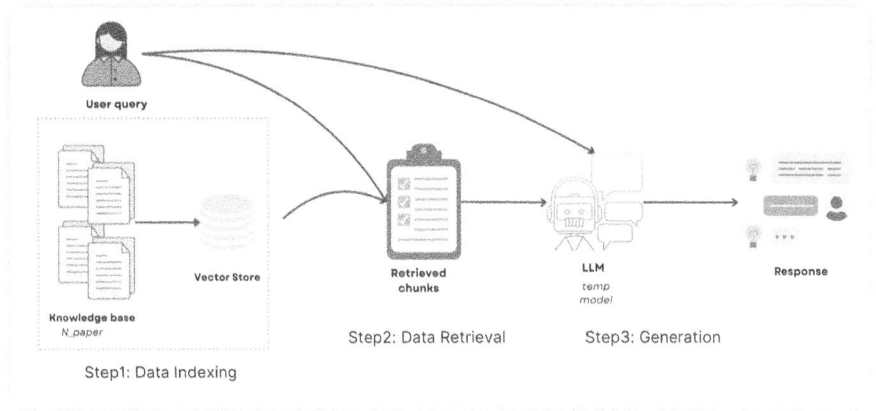

Fig. 1. RAG pipeline with three hyperparameters: $N_{paper}, temp$ and $model$

In Step 3, the retrieved chunks serve as a context for LLMs to generate the answer for the user query.

In our approach, the documents selected for the knowledge base in Step 1 are scientific papers that inherit domain knowledge for ontology engineering. One of the pain points in RAG systems is the missing content in the knowledge base [4], which is also a key challenge in our RAG approach: how to select scientific papers relevant to generate CQs for a specific domain ontology. There are three principals for selecting scientific papers in our approach: 1) these papers are relevant to the domain of the target ontology; 2) these papers help to explicitly define the scope and requirements of the ontology; 3) the format of the content of these papers should be processable in the RAG system.

To gain a deeper understanding of the effect of papers in the knowledge base in our RAG approach, we set the number of papers (N_{paper}) as a hyperparameter to evaluate its impact on the performance of the RAG approach to generate CQs. Our RAG approach includes two additional hyperparameters: temperature ($temp$) and the model name of the selected LLM ($model$). The temperature parameter ranging from 0 to 2 is used to control the randomness of LLMs' output. There are various open-source LLMs, such as Google's Gemma, as well as closed-source LLMs, like OpenAI's GPT, available for implementing our RAG approach. For experiments, we choose gpt-4o since it is one of the most advanced LLMs.

3.2 Prompt Engineering

In the field of LLMs, a prompt serves as an input that directs the model's generation of responses. The use of prompting techniques involves carefully formulating these prompts to optimize the effectiveness of LLMs. This process requires intentional structuring and wording of prompts to correspond with the model's abilities and the task description. Prompts significantly affect the performance of LLMs especially with zero-shot prompting [7]. Since LLMs are sensitive to prompt, designing a good prompt is another key challenge in our approach. For the task of generating CQs, we use zero-shot prompting and consider that a good prompt template in our RAG approach should consist of the following five components.

- **The role of the LLM** In our approach, the LLM is considered as an expert in a specific domain.
- **The purpose of the ontology/KG** The purpose of the ontology/KG is important for LLMs to understand the requirements and scope that the CQs should be covered.
- **The definition of CQ** CQ is a technical term in ontology engineering with a special meaning. Explicitly definition of the CQ in the prompt helps LLMs to better understand the task.
- **The task description** The number of generative CQs should be determined for each ontology engineering task.
- **The output format** Specifying the structure of the output is beneficial for the analysis and evaluation of the generated output.

These components constitute the following template with four variables to be determined for each ontology engineering task in our approach. Variables are enclosed in curly braces as shown in Listing 1.

Listing 1. Prompt template with four variables

```
You are an expert in {domain name}.
Your purpose is to {purpose of the ontology}.
A competency question is {definition of CQs}.
Derive {number of CQs} competency questions for the above
    -mentioned ontology (or knowledge graph), using the
    provided documents.
Return ONLY the competency questions, no other text.
```

4   Experiment

To evaluate our RAG approach from Sect. 3, we conduct two experiments, where we replicate two domain expert-driven ontology engineering tasks. We choose this setup since these existing experiments provide us with a set of ground-truth CQs identified manually by experts to compare our results to. Details about the datasets and codes could be found in this repository[1].

4.1   Task Description

We take two ontology engineering tasks to evaluate our approach for generating CQs. The first is the construction of a knowledge graph of empirical research

---

[1] https://anonymous.4open.science/r/GenCQs/README.md.

in requirement engineering(RE), namely KG-EmpiRE [8]. In this paper, the authors constructed the KG-EmpiRE with the purpose of providing the community with the state and evolution of empirical research in RE. The KG-EmpiRE was evaluated against 77 CQs manually derived by three domain experts from a published visionary paper about how researchers should conduct empirical research in RE [13]. The second is the construction of a core reference ontology in Human-Computer Interaction (HCI), namely HCIO [5]. In this paper, the authors constructed the HCIO with the purpose of clarifying the main concepts involved in the HCI phenomenon. The HCIO was evaluated against 15 CQs identified by ontology engineers using the methods described in SABiO [2]. Examples of these CQs identified by domain experts could be found in Table 1 with column name CQ_{gt}.

4.2   Hyperparameters Setting

As mentioned in Sect. 3.1, the selection of documents for the knowledge base in our RAG pipeline is very important.

For the KG-EmpiRE, we follow the methodology of how the authors of KG-EmpiRE derived the ground-truth CQs. Since the purpose of KG-EmpiRE is to capture the state and evolution of empirical research in requirement engineering, the authors select a visionary paper [13] to identify 77 CQs. We also select this visionary paper as one of the most important documents in the knowledge base. To investigate the impact of number of papers in our RAG approach, we also include other related publications on the state and evolution of the topic mentioned in the KG-EmpiRE paper.

For HCIO, since the authors of HCIO do not explicitly mention how these 15 CQs are identified, we select the referenced papers mentioned in the HCIO papers [5] that describe how other relevant ontologies are developed.

All selected referenced papers are in PDF formats. The hyperparameter N_{paper} was set to 1, 2, 3, 4, 5 and 10. Since gpt-4o is the latest model of OpenAI's GPT models, we set the hyperparameter *model* to gpt-4o. Temperature *temp* is set to 0.5, 0.75, 1.0, 1.25 and 1.5. Each experiment, for every hyperparameter configuration, was repeated 10 times.

4.3   Variable Setting for Prompts

We design prompts for the two tasks based on the prompt template described in Sect. 3.2. This template includes four variables that need to be determined. The *domain name* is chosen based on the selected task. The *number of CQs* matches the number of ground-truth CQs provided by domain experts. For the *definition of CQs*, we take the definition of an informal CQ in [15], a competency question is a natural language question that specifies the requirements of an ontology and can be answered by that ontology. For the *purpose of the ontology*, we refer to the original papers of KG-EmpiRE [8] and HCIO [5], which elaborate the objectives of the corresponding ontology or knowledge graph.

Listing 2 and Listing 3 present the prompts used to generate the CQs for KG-EmpiRE and HCIO, respectively.

Listing 2. Prompt for KG-EmpiRE

```
You are an expert in Requirements Engineering.
Your purpose is to organize scientific data in an openly
    available and long-term way with respect to building,
    publishing, and evaluating an initial knowledge graph of
    empirical research in Requirement Engineering. To achieve this
    goal, you need to create a knowledge graph which enables
    sustainable literature reviews to synthesize a comprehensive,
    up-to-date, and long-term available overview of the state and
    evolution of empirical research in Requirement Engineering.
A competency questions is a natural language question that
    specifies the requirements of an ontology and can be answered
    by that ontology.
Derive 77 competency questions for the above mentioned
    ontology (or knowledge graph), using the provided
    documents.
Return ONLY the competency questions, no other text.
```

Listing 3. Prompt for HCIO

```
You are an expert in Human-Computer Interaction.
Your purpose is to develop a referece ontology about the
    human-computer interaction phenomenon. This ontology is
    grounded in Unified Foundation Ontology and reuses concepts
    from the core System and Software Ontology to represent the
    very high-level core concepts in the Human-Computer
    Interaction and serve as a reference to the HCI domain, with
    the aim of making a clear and precise definition of domain
    concepts for the purpose of communication, learning and
    problem-solving.
Competency questions are a natural language question that
    specifies the requirements of an ontology and can be answered
    by that ontology.
Derive 15 competency questions for the above mentioned
    ontology (or knowledge graph), using the provided
    documents.
Return ONLY the competency questions, no other text.
```

4.4   Evaluation

We use precision to evaluate the quality of LLM-generated CQs against a set of ground-truth CQs designed by domain experts. In addition, we use consistency to evaluate the impact of different temperature settings for the task.

We compared the generative CQs (CQ_{gen}) of the LLM to each CQ in the ground truth (CQ_{gt}) and consider a CQ_{gen} as valid if it is sufficiently similar to at least one CQ_{gt}. For the similarity score, we use cosine similarity between the embedding of CQ_{gen} and CQ_{gt} calculated using SentenceBERT [12]. Similar to [11], we define a threshold θ above which we consider a CQ_{gen} to be valid. Here we choose the same $\theta(0.6)$ as in [11].

Table 1. Examples of generative CQs and their matched ground truth CQ with highest cosine similarity scores for two domain ontology engineering tasks

Domain	CQ_{gen}	CQ_{gt}	cos	valid CQ_{gen}
hci	What are the primary components of a Human-Computer Interaction system?	What does make up the user interface of an interactive computer system?	0.7393	yes
hci	What methodologies exist for building ontologies in the HCI domain?	What is a complex interactive computer system?	0.3467	no
re	How has the use of empirical methods in RE evolved over time?	How often are which empirical methods used over time?	0.8245	yes
re	What are the typical outcomes of empirical RE studies on process maturity?	Which sub-fields of SE and RE do the empirical studies cover over time?	0.4718	no

Precision measures the accuracy of the CQs generated by the LLM. It is the ratio of true positives to the total number of CQs generated by the LLM. The precision of the CQs generated by the LLM can be defined as follows:

$$\text{Precision} = \frac{TP}{TP + FP} \tag{1}$$

True positives (TP) is the number of valid CQ_{gen} and false positives (FP) is the number of invalid CQ_{gen}.

Table 1 shows some examples of the CQ_{gen} and their matched CQ_{gt} with cosine similarity scores for two domain engineering tasks.

The consistency in this task refers to how similar or stable the generated CQs are across multiple runs for each temperature setting. we use task performance variance and text similarity variance to measure the consistency of the LLM's output across different temperatures. The variance in task performance is defined as the standard deviation of precision for all iterations in each temperature setting, denoted as $std_{precision}$. The variance in text similarity is defined as the standard deviation of cosine similarity of the generate text across different temperature, denoted as std_{cosine} Since we run the experiments with each setting for 10 times, we take the average of each metric.

Additionally, we perform an Analysis of Variance (ANOVA) test to assess the significance of N_{paper} and $temp$ on the task performance.

5   Results and Discussion

5.1   Performance of Generating CQs

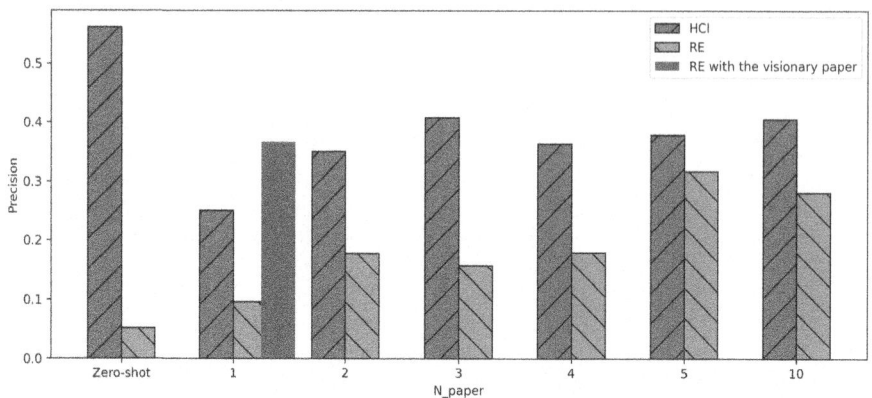

Fig. 2. Precision of using RAG with gpt-4o to generate CQs, compared to zero-shot prompting

Figure 2 shows the precision of our RAG approach, compared to zero-shot prompting in generating CQs for two domain ontology engineering tasks, with different number of papers in the knowledge base for the RAG.

As a first look, we observe that for the task in the RE domain, our RAG approach performs much better than zero-shot prompting. As N_{paper} increased, there is a noticeable trend where precision increase marginally. These suggest that the addition of domain knowledge could enhance the understanding capacity of LLMs for generating CQs for domain ontology engineering. In particular, the best precision is achieved when we use the only visionary paper as input to the knowledge base in the RAG pipeline, following the methodology of the KG-EmpiRE paper to identify ground-truth CQs. These indicate that with a good selection of papers in the knowledge base, small size of a knowledge base could achieve good performance, which is very important from the perspective of token cost in closed-source LLMs such as OpenAI's GPT models.

For the precision of the task in the HCI domain, zero-shot prompting yields the highest precision, marginally better than our RAG approach across all N_{paper}. Similar to the performance of the task in the RE domain, increasing the number of papers N_{paper} ranging from 1 to 10 generally improves the precision, but does not surpass the precision achieved with zero-shot prompting. Therefore, taking into consideration of the precision performance and the token cost for processing the documents in knowledge base, our RAG approach might not fit for generating CQs for HCIO, compared to zero-shot prompting.

From the perspective of zero-shot prompting, we observe that the precision in HCI is much higher than the precision in RE, which we think is due to the degree of abstraction of the target ontology or knowledge graph. The more concrete the ontology/KG is, the more domain knowledge is required for LLMs to perform well in the tasks of generating CQs for ontology engineering. For instance, the purpose of the HCIO is to develop a reference ontology to represent the core concepts in HCI, while the purpose of the KG-EmpiRE is to construct a knowledge graph to capture the state and evolution in RE. More domain knowledge such as specific methods used in RE is required to construct the KG-EmpiRE so as to answer the example CQ_{gt} shown in Table 1, *How often are which empirical methods used over time?*. Therefore, our RAG approach outperforms zero-shot prompting in generating CQs for KG-EmpiRE, while zero-shot prompting outperforms the proposed RAG approach in generating CQs for HCIO.

In general, our RAG approach works well in the task of generating CQs for more concrete ontologies/KGs, compared to zero-shot prompting. Moreover, increasing the number of papers N_{paper} in the RAG pipeline generally improves the precision of generating CQs for domain ontologies/KGs. The ANOVA test results also confirm that N_{paper} has a significant impact on the task performance ($p < 0.001$).

5.2 Consistency of LLMs

Figure 3 shows the standard deviation of precision for task performance and the standard deviation of cosine similarity for the generated text with different temperature settings in two domain ontology engineering tasks.

Apparently, there are no obvious patterns about how consistency changes by different temperatures regardless of different consistency metrics, which contrasts with the assumption that with higher temperature, less probable tokens are more likely to be sampled, resulting in more random outputs. This suggests that the temperature setting would not affect the task performance of generating CQs in our RAG pipeline. The ANOVA test results also confirm that *temp* doesn't have a significant impact on the task performance ($p > 0.05$).

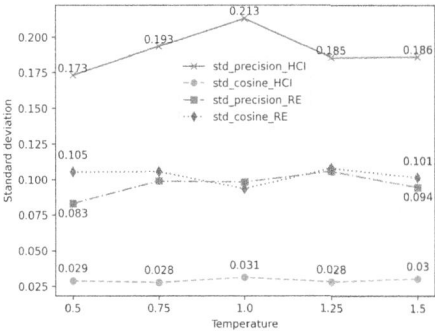

Fig. 3. Standard deviation of precision for the task performance and standard deviation of cosine similarity for generated text with different temperature.

From the perspective of different domains, the vertical distance between $std_{precision}$ and std_{cosine} in RE is significantly smaller than that observed in HCI. This suggests a reduced difference among two standard deviation for RE as opposed to HCI across the temperature range. This phenomenon may be attributed to the quantity of CQ_{gt}. Specifically, with 77 CQ_{gt} in RE, there is a higher likelihood that the 77 CQ_{gt} generated over 10 iterations exhibit overlap.

6   Conclusion

This study aimed to examine the capabilities of retrieval-augmented generation (RAG)-based large language models (LLMs) to generate competency questions (CQs) for ontology engineering. Additionally, we explored how various hyperparameters within the RAG pipeline influence the task performance. A prompt template with four variables was specifically designed to direct LLMs in generating CQs for domain ontologies and knowledge graphs. Using one LLM (gpt-4o), two LLMs techniques (zero-shot prompting and RAG) and five temperature settings, we replicated two expert-driven ontology engineering tasks from different domains. Experimental results revealed that our RAG approach works well in the task of generating CQs for concrete ontologies/KGs that required more domain knowledge, such as generating CQs for KG-EmpiRE, compared to zero-shot prompting. Moreover, increasing the number of papers N_{paper} in the RAG pipeline generally improves the precision of generating CQs for domain ontologies/KG. It is interesting to note that the temperature setting does not have a significant impact on our approach.

Our RAG approach accelerates ontology engineering by automatically generating CQs. The generated CQs can serve as candidate CQs for domain experts in the design phase of ontology engineering and can also be utilized to evaluate existing ontologies and knowledge graphs. Future work will focus on using our RAG pipeline for generating CQs in more domain ontology engineering tasks to investigate the generalization of our approach. Furthermore, due to the token cost of OpenAI's GPT models, we would like to explore the capability of open-source LLMs, such as Meta's Llama and Google's Gemma for generating CQs.

References

1. Alharbi, R., Tamma, V., Grasso, F., Payne, T.: An experiment in retrofitting competency questions for existing ontologies. In: Proceedings of the 39th ACM/SIGAPP Symposium on Applied Computing, pp. 1650–1658 (2024)
2. de Almeida Falbo, R.: SABiO: systematic approach for building ontologies. In: ONTO.COM/ODISE@FOIS (2014)
3. Antia, M.J., Keet, C.M.: Automating the generation of competency questions for ontologies with AgOCQs. In: Ortiz-Rodriguez, F., Villazón-Terrazas, B., Tiwari, S., Bobed, C. (eds) Iberoamerican Knowledge Graphs and Semantic Web Conference, pp. 213–227. Springer, Cham (2023). https://doi.org/10.1007/978-3-031-47745-4_16

4. Barnett, S., Kurniawan, S., Thudumu, S., Brannelly, Z., Abdelrazek, M.: Seven failure points when engineering a retrieval augmented generation system. In: Proceedings of the IEEE/ACM 3rd International Conference on AI Engineering-Software Engineering for AI, pp. 194–199 (2024)
5. Costa, S.D., Barcellos, M.P., de Almeida Falbo, R., Conte, T., de Oliveira, K.M.: A core ontology on the human-computer interaction phenomenon. Data Knowl. Eng. **138**, 101977 (2022)
6. Gruninger, M.: Methodology for the design and evaluation of ontologies. In: International Joint Conference on Artificial Intelligence (1995)
7. Jin, W., Cheng, Y., Shen, Y., Chen, W., Ren, X.: A good prompt is worth millions of parameters: Low-resource prompt-based learning for vision-language models. arXiv preprint arXiv:2110.08484 (2022)
8. Karras, O., Wernlein, F., Klünder, J., Auer, S.: Divide and conquer the empire: a community-maintainable knowledge graph of empirical research in requirements engineering. arXiv preprint arXiv:2306.16791 (2023)
9. Keet, C.M., Mahlaza, Z., Antia, M.-J.: CLaRO: a controlled language for authoring competency questions. In: Garoufallou, E., Fallucchi, F., William De Luca, E. (eds.) MTSR 2019. CCIS, vol. 1057, pp. 3–15. Springer, Cham (2019). https://doi.org/10.1007/978-3-030-36599-8_1
10. Lewis, P., et al.: Retrieval-augmented generation for knowledge-intensive NLP tasks. Adv. Neural. Inf. Process. Syst. **33**, 9459–9474 (2020)
11. Rebboud, Y., Tailhardat, L., Lisena, P., Troncy, R.: Can LLMS generate competency questions? In: ESWC 2024, Extended Semantic Web Conference (2024)
12. Reimers, N., Gurevych, I.: Sentence-BERT: sentence embeddings using Siamese BERT-networks. arXiv preprint arXiv:1908.10084 (2019)
13. Sjoberg, D.I., Dyba, T., Jorgensen, M.: The future of empirical methods in software engineering research. In: Future of Software Engineering (FOSE 2007), pp. 358–378. IEEE (2007)
14. Studer, R., Benjamins, V., Fensel, D.: Knowledge engineering: principles and methods. Data Knowl. Eng. **25**(1), 161–197 (1998)
15. Uschold, M., Gruninger, M.: Ontologies: Principles, methods and applications. The knowledge engineering review **11**(2), 93–136 (1996)
16. Wiśniewski, D., Potoniec, J., Ławrynowicz, A.: Bigcq: A large-scale synthetic dataset of competency question patterns formalized into sparql-owl query templates. arXiv preprint arXiv:2105.09574 (2021)
17. Wiśniewski, D., Potoniec, J., Ławrynowicz, A., Keet, C.M.: Analysis of ontology competency questions and their formalizations in SPARQL-OWL. J. Web Semant. **59**, 100534 (2019)

Modeling Modern and Historical Data as a Knowledge Graph: A Case Study for Earthquake Data

Iosif Oikonomakis[1,2] , Pavlos Fafalios[1,3] , Michalis Mountantonakis[1,2] , and Yannis Tzitzikas[1,2(✉)]

[1] Information Systems Laboratory FORTH-ICS, Heraklion, Greece
{sifisoik,fafalios,mountanton,tzitzik}@ics.forth.gr
[2] Computer Science Department University of Crete, Heraklion, Greece
[3] Technical University of Crete, Chania, Greece

Abstract. Historical data are sparse and vague making their collection and analysis difficult. To come up with a methodology for handling such data, in this paper we elaborate on this problem by considering the requirements and challenges for building a Knowledge Graph that contains data about both modern and *historical earthquakes*. We discuss the requirements and challenges, and we report the main observations concerning uncertainties by analyzing the documentation of ancient earthquakes that hit the island of Crete. Afterwards, we analyze representation approaches and related ontologies and then we present a modeling approach that can tackle the requirements. We showcase the feasibility of the approach by implementing it using RDF and we share publicly the result.

Keywords: Historical Data · Modeling Uncertainty · Earthquakes · Knowledge Graphs · CIDOC-CRM family of models

1 Introduction

Historical data are sparse and vague making their representation and analysis difficult. To come up with a methodology for handling such data, in this paper we elaborate on this problem by considering the requirements and challenges for building a Knowledge Graph that contains data about both modern and *historical earthquakes* for the region of Crete. As regards earthquake data, there is a detailed list and characterization of roughly all earthquakes that happened after 1900 in various data repositories[1]. However, for the earthquakes that happened earlier, the information is vague and in many cases it is described in books, like [7,8]. Figure 1 shows indicative textual descriptions that are found in such books, translated to English.

---

[1] E.g. at https://earthquake.usgs.gov/earthquakes/search/ and
http://www.geophysics.geol.uoa.gr/stations/gmapv3_db/index.php?lang=en.

M. Sfakakis et al. (Eds.): MTSR 2024, CCIS 2331, pp. 82–94, 2025.
https://doi.org/10.1007/978-3-031-81974-2_7

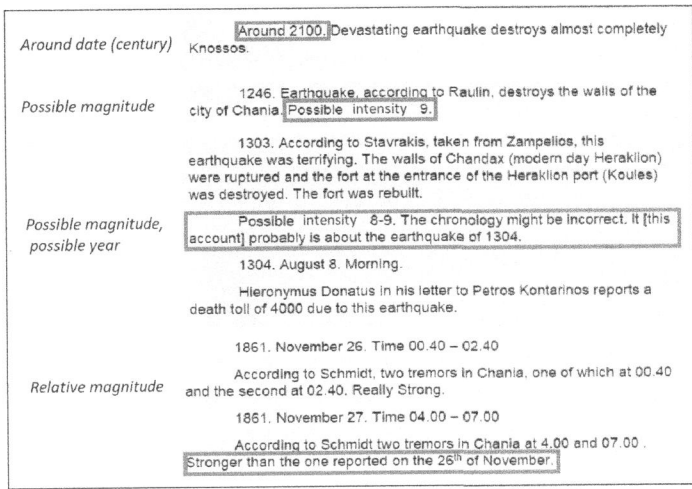

Around date (century)	Around 2100. Devastating earthquake destroys almost completely Knossos.
Possible magnitude	1246. Earthquake, according to Raulin, destroys the walls of the city of Chania. Possible intensity 9.
	1303. According to Stavrakis, taken from Zampelios, this earthquake was terrifying. The walls of Chandax (modern day Heraklion) were ruptured and the fort at the entrance of the Heraklion port (Koules) was destroyed. The fort was rebuilt.
Possible magnitude, possible year	Possible intensity 8-9. The chronology might be incorrect. It [this account] probably is about the earthquake of 1304.
	1304. August 8. Morning.
	Hieronymus Donatus in his letter to Petros Kontarinos reports a death toll of 4000 due to this earthquake.
	1861. November 26. Time 00.40 – 02.40
Relative magnitude	According to Schmidt, two tremors in Chania, one of which at 00.40 and the second at 02.40. Really Strong.
	1861. November 27. Time 04.00 – 07.00
	According to Schmidt two tremors in Chania at 4.00 and 07.00. Stronger than the one reported on the 26th of November.

Fig. 1. Indicative descriptions of ancient earthquakes from [8] translated to English.

We can observe information expressed at various levels of detail and precision: dating at century level, statements with magnitude intervals, relative magnitude, statements about the provenance of information, etc. There is no principled and straightforward method to express this information as a KG (Knowledge Graph) and exploit it at the query/analytics level. Consequently there is a need for a methodology for constructing KGs with *both precise* and *imprecise* data for the benefit of analysis and historical research. The main research question is: *what kind of modeling facilitates representation, reasoning and analytics over KGs that contain precise and imprecise data?*

Regarding our contribution, we i) analyze our main observations about the needed requirements by analyzing the contents of books that document ancient earthquakes, ii) discuss possible representation approaches, iii) present our proposed representation based on CIDOC-CRM (ISO 21127)[2] [3] and its extensions, and iv) showcase the adequacy of the model by showing how it can be used to model ancient earthquakes and to query such data.

The rest of this paper is organized as follows: Sect. 2 describes the motivating scenario and the methodology that we followed. Section 3 discusses the various representation approaches. Section 4 describes and proposes the modeling approach. Section 5 provides indicative examples, Sect. 6 discusses implementation, and finally, Sect. 7 concludes the paper.

2   Motivating Scenario and Methodology

We adopted the following methodology: (a) collect the list of questions that we would like to be answerable (for both ancient and modern earthquakes), (b) find the available sources (both digital and printed books), (c) inspect the data they

---

[2] https://www.cidoc-crm.org/.

have, and (d) evaluate various representation and modeling approaches. Below we provide information for (a)-(c), while (d) is described in Sect. 3.

2.1 Initial Competency Questions

We started by forming a list of competency questions that we would like to be answerable, for being able to analyze earthquake data and building such applications. Below we list the more indicative ones.

Basic-Info Analytic Queries

• Earthquakes with intensity ≥ 6 before 1800, whose focus fall into a given area/s. For each of their key properties (location, magnitude, depth) provide their precision, and the provenance of the information

• Sum and maximum magnitude of earthquakes with focus (epicenter) in Crete by month.

Provenance-based Analytic Queries

• Earthquakes mentioned in Source X, that come from Source Y.

• Earthquakes mentioned in Source X that are wrong (wrong date/ location/-magnitude) according to Book Y.

• Sources that contain information about the earthquake X, organized chronologically, and accompanied by the corresponding citation network.

2.2 Data Sources and Data Collection

We collected data from several data sources and for many earthquakes, as described below.

Data Sources. Earthquake data from 1900 and onward was mainly gathered from two sources, from the earthquake catalogues of the United States Geological Survey (USGS)[3] and from the earthquake catalogues of the University of Athens (UoA)[4]. Finding data about earthquakes before 1900 was quite challenging. We managed to collect data about earthquakes before 1900 (for the island of Crete) mainly from two sources, a book about Cretan (ancient and modern) earthquakes [7] and an article from 1950 published in a Cretan journal [8].

Data Collection Process. For the needs of our analysis we decided to download from USGS all earthquakes of magnitude 3 or above, according to the rectangle drawn on a map from latitude 34.666 N - 35.934 N and longitude 23.138 E - 26.676 E, from all the datasets contained on those sites. The coordinates were chosen such that they contain the island of Crete and the sea near it, up to at least 30 km from Crete's coast.

From the book and the article, we had to manually collect information about all earthquakes listed and their citations.

Size of Collected Data. From USGS we collected 733 earthquakes, from [7] 219 earthquakes, while from [8] 271 earthquakes. In total, we have 1223 descriptions of earthquakes.

---

[3] https://earthquake.usgs.gov/earthquakes/search/.

[4] http://www.geophysics.geol.uoa.gr/stations/gmapv3_db/index.php?lang=en.

2.3   Observations

Here, we describe the different levels of detail and precision that we have noticed by reading the books for the ancient earthquakes that hit the island Crete.

- **A. Dating Uncertainty**: In such a case, there is no evidence about the exact year or even century of the earthquake.
- **B. Magnitude/Depth Uncertainty**: In such cases, the sources do not provide the exact magnitude or/and depth of an earthquake, but a magnitude interval (e.g., 8–9 Richter). Moreover, in some cases there can be a comparison with other earthquakes that can aid us to estimate the magnitude/depth (e.g. "stronger than the one on the 26th of November").
- **C. Location Uncertainty**: For a given earthquake, there can be an uncertainty for the exact location of the earthquake, e.g."Southeast of Santorini".
- **D. Provenance of Information**: For the same earthquake one or more sources can either agree or disagree with one or more key characteristics of the earthquake (location, magnitude, depth, etc.). This becomes even harder for ancient earthquakes.

The key requirement is to model these different levels of granularity, precision, as well as the provenance, for aiding the query formulation process and the presentation and visualization of results (of plain or analytic queries).

3   Representation and Modeling Approaches

3.1   Knowledge Graphs Limitations

Current KGs are based on the W3C standard RDF (Resource Description Framework) and OWL, which essentially offer a labeled directed graph data model. However, the expressiveness of this data model is limited: it does not allow quantitative statements, i.e., it cannot host data associated with degrees that express various kinds of uncertainty (probability, trust, etc.). This limits the applicability, and thus the value of KGs, since we cannot host in a disciplined manner information that has been produced by information extraction and data mining techniques. Existing solutions (like reification) have not been widely adopted due to several limitations, e.g. they do not allow inferences on (reified) triples (important for producing new knowledge) and require an addition of a large number of triples to annotate a single statement (enlarging the already large dataset). Also, current technology for KGs does not offer any intrinsic mechanism for hosting (and properly managing) knowledge expressed in different levels of granularity and nested provenance levels (i.e. provenance of the provenance). There are only a few works that elaborate on fuzzy or probabilistic KGs (a review of the basic concept and definitions of knowledge reasoning and the methods for reasoning over KGs, including fuzzy extensions, is given by Chen et al., 2020 [1]), however they have not reached a level of maturity to enable their application in real datasets. There is also a recent W3C proposal, under the name RDF-Star[5], that extends RDF with a way to make statements about other statements, and

---

[5] https://www.w3.org/2022/08/rdf-star-wg-charter/.

this can be exploited for associating an RDF edge (triple) with scores, weights, temporal aspects and provenance.

However the general question that arises is: how to select what approach to use for modeling various levels of granularity/precision and provenance? The one extreme is to tackle all such aspects at the conceptual modeling level (i.e. at the level of the ontology); the other extreme is to tackle them at the data model level (i.e. adopt a data model more expressive than RDF). A deeper understanding is required for deciding (based on the characteristics of the application context) what approach (or what kind of hybrid approach) is beneficial to adopt. In this paper, we investigate the conceptual modeling level.

3.2   Ontologies Related to Earthquakes

As regards ontology-based modeling of earthquakes, there are some works for modeling various perspectives of earthquakes. This includes a) General Emergency Management ontologies, like SOFERS emergency response system [5] and the Emergency Case Ontology Model [12], b) Earthquake Emergency Management Ontologies, like EEM, an ontology for modeling sensors and actuators (for evaluating both the earthquake entity and to respond to the emergency) and EDER, a disaster response geo-ontology [9], c) Earthquake Engineering ontologies for Research [4] and for building seismic risk assessment [11], d) Earthquake Emergency Training ontologies, for example a drill script design ontology [2]. The aforementioned ontologies focus on particular aspects, they cannot document all information about an earthquake, do not meet our requirements (as listed in §2.1), and cannot tackle the difficulties (as listed in §2.3).

In addition, there exists e) a data warehousing ontology [6], created for the purpose of storing earthquake data and predicting earthquakes. We found one existing attempt at creating an f) Earthquake LOD, using recent datasets from the USA and Japan, with the purpose of improving the discovery and retrieval of earthquake data [10]. While these ontologies serve the purpose of storing earthquake data from different datasets, they are still not extensive enough for our case, as there is no planning for earthquakes before 1900, ambiguity in data and conflict between observatories and sources. The data warehousing ontology does not even account for earthquake data sources. There exists also QuakeML[6], an XML format for exchanging seismological data, but it has not been modeled in RDF.

It is also worth mentioning CRMsci, the "Scientific Observation Model"[7], which is a formal ontology, that uses and extends the CIDOC-CRM, intended to be used as a global schema for integrating metadata about scientific observation, measurements and processed data in descriptive and empirical sciences such as biodiversity, geology, geography, archaeology, cultural heritage conservation and others in research IT environments and research data libraries.

Last, CRMinf (the "Argumentation Model")[8] is another official extension of CIDOC-CRM that is closely related to CRMsci. It is intended to be used

---

[6] https://quake.ethz.ch/quakeml/.
[7] https://www.cidoc-crm.org/crmsci/.
[8] https://www.cidoc-crm.org/crminf/.

as a global schema for integrating metadata about argumentation, inference making, belief adoption and provenance assessment. In this paper we propose the *combined use* and *light extension* of CIDOC-CRM, CRMsci and CRMinf.

4 The Proposed Modeling

Based on the requirements and the competency questions, we decided to use CIDOC-CRM and its compatible extensions CRMsci and CRMinf. CIDOC-CRM is a well developed and recognized ontology providing us an ontological base for our model (we represent earthquakes as a subclass of E5 Event). CRMsci is necessary, since a class for measurements of temporal entities is required, while CRMinf is used for representation of provenance and uncertainty. We shall call our model **CRM-EQ**. The main concepts that it captures are shown in Figure 2. In brief, we mainly use classes and properties from the aforementioned models, plus some original classes and properties that extend CIDOC-CRM and CRMsci to facilitate the needs of our own model. A more detailed overview of CRM-EQ (also annotated with examples of instances for each class) is shown in Fig. 3. Below, we provide details on how we model each type of information.

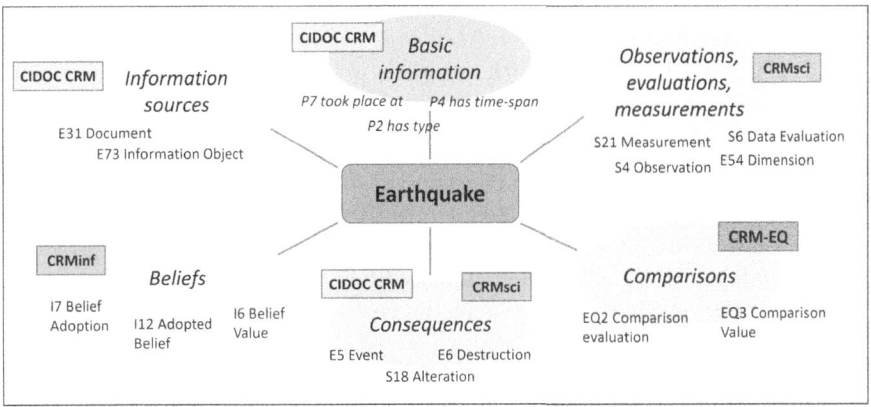

Fig. 2. Overview of modeled information.

Modeling Basic Earthquake Information First, for representing an instance of an earthquake, we define a new class with the name `EQ1 Earthquake` as a subclass of the CIDOC-CRM class `E7 Event`.[9] Then, we make use of the CIDOC-CRM properties *P7 took place at*, *P4 has time-span* and *P2 has type* (inherited from super-classes of E7 Event) for representing the general location

---

[9] We prefer defining a new class instead of directly using E7 Event together with the property *P2 has type*, as it makes querying more efficient and because we reserve the P2 property for defining the type of an earthquake (e.g. aftershock).

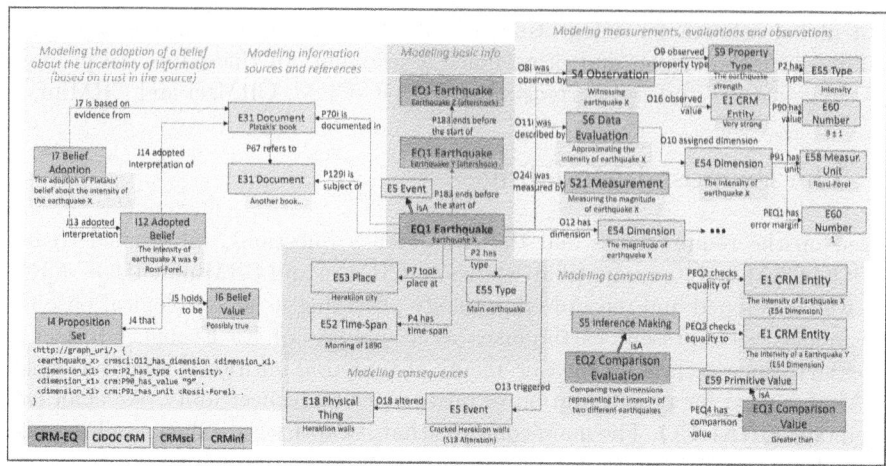

Fig. 3. The CRM-EQ model.

which suffered damages, e.g. Crete (the island) or Arkalochori (town in the Heraklion regional unit of Crete)[10], its timestamp in any granularity level (e.g. year, year and month, date, etc.), and one or more types (e.g. aftershock, tectonic, etc.). We can also use the property *P183 ends before the start of* for connecting an earthquake to aftershocks, or the property *P9 consists of* if we consider an earthquake as a set of distinct shocks/earthquakes.

Modeling Measurements, Evaluations and Observations. We make use of CRMsci which offers classes and properties for describing measurements for events (S21 Measurement), evaluations based on established hypotheses and inference rules (S6 Data Evaluation) as well as general observations providing additional information about an earthquake (S4 Observation). These constructs allow us to represent characteristics of the earthquake together with metadata information, such its magnitude (and which observatory measured it), its intensity, etc. Here, the new property *PEQ1 has error margin* can be used to assign an error margin to a recorded dimension.

Modeling Information Sources. For historical earthquakes that are documented in archival sources and books (known to have occurred prior to the early 20th century), we need to retain the data provenance information. This is important for the verification and the long-term validity of research findings that have made use of this data. To capture such information, we can make use of constructs of the core CIDOC-CRM model. In particular, we can link an earthquake with a document (E31 Document) that provides information about it using the property *P70 documents (is documented in)*, or using the property *P129 is about (is subject of)* if the earthquake is the primary subject of the document. Also, we can link a document with other documents it refers to (or other referred

---

[10] Notice that this location might be different from the epicenter of the earthquake.

types of entities, in general) using the property *P67 refers to (is referred to by)*. Additional (metadata) information can be included using existing CIDOC-CRM constructs, such as who wrote the book, when, etc.

Modeling Beliefs on Earthquake Characteristics. We have seen that historical information about earthquakes, as documented in books, is expressed in various levels of detail and precision. To maintain the full provenance chain of information, we use the CRMinf model which supports the structured description of beliefs/propositions of variable certainty as documented in books or other information sources (using the classes `I7 Belief Adoption`, `I12 Adopted Belief`, `I4 Proposition Set`, and `I6 Belief Value`). This implies a trust to the considered information source(s).

Modeling Consequences. For representing the consequences of an earthquake, e.g., damages and destructions, we can use the property *O13 triggered* of CRMsci for linking an event (an earthquake in our case) with other events occurred due to the earthquake and with the physical things that altered by this activity.

Modeling Comparisons. Comparing historical earthquakes is quite common due to the absence of precise information about an earthquake characteristic. An example is the witnessing that an earthquake was stronger than another earthquake. We provide new classes and properties for supporting the description of such information, in particular the class `EQ2 Comparison Evaluation` which is linked to the two entities under comparison using the properties *PEQ2 checks equality of* and *PEQ3 checks equality to*, and to an instance of the class `EQ3 Comparison Value` using the property *PEQ4 has comparison value*.

Shortcuts. We provide a set of shortcut properties (see Fig. 4), each one representing a deduction/join of a long data path. These properties are introduced for the cases where there is less detailed knowledge (that would allow for full data path description), while it can also highly accelerate data querying. For example, the property *PEQ8 has documented possible dimension* is a shortcut of the fully developed path: `EQ1 Earthquake` - *P70i is documented in* - `E31 Document` - *J14 adopted interpretation of* - `I12 Adopted Belief` - {*J4 holds to be* ="Possibly true"*, J4 that* = <propositions describing an earthquake dimension>}.

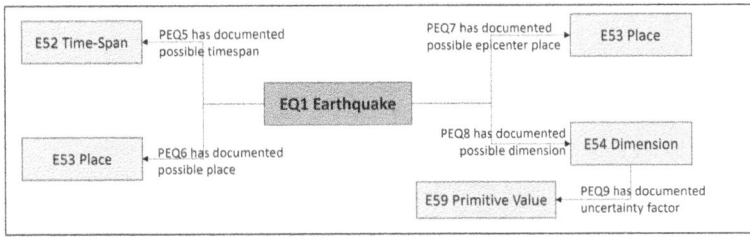

Fig. 4. Shortcuts of CRM-EQ model.

5   Examples of Modelling Modern and Ancient Earthquakes

5.1   Example 1: Modeling a Relatively Modern Earthquake

In Fig. 5 we can see how we can model the basic information of a modern (20th century) earthquake, where we do not have to deal with any uncertainty. We can see how we model information about the earthquake, like place, epicenter, date and measurements, along with the source of the information regarding the earthquake. In Fig. 6 we can see how we model the measurements (intensity, duration, quake movement type, quake direction) regarding the earthquake in a specific location, Malia in our example.

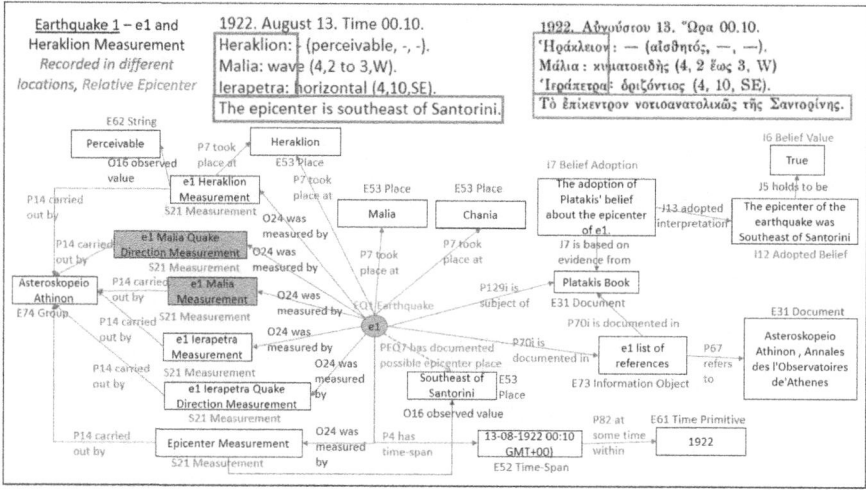

Fig. 5. 20th Century Earthquake - General information and Heraklion measurement

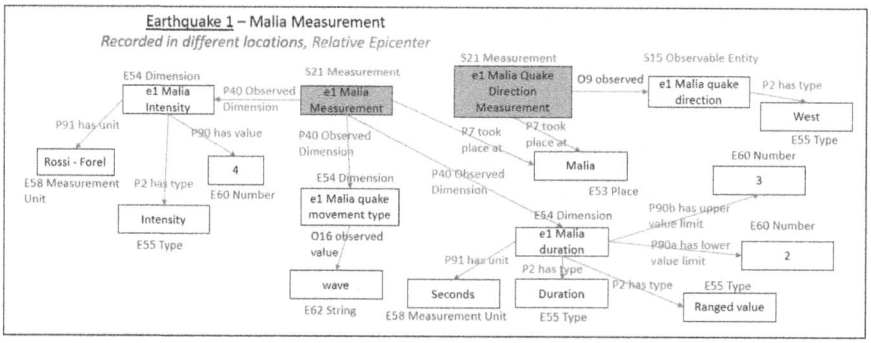

Fig. 6. 20th Century Earthquake - Malia measurement

5.2 Example 2: Modeling Uncertain Intensity and Caused Damages

In Fig. 7 we can see how we model a statement about the possible intensity of an earthquake. Note how we model uncertainty, i.e. we associate the statement about intensity with a tag "Possible". Classes from CRMinf are used to model uncertainty and shortcut properties, shown in dotted lines, are used to quickly connect uncertainty values with the corresponding entity, intensity in this case. Additionally, we can see how we model the damages caused by this earthquake (the earthquake triggers an alteration/destruction or death event).

5.3 Example 3: Modeling Time Uncertainty and Possible Earthquake Equivalences

In Fig. 8 we can see a more complex example, with various kinds of uncertainty. In particular we show how we model the third book excerpt in Fig. 1. Apart from ranged intensity uncertainty, here we can see how we model uncertainty as regards the time point/period, and uncertainty as regards equivalence with another reported earthquake $e4$, shown in Fig. 9.

Figure 10 shows an example on how to model the adoption of a documented belief about the wrong date of an earthquake. Indeed, we adopt the belief in the Platakis book that the date of an earthquake that hit Heraklion is not 1303-08-08 as sourced from Stavrakis' book. In the RDF data model, the proposition set can be implemented using named graphs. Similarly, we can model the adoption of a belief about the possible magnitude, intensity or epicenter of an earthquake, the adoption of a belief that two earthquakes mentioned in different sources are probably the same earthquake, etc. This allows tracking (and querying) the full provenance chain of uncertain or false information as documented in sources.

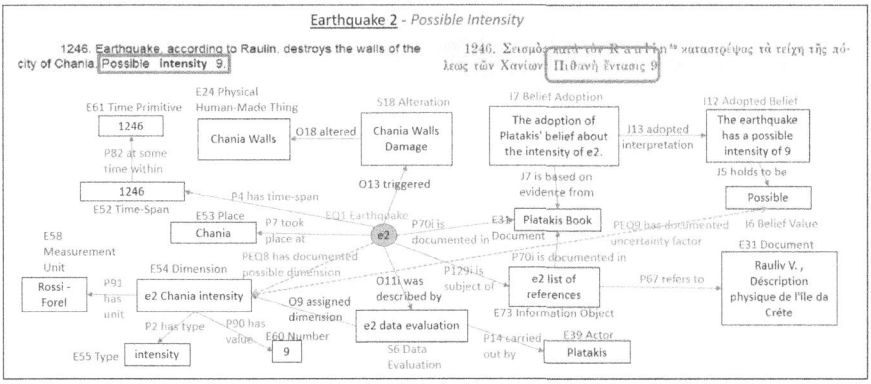

Fig. 7. 1246 earthquake. Modelling uncertainty and damages.

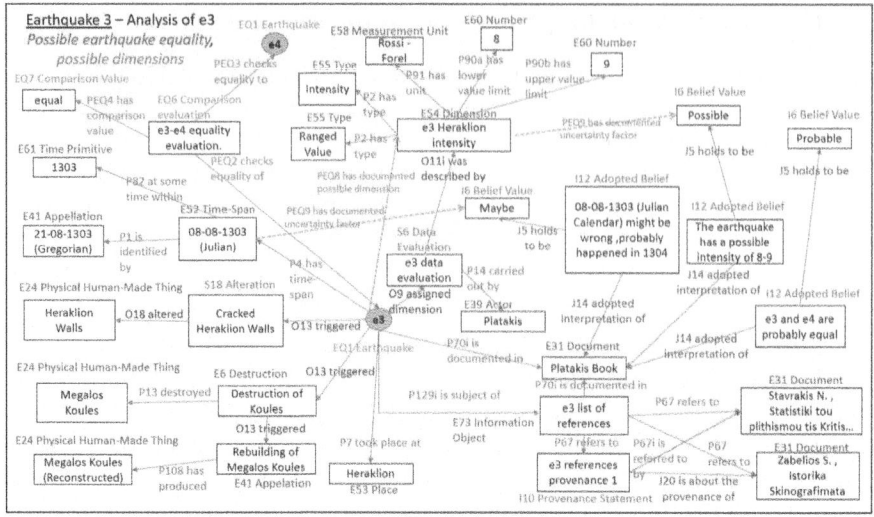

Fig. 8. 1303 earthquake(e3)

6 Implementation and Application

We have implemented the proposed modeling approach. In particular we have created the ontology described. Using that ontology we have documented the earthquakes described in the previous section. These data are publicly available[11], including a .ttl file that contains the RDF representation of all earthquakes described in §5. We have tested the ontology and the earthquake description by trying to formulate the competency questions described in §2.1. For reasons of space, below we show only the following query:

"Give me all earthquakes with intensity $>= 6$ before 1800, whose focus falls into Crete. For each earthquake, give the following information: date, place,

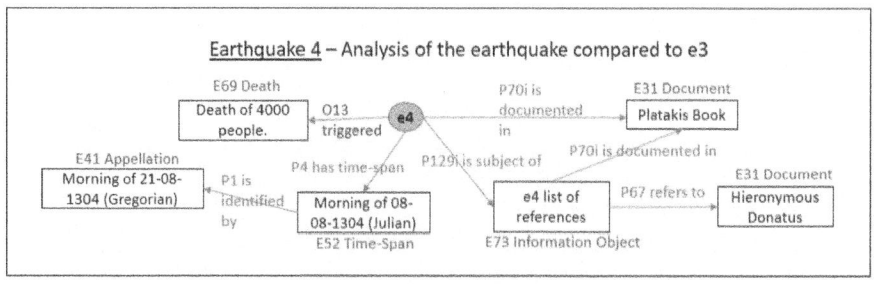

Fig. 9. 1304 earthquake(e4)

---

[11] https://demos.isl.ics.forth.gr/crm-eq.

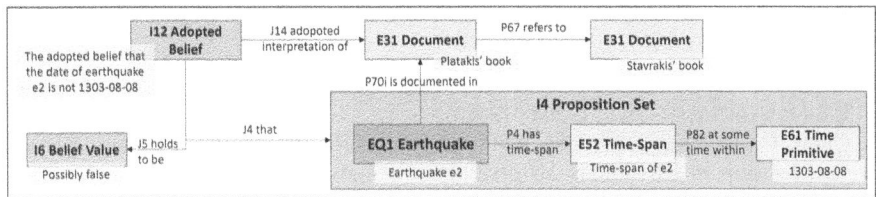

Fig. 10. Modeling the adoption of a belief about the wrong date of an earthquake.

intensity, uncertainty factor (if any), information sources" can be expressed in SPARQL as:

```
 1  SELECT ?eq ?date ?place ?intensity ?uncertainty ?source_title
 2  WHERE {
 3      ?eq a eq:EQ1_Earthquake ; crm:P4_has_time-span ?timespan ; crm:P7_took_place_at ?place .
 4      ?place crm:P89_falls_within eq:Crete.
 5      ?timespan crm:P82_at_some_time_within ?date . FILTER (year(?date)<1800) .
 6      ?eq crmsci:O12_has_dimension ?intDim .
 7      ?intDim crm:P2_has_type eq:intensity ;
 8             crm:P90_has_value ?intensity . FILTER(?intensity >= 6) .
 9      OPTIONAL { ?intDim eq:PEQ9_has_documented_uncertainty_factor ?uncertainty } .
10      OPTIONAL { ?source crm:P70_documents ?eq ; crm:P102_has_title ?source_title } }
```

Note here that, for exploiting the full power of RDF and SPARQL and also simplifying query writing, the underlying engine/triplestore should have inference enabled for the *rdfs:subClassOf, rdfs:subPropertyOf* and *owl:sameAs* relationships, as well as have the required inclusion relationships between toponyms materialised so that the queries work correctly. For example, the above query will not return earthquakes that took place at Heraklion, if inclusion relationships between toponyms have not been materialized (i.e. the relation that Heraklion falls within Crete). Similarly the query will not return uncertain dimensions that make use of the property *PEQ8 has documented possible dimension* (subproperty of *O12 has dimension*), if *subPropertyOf* inference is not enabled.

7   Concluding Remarks

In this paper, we presented an approach for handling historical data which are sparse and vague. In particular, we focused on a case study for earthquake data for the island of Crete. Indeed, we discussed the requirements and challenges for building a Knowledge Graph for the mentioned data, a list of competency questions and we recorded the main observations concerning uncertainties. Afterwards, we analyzed representation approaches and related ontologies and then we presented the proposed representation for making it feasible to provide an answer to the competency questions. We have showcased the feasibility of the approach by implementing it using RDF. As a future work and research, we plan to produce and make publicly available a complete dataset about all earthquakes in Crete (the 1223 earthquakes described in §2.2), and to investigate various analytic and visualization services that are suitable for uncertain data.

References

1. Chen, X., Jia, S., Xiang, Y.: A review: knowledge reasoning over knowledge graph. Expert Syst. Appl. **141**, 112948 (2020)
2. Chou, C.C., Jeng, A.P., Chu, C.P., Chang, C.H., Wang, R.G.: Generation and visualization of earthquake drill scripts for first responders using ontology and serious game platforms. Adv. Eng. Inform. **38**, 538–554 (2018)
3. Doerr, M.: The CIDOC conceptual reference module: an ontological approach to semantic interoperability of metadata. AI Mag. **24**(3), 75–75 (2003)
4. Hasan, R., Farazi, F., Bursi, O.S., Reza, M.S.: A faceted lightweight ontology for earthquake engineering research projects and experiments. In: Taucer, F., Apostolska, R. (eds.) Experimental Research in Earthquake Engineering. GGEE, vol. 35, pp. 11–19. Springer, Cham (2015). https://doi.org/10.1007/978-3-319-10136-1_2
5. Liu, Y., Chen, S., Wang, Y.: SOFERS: scenario ontology for emergency response system. J. Netw. **9**(9), 2529 (2014)
6. Nimmagadda, S.L., Dreher, H.: Ontology based data warehouse modeling and mining of earthquake data: prediction analysis along Eurasian-Australian continental plates. In: 2007 5th IEEE International Conference on Industrial Informatics, vol. 1, pp. 597–602 (2007). https://doi.org/10.1109/INDIN.2007.4384825
7. Papadopoulos, G.A.: A Seismic History of Crete. The Hellenic Arc and Trench - Earthquakes and Tsunamis: 2000 BC - 2011 AD. Ocelotos, Athens (2011)
8. Platakis, E.K: Oi Seismoi tis Kritis apo ton Arxaiotaton mexri ton Kath' Imas Xronon. **4**, 494–496 (1950). vol. D. Andreas G, Kalokairinos
9. Spalazzi, L., Taccari, G., Bernardini, A.: An internet of things ontology for earthquake emergency evaluation and response. In: 2014 International Conference on Collaboration Technologies and Systems (CTS), pp. 528–534. IEEE (2014)
10. Uematsu, H., Takeda, H.: Earthquake ontology and LOD (2023). http://www-kasm.nii.ac.jp/papers/takeda/23/uematsu23ijckg.pdf
11. Xu, M., Zhang, P., Cui, C., Zhao, J.: An ontology-based holistic and probabilistic framework for seismic risk assessment of buildings. Buildings **12**(9), 1391 (2022)
12. Yang, P., Wang, W., Dong, C.: Application of emergency case ontology model in earthquake. In: 2009 International Conference on Management and Service Science, pp. 1–5. IEEE (2009)

Towards a Knowledge Graph for Models and Algorithms in Applied Mathematics

Björn Schembera[1]([envelope]) [ORCID], Frank Wübbeling[2] [ORCID], Hendrik Kleikamp[2] [ORCID],
Burkhard Schmidt[3] [ORCID], Aurela Shehu[3] [ORCID], Marco Reidelbach[5] [ORCID],
Christine Biedinger[4] [ORCID], Jochen Fiedler[4] [ORCID], Thomas Koprucki[3] [ORCID],
Dorothea Iglezakis[6] [ORCID], and Dominik Göddeke[1,7] [ORCID]

[1] Institute of Applied Analysis and Numerical Simulation, University of Stuttgart, Stuttgart, Germany
`{bjoern.schembera,dominik.goeddeke}@ians.uni-stuttgart.de`
[2] Institute of Applied Mathematics: Analysis and Numerics, University of Münster, Münster, Germany
`{frank.wuebbeling,hendrik.kleikamp}@uni-muenster.de`
[3] Weierstrass Institute for Applied Analysis and Stochastics, Berlin, Germany
`{burkhard.schmidt,aurela.shehu,thomas.koprucki}@wias-berlin.de`
[4] Fraunhofer Institute for Industrial Mathematics, Kaiserslautern, Germany
`{christine.biedinger,jochen.fiedler}@itwm.fraunhofer.de`
[5] Mathematics of Complex Systems, Zuse Institute Berlin, Berlin, Germany
`reidelbach@zib.de`
[6] University Library, University of Stuttgart, Stuttgart, Germany
`dorothea.iglezakis@ub.uni-stuttgart.de`
[7] Stuttgart Center for Simulation Science (SC SimTech), University of Stuttgart, Stuttgart, Germany

Abstract. Mathematical models and algorithms are an essential part of mathematical research data, as they are epistemically grounding numerical data. To make this research data FAIR, we present how two previously distinct ontologies, MathAlgoDB for algorithms and MathModDB for models, were merged and extended into a living knowledge graph as the key outcome. This was achieved by connecting the ontologies through computational tasks that correspond to algorithmic tasks. Moreover, we show how models and algorithms can be enriched with subject-specific metadata, such as matrix symmetry or model linearity, essential for defining workflows and determining suitable algorithms. Additionally, we propose controlled vocabularies to be added, along with a new class that differentiates base quantities from specific use case quantities. We illustrate the capabilities of the developed knowledge graph using two detailed examples from different application areas of applied mathematics, having already integrated over 250 research assets into the knowledge graph.

Keywords: Research Data Management · Ontologies · Knowledge Graphs · Mathematical Models · Mathematical Algorithms

1   Introduction

Data and knowledge driven approaches constitute the fourth paradigm of science [20]. Computer simulations generate vast amounts of data, big measurement data are recorded in physics, and statistical data are collected in social science cohort studies, among others. For scientific reasoning, generation, processing and analysis of data is becoming essentially important. Moreover, sharing and citing research data is increasingly acknowledged as a key part of the scientific process [10]. To enable this and to ensure good scientific practice, research data must be documented and stored in accordance with the FAIR principles [43] as a means to avoid dark data [35]. In particular, all relevant information that has led to a scientific finding must be documented in order to be able to replicate and reproduce the result at a later date or by third parties [4,33].

Specifically in branches of science using mathematical methods, research data take many forms. Mathematics is typically still associated with classical mathematical artifacts, i.e. documents with mathematical proofs and formulae. However, this definition falls short, as applied mathematics produce data based on numerical methods. These particular fields rely on mathematical models and algorithms for the generation of numerical or symbolic data [8,42]. A comprehensive overview of types of mathematical research data can be found in [10].

For a complete epistemic understanding, all models and solution algorithms must be documented. This knowledge, which goes beyond reproducibility, supports tackling similar problems or improving efficiency by identifying alternate, competing or complementing models and solution schemes. The conceptual foundations for semantic knowledge representation for these research assets were laid in [36,37], where an ontology for mathematical models and algorithms was proposed. Building on this work, we present a matured version of a joint ontology of models and algorithms stemming from applied mathematics, and a Knowledge Graph (KG) with to date more than 2000 elements, ready for production service. To this end, the paper is structured as follows: Sect. 2 reviews related work, followed by Sect. 3 which discusses the preliminary work and details our extensions and ontology merging. Section 4 describes the transition to a data-driven KG along use cases. Section 5 concludes with a summary and outlook.

2   Related Work

The use of ontologies in mathematics is still limited, as the importance of making all research data FAIR has only recently gained broader acceptance. Preliminary work in the area of mathematical models exists, e.g. introducing taxonomic classification of mathematical artifacts [13], which were eventually merged with succeeding educational approaches [23,24]. Other didactic uses of ontologies for mathematical learning can be found in [44,45]. However, since these ontologies are primarily educational and taxonomic, they do not include many mathematical objects relevant to our work.

In addition, there are many subject-specific ontologies for mathematical models from a certain domain, e.g., plasma physics [39], biology [9,21], Neural Networks [30], in a mechanistic context [40,41] or for models built on interval data [12]. In contrast, our approach is broader and more flexible and aims to create a general ontology for mathematical models and (numerical) algorithms. Our ontology is designed to be modular to possibly connect with other ontologies and knowledge frameworks, such as those for software and hardware, in the context of Linked Open Data [7].

Based on the assumption that mathematical papers hold research data, Open Mathematical Documents [25] introduce a semantic markup format defining an ontology for mathematical documents. A more general approach to representing these semantics is the use of *Model Pathway Diagrams* (MPDs) [26]. MPDs can be viewed as preliminary work leading to our development of an ontology for mathematical models and algorithms.

The Algorithms Metadata Vocabulary [11] is designed from a computer science perspective presenting detailed knowledge about algorithms, including characteristics such as loop constructs or data structures. The MEX Algorithm Ontology [16] focuses on representing the algorithmic information present in a basic machine learning experiment. While these details are crucial for developers, computer and ML scientists, our focus is solely on mathematical algorithms.

The work presented is being driven by the *Mathematical Research Data Initiative* (MaRDI) [42], a consortium within the *National German Research Data Infrastructure* (NFDI) [19]. The goal of the NFDI is a linked data infrastructure and semantic technology built by discipline-specific consortia. The NFDI Core Ontology [34] describes and connects research outputs like datasets, software as well as events with agents and their roles and scientific domains. The Open Research KG (ORKG) [3] describes scientific papers of different domains in a semantic way, making it easier to find and compare. As mathematical models and algorithms are intensively used in engineering, the ontology metadata4ing [2], allows to connect research outputs with agents, methods, tools and the object of research via provenance tracking.

3   Merging MathModDB and MathAlgoDB

This section reviews the ontologies for mathematical models and algorithms from [36,37] and presents their extension and redesign. The updated ontology serves as the data model for the KG discussed in Sect. 4, with AlgoData now renamed to MathAlgoDB.

3.1   Previous Ontology Structure and Their Shortcomings

In [36], mathematical models have been identified as one of the central categories of mathematical research data and the *Mathematical Models Ontology* (MathModDB) has been developed, with its essential classes being *Mathematical*

Model, Mathematical Formulation, Quantities, Application Problem and *Application Domain*. The same holds true for numerical algorithms, leading to the *MathAlgoDB* ontology with its essential classes being *Algorithm, Algorithmic Problem, Software, Benchmark* and *Publication*. These class names showed some inconsistencies with other common standard nomenclature, such as Wikidata[1] and the ORKG[2]. Hence, minor modifications of the original design were made by renaming the classes *Application Domain* to *Research Field* and *Application Problem* to *Research Problem*.

Major adjustments became necessary as a result of the considerations described in the following. Solving an application problem via modeling (represented in MathModDB) requires addressing algorithmic problems (represented in MathAlgoDB). In [36], this connection was made through the relation *uses algorithmic subproblem* and its inverse *used by model problem*, representing the process where mathematical modeling is followed by solving model equations with a numerical algorithm via the class *Algorithmic Problem*. In [36], it was already mentioned that distinguishing between a mathematical problem and an algorithmic one can be challenging. Sometimes, specific *Mathematical Model* in MathModDB had no corresponding *Algorithmic Problem* in MathAlgoDB. In such cases, the mathematical problem needed to be added to MathAlgoDB as an *Algorithmic Problem*. In this respect, there are strong canonical connections between the two ontologies, which were additionally specified during the further development, as presented in the upcoming sections. In the course of this consideration, the *Algorithmic Problem* class was also renamed *Algorithmic Task* for the sake of harmonization.

3.2   Computational Tasks as the Missing Link

In the preliminary work, MathModDB as the ontology for mathematical models and MathAlgoDB as the ontology for algorithms were rather separate developments. However, since they represent two sides of the same epistemic coin, they have been unified in this approach, see Fig. 1.

This is evident as the connections between the two parts are now made through several classes. First, a *Computational Task* class had to be introduced, which is complementary to the *Algorithmic Task* class and represents the semantic information content that a specific computational task is closely related to an algorithmic problem class. For example, the *Computational Task* of calculating the time evolution of a dynamical system model is directly linked to the *Algorithmic Task* of solving coupled ordinary differential equations.

Second, the *Publication* class originally developed for MathAlgoDB is now also linked to MathModDB, since where a mathematical model (or any of its parts) was invented, analyzed, studied, surveyed or used in the literature is a crucial reference information for researchers.

---

[1] https://www.wikidata.org/wiki/Q2465832.

[2] https://orkg.org/fields.

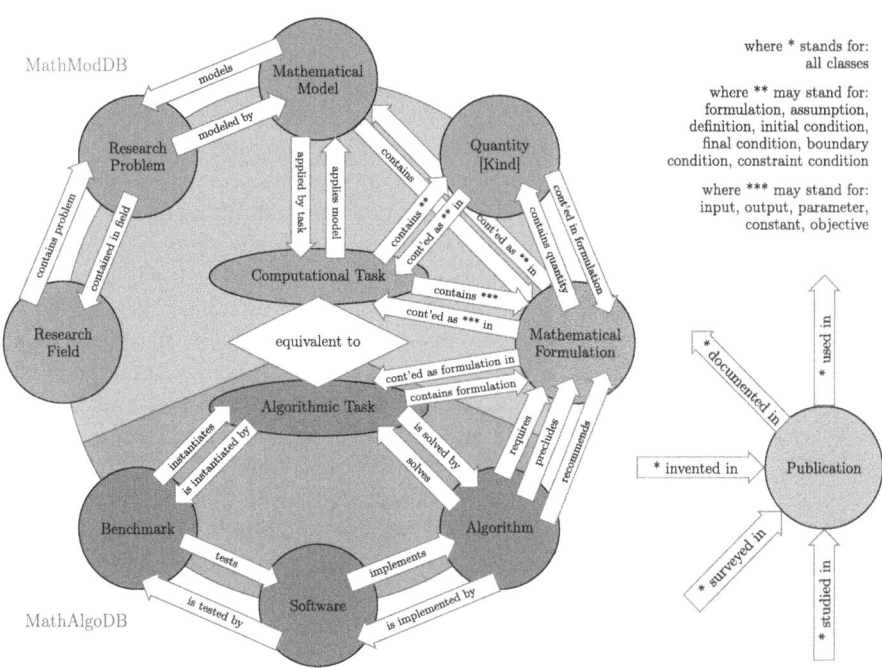

Fig. 1. Schematic display of the joint ontology for mathematical models and algorithms. Classes and important relations are depicted.

Third, as the properties of mathematical formulations and the quantities contained in them are highly relevant for the selection of potential solution algorithms, a corresponding relation between *Mathematical Formulation* and *Algorithmic Task* was introduced.

3.3   Role of Quantities in Mathematical Knowledge Representation

As stated in the previous section, quantities play a decisive role in mathematical expressions as they give models their actual semantic meaning. Hence, next to the *Quantity* class, the *Quantity Kind* class was introduced. In this way, we enhance clarity and precision in the semantic representation by categorically separating basic quantities from the specific quantities that occur in the use cases. For example, the electrical membrane potential of a cell, which occurs as a quantity in one of the bio-physiological use cases, is a specialization of the quantity *Electrical Potential*. In electrostatics, the difference in this potential between two points is given by the basic quantity *Voltage*, which is an individual of the *Quantity Kind* class. *Voltage* then refers to the corresponding entries in the controlled vocabulary QUDT[3] [17, 22] and in Wikidata[4].

---

[3] https://qudt.org/vocab/quantitykind/Voltage.
[4] https://www.wikidata.org/wiki/Q25428.

3.4   Metadata Enrichment for Mathematical Models

The existing ontologies were revised with regard to the integration of external information sources, in particular controlled vocabularies. This is intended to drive the enrichment of the KG with metadata in an unambiguous way. The information was added either as data properties or annotation properties - depending on whether the information can be used to make new findings in reasoning or it should only be available to users. Individuals from the *Quantity* class can now be equipped with IDs from QUDT. Only if quantities are clearly presented, potential risks of incorrect units or misinterpretation, which have already led to issues elsewhere [18], can be avoided. In addition, individuals in the *Research Field* class can now be assigned identifiers from the German Research Foundation (DFG) [1], Mathematics Subject Classification (MSC) [28] and Physics Subject Headings (PhySH) [38] classification systems. Furthermore, it is now possible to link individuals with their equivalents in Wikidata.

Subject-specific metadata can also be integrated, such as a natural language description as a comment and links to Wikipedia or Wikidata as annotations for individuals of any class. Moreover, individuals of the *Mathematical Formulation* class can hold the specific mathematical expression in LaTeX or MathML, and all symbols are broken down into quantities. For all these quantities, relevant metadata can be attached, for instance marking whether a quantity is a scalar, vector, matrix or a higher order tensor, and, for example, to indicate its matrix structure and more special properties. Individuals of the *Mathematical Formulation* and the *Mathematical Model* class can both hold relevant properties as metadata, such as the order of the model equations, but also whether they are linear, convex, homogeneous, just to name a few.

3.5   Metadata Enrichment for Mathematical Algorithms

One major goal of MathAlgoDB is the proposition of a catalog with appropriate numerical algorithms for a concrete research problem. As stated, mathematical modeling boils down to a computational task containing a formulation with quantities. The formulation will be general (e.g. "solve ordinary differential equation"), but the modeling will provide additional properties for the formulation (e.g. stiff/non-stiff, scalar, first order, linear) or the quantities involved (e.g. the system matrix A, in the formulation of a linear *Ordinary Differential Equation* (ODE) $y' = Ay$, is symmetric) and are now available through MathModDB.

In order to use that information, several changes were made to MathAlgoDB, mostly related to the algorithm selection for specific application tasks. We need to augment the information on algorithms that is currently present, with information about (the properties of) the objects it handles as input or output. For instance in the case of linear equations, for the mathematical formulation of "solve $Ax = b$ for x":

- General algorithms like LU decomposition works for all square and invertible matrices.

- Conjugate Gradient requires A to be *symmetric and positive definite* (s.p.d.).
- If A is Toeplitz, solving with Trench's algorithm is recommended.
- Expectation Maximization/Maximum likelihood type algorithms are generally applicable for problems with a positivity constraint on A and x, but particularly recommended provided b is Poisson–distributed.

In the preliminary approach, this was implemented by using named tasks and subtasks, defining a general **linear equation task** and a **linear equations for s.p.d. matrices** subtask. As we showed, this is an approach that works fine for purely theoretical considerations and follows the structure of typical textbook derivations of algorithms.

However, this implies that no automatic assignment of models to computational tasks or algorithms is possible. The new approach defines properties for the quantities involved in an algorithm, and thus can use the information provided by the model. Next, we give an example of a tomography problem. Since the underlying model is linear, after discretization, the problem will always reduce to a simple **linear equation task** and using general algorithms would be a mistake.

Example 1 (Computerized Tomography of synthetic parallel data).

- Computational Task: In the formulation of a linear system $Ax = b$, solve for x.
- Property 1: The formulation stems from (a discretization of) the Radon transform.
- Property 2: The Radon transform has been sampled using parallel beam geometry.
- Property 3: A is sparse.
- (Plain) Filtered backprojection algorithm requires the first two properties. It is **recommended** in this case.
- Algebraic Reconstruction/Kaczmarz' algorithm requires property one, but does not make use of the sampling structure. It is **possible**, but not recommended.
- (Plain) conjugate gradient requires A to be symmetric, which is not the case here. It is **unusable** (at least directly).

For this case, filtered backprojection should be selected. MathAlgoDB also provides links to various implementations.

This simple example shows that it is hardly possible to predefine available properties. Each community or application case will have to be able to define their own property set, which precludes us from defining this within the ontology.

In order to materialize this idea in the graph, we link *Algorithmic Task* to the *Mathematical Formulation* class by object properties. The formulations then contain data properties which are interpreted based on the object property. We define:

- **requires**: All properties listed are required for the algorithm.

- **recommends**: If the properties are satisfied, the algorithm is preferred.
- **precludes**: When this property is present, the algorithm cannot be used.

Example 2. In the case of initial value problems for ODEs, Runge-Kutta methods are the primary choice. They differ on whether or not can handle stiffness, and on convergence order, in turn requiring smoothness of solutions of the ODE. In terms of the ontology:

- Forward Euler precludes stiffness.
- Backward Euler is recommended when the ODE is stiff.
- RK4 requires smoothness of (at least) order 4, precludes stiffness and is recommended when the smoothness is of order 4.

For the algorithm selection, an appropriate SPARQL query yields all algorithms and implementations that solve the mathematical task, satisfy all required properties, do not conflict with precluded properties, possibly sorted by the recommended property. The last one is important – note that the most general algorithms will always show up here, but will usually be inappropriate due to running time or precision.

4 Living Knowledge Graph of Models and Algorithms

As of mid August 2024, more than 120 mathematical models and over 200 algorithms have been added as individuals, turning the conceptual ontology into a living KG. The models stem from diverse research fields such as continuum mechanics, semiconductor physics, enzyme kinetics or biophysics. Two examples are presented in the Sects. 4.1 and 4.2, Although the majority of use cases derive from the field of numerical mathematics, it was prototypically shown in [32] that the KG can also be used to capture a Logical Data Analysis algebraic modeling workflow, rooted in the Digital Humanities, representing research from Egyptology.

Up to now, the current data corpus consists of manually maintained, curated information only. This is primarily due to the high demands placed on the data quality of an algorithm and model database. High data quality is of great importance for third parties to be able to rely on the information and to use the contained information for their own research or for verification purposes. However, we are aware that this is a limitation in our approach and will evaluate in future work a semi-automatic approach similar to the one proposed in the neighboring NFDI consortium for catalysis [5,6]. In addition, the templates described in Sect. 4.3 serve as preparatory work for a semi-automated collection of model data.

The implementation and data ingest of MathModDB was initally only conducted using Protégé [29]. MathAlgoDB is based on an Apache Jena Fuseki with a web interface in the Django framework. The data ingest and SPARQL endpoints are described in Sect. 4.3.

4.1   Use Case: From Falling Apples to Moving Planets

As an illustrative example, we consider the famous story of Sir Isaac Newton being inspired to formulate his theory of gravitation by watching the fall of an apple from a tree in the year 1666. We have implemented this within the MathModDB KG by including a *Research Field* named "Pomology" (science of fruits) containing "Gravitational Effects on Fruit" as a specific *Research Problem*. Currently, there is a choice of two *Mathematical Models* addressing this problem, i.e., "Free Fall Models" without and with the effect of air drag, both of them assuming constant gravitation. The former one, actually dating back to Newton, contains the simple "Free Fall Equation", $\dot{v} = g$, as a *Mathematical Formulation*. That equation contains the (time-derivative of the) free fall velocity v and the gravitational acceleration g. Obviously, these two *Quantities* are assigned to the *Quantity Kinds* velocity and acceleration, respectively. The free fall model with air drag may be described by the nonlinear equation $\dot{v} = g - \frac{\rho C_D A v^2}{2m}$ which, in addition to the case without drag, contains the density of air ρ, the drag coefficient C_D, the cross section A and the mass of the apple m. Within the context of these "Free Fall Models", several different *Computational Tasks* can be formulated, e.g., how long does it take for an apple to reach the ground, or with which velocity will it hit the ground. While the above equations are so simple that they can be solved analytically, in more realistic free fall models the underlying equations have to be solved numerically, which falls into the realm of the MathAlgoDB KG containing suitable numerical solvers for ordinary differential equations such as the Runge Kutta family of algorithms.

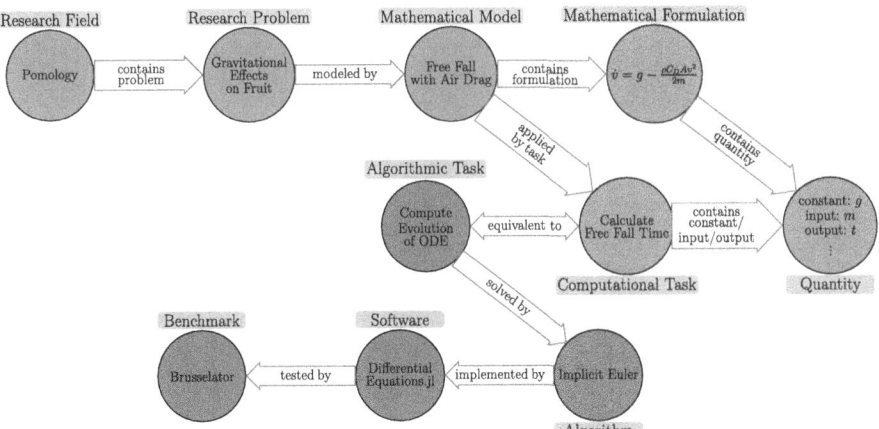

Fig. 2. Schematic display of the sample use case 4.1 free fall model in pomology in the joint ontology. For reasons of clarity, we will limit ourselves here to the essential entries and not show all connections, classes and quantities.

In the case of the simple Free Fall Model in vacuum, virtually every scheme for solving ODEs can be applied. Following the example 2 in 3.5, the simplest one (Forward Euler) could be used, if no order property is specified in the model.

For the air drag model (see Fig. 2), we treat the equation as being stiff due to the nonlinearity. Since in the Forward Euler algorithm stiffness is a precluded property, it cannot be used in that case. However, Backward Euler is a possible algorithm for stiff ODEs, and it will be therefore proposed by MathAlgoDB.

Note that for both examples, the model **should** specify a smoothness class which would then trigger recommendation of a higher order Runge-Kutta scheme (such as RK4).

The following SPARQL query can be used to find all algorithms with their respective *Computational Task* and *Algorithmic Problem* that can be applied when considering the *Research Problem* of gravitational effects on fruits. Here, for simplicity, we only implement the "precludes" relation in order to exclude the explicit Runge-Kutta schemes for stiff equations:

```
PREFIX madb: <https://mardi4nfdi.de/mathalgodb/0.1#>
PREFIX mmdb: <https://mardi4nfdi.de/mathmoddb#>
SELECT ?mod ?task ?prob ?form ?alg
WHERE {
  mmdb:GravitationalEffectsOnFruit mmdb:modeledBy ?mod .
  ?task mmdb:appliesModel ?mod .
  ?task mmdb:equivalentTo ?prob .
  ?form mmdb:containedAsFormulationIn ?mod .
  ?alg madb:solves ?prob .
  FILTER (  # implements the 'precludes' relation
    NOT EXISTS {
      ?alg madb:precludes ?precForm .
      FILTER (
        NOT EXISTS {
          ?precForm ?a ?b .
          FILTER (CONTAINS(STR(?a), STR(mmdb:)))
          FILTER (
            NOT EXISTS {
              ?form ?a ?b .
      })})})}
```

This query gives the expected output:

mod	task	prob	form	alg
FreeFallModelAirDrag	FreeFallDetermineVelocity	ComputeEvolutionODE	FreeFallEquationAirDrag	RKim11
FreeFallModelVacuum	FreeFallDetermineVelocity	ComputeEvolutionODE	FreeFallEquationVacuum	RKex11
FreeFallModelVacuum	FreeFallDetermineVelocity	ComputeEvolutionODE	FreeFallEquationVacuum	RKim11
FreeFallModelVacuum	FreeFallDetermineVelocity	ComputeEvolutionODE	FreeFallEquationVacuum	RK44kutta

4.2 Use Case: Like a Virus Romanization of Northern Tunesia

From 146 BC to 350 AD, Roman culture spread across Northern Tunisia. Today, this can be traced by looking at archaeological evidence and historical records such as the administrative status of cities. In the *Research Field* of Roman Archaeology, this phenomenon is studied under the *Research Problem* of "Romanization Spreading in Northern Tunisia".

In [27], the spreading was modeled using a susceptible-infected (SI) model from the epidemiology domain on interregional networks with a time-dependent spreading rate. In this *Mathematical Model* the state of each region m at time t is given by $s_m(t)$, the number of susceptible (non-Romanized) cities, and $i_m(t)$, the number of infected (Romanized) cities. The change in the number of susceptible and infected cities over time is described by the following *Mathematical Formulation*s,

$$\frac{ds_m(t)}{dt} = -s_m(t)\alpha(t) \sum_{n=1}^{N_R} G_{m,n} i_n(t)$$

$$i_m(t) = P_m - s_m(t)$$

with $\alpha(t)$, G, P_m and N_R denoting the *Quantities* time-dependent spreading rate, interregional contact network, total number of cities in region m, and total number of regions, respectively.

Two *Computational Task*s are associated with the model. These are: 1) the determination of approximate spreading curves $\phi(t)$ using arbitrary parameters for G and $\alpha(t)$ in a first-order Runge-Kutta scheme and 2) the determination of optimal parameters G and $\alpha(t)$ with respect to the real-world data using the Prescaled Metropolis-Adjusted Langevin Algorithm to minimize a loss function.

The initial value ODE problem in MathAlgoDB can be handled as in the Free Fall Model. Properties of the problem that would hint to use the Langevin Algorithm are high dimension, smoothness and availability of strong gradient information.

4.3 Data Flows in the Knowledge Graph

Templates were developed that facilitate the process for researchers wishing to add mathematical models to the MathModDB in order to make these models FAIR. They are provided as Markdown files and are designed to have a low entry barrier, allowing users with little to no experience to get started easily while guaranteeing the important details of the mathematical model are gathered. The filled-in templates then serve as a basis for a further semantically annotated standardized description of the model employing the MathModDB ontology.

MaRDMO [31] is an extension of the Research Data Management Organiser [14], the most widely used tool for data management planning in Germany [15], facilitating the documentation of interdisciplinary workflows. It offers a standardized questionnaire and integrates with resources like the MaRDI Portal[5], Wikidata, and other knowledge bases. Utilizing the MathModDB ontology, MaRDMO allows the documentation of mathematical models either independently or as part of larger workflows. It facilitates seamless integration with the KG by connecting existing model entities and creating new ones when necessary [32]. This capability positions MaRDMO as a user-friendly and interdisciplinary interface to explore and contribute to the KG.

---

[5] https://portal.mardi4nfdi.de/wiki/Portal.

The MathAlgoDB KG can be accessed via a web interface which can be used to retrieve information and browse the graph. Furthermore, the web interface has recently been extended to allow for the addition of new data into the KG. The joint ontology including the examples shown above is available at https:// mtsr2024.m1.mardi.ovh/. The SPARQL query shown in Sect. 4.1 can be sent to the corresponding SPARQL port at https://sparql.mtsr2024.m1.mardi.ovh/ mathalgodb/query in order to obtain the results presented above.

5   Conclusion and Outlook

We have extended the original design for semantically representing mathematical models and algorithms by merging the two previosuly distinct ontologies MathAlgoDB and MathModDB into a living KG. The key extensions presented include renaming of classes for harmonization, introducing a Computational Task class as the missing but crucial link between MathModDB and MathAlgoDB, incorporating controlled vocabularies for the *Research Field* and *Quantity Kind* classes, and enabling metadata enrichment for both models and algorithms. This allows for a comprehensive representation of modeling and simulation research assets across various scientific fields. In addition to the more than 250 research assets already integrated, we have demonstrated the KG's capabilities through three examples from different areas of applied mathematics. This comprehensive representation now supports more complex models, like planetary dynamics, and suggests future expansions to include theoretical concepts such as gravitational theory and classical mechanics.

While primarily focused on numerical mathematics, future work will adapt the ontology to other mathematical areas, particularly those stemming from MaRDI and NFDI. Limitations include implicit handling of discretization and the manual, time-consuming data ingestion process, which we aim to partially automate. As discretization is an essential part of numerical mathematics and it impacts the numerical algorithm, its integration into the KG will become a top priority in our future work. This should enable the specific discretization methodology to be documented, i.e. whether grid-, particle-based or other methods were used. Our near future project work plan also includes the integration of the graph into the MaRDI portal, allowing the assignment of persistent IDs for models and algorithms.

Acknowledgments. The co-authors C.B., J.F., M.R., A.S., B.S., B.S. acknowledge funding by MaRDI, funded by the DFG (German Research Foundation), project number 460135501, NFDI 29/1 "MaRDI - Mathematische Forschungsdateninitiative". The co-authors H.K. and F.W. acknowledge funding by the DFG under Germany's Excellence Strategy EXC 2044-390685587, Mathematics Münster: Dynamics- Geometry-Structure.The co-author D.G. acknowledges funding by the DFG under Germany's Excellence Strategy EXC 2075: Data-Integrated Simulation Science (SimTech), project number 390740016.

References

1. The DFG subject area structure. https://www.dfg.de/en/research-funding/proposal-funding-process/interdisciplinarity/subject-area-structure
2. Arndt, S., et al.: Metadata4ing: an ontology for describing the generation of research data within a scientific activity (2023). https://doi.org/10.5281/zenodo.5957104
3. Auer, S., Kovtun, V., Prinz, M., Kasprzik, A., Stocker, M., Vidal, M.E.: Towards a knowledge graph for science. In: Proceedings of the 8th International Conference on Web Intelligence, Mining and Semantics, pp. 1–6 (2018). https://doi.org/10.1145/3227609.3227689
4. Baker, M.: 1,500 scientists lift the lid on reproducibility. Nature **533**(7604), 452–454 (2016). https://doi.org/10.1038/533452a
5. Behr, A.S., Borgelt, H., Kockmann, N.: Ontologies4Cat: investigating the landscape of ontologies for catalysis research data management. J. Cheminform. **16**(1), 16 (2024). https://doi.org/10.1186/s13321-024-00807-2
6. Behr, A.S., Völkenrath, M., Kockmann, N.: Ontology extension with NLP-based concept extraction for domain experts in catalytic sciences. Knowl. Inf. Syst. **65**(12), 5503–5522 (2023)
7. Berners-Lee, T.: Linked data (2007). https://www.w3.org/DesignIssues/LinkedData.html
8. Boege, T., et al.: Data management planning in the German mathematical community. Eur. Math. Soc. Mag. **130**, 40–47 (2023). https://doi.org/10.4171/mag/152
9. Chelliah, V., Laibe, C., Le Novère, N.: Biomodels database: a repository of mathematical models of biological processes. In: Silico Systems Biology pp. 189–199 (2013). https://doi.org/10.1007/978-1-62703-450-0_10
10. Conrad, T.O., Ferrer, E., Mietchen, D., Pusch, L., Stegmüller, J., Schubotz, M.: Making mathematical research data FAIR: pathways to improved data sharing. Sci. Data **11**(1), 676 (2024). https://doi.org/10.1038/s41597-024-03480-0
11. Dutta, B., Patel, J.: Algorithm metadata vocabulary: a representational model and metadata vocabulary for describing and maintaining algorithms. J. Inf. Sci. (2022). https://doi.org/10.1177/01655515221116557
12. Dyvak, M., Melnyk, A., Rot, A., Hernes, M., Pukas, A.: Ontology of mathematical modeling based on interval data. Complexity **2022**, 1–19 (2022). https://doi.org/10.1155/2022/8062969
13. Elizarov, A., Kirillovich, A., Lipachev, E., Nevzorova, O.: Digital ecosystem OntoMath: mathematical knowledge analytics and management. In: Kalinichenko, L., Kuznetsov, S.O., Manolopoulos, Y. (eds.) DAMDID/RCDL 2016. CCIS, vol. 706, pp. 33–46. Springer, Cham (2017). https://doi.org/10.1007/978-3-319-57135-5_3
14. Engelhardt, C., Enke, H., Klar, J., Ludwig, J., Neuroth, H.: Research data management organiser. In: Proceedings of the 14th International Conference on Digital Preservation, pp. 25–29 (2017)
15. Enke, H., Hausen, D., Henzen, C., Jagusch, G., Krause, C., Schönau, S., et al.: Data management planning: concept for setting up a working group in the NFDI section common infrastructures. Zenodo (2023). https://doi.org/10.5281/zenodo.7540682
16. Esteves, D., et al.: Mex vocabulary: A lightweight interchange format for machine learning experiments, vol. 10, no. 1145/2814864, pp. 2814883 (2015)

17. Foster, M.P.: Quantities, units and computing. Comput. Stand. Interfaces **35**(5), 529–535 (2013). https://doi.org/10.1016/j.csi.2013.02.001, https://www.sciencedirect.com/science/article/pii/S0920548913000160

18. Harish, A.: When NASA lost a spacecraft due to a metric math mistake. https://www.simscale.com/blog/nasa-mars-climate-orbiter-metric/

19. Hartl, N., Wössner, E., Sure-Vetter, Y.: Nationale forschungsdateninfrastruktur (nfdi). Informatik Spektrum **44**(5), 370–373 (2021). https://doi.org/10.1007/s00287-021-01392-6

20. Hey, T.: The fourth paradigm - data-intensive scientific discovery. In: Kurbanoğlu, S., Al, U., Erdoğan, P.L., Tonta, Y., Uçak, N. (eds.) E-Science and Information Management, pp. 1–1. Springer, Berlin Heidelberg, Berlin, Heidelberg (2012)

21. Inizan, O., Fromion, V., Goelzer, A., Saïs, F., Symeonidou, D.: An ontology to structure biological data: the contribution of mathematical models. In: Research Conference on Metadata and Semantics Research, pp. 57–64. Springer (2021). https://doi.org/10.1007/978-3-030-98876-0_5

22. Keil, J.M., Schindler, S.: Comparison and evaluation of ontologies for units of measurement. Semant. Web **10**(1), 33–51 (2019). https://doi.org/10.3233/SW-180310

23. Kirillovich, A., Falileeva, M., Nevzorova, O., Lipachev, E., Dyupina, A., Shakirova, L.: Prerequisite relationships of the ontomathedu educational mathematical ontology. In: Figueroa-García, J.C., Díaz-Gutierrez, Y., Gaona-García, E.E., Orjuela-Cañón, A.D. (eds.) Applied Computer Sciences in Engineering, pp. 517–524. Springer International Publishing (2021). https://doi.org/10.1007/978-3-030-86702-7_44

24. Kirillovich, A., Nevzorova, O., Falileeva, M., Lipachev, E., Shakirova, L.: Ontomathedu: a linguistically grounded educational mathematical ontology. In: Benzmüller, C., Miller, B. (eds.) Intelligent Computer Mathematics, pp. 157–172. Springer International Publishing, Cham (2020)

25. Kohlhase, M.: OMDoc – An open markup format for mathematical documents [Version 1.2], LNAI, vol. 4180. Springer Verlag (2006). https://doi.org/10.1007/11826095

26. Koprucki, T., Kohlhase, M., Tabelow, K., Müller, D., Rabe, F.: Model pathway diagrams for the representation of mathematical models. Opt. Quant. Electron. **50**(2), 1–9 (2018). https://doi.org/10.1007/s11082-018-1321-7

27. Kostré, M., Sunkara, V., Schütte, C., Conrad, N.D.: Understanding the romanization spreading on historical interregional networks in northern Tunisia. Appl. Netw. Sci. **7**(53) (2022).https://doi.org/10.1007/s41109-022-00492-w

28. Lange, C., et al.: Bringing mathematics to the web of data: the case of the mathematics subject classification. In: Simperl, E., Cimiano, P., Polleres, A., Corcho, O., Presutti, V. (eds.) ESWC 2012. LNCS, vol. 7295, pp. 763–777. Springer, Heidelberg (2012). https://doi.org/10.1007/978-3-642-30284-8_58

29. Musen, M.A.: The protégé project: a look back and a look forward. AI matters **1**(4), 4–12 (2015). https://doi.org/10.1145/2757001.2757003

30. Nguyen, A., Weller, T., Färber, M., Sure-Vetter, Y.: Making neural networks FAIR (2020). https://arxiv.org/abs/1907.11569

31. Reidelbach, M., Ferrer, E., Weber, M.: MaRDMO plugin - document and retrieve workflows using the MaRDI Portal. In: Proceedings of the 1st Conference on Research Data Infrastructure (CoRDI) - Connecting Communities (2023). https://doi.org/10.52825/cordi.v1i.254

32. Reidelbach, M., Schembera, B., Weber, M.: Towards a fair documentation of workflows and models in applied mathematics. In: Buzzard, K., Dickenstein, A.,

Eick, B., Leykin, A., Ren, Y. (eds.) Mathematical Software – ICMS 2024, pp. 254–262. Springer Nature Switzerland (2024). https://doi.org/10.1007/978-3-031-64529-7_27

33. Riedel, C., Geßner, H., Seegebrecht, A., Ayon, S.I., Chowdhury, S.H., Engbert, R., Lucke, U.: Including data management in research culture increases the reproducibility of scientific results. INFORMATIK 2022 (2022). https://doi.org/10.18420/inf2022_114

34. Sack, H., et al.: Knowledge graph based RDM solutions. In: Proceedings of the 1st Conference on Research Data Infrastructure (CoRDI) - Connecting Communities (2023). https://doi.org/10.52825/cordi.v1i.371

35. Schembera, B., Durán, J.M.: Dark data as the new challenge for big data science and the introduction of the scientific data officer. Philos. Technol. **33**, 93–115 (2020). https://doi.org/10.1007/s13347-019-00346-x

36. Schembera, B., et al.: Ontologies for models and algorithms in applied mathematics and related disciplines. In: Garoufallou, E., Sartori, F. (eds.) Communications in Computer and Information Science, pp. 161–168. Springer Nature Switzerland, Cham (2024). https://doi.org/10.1007/978-3-031-65990-4_14

37. Schembera, B., et al.: Building ontologies and knowledge graphs for mathematics and its applications. In: Proceedings of the 1st Conference on Research Data Infrastructure (CoRDI) - Connecting Communities (2023). https://doi.org/10.52825/cordi.v1i.255

38. Smith, A.: Physics subject headings (PhySH). Knowl. Organ. **47**(3), 257–266 (2020). https://doi.org/10.5771/0943-7444-2020-3-257

39. Snytnikov, A., Glinskiy, B., Zagorulko, G., Zagorulko, Y.: Ontological approach to formalization of knowledge in computational plasma physics. J. Phys: Conf. Ser. **1640**, 012013 (2020). https://doi.org/10.1088/1742-6596/1640/1/012013

40. Suresh, P., Hsu, S.H., Akkisetty, P., Reklaitis, G.V., Venkatasubramanian, V.: OntoMODEL: ontological mathematical modeling knowledge management in pharmaceutical product development, 1: conceptual framework. Ind. Eng. Chem. Res. **49**(17), 7758–7767 (2010). https://doi.org/10.1021/ie100246w

41. Suresh, P., Joglekar, G., Hsu, S., Akkisetty, P., Hailemariam, L., Jain, A., Reklaitis, G., Venkatasubramanian, V.: Onto MODEL: Ontological mathematical modeling knowledge management. In: Computer Aided Chemical Engineering, vol. 25, pp. 985–990. Elsevier (2008). https://doi.org/10.1016/S1570-7946(08)80170-8

42. The MaRDI consortium: MaRDI: Mathematical Research Data Initiative Proposal (2022). https://doi.org/10.5281/zenodo.6552436

43. Wilkinson, M.D., et al.: The FAIR guiding principles for scientific data management and stewardship. Sci. Data **3**(1), 1–9 (2016). https://doi.org/10.1038/sdata.2016.18

44. Zang, Z., Ma, T.: Research and Application of Mathematical Knowledge Graph Based on Ontology Learning. In: Liu, Q., Liu, X., Cheng, J., Shen, T., Tian, Y. (eds.) Proceedings of the 12th International Conference on Computer Engineering and Networks. pp, 1387–1394. Springer Nature, Singapore (2022). https://doi.org/10.1007/978-981-19-6901-0_147

45. Zwaneveld, B.: Structuring mathematical knowledge and skills by means of knowledge graphs. Int. J. Math. Educ. Sci. Technol. **31**(3), 393–414 (2000). https://doi.org/10.1080/002073900287165

Developing Datasets for Training OCR/HTR Models for the Late 19th Century Greek Texts

Georgios Roukas$^{(\boxtimes)}$ ⓘ and Michalis Sfakakis$^{(\boxtimes)}$ ⓘ

Department of Archives, Library Science and Museology, Ionian University, Corfu, Greece
{alm.mpci2201,sfakakis}@ionio.gr

Abstract. Historical documents are vital for preserving cultural information. To access their content, OCR and HTR technologies transcribe them into text. Challenges arise with handwritten texts due to varied writing styles. This study develops two corpora to train models for 19th-century Greek texts. The first dataset includes printed texts from the "Ellinomnimon" archive, and the second comprises handwritten documents from the Lasithi Demogerontia archives. Moreover, using the Transkribus platform, two models were iteratively refined, enhancing their ability to transcribe Greek historical documents from 1800 to 1870.

Keywords: text transcription · machine learning · optical recognition · OCR · HTR · CER · Transkribus

1 Introduction

Historical documents are valuable information sources for human culture and collective memory. To preserve and access these information sources, digital representations of the historical documents are collected and organized in digital repositories. Although the number of scanned historical documents is huge, in order to process their content and unveil the wealth of information incorporated into them, the scanned images must be transcribed into their equivalent text forms (i.e. digital transcripts). Optical Character Recognition (OCR) [1] and Handwritten Text Recognition (HTR) [2] technologies were developed to produce digital transcripts of images of printed or handwritten texts. Recognition of characters, especially handwritten ones is difficult due to variability in writing styles, text layouts and cursive representation of characters among others, with respect to specific language [3, 4]. The development of deep neural networks in the field of image processing has impressively improved OCR/HTR, especially on modern printed texts, providing also a wide range of specialized models for different needs including printed or handwritten texts in many different languages from 19th-century and earlier.

Even though models capable of performing automatic transcription in Modern Greek language exist, there is no suitable model to produce digital transcripts neither for printed nor for handwritten Greek texts written in 19th-century and earlier. To address these issues, this work presents the development and the assessment of two preliminary small text corpora in order to train and specialize properly existing models for both printed and handwritten Greek historical documents produced between 1800 and 1870.

M. Sfakakis et al. (Eds.): MTSR 2024, CCIS 2331, pp. 110–115, 2025.
https://doi.org/10.1007/978-3-031-81974-2_9

The first dataset (PDS), consisting of printed text was prepared as part of our work aiming to extract entities and provide full text access to the documents of the digital archive "Ellinomnimon", which contains a wealth of Greek documents from the 17th to 19th century. The second dataset (HDS) consists of handwritten documents from the archives of the Lasithi Demogerontia in Crete, Greece, which deal with property lease auctions by Monasteries in Lasithi. Both datasets were developed iteratively, starting with a small number of manually transcribed pages and then extended by a semi-automated process using models trained with them. The Transkribus[1] platform was used to select and specialize already trained models for other languages, as well as to assess the datasets [5].

The paper structure is as follows. The following section presents the methodology followed, while the subsection describes the datasets and how they were used with Transkribus to produce trained models. The next section presents the results of the project while some concerns identified during the development of the project are also mentioned.

2 Methodology and Training Datasets Development

The production or specialization of existing OCR/HTR models requires proper datasets, containing all the language specific characters, symbols and styles used in texts, in order to train the underlying Machine Learning algorithms. A typical digital transcription process starts by recognizing the text regions and lines by applying text line segmentation approaches and then converts these image segments into textual representations [6, 7].

As already mentioned, to develop our datasets for transcribing printed and handwritten Greek historical documents produced between 1800 and 1870 the Transkribus platform was used. Transkribus is an advanced platform for analyzing historical documents, encompassing various research areas such as layout analysis and handwritten text recognition [8]. It also includes OCR and HTR systems. Although Transkribus offers a variety of models for transcribing printed and handwritten texts in many languages and time periods, none of them was able to recognize Greek texts. Therefore, this work reports on the development and the assessment of the two training datasets, as well as on the specialization of existing models in Transkribus for transcribing printed and handwritten Greek historical documents produced between 1800 and 1870.

For each dataset, as depicted in Fig. 1, starting with a small number of manually transcribed pages, a model was selected for training with Greek texts, either printed or handwritten, from Transkribus. Then, by applying the specialized model, the produced transcriptions were evaluated and corrected by domain experts. These corrected documents were incorporated into the original dataset and the specialized model was trained again. The procedure was repeated until an efficient specialized model was generated. It is worth noting that while several digitized pages of historical documents were found for printed texts, locating quality images for handwritten material proved extremely difficult.

---

[1] URL (accessed August 15, 2024): https://www.transkribus.org/.

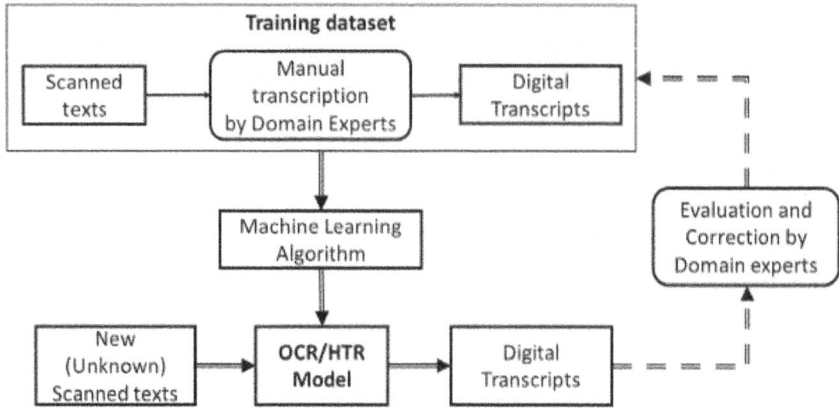

Fig. 1. Workflow for the development of the training datasets and OCR/HTR models

2.1   Extending Training Datasets and Specializing OCR/HTR Models

Transkribus offers trained models for transcribing handwritten and printed texts in various languages [9]. Since models are designed to recognize specific writing styles, reusing them for different documents while maintaining a low Character Error Rate (CER) can be challenging [10].

It is evident that there is a need for training and customizing models in Transkribus, especially in Greek. Thus, the models used primarily, as well as all other models dedicated to other languages and time periods, failed to recognize and transcribe most of Greek characters, especially those with polytonic characters. Therefore, for the printed Greek historical documents, the model "Noscemus GM 6" was used as the specialization model, while for the handwritten documents the model "Ligorio 0.3 PyL" was used, as they indicated in their description that they could recognize Greek characters.

The Transkribus system evaluates the accuracy of the automatic transcription of a page using a model with the Character Error Rate (CER). The CER is defined as the difference in characters between the correctly transcribed page (ground truth) and the one automatically generated using the model. Any character that is missing (comma, letter, number), or differs from the corresponding correct character such as a "u" instead of a "v" or even an uppercase letter instead of a lowercase letter, is included in the difference. In the best cases, a sufficiently trained model can produce automated transcriptions of printed material with a CER of less than 5% (meaning that 95% of the characters are correct). Results from models trained on printed material can be even better, reaching a CER of 1–2%.

Thus, for both datasets, the models started to be improved by adding a few more training data at a time. As for the printed texts, based on *Noscemus GM 6* model, the first time the system was trained on 10,775 words in lower case, while the final model was trained on 20,917 words in upper and lower case, numbers and different writing styles. In this way, a CER of 1.1% was achieved on the training data and 1.6% on the validation data. The gradual enrichment process for training the model is shown in the following table (Table 1):

Table 1. Models created for printed documents based on *Noscemus GM 6* model.

Model Name	Training Words	Style	CER
Printed 1	10.775	Lowercase	1.40%
Printed 2	10.686	+Uppercase	2.60%
Printed 3	20.917	+Numbers, different styles	1.60%

In the graph below, we can observe that the system converged quite quickly when trained on the printed text corpus. In almost 30 training epochs it had already become quite familiar with the printed characters presented to it (Fig. 2).

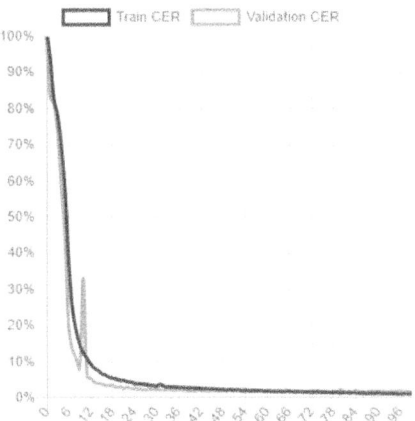

Fig. 2. Graph of the 3rd model for printed documents (x: epochs, y: percentage of CER)

The system was also trained on handwritten texts based on Ligorio 0.3 PyL model. Initially, 46 pages were selected for training, followed by 55 pages. Specifically, the model was trained on 6,534 words and later on 8,601 words. The achieved CER was 11% on the training data and 26.6% on the validation data. It is important to note that handwritten models benefit from a larger volume of diverse text to improve accuracy. Manual transcription was necessary due to the lack of ready-made transcriptions.

The following table summarizes the results for handwritten documents (Table 2):

Table 2. Models created for handwritten documents based on *Ligorio 0.3 PyL* model.

Model Name	Training Words	Style	CER
Handwritten 1	6.534	46 pages	33.30%
Handwritten 2	8.601	55 pages	22.60%

The graph in the case of manuscripts shows very different lines from those for printed documents, indicating that the algorithm converges much slower than the algorithm for the printed documents. Thus, we observe that the system continues to learn from the first training epoch to the 100th epoch. Here the training process needs more training epochs precisely because of the special characteristics of manuscript texts (Fig. 3).

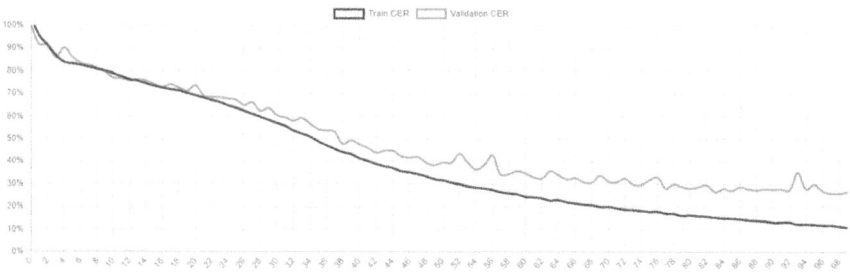

Fig. 3. Graph of the 2nd model for handwritten documents (x: epochs, y: percentage of CER)

3   Conclusion and Discussion

While perfecting models may not be critical, general models trained with Transkribus are still valuable for speeding up transcription processes. Sharing these models on the Transkribus platform allows researchers to benefit from existing models. If the academic community collaborates to create and share more models, it could greatly enhance the digital transcription of older texts, despite some limitations.

One major limitation is the lack of well-digitized texts and corresponding transcriptions. Training a model takes time, but having transcriptions available would significantly reduce this time and improve the training process.

For this project a manual process was used to select and transcribe digital images to serve as the initial training data for an automatic transcription system. For printed and handwritten documents, texts with various writing styles, fonts, and layouts were chosen.

Two optical character recognition models (OCR and HTR) were then specialized within the Transkribus system, one for printed documents and another for handwritten ones. Images of digitized documents and their transcriptions were submitted, and the models were trained using machine learning techniques. Newly scanned documents were automatically transcribed and evaluated, and the transcribed texts were corrected and combined with previous data as "ground truth" for training again the models. This iterative process aimed to reduce the Character Error Rate (CER) and create better recognition models.

The results confirmed that larger training datasets lead to lower CER. Achieving a low CER is possible when the model is trained on a specific writing style. This applies to both printed and handwritten materials. While no model can recognize all language variations, this work is a starting point for Greek language transcription using machine learning. As technology advances, better-trained models will likely achieve even lower CER and improve transcription accuracy across various document types.

References

1. Mori, S., Suen, C.Y., Yamamoto, K.: Historical review of OCR research and development. Proc. IEEE **80**(7), 1029–1058 (1992). https://doi.org/10.1109/5.156468
2. Romero, V., Sánchez, J., Bosch, V., Depuydt, K., de Does, J.: Influence of text line segmentation in handwritten text recognition. In: 2015 13th International Conference on Document Analysis and Recognition (ICDAR), pp. 536–540. IEEE, Tunis, Tunisia (2015). https://doi.org/10.1109/ICDAR.2015.7333819
3. Shanthi, N., Duraiwamy, K.: Performance comparison of different image sizes for recognizing unconstrained handwritten tamil characters using SVM. J. Sci. **3**(9), 760–764 (2007)
4. Martínek, J., Lenc, L., Král, P.: Building an efficient OCR system for historical documents with little training data. Neural Comput. Appl. (2020)
5. Muehlberger, G., et al.: Transforming scholarship in the archives through handwritten text recognition: transkribus as a case study. J. Document. **75**(7), 954–976 (2018). https://doi.org/10.1108/JD-07-2018-0114
6. Springmann, U., Najock, D., Morgenroth, H., Schmid, H., Gotscharek, A., Fink, F.: OCR of historical printings of Latin texts: problems, prospects, progress. In: DATeCH 2014: Proceedings of the First International Conference on Digital Access to Textual Cultural Heritage, pp. 71–75. Association for Computing Machinery, Madrid, Spain (2014). https://doi.org/10.1145/2595188.2595205
7. Omidiora, E.O., Adeyanju, I.A., Fenwa, O.D.: Comparison of machine learning classifiers for recognition of online and offline handwritten digits. Comput. Eng. Intell.t Syst. **4**(13), 39–47 (2013)
8. Mühlberger, G., Colutto, S., Kahle, P.: Handwritten Text Recognition (HTR) of historical documents as a shared task for archivists, computer scientists and humanities scholars. The Model of a Transcription & Recognition Platform (TRP). Austria: University of Innsbruck (2014)
9. Jander, M.: Handwritten Text Recognition - Transkribus: A User Report. eTrap. Ανάκτηση από, Göttingen, Germany (2016) https://www.etrap.eu/wp-content/uploads/2016/11/TrAIN-Transkribus_User_Report-2016.pdf
10. Memon, J., Sami, M., Ahmed Khan, R., Uddin, M.: handwritten optical character recognition (OCR): a comprehensive systematic literature review (SLR). IEEE Access (8), 142642–142668 (2020). https://doi.org/10.1109/ACCESS.2020.3012542

JobHive: A Semantic Path-Based Platform for E-Recruitment Recommendation

Hakim Mokeddem[✉][iD], Benelhadj Djelloul Mama Saadia[iD],
and Gouaouri Mohammed Dhiya Eddine[iD]

Ecole Nationale Supérieure d'Informatique, BP 68M, 16309 Oued-Smar,
Algiers, Algeria
{h_mokeddem,im_benelhadjdjelloul,im_gouaouri}@esi.dz

Abstract. This paper presents JobHive, a recommender system based on knowledge graphs to provide improved recommendations by aligning candidate resumes with job requirements, considering both explicit and implicit skills. By integrating semantic similarity computations, the system ensures comprehensive match quality for job seekers and employers.The matching algorithm calculates a similarity score between job offers and resumes by comparing skills, experience, and inferred skills. It uses a Transformer-based Sequential Denoising Auto-Encoder (TSDAE) for contextualized understanding, which generates comprehensive representations of entities to improve semantic similarity assessments. Additionally, the algorithm uses a knowledge graph to understand connections between entities, allowing it to find the best matches by considering both direct and indirect relationships.

The evaluation of the matching algorithm for JobHive demonstrated its effectiveness in ranking resumes according to job offers. Tested with 40 job offers and 240 resumes, the algorithm achieved high relevance scores, indicating it closely matched manual rankings.

Keywords: e-recruitment · recommender system · ontology · knowledge graph · semantic similarity

1 Introduction

Recommender systems have become indispensable in the e-recruitment domain, providing significant advantages to both job seekers and employers. These systems generate personalized recommendations, aligning job seekers with suitable job opportunities and assisting employers in efficiently identifying potential candidates.

Traditional recommender systems rely on explicit qualifications listed in job offers and resumes. For example, content-based recommender systems use job description details and user profiles to make job recommendations [8]. On

M. Sfakakis et al. (Eds.): MTSR 2024, CCIS 2331, pp. 116–126, 2025.
https://doi.org/10.1007/978-3-031-81974-2_10

the other hand, collaborative filtering-based recommender systems, suggest job opportunities by considering the behavior and preferences of similar users [3].

However, these systems have limitations due to their lack of semantic understanding. They mainly match qualifications based on predefined criteria and keywords, without understanding the semantic context, leading to the omission of relevant qualifications that are not explicitly mentioned.

To overcome this limitation, incorporating ontologies in the human resources domain can enhance the recruitment process by aligning candidate profiles with job requirements more effectively. Using formal semantic representations through ontologies allows for a structured depiction of the semantic relationships between various job titles and the corresponding skills required.

This paper introduces JobHive, a recommender system that leverages links between skills, jobs and new AI techniques to compute semantic similarity. By using knowledge graphs, JobHive provides enhanced recommendations by aligning candidate resumes with job requirements and suggesting suitable job opportunities to candidates. The integration of semantic similarity computations ensures that even implicitly related qualifications are considered, thereby improving the overall match quality for both job seekers and employers.

This paper is structured as follows: Sect. 2 provides an overview of relevant works on recommendation systems in the e-recruitment domain. In Sect. 3, we introduce the knowledge graph. Section 4 presents the recommendation algorithm based on the knowledge graph. Section 5 details the evaluation of the proposed algorithm and the implementation of the JobHive system.

2   Related Works

Knowledge-based recommender systems in E-recruitment can be categorized into three main types based on the techniques they use: semantic similarity-based systems, rule-based systems and embedding-based systems.

Semantic Similarity-Based Systems. In the E-recruitment domain, the recommendation of job offers involves calculating the similarity between jobs or skills in most cases. The authors in [4] developed a knowledge graph that represents skills and occupations by using ISCO and ESCO [11] ontologies. This graph was further enhanced by incorporating data from job offers. The graph consists of two main types of concepts: occupations and skills. The relationship between an occupation (O) and a skill (C) signifies that the occupation (O) requires the skill (C). To establish a measure of similarity between two skills, a similarity link was created using the Jaccard distance. Subsequently, the Dijkstra algorithm was employed on this graph to identify the shortest path between two skills, thereby constructing a recommendation model that assists employees in transitioning between jobs.

The similarity algorithm developed by [7] uses the structure of a skill ontology to determine the similarity between two skills, resulting in a score between a resume and a job offer. The system developed by the authors provides recruiters with the flexibility to adjust the weight assigned to different skills when evaluating candidate profiles.

The model proposed in [9] uses graph similarity and is constructed based on a computer science domain ontology. For every published job offer, the system calculates a score for the candidate's resume, considering both technical and soft skills.

Rule-Based Systems. This category of recommendation systems uses inference rules on an ontology or a knowledge graph to generate recommendations. In [10], the authors proposed a recommendation system specifically designed for disabled individuals in E-recruitment. The system incorporates an ontology that conceptualizes their profiles and occupations. The recommendation algorithm extracts information about the user's performance and occupation conditions from the ontology using SPARQL. The list of recommendations is generated by applying rules to the extracted knowledge using the SWRL language [5].

Embedding-Based Systems. Knowledge graph embedding refers to the process of transforming the entities and relationships in a knowledge graph into vector representations. These vector representations, known as embeddings, capture the semantic relationships and properties of the entities and relationships in the graph.

The authors in [2] proposed a recommender system for job transitions. They constructed three knowledge graphs: a job transition network, a job-skill network, and a skill co-occurrence network. The authors then proposed an embedding algorithm for these three graphs, which learns vector representations of occupations and skills. These vectors represent job offers and resumes, enabling the calculation of similarity and the generation of recommendations.

3   The Knowledge Graph

We generated a knowledge graph based on a human resources ontology [1], using a dataset comprising resumes and job offers from the IT domain. This dataset includes 300,000 profiles extracted from the Emploitic.com[1] database.

The ontology is structured into two main pillars: Occupation, representing specific jobs, and Skill, denoting competences associated with particular occupations. Occupations are linked to skills via the *Requires* relationship and to similar occupations through the *Is_Similar_To* relationship. Similarly, skills are connected to each other using the *Is_Similar_To* link. Each link in the ontology is assigned a weight to reflect the relevance of the relationship. The weight is determined using the Jaro-Winkler similarity metric [6].

The figure below shows an example of the knowledge graph (Fig. 1).

The graph illustrates two occupations: Web Developer and Front-End Developer, connected to each other via an *Is_Similar_To* relationship with a specified weight. Additionally, both occupations require specific skills. For instance, the

---

[1] https://www.emploitic.com/.

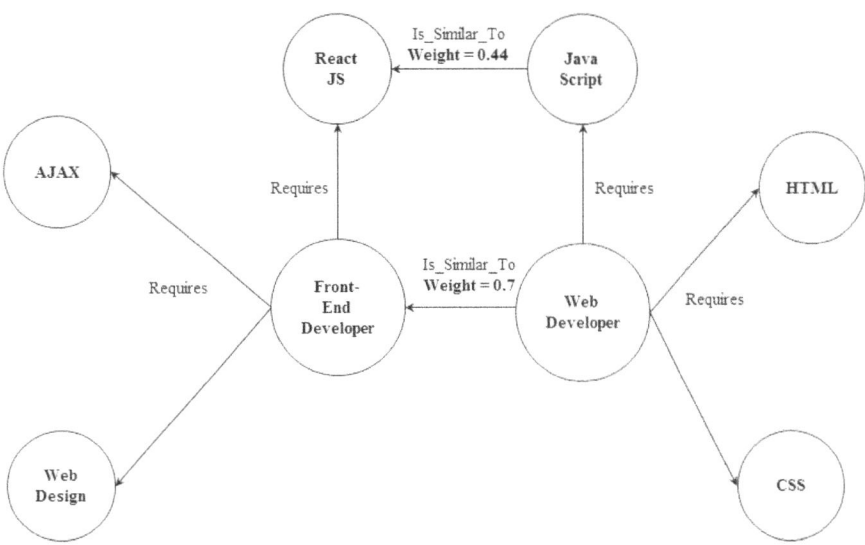

Fig. 1. Example of the knowledge graph

Web Developer occupation necessitates skills in HTML, CSS, and JS. Each skill can be interconnected with another using an *Is_Similar_To* relationship, which is assigned a particular weight.

4   The Matching Algorithm

The matching algorithm for a job offer calculates a similarity score between the job offer and candidates' resumes. This score incorporates the similarity in skills and experience, as well as implicit skills that can be inferred from the candidates' experience mentioned in their resumes.

4.1   The Matching Formula

The formula for evaluating the compatibility of a resume C with a job offer O is defined as follows:

$$Matching(O,C) = \frac{a \cdot SkillsSim + b \cdot ExperienceSim + c \cdot ImplicitSkillsSim}{a + b + c}$$

(1)

The functions *SkillsSim* and *ExperienceSim* evaluate how similar the skills and experience listed in the resume are to those required by the job offer, respectively. The function *ImplicitSkillsSim* measures the similarity of implicit skills inferred from the experience detailed in the resume. The weights a, b, and c indicate the relative importance of each component in the algorithm.

We present now the calculation of the functions *SkillsSim*, *ExperienceSim*, and *ImplicitSkillsSim*. For simplicity, we focus on *SkillsSim*, as the other functions are computed similarly.

The *SkillsSim* function calculates the average similarity of skills by finding the highest similarity score between each skill required in the job offer O and the skills listed in the resume C. The average of these maximum similarity scores is then computed.

$$SkillsSim = Average(Max(Similarity(s_o, s_c^j) \mid j \in \{1, 2, .., n\}})) \quad (2)$$

In this equation, s_o represents a skill required by the job offer O, s_c^j represents a skill mentioned in the resume C and n represents the number of skills in the resume.

4.2 Entity Similarities

The *Similarity* function calculates similarities between two entities. As shown in the figure below, this function operates by extracting entities (such as skills and experience) from both the job offer and the resume. For each entity, if the extracted entities from the job offer and resume are syntactically identical, the similarity score is set to 1. If the entities are not identical, a semantic similarity model is used to compute the score. Additionally, if the entities exist in a graph, a graph similarity function is applied (Fig. 2 and 3).

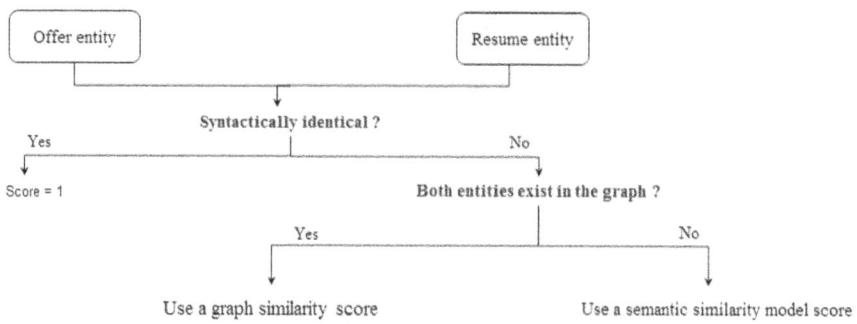

Fig. 2. Calculation of entity similarities

Case 1: Entities Do Not Exist in the Graph. In cases where entities do not exist in the graph, we use a semantic similarity model to calculate similarity scores. The development of this model has been carried out in three steps:

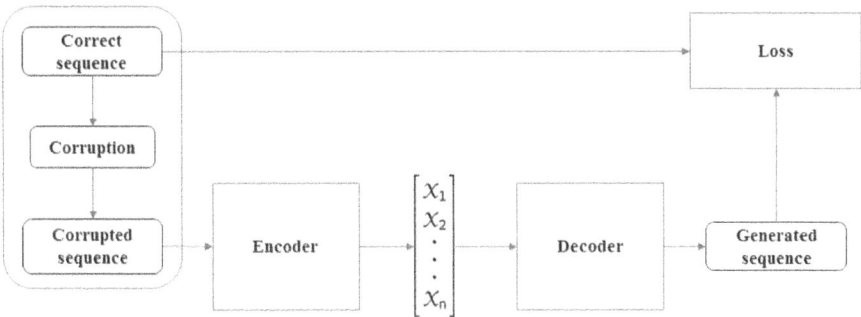

Fig. 3. Sequential Denoising Auto-Encoder Architecture

1. Data Collection. Data for model training is sourced from diverse platforms like OpenAI GPT, Write Sonic, and DBPedia. Entities are extracted from the knowledge graph, and their descriptions are used to enrich the training dataset. Named Entity Recognition (NER) models are developed using data of LinkedIn job offers to identify and annotate entities like skills and occupations.
2. Model Architecture. The chosen model, a Transformer-based Sequential Denoising Auto-Encoder (TSDAE) [12], is highlighted for its ability to generate contextualized representations of entities. This ensures nuanced understanding of semantic relationships among words based on their contextual usage. In addition, the model's reliance on unsupervised learning techniques underscores its adaptability in domains lacking labeled datasets, thereby enhancing its robustness in generating accurate semantic similarities for effective job recommendations.

   The main advantage of this model and any transformer-based model is that it generates contextualized representations, meaning a word has multiple representation vectors depending on the context in which the word appears.

   The figure below illustrates the mechanism of model training. It takes as input a list of sequence pairs, where each pair consists of a clean sequence and a corrupted sequence. The clean sequence is the original sequence, while the corrupted sequence is a version of the original sequence that has been altered. The sequences can be corrupted using various strategies such as word deletion, word replacement, and word swapping. The encoder is a transformer-based model that generates a representation of the corrupted sequence. This representation is a vector that captures important information about the sequence. As for the decoder, it attempts to reproduce the correct sequence using only the representation generated by the encoder.
3. Semantic Similarity Calculation. Semantic similarity between entities is computed using cosine similarity between their vector representations generated by the model.

The calculation formula for the semantic similarity between two entities x and y is as follows:

$$Similarity(x, y) = cosine\_similarity(sts(x), sts(y)) \qquad (3)$$

where, sts represents the vector representation of an entity using the semantic similarity model.

Case 2: Entities Exist in the Graph. When entities are present in the graph, there are three possible scenarios:

1. If x and y reference the same node in the knowledge graph, then

$$Similarity(x, y) = 1 \qquad (4)$$

2. If there is a *Is_Similar_To* or *Requires* link between x and y, then *Similarity(x, y)* is assigned the score of that link.
3. Otherwise, we compute the similarity between the representation vectors of entities using our similarity model. Then, we compute the value of *max_score_path* between x and y which is computed as follows:

$$max\_score\_path = \frac{shortest\_path\_weight(x, y)}{path\_length} \qquad (5)$$

In this case, the formula of the *Similarity* function is:

$$Similarity(x, y) = \frac{cosine\_similarity(sts(x), sts(y)) + max\_score\_path(x, y)}{2}. \qquad (6)$$

Through *max_score_path*, we aim to find the most optimal path (the largest similarity score value) between two entities in the knowledge graph. The average of the weights of the links in this path represents the similarity between these entities. Since the scores of the links in the knowledge graph represent a similarity of less than 1, we can use Dijkstra's algorithm to find the shortest path.

For example, as shown in the figure below, there is no direct link between the JQuery and Web Dev nodes. We can extract the shortest path using complementary links that connect between intermediate nodes (in this case, JavaScript) (Fig. 4).

5   Evaluation and Implementation

This section covers the evaluation of the matching algorithm and the implementation of the JobHive recommender system.

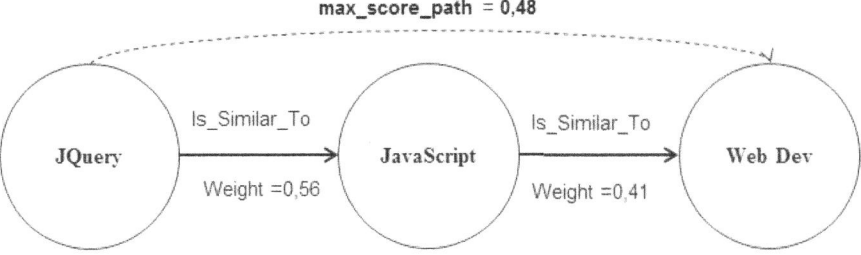

Fig. 4. Calculation of entity similarities

5.1 Evaluation of the Matching Algorithm

To evaluate the matching algorithm, we selected 40 representative job offers in the IT domain and paired them with 240 resumes. For each job offer, we manually classified 6 resumes based on their relevance to the offer. The matching algorithm under evaluation was then tasked with ranking these resumes according to their estimated relevance. To compare the algorithm's predicted ranking with the correct ranking, we calculated evaluation metrics such as the Mean Precision at k ($mp@k$) and the Normalized Discounted Cumulative Gain at k ($ndcg@k$).

The evaluation results showed that the system is effective at ranking the resumes based on their relevance to job offers. With a score of **0.775** for **mp@3**, the system demonstrates its ability to identify relevant resumes within the top three positions, indicating that a substantial portion of the top-ranked resumes were indeed pertinent to the job offers. The **0.799** score for *ndcg@3* further highlights the system's capability in terms of ranking quality, suggesting that the order in which resumes were ranked closely aligned with an ideal ranking, especially in the top three positions.

5.2 Implementation of JobHive

This section focuses on the implementation of our solution, detailing the steps and technical aspects involved in developing each key component. We cover the creation and preparation of the knowledge graph, the data collection process, and the development of both the backend and frontend of the JobHive platform.

The first step of our implementation involved generating and preparing the knowledge graph, which serves as the knowledge base for our recommendation system. We followed an established process for generating the graph. Once created, the knowledge graph is stored in a dedicated *Neo4J* container. Using the *Cypher* query language, we can efficiently query the graph and extract useful information to feed into our recommendation system.

The second step involves implementing the data collector, which is designed to collect and store entity descriptions. This component retrieves descriptions

from diverse data sources. Once collected, these descriptions are stored to facilitate easy access to the information required for subsequent steps, such as training
the semantic similarity model.

The recommendation algorithm was developed as a flexible REST API. Backend services were built using the FastAPI framework, chosen for its high performance and development ease. Each service focuses on essential system tasks
within a service-oriented architecture, offering flexibility to employ various technologies.

When a candidate applies for a job, the matching score between the CV and
the job is calculated and stored in the database. As illustrated in the figure
below, the recruiter can view the applications ordered by their relevance scores
(Fig. 5).

Fig. 5. Recommended candidates in JobHive

6   Conclusion and Future Works

In this paper, we developed a knowledge graph-based matching algorithm within
the JobHive platform using data from the e-recruitment platform Emploitic.com.

Our matching algorithm presents a promising approach to improving the
recruitment process in the IT domain. By integrating an ontology that encompasses occupations and skills, we created a framework for evaluating the compatibility between job offers and candidate resumes.

The matching algorithm evaluates the compatibility between job offers and
candidates' resumes by calculating a similarity score. This score considers skills,

experience, and implicit skills inferred from a candidate's resume. The algorithm employs three primary similarity measures: *SkillsSim*, *ExperienceSim*, and *ImplicitSkillsSim*, each weighted according to their importance. These measures use a combination of syntactic matching and semantic analysis through a Transformer-based Sequential Denoising Auto-Encoder (TSDAE) model, which captures contextual relationships between entities.

Additionally, when entities are present in a knowledge graph, the algorithm exploits graph-based techniques to further refine similarity scores. This includes leveraging direct and indirect links between entities to assess semantic proximity. The integration of these methods allows the algorithm to uncover both explicit and implicit skills, offering a comprehensive assessment of job-candidate compatibility.

The evaluation results of the matching algorithm demonstrate that the algorithm effectively ranks resumes in a manner closely aligned with manual assessments. The high scores for metrics like Mean Precision and Normalized Discounted Cumulative Gain, highlight the algorithm's ability to prioritize the most relevant candidates for a given job offer.

Overall, the integration of semantic similarity models and graph-based techniques provides a comprehensive understanding of candidate-job offer compatibility, enhancing the recruitment process. Future work will focus on expanding the ontology to cover additional domains, refining the semantic similarity models, and exploring advanced machine learning techniques to further enhance recommendation accuracy.

References

1. Boudjedar, S., Bouhenniche, S., Mokeddem, H., Benachour, H.: Automatic human resources ontology generation from the data of an e-recruitment platform. In: Metadata and Semantic Research: 14th International Conference, MTSR 2020, Madrid, Spain, December 2–4, 2020, Revised Selected Papers 14, pp. 97–109. Springer (2021)
2. Dave, V.S., Zhang, B., Al Hasan, M., AlJadda, K., Korayem, M.: A combined representation learning approach for better job and skill recommendation. In: Proceedings of the 27th ACM International Conference on Information and Knowledge Management, pp. 1997–2005 (2018)
3. Elahi, M., Ricci, F., Rubens, N.: A survey of active learning in collaborative filtering recommender systems. Compu. Sci. Rev. **20**, 29–50 (2016)
4. de Groot, M., Schutte, J., Graus, D.: Job posting-enriched knowledge graph for skills-based matching. arXiv preprint arXiv:2109.02554 (2021)
5. Horrocks, I., Patel-Schneider, P.F., Boley, H., Tabet, S., Grosof, B., Dean, M., et al.: SWRL: a semantic web rule language combining OWL and RuleML. W3C Member Submission **21**(79), 1–31 (2004)
6. Jaro, M.A.: Advances in record-linkage methodology as applied to matching the 1985 census of Tampa, Florida. J. Am. Stat. Assoc. **84**(406), 414–420 (1989)
7. Mentec, F., Miklós, Z., Hervieu, S., Roger, T.: Conversational recommendations for job recruiters. In: Knowledge-Aware and Conversational Recommender Systems (2021)

8. Pazzani, M.J., Billsus, D.: Content-based recommendation systems. In: The Adaptive Web: Methods and Strategies of Web Personalization, pp. 325–341 (2007)
9. Phan, T.T., Pham, V.Q., Nguyen, H.D., Huynh, A.T., Tran, D.A., Pham, V.T.: Ontology-based resume searching system for job applicants in information technology. In: Advances and Trends in Artificial Intelligence. Artificial Intelligence Practices: 34th International Conference on Industrial, Engineering and Other Applications of Applied Intelligent Systems, IEA/AIE 2021, Kuala Lumpur, Malaysia, July 26–29, 2021, Proceedings, Part I 34, pp. 261–273. Springer (2021)
10. Shishehchi, S., Banihashem, S.Y.: JRDP: a job recommender system based on ontology for disabled people. IJTHI **15**(1), 85–99 (2019)
11. le Vrang, M., Papantoniou, A., Pauwels, E., Fannes, P., Vandensteen, D., De Smedt, J.: ESCO: boosting job matching in Europe with semantic interoperability. Computer **47**(10), 57–64 (2014)
12. Wang, K., Reimers, N., Gurevych, I.: TSDAE: using transformer-based sequential denoising auto-encoder for unsupervised sentence embedding learning. In: Conference on Empirical Methods in Natural Language Processing (2021). https://api. semanticscholar.org/CorpusID:233231435

Track on Open Repositories, Research Information Systems and Data Infrastructures

Making Sense of Metadata Mess: Alignment and Risk Assessment for Diatom Data Use Case

Kio Polson[1]([✉]) [iD], Marina Potapova[2] [iD], Uttam Meena[3], Chad Peiper[1] [iD], Joshua Brown[4] [iD], Joshua Agar[3] [iD], and Jane Greenberg[1] [iD]

[1] Metadata Research Center, Drexel University, Philadelphia, PA, USA
{kp3272,cep98,jg3243,mp895,jca92}@drexel.edu
[2] Academy of Natural Sciences of Drexel University, Philadelphia, PA, USA
[3] College of Engineering, Drexel University, Philadelphia, PA, USA
um44@dragons.drexel.edu
[4] Oak Ridge National Lab, Oak Ridge, TN, USA
brownjs@ornl.gov

Abstract. Biologists study Diatoms, a fundamental algae, to assess the health of aquatic systems. Diatom specimens have traditionally been preserved on analog slides, where a single slide can contain thousands of these microscopic organisms. Digitization of these collections presents both metadata challenges and opportunities. This paper reports on metadata research aimed at providing access to a digital portion of the Academy of Natural Sciences' Diatom Herbarium, Drexel University. We report results of a 3-part study covering 1) a review of relevant metadata standards and a microscopy metadata framework shared by Hammer et al., 2) a baseline metadata alignment mapping current diatom metadata properties to standard metadata types, and 3) a metadata risk analysis associated with the course of standard data curation practices. This research is part of an effort involving the transfer of these digital slides to an new system, DataFed, to support global accessible. The final section of this paper includes a conclusion and discusses next steps.

Keywords: Microscope Slides · Diatoms · Reproducibility · Optical Microscopy · Preservation Metadata · Herbarium · Image Files · Digitization · Water–Sampling

1 Introduction

Creating and managing high quality metadata is essential for supporting digital life-cycle management and the FAIR principles [17]. These aims inform a current initiative involving the Academy of Natural Sciences' Diatom Herbarium (ANS Diatom Herbarium), Drexel University. Diatoms are a fundamental algae, which remove carbon dioxide from the atmosphere through photosynthesis. Researchers focused on diatoms collect and preserve water samples on slides.

M. Sfakakis et al. (Eds.): MTSR 2024, CCIS 2331, pp. 129–140, 2025.
https://doi.org/10.1007/978-3-031-81974-2_11

They use microscopy technology to observe diatom microorganisms. Today, the ANS Diatom Herbarium contains well over 300,000 slides and is recognized as one of the most extensive diatom collections in the United States. In 2009, with the support of the U.S. National Science Foundation, the creators of this collection undertook a project to digitize 6,000 slides, a subset of the collection. The aim was to make the collection more globally accessible.

Indeed, the digitization of these diatom slides was an important step toward increased collection access and data sharing, although this activity revealed a number of significant challenges related to collection organization and curation. The main challenges stem from the fact that a diatom specimen is microscopic. Biological database software generally assumes that a slide simply captures a single specimen or organism, while a diatom slide may contain thousands of microscopic specimens. Given this challenge and the absence of a unified technology supporting project needs, the ANS team was required to develop a system with a unique combination of microscope hardware, digitization hardware, and digitization software. The workflows, metadata gathering, and processing activities were conducted in house, as software libraries accounting for this specific use case are not available.

In early 2024, a new effort was launched to enhance access to the ANS Diatom Herbarium and address these noted challenges. This current initiative involves information and computer scientists and diatom experts, with key aims to: 1) advance the management of the ANS Diatom Herbarium, and 2) support global access to this unique collection. The collaboration is connected with a more recent NSF project, 'Development of a Platform for Accessible Data-Intensive Science and Engineering.' A major component of the larger NSF project is to develop a metadata infrastructure for porting the digital collection to a developing system, called DataFed [15]. This paper discusses the current metadata research activities specific to the ANS Diatome Herbarium collection. We report on our review of metadata standards, a baseline metadata alignment, and a metadata risk analysis. The sections that follow cover these three activities, followed by a discussion and a conclusion.

2   Review of Metadata Standards

Over the last 15 years, there's been a significant increase in metadata activities across science. One key motivator is to improve support for research reproducibility [1]. As a result, a number of community-driven metadata standards, including efforts in microscopy have emerged. These relatively new standards typically gather a series of microscopy activities under a single unit known as an "imaging experiment." Hammer et al. [4] explain that the evolving metadata landscape for an imaging experiment has the following three categories:

- Experimental and Sample Metadata (documents sample preparation)
- Microscopy Metadata (documents image data acquisition)
- Analysis Metadata (documents image analysis)

These categories provide a framework that informs our review, whereby a digitized diatom slide, or a set of slides, fall specifically under the "imaging experiment" label. A chief goal here is to provide as much context as possible for the digitized slides, thus, enabling diatom researchers around the world to conduct analytical experiments using these published slides.

3 Relevant Metadata Standards

In recent years, there have been two major schemas relevant to microscopy: the Open Microscopy Environment (OME) [11] and Digital Imaging and Communications in Medicine (DICOM) [2]. Darwin Core (DwC) [16], which is used for scientific samples is also relevant for sample metadata.

The OME appears is the most aligned with the needs of the diatom team. Currently, the main file format that the OME supports is called OME-TIFF [10]. This file format stores image information and pixels in a TIFF file, bundled together with metadata that strictly adheres to the OME Data model [9] in an XML serialization. Figure 1 presents a high-level overview of these OME standards.

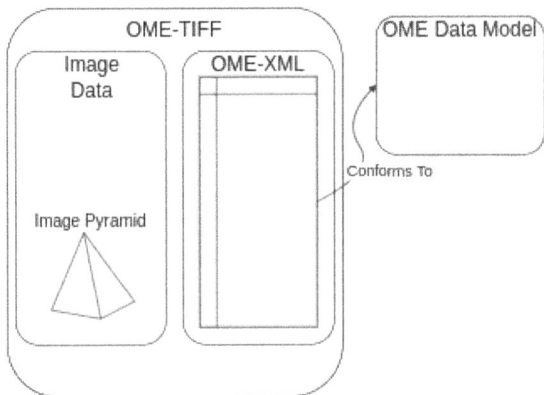

Fig. 1. High-level Overview of current OME Standards

While OME-TIFF is the current standard, recent efforts point to a new file format, OME-Zarr [6]. This development is supported by working group focusing on OME Next Generation File Formats (OME-NGFF) [8]. Research indicates that OME-NGFF will have three major improvements when compared with OME-TIFF. First, instead of relying on TIFF based images that need to keep track of multidimensional images in one file, the new standard will move to a Zarr [18] based file format. Zarr is a file format where any number of imaging dimensions and image sizes can be handled using well-structured folders. This Zarr file format is also easier to store and access from cloud computing solutions.

Second, instead of using XML based metadata, the OME Data Model aims to adhere to a Resource Description Framework (RDF) [5]. Third, the OME Data Model would be expanded to account for the changes in microscopy technology that has emerged since 2016. The most likely candidate for how the OME Data Model would be extended comes from a joint collaboration between the 4D Nucleome Initiative (4DN), the BioImaging North America (BINA) and the OME, to form the 4DN-BINA-OME (NBO) framework [4].

In addition to these OME-TIFF updates, this effort emphasizes the need for extensibility in microscopy metadata. Underlying reasons include supporting quality and reproducibility [7], complex biomedical tissue imaging [14], and basic information for interoperable archiving [13].

In addition to OME, advances have also been made with DICOM as a metadata standard for microscopy [3]. DICOM has been used in the biomedical community and supports robust file format and file transfer protocols. OME lacks the same level of rigor compared to DICOM, especially regarding the transfer of data at time of publication. Overall, DICOM offers a more developed suite of standards, although it does not fully support the needs of the ANS Diatom Herbarium.

Finally, it is important to mention the Darwin Core. The Darwin Core (DwC) is globally recognized and used for scientific samples, including museum specimens, and serves as the baseline standard for the ANS Diatom Herbarium. The diatom team has extended this standard in-house to improve the metadata quality of their collection [12].

4   Baseline Metadata Alignment

The baseline metadata alignment that follows builds on the Hammer et al. framework. Hammer et al. present a set of subdivisions (also known as types) of metadata beyond *sample metadata, microscopy metadata,* and *analysis metadata.* They further break down"microscopy metadata" into two subcategories, *provenance metadata* and *quality control metadata.* "Provenance metadata" in microscopy is further subdivided into three more categories of metadata: *microscope hardware specifications metadata, image acquisition settings metadata,* and *image structure metadata.* The ANS Diatom Herbarium work has also identified and captured "scanning metadata," which is not part of the Hammer et al. framework. Below is a tree structure of Hammer et al. framework and how it aligns with our diatom use case, followed by a key Table 1 to support interpretation:

- **Sample Metadata (D)**
- Microscopy Metadata
  - Provenance Metadata
    - **Microscope Hardware Specifications Metadata (D)**
    - **Image Acquisition Settings Metadata (D)**
    - **Image Structure Metadata (D)**
    - *Scanning Metadata (X)*
  - Quality Control Metadata
- Analysis Metadata

Table 1. Key of Metadata Alignment Tree

Style	Part of Hammer et al. Framework	Part of Diatom Metadata
· Normal Text	Yes	No
· **Bold (D)**	Yes	Yes
· *Italics (X)*	No	Yes

4.1 Sample Metadata

Sample metadata includes any descriptive, structural, or provenance metadata that relates to information about the water on glass slides used for viewing diatoms under a microscope. Sample metadata has been stored in a database that capture's the complexity of this information. Attributes like: water sample original location, time and date of collection, name of person who collected sample, ID given to (and printed on) slide, etc.

The information contained in this database is extremely rich and critically important to the diatom team. The structure of this metadata is loosely based on the Darwin Core metadata schema, with several modifications to account for the microscopic nature of a specimen. At a high-level view, the most general entity is the 'locality' which defines which body of water is being discussed. Each 'locality' can have multiple 'gathering events.' Each 'gathering event' corresponds to a sample of water. Two 'gathering events' can occur at the same 'locality' and at the same time, at different body of water locations, or at the same exact location at a 'locality' but collected at different times. Finally, each sample from a gathering event can produce multiple 'collection objects.' A collection object can be a slide prepared for a microscope or a sub-sample where the water has gone through some 'preparation' and placed in a smaller container. Each 'collection object' has an ID printed directly on the physical object, and this ID is the same one that is in the database. Furthermore, this same ID is also associated with the scan of the slide, which is discuss later. The basic taxonomic structure described above is presented in Fig. 2.

Sample metadata is contained in a MySQL Database. The database has at most twenty-nine tables, although the key architect is not accessible. Unfortunately, the lack of contact means it is unclear how many of these tables are used by the schema, or are relics of previous versions that were never deleted.

Additional challenges stem from File Maker Pro, which provides a front-end allowing users to view database contents. File Maker Pro has had a number of significant updates since the database was first constructed and modified support for certain tasks. Given various project constraints, neither the database structure nor the templates generated in the previous File Maker Pro version have been updated for the current database. This situation presents backwards compatibility issues for ANS Diatom Herbarium team members seeking navigating their previously collected sample metadata. Templates supporting certain functionalities in File Maker Pro versions no longer offer the same support. As a result, diatom team members need to learn and develop new workarounds to

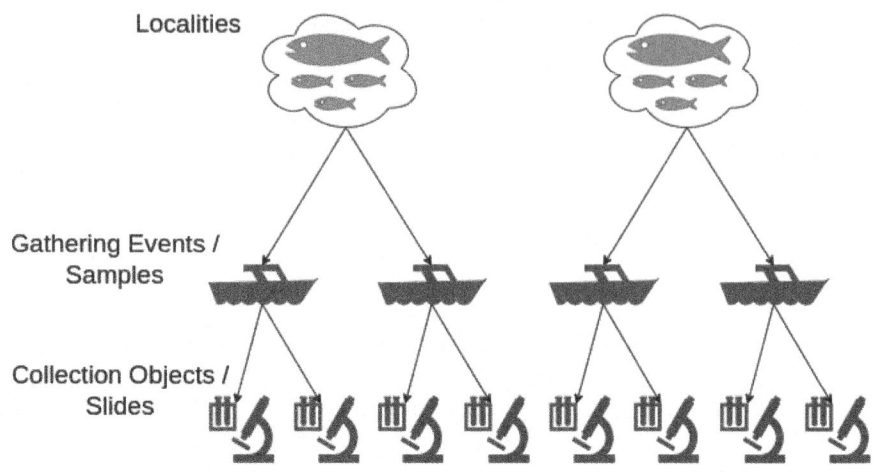

Fig. 2. Sample Metadata Data Structure for the ANS Diatom Herbarium

accomplish their goals. One key challenge is batch editing sample metadata areas that need to be cleaned and updated.

4.2 Microscope Hardware Specifications Metadata

'Microscope hardware specifications metadata' contains descriptive metadata about the microscope hardware specification the diatom team used when they conducted the scan of a slide. The microscope hardware specification is critical to scientists studying slide scans, given the impact on interpreting and understanding diatom characteristics. The specification settings are not automatically and adequately captured by the scanning software. The scanning software records some parts of the microscope, like the focus dial. However, a human has to manually change the illumination of the stage and the lens magnification, and this specification metadata has to be recorded separately.

The diatom team has chosen an innovative way to ensure the physical settings and calibration of the microscope stay with the scan of a slide. Once a scan is completed, the diatom team needs to name the folder which contains all the files and images associated with a single scan. The name selected for this folder is one that combines these microscope hardware specifications metadata together, with an underscore '_' between metadata elements. The precise order and inclusion of metadata changed over time, although the most recent version follows the following pattern.

```
[Slide ID]_[Sample ID]_[Magnification]_[Illumination]_
[Focal plane capture mode]_[Number of focal planes]_
[Distance between focal planes]
```

Following is an outline of these components and a brief definition:

`Slide ID` – A unique series of letters and numbers printed on the physical slide and recorded in the Sample Metadata Database

`Sample ID` – A unique series of letters and numbers printed on the bottle of water which contains the water that had originally produced the slide in question

`Magnification` – Lens used for scan which magnifies the image

`Illumination` – The method used to illuminate the slide for imaging

`Focal plane capture mode` – Either 'Zstack' or 'Zbest'. Defines strategy for capturing focal planes

`Number of focal planes` – When capturing multiple focal planes, indicates how many focal planes were captured

`Distance between focal planes` – Defines how gradual focal plane would change between images taken

Each scan compiles this information into the folder name. The exact schema changed over time, however, given the reliance on manual metadata generation and the and the titles were prone to human error. Still, this was a relatively effective way to keep some hard coded metadata to stay with each scan.

4.3 Image Acquisition Settings Metadata

For the diatom use case, digitization is a type of image acquisition. When digitizing diatom slides, there are additional software settings that the diatom experts can specify to ensure a clear image is captured. We refer to these settings as the 'image acquisition settings.' The type of metadata includes a combination of technical, preservation and descriptive metadata relating to the software used when creating a scan of a slide. The software produces technical metadata which details some descriptive and preservation metadata related to calibrating the software itself for a scan.

This calibration has many components that are recorded for each scan. Specifically, there are 107 different fields across six categories. For the Diatom team, once the software was calibrated for one slide, this calibration would usually work for following slides as well. Occasionally, something would change, though, and the software would need to be recalibrated in order to produce a professional scan. The majority of data captured is contained in an automatically generated file after a scan is complete. This file has relevant metadata that appears to be most at risk of getting lost in the process of data curation.

4.4 Image Structure Metadata

As the digitization of a slide is taking place, multiple images are captured that will later be stitched together. In the diatom use case, the component images are referred to as 'tiles.' These tiles can eventually be recompiled similar to a large jigsaw puzzle, usually twenty tiles by twenty tiles. In addition, in order to get the most clarity to see each diatom in a slide, it was necessary to take images on multiple focal planes. Thus, digitization not only captures tile images that would make up a single larger image, or one jigsaw puzzle, it has to recreate an additional dimension. The tiles frequently make up multiple full images or multiple jigsaw puzzles stacked one on top of the other. There could be a variable number of these image stacks according to the assessment of diatom experts to optimize how many diatoms are visible on each slide. All of this complexity needed to be recorded to document the image structure. Thus, the image structure metadata was any metadata that kept track of which tile needed to go where in the final stack of images.

This metadata was automatically generated by the software into a text file. This file captures the full complexity of where exactly each component image for a slide scan was taken in space and how that measurement in micrometers translates to the number of pixels in the slide. The file proved to be a critical piece of metadata for each scan when reconstructing the original image, and was also at risk of getting lost or deleted in the process of data curation.

4.5   Scanning Metadata

Finally, the scanning metadata is any descriptive or provenance metadata relating to the scanning and digitization event. Once the slide is on the stage, the microscope hardware is properly calibrated, and the digitization software is properly calibrated, a person can initiate the scanning process. This step of actually taking the scan also produces metadata.

An Excel spreadsheet was used for capturing this scanning metadata. For the diatom team accomplishing the scans of these slides, it is useful for them to have a method to record when a scan has been completed and for which slide. At first, this spreadsheet was very sparse and only had a boolean record of whether a slide had been scanned or not. Since our collaboration started, a new spreadsheet was created which also included fields of what date was a scan taken, who was the student who took the scan of a slide, along with some image acquisition settings metadata for redundancy. The image acquisition settings metadata was repeated in the Excel spreadsheet so that the folder name could be automatically generated to try to avoid some human error in the naming conventions. This amount of redundancy seemed appropriate for this use case.

5   Metadata Risk Assessment

The ongoing diatom collaboration made evident that the overall size and scope of this project introduces many technical issues that present potential road blocks to other research that seeks to use the ANS Diatom Herbarium digital slides. These include: 1. issues of storage space, 2. metadata loss, 3. metadata inconsistency, 4. suppression of metadata maintenance, and 5. missing metadata. Clear identification and articulation of these challenges in integral to addressing them and mitigating risk in future projects, given the speed at which technology changes.

5.1   Storage Space and Potential Data Loss

A single scan for microscopy imaging and digitization project is quite extensive. For example, the scan of a single slide regularly in the ANS Diatom Herbarium took up least twenty gigabytes of space, and this was a project, attempting to scan and digitize only 6,000 slides. This implies needing at least 100 terabytes of storage space somewhere. Unfortunately, the diatom team ran out of server space part way through the process of digitizing and had to start storing slides on external hard drives. The use external drives reduced the capacity for metadata backups and increases the opportunity for file corruption. This limitation required the team to find ways for each scan to take up less space, or to add more storage space.

Because some scans of slides are only stored on external hard drives, both data and metadata alike are at risk of being corrupted without being backed up. Whenever possible, original data and metadata should both be kept on working computers and backed up in multiple places to help with the preservation and sustainability of data.

5.2   Metadata Loss from Image Conversion

Each microscope imaging solution has its own proprietary file format for saving a microscope image. This means that for future use, the images have to be converted to a format which is easier to view. In microscopy, the popular solution is to use OME-TIFF. This is an open source file format specifically for making it easier to view microscopy images. However, there is no, one size fits all, way to take raw image files from unique microscope setups and easily turn them into OME-TIFF files. In the diatom case, lots of technical work has to be done in order to properly convert the images. This meant extra time and money spent on creating a workflow for this conversion.

The original solution that the diatom team had devised to convert scanned slides to OME-TIFF lost all image acquisition settings metadata and all the image structure metadata in the process. While this metadata might not have been a priority for the diatom team, it could still be important down the road for digital reconstruction or for the details that are available about the focal length. For this reason, it has proven important to consult with information scientists, or to have a metadata review process to ensure that no metadata gets lost in the conversion process.

5.3   Metadata Inconsistency from Human Error

As was mentioned earlier, the naming convention of the folders changed over time as the diatom team was honing in on their scanning methodology. These were not significant changes, but it does mean that the naming convention listed in this paper could not be relied upon for all scans of slides. This can interfere with future search functionality if left unchanged. With this deeper understanding of the metadata involved, it should then be possible to clean these folder names as a subproject of this initiative. Furthermore, creating systems and workflows that can minimize human error can also be important in the stewarding of metadata.

5.4 Suppressed Metadata Maintenance from Bad User Interface (UI)

As was mentioned earlier, the original architect of the MySQL Database containing the sample metadata was no longer in contact with the diatom team. For a considerable amount of time, this meant that the entire database was essentially inaccessible without the right credentials. Even once access was obtained, access was still limited by the changes to File Maker Pro that had occurred since the original File Maker Pro files had been created. These limitations made accessing, updating, and correcting the database incredibly difficult.

The diatom team includes committed stewards wit metadata expertise, although the User Interface (UI) tools have been cumbersome and make metadata update and maintenance tasks extremely challenges. While a new UI for the existing MySQL database is needed, development and implementation require resources and time, presenting a new set of challenges. Overall, this challenge underscores importance of good UI for proper metadata management.

5.5 Missing Metadata

Finally, the OME comparison work allowed us to identify metadata that was not currently being recorded. The OME data model allows for there to be information recorded about such concepts as the digitization project itself, called the 'project'; the people who have been involved in the digitization project, referred to as 'experimenters'; and the make and model of all the hardware involved in the digitization process referred to as the 'instruments'.

For example, the exact make and model of microscope, microscope camera, and magnification lens were not recorded anywhere. While these pieces of information may not immediately appear relevant, they could still be relevant to future research. For example, a researcher might be curious about something like image quality across multiple microscopes, or maybe identifying watermarks, or digital signatures of particular microscopes to help determine where an unlabeled slide was originally taken. The exact scanning methodology or process is not recorded anywhere, either. Metadata should always be a balance between what is potentially relevant, and what is practical for collection. Therefore, it is possible that in this diatom use case, metadata detailing the scanning process may not be practical for collection. However, hardware does seem like a piece of information worth recording in a metadata form, even if the process or methodology only gets recorded in a paper rather than in the metadata of each scan.

6   Conclusion and Next Steps

This paper has reported on metadata research pursued in support of ongoing work to transfer the digital component of the ANS Diatom Herbarium collection to the DataFed platform. Metadata is critical to providing global access to this collection, supporting diatom research activities, and ensuring a robust infrastructure within the 'Development of a Platform for Accessible Data-Intensive Science and Engineering' initiative. Background research revealed the value of the Open Microscopy Environment (OME) metadata standard, as well as aspects of the Digital Imaging and Communications in Medicine (DICOM) and Darwin Core (DwC) metadata standard. The baseline metadata alignment examined the complexity of the current ANS Diatom Herbarium metadata structure covering sample metadata, microscope hardware specifications metadata, image acquisition settings metadata, image structure metadata, and scanning metadata and contextualized them by mapping to the following five key types of metadata: descriptive metadata, structural metadata, provenance metadata, technical metadata, and preservation metadata. Additionally, metadata risk analysis revealed a set of concerns with the current state of metadata that cover storage space and potential data loss, metadata loss from image conversion, metadata inconsistency from human error, suppressed metadata maintenance from an insufficient user interface, and missing metadata.

These efforts have helped our team consider potential solutions, some of which we have already pursed, such as updating the Excel software and improving the image conversion python scripts. These scripts have been prepared, and our next step is to implement them, as we further develop the DataFed mechanism for ANS Herbarium collection on use.

In moving forward, next steps include addressing administrative aspects of collection sharing and improving the underlying python scripts which convert images to OME-TIFF. Our next steps are guided by a measure that aids diatom researchers both locally and globally, with the overall aim of supporting research advances and knowledge discovery.

Acknowledgement. This work is supported by NSF-OAC #2320600 and Metadata Research Center

References

1. Baker, M.: 1,500 scientists lift the lid on reproducibility. Nature **533**(7604), 452–454 (2016). https://doi.org/10.1038/533452a
2. DICOM. https://www.dicomstandard.org. Accessed 31 July 2024
3. Gupta, Y., Costa, C., Pinho, E., Silva, L.B.: DICOMization of proprietary files obtained from confocal, whole-slide, and FIB-SEM microscope scanners. Sensors **22**(6), 2322 (2022). https://doi.org/10.3390/s22062322
4. Hammer, M., et al.: Towards community-driven metadata standards for light microscopy: tiered specifications extending the OME model. Nat. Methods **18**(12), 1427–1440 (2021). https://doi.org/10.1038/s41592-021-01327-9
5. Kobayashi, N., Moore, J., Onami, S., Swedlow, J.R.: OME core ontology: an OWL-based Life science imaging data model. In: Workshop on Semantic Web Applications and Tools for Life Sciences (2019). https://scholar.archive.org/work/xnvkzeuqzbg4de6fovmyawjpmm

6. Moore, J., et al.: OME-Zarr: a cloud-optimized bioimaging file format with international community support. Histochem. Cell Biol. **160**(3), 223–251 (2023). https://doi.org/10.1007/s00418-023-02209-1

7. Nelson, G., et al.: QUAREP-LiMi: a community-driven initiative to establish guidelines for quality assessment and reproducibility for instruments and images in light microscopy. J. Microscopy **284**(1), 56–73 (2021). https://doi.org/10.1111/jmi.13041

8. Next-generation file formats (NGFF): NGFF Documentation. https://ngff.openmicroscopy.org/. Accessed July 26 2024

9. OME XML Schema June 2016 Version 2, OME XML Schema June 2016 (2016). https://www.openmicroscopy.org/Schemas/Documentation/Generated/OME-2016-06/ome.html

10. The Open Microscopy Environment: The OME-TIFF format, OME Data Model and File Formats 5.6.3 Documentation (2023). https://docs.openmicroscopy.org/ome-model/5.6.3/ome-tiff/

11. The Open Microscopy Environment: The Open Microscopy Environment. Retrieved 31 July 2024. https://www.openmicroscopy.org/index.html

12. Potapova, M.G., Lee, S.S., Spaulding, S.A., Schulte, N.O.: A harmonized dataset of sediment diatoms from hundreds of lakes in the northeastern United States. Sci. Data **9**(1), 540 (2022). https://doi.org/10.1038/s41597-022-01661-3

13. Sarkans, U., et al.: REMBI: recommended metadata for biological images-enabling reuse of microscopy data in biology. Nat. Methods **18**(12), 1418–1422 (2021). https://doi.org/10.1038/s41592-021-01166-8

14. Schapiro, D., et al.: MITI minimum information guidelines for highly multiplexed tissue images. Nat. Methods **19**(3), 262–267 (2022). https://doi.org/10.1038/s41592-022-01415-4

15. Stansberry, D., Somnath, S., Breet, J., Shutt, G., Shankar, M.: DataFed: towards reproducible research via federated data management. In: 2019 International Conference on Computational Science and Computational Intelligence (CSCI), pp. 1312–1317 (2019). https://doi.org/10.1109/CSCI49370.2019.00245

16. Wieczorek, J., et al.: Darwin core: an evolving community-developed biodiversity data standard. PLOS ONE **7**(1), e29715 (2012). https://doi.org/10.1371/journal.pone.0029715

17. Wilkinson, M.D., et al.: The FAIR guiding principles for scientific data management and stewardship. Sci. Data **3**(1) (2016). https://doi.org/10.1038/sdata.2016.18

18. Zarr. https://zarr.dev/. Accessed 25 July 2024

A Health Tourism Ontology Framework for Versatile Applications

Sofia Gkevreki$^{(\boxtimes)}$ ⓘ, Vasiliki Fiska ⓘ, Spiros Nikolopoulos ⓘ,
and Ioannis Kompatsiaris ⓘ

Information Technologies Institute, Centre for Research and Technology Hellas,
6th Km Charilaou-Thermi, 57001 Thessaloniki, Greece
{sgkevreki,vickyfi,nikolopo}@iti.gr
https://bhv.iti.gr

Abstract. Our world is becoming more interconnected everyday and there is an increasing demand for smart solutions on diverse data management. Ontology-based systems enhance data interoperability and analysis across various domains and platforms. In healthcare, they enable the integration of patient records, medical histories, and treatment plans across various providers, thereby improving care quality and patient outcomes. In the tourism industry, they facilitate the effective management of travel information, lodgings and activity options, leading to more personalized and efficient travel experiences. A unified Health Tourism ontology is presented in this manuscript aiming to enhance the overall quality of life by offering personalized health and wellness travel experiences that cater to individual needs and preferences. This paper details the design, implementation, and utilization of the proposed ontology, exploring its application in a Health Tourism application and its potential for broader use in other domains requiring structured data management and interoperability.

Keywords: Ontology Design · Data Integration · Knowledge Representation · Semantic Web · Health Tourism

1 Introduction

Ontologies are fundamental to data management and knowledge representation, allowing systems to exchange and integrate information [1] by offering formal frameworks for organizing information, establishing connections, and promoting interoperability across several systems and domains [2]. In today's interconnected world, managing and integrating several data sources is critical [3]. In the healthcare sector, there is a need to ease the integration of patient records, medical histories, and treatment plans among many healthcare providers to improve care quality and patient outcomes [4]. While in the tourism sector, enabling effective management of travel information, accommodation details, and activity options, can lead to more personalized and efficient travel experiences [5].

A unified Health Tourism (HT) ontology, which combines the needs of the two aforementioned sectors, can improve people's overall quality of life by enabling comprehensive, personalized health and wellness travel experiences, facilitating the integration of medical and wellness data with travel and accommodation services, and ensuring that individuals receive tailored recommendations that meet their specific health needs and preferences. This holistic approach recognizes the unique value proposition of the growing industry [6–8] of HT: it goes beyond mere medical care, harnessing the inherent therapeutic benefits of travel itself [9], maximizing the positive impact on the traveler's overall well-being.

The presented manuscript describes the design and development of a versatile ontology, intended at supporting HT applications that optimize service discovery for users seeking medical and tourism options, but inherently extensible to a variety of other domains. By adopting this data structure, stakeholders in both healthcare and tourism may provide more coordinated and user-centric services, resulting in better health results and more enjoyable travel experiences.

The proposed approach enables any application to create customized HT experiences. Ontological reasoning uses logical rules and contributes to developing intelligent relationships and semantic interoperability. Since planning a HT trip can be complex, involving coordination between healthcare providers, travel agencies, and accommodation services, the ontology helps to simplify these processes and to provide straightforward medical and travel solutions. Upon analyzing various studies on similar ontologies [10–14], it becomes evident that while there are a few available, none specifically address the contents of a complete HT experience, such as medical services and specialties, accommodation and health providers, accommodation features and amenities, places, landscapes and activities. Such integration can be of great importance in promoting not just HT, but also the medical and travel sectors themselves.

The paper is organized as follows. Section 2 presents the design of the HT ontology, detailing its core components and domain-specific modules, while also outlining the interoperability layer for seamless data integration. Section 3 delves and discusses the Ontology Principles, emphasizing reusability and expandability as guiding forces for the ontology's design. To illustrate its practical application, Sect. 4 introduces an example use case, showcasing how the ontology can be used to deliver personalized HT experiences.

2   Health Tourism Ontology Design

The development aims to create a universal and rich ontology suitable for any context or use case involving health and tourism data. The proposed design follows a modular and layered approach, which allows for both core and domain-specific extensions. As detailed in Fig. 1, it incorporates an expressive schema to describe various aspects of HT offerings. By exploiting this design, any application can identify HT solutions that directly address the user needs. This intelligence of the system is further enhanced by the ontology's reasoning capabilities, extracting knowledge from the data to personalize user experiences. The

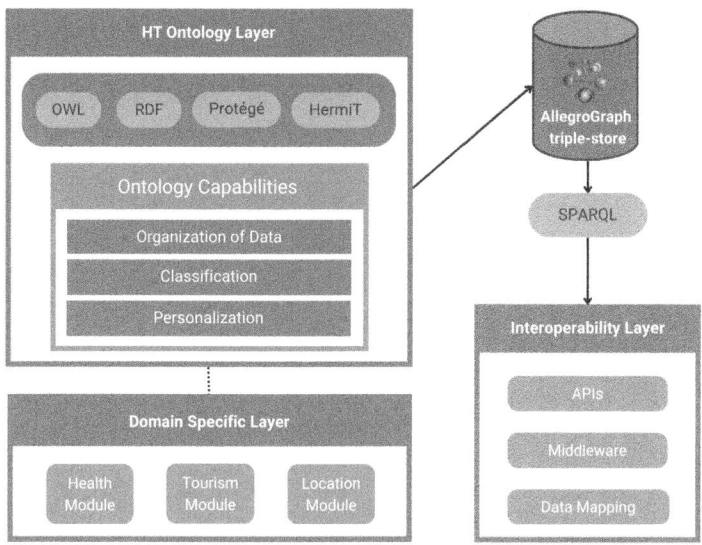

Fig. 1. Architecture design of the proposed HT ontology

proposed HT Ontology design comprises three main components: the core HT ontology, domain-specific modules, and the interoperability layer.

2.1 The Core HT Ontology Layer

The core HT Ontology Layer forms the foundation of the system's intelligence, enabling it to understand and manage data effectively. It uses advanced technologies to build a powerful knowledge base, allowing the platform to interpet and manage information efficiently. The implementation integrates OWL[1] for robust knowledge representation and RDF[2] as a framework for representing resources and their properties. Protégé [15] was used to build the main concepts of the ontology. Its built-in inference engine verified the logical consistency of the relationships defined within the ontology [15]. Advanced semantic reasoning was achieved with the HermiT reasoner [16]. These technologies (as illustrated in Fig. 1) proved useful in ensuring standardized data organization and semantic interoperability.

The HT ontology demonstrates several key capabilities, including data organization, classification, and personalization. A well-defined structure allows the system to easily locate and access HT information. Classification enables the automatic categorization of data based on predefined rules, facilitating the organization and grouping of similar data for better understanding. Personalization allows the ontology to capture user preferences and relationships between data

---

[1] OWL Web Ontology Language Reference.
[2] Resource Description Framework (RDF).

points, enabling customized user experiences. These capabilities are particularly beneficial for platforms that require structured and accessible data, data processing, and personalized user experiences, thereby enhancing overall functionality and user satisfaction in the HT domain.

2.2 Domain-Specific Layer

Modules. Building upon the core ontology, domain-specific modules extend the framework to meet the particular needs of specific domains. The following key modules are essential.

- The Health Module extends the core ontology with concepts specific to healthcare. It encompasses medical services, medical experts and health-related data, enabling detailed and personalized searches for patients seeking medical treatments.
- The Travel Module relates to all aspects of planning and booking travel arrangements, such as accommodation, activities and experiences.
- The Location Module enhances the core ontology's geo-location concepts, enabling location-based searches for entities related to HT.

Structure. The proposed ontology establishes a structured framework for organizing and representing information pertinent to HT. This concept facilitates the management, processing, and retrieval of data, while the underlying semantics enable the system to draw logical conclusions and exhibit intelligent behavior. A presentation of the ontology's top-level classes and structural components is provided in Table 1.

Table 1. Main top-level classes.

Class	Description
Provider	Categorizes entities that offer HT services
MedicalSpecialty	Categorizes fields within medicine
MedicalService	Categorizes medical treatments and procedures
Activity	Actions or experiences during a travel
Place	Categorizes a wide range of locations and landscapes
Amenity	Amenities offered by accommodation providers entities
Room	Room entities that are offered by accommodation providers
AccommodationFeature	Categorizes a range of features within an accommodation

Key components include the Provider class, categorizing service providers like medical experts and accommodation providers. The MedicalExpert class is further linked to MedicalSpecialty and MedicalService classes (see Fig. 2 and Fig. 3), enabling detailed categorization and personalized searches for patients. Similarly, the AccommodationProvider class connects with Room, Amenity (see Fig. 4), and AccommodationFeature classes for structured information about lodging options.

The ontology also includes an Activity class for recommending experiences. This class is further categorized into Eating (considering dietary needs) and Life-Activity (see Fig. 5), allowing for personalized recommendations based on user preferences. Finally, the Place class serves as the foundation for location-related data, including geographical data (see Fig. 5), landscapes, and physical places relevant to HT (e.g., airports, medical institutions, addresses). This structured approach facilitates efficient search and retrieval of information based on location and user needs and allows for future iterations of the ontology.

Data Collection. Tripadvisor[3], a widely used digital guide for tourists, informed activity selection (activities, attractions, food) for relevant user recommendations. Hotels.com[4] Provider API accessed through RapidAPI[5] was employed to provide details on accommodation options (providers, amenities, types, features). Medical services data came primarily from industry platforms like Doctoranytime[6] (a platform that assists users in finding and booking appointments with healthcare professionals) and MedicalTourism[7], a leading platform for HT information. Supplementary, extensive web searches were conducted to augment the data collection process for all classes within the ontology, ensuring comprehensive coverage and accuracy across medical services, activities, accommodations, places and user preferences.

2.3   Interoperability Layer

In the context of the HT ontology, the interoperability layer employs APIs and Middleware to facilitate interactions between different parts of any platform and the ontology, enabling access to the stored data. Data mapping translates data from various sources into a format that aligns with the concepts and relationships defined within the HT ontology. This layer serves as a bridge, allowing platforms to access and utilize stored HT data, thereby empowering patients and providers in the HT ecosystem to tap into a broader pool of accurate and consistent information.

This layer is also designed to address semantic interoperability, achieving semantic consistency across different systems [17] and enhancing data quality, scalability and cross-domain integration, overall creating a solid foundation for future innovations in the domain.

---

[3] Tripadvisor.
[4] Hotels.com.
[5] RapidAPI.
[6] Doctoranytime.
[7] MedicalTourism.

SPARQL is employed for querying and retrieving RDF data stored within the ontology [18]. AllegroGraph[8], chosen for its scalability, performance, and support for SPARQL queries, serves as the triplestore for storing and managing the RDF data representing the ontology. By working together, these technologies empower the HT ontology to not only intercommunicate but also to deliver a personalized user experience providing a homogeneous view across multiple HT systems.

3   Ontology Principles

3.1   Reusability

The ontology is designed with reusability as a core principle. This allows for its adaptation to various contexts within both medical and tourism domains.

It establishes a common vocabulary for medical specialties and services, which can be utilized within various medical systems. Currently containing over 600 classes related to medical services (Fig. 2) and representing different areas of medical expertise, specialties and sub-specialties (Fig. 3), the ontology ensures extensive coverage and facilitates interoperability. Offering a standardized vocabulary, the ontology achieves data exchange between different healthcare systems. Grouping medical services by specialty category creates a knowledge base, allowing related fields to share information.

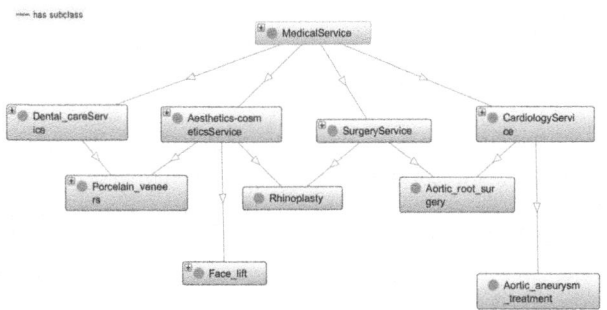

Fig. 2. Medical services in the HT ontology

In the same manner, the ontology can be extended to categorize and classify accommodation options within the tourism domain. This would establish a common vocabulary for accommodation types, amenities, features, rooms and their attributes (Fig. 4). This knowledge base allows travel agencies, booking platforms, and accommodation providers to utilize a standardized system for describing their offerings.

---

[8] AllegroGraph.

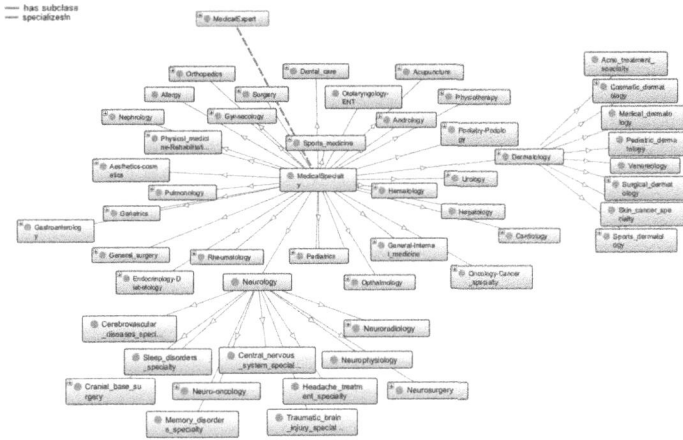

Fig. 3. Medical specialties in the HT ontology

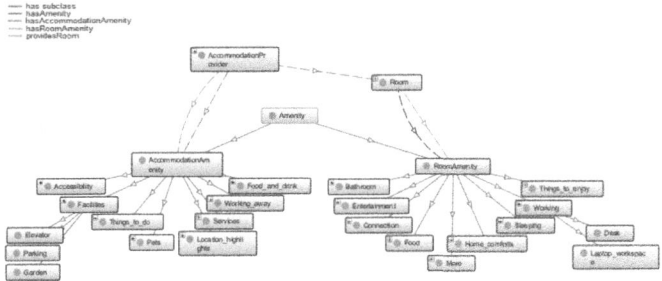

Fig. 4. Accommodation options in the HT ontology

Activities represented in this ontology serve to structure and recommend experiences for health tourists, but it can also be used across various domains, including tourism and related fields. A key component is the ontology's representation of eating options, encompassing diverse dietary options, supporting dining reservation platforms, restaurant review applications, and travel planning websites by categorizing and suggesting dining experiences considering the tourists' specific dietary needs and preferences. Containing a comprehensive catalog of activities commonly pursued by tourists (Fig. 5), the ontology empowers different platforms to curate personalized itineraries, recommend points of interest, and facilitate seamless booking processes. Standardizing the classification and description of activities, experiences, and adventures simplifies the booking process for tourists but also strengthens collaboration and data exchange among tourism stakeholders, enhancing the breadth and quality of tourism offerings available.

The HT ontology incorporates detailed location information and categorization (Fig. 5) that can be applied to many fields beyond tourism and medical services. Recommendation systems can personalize suggestions for nearby points of interest. Mapping services across various platforms that require search features can utilize this class to store geographical information, thereby improving the accuracy and relevance of search results. The versatility of this class can be extended to rout planning, navigation, location monitoring, distance calculation. This reusability ensures that the ontology remains relevant and useful in diverse applications, promoting consistency and interoperability.

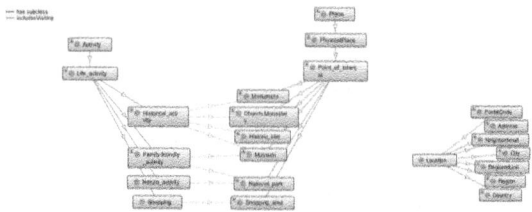

Fig. 5. Activities and Location in the HT ontology

3.2   Expandability

The modular architecture of the HT ontology allows for expansion to accommodate emerging trends, technological advancements, and evolving user requirements. This flexibility facilitates the addition of new concepts, classes, and properties as needed. By creating specialized domain-specific modules, the ontology can be tailored to meet the unique requirements of these sectors while maintaining consistency with the core framework.

As new medical specialties emerge or existing ones evolve, the ontology can be easily updated to incorporate these changes, ensuring that it remains current and comprehensive. In the tourism domain, the ontology can be extended to include new categories of accommodation options, attractions, travel services, and emerging travel trends.

The framework's flexibility also facilitates its application to new domains. By leveraging the foundational structure of existing classes and properties, the ontology can be adapted to fit the requirements of different fields.This adaptability promotes knowledge sharing, accelerating the development of domain-specific ontologies while maintaining consistency across diverse applications.

While this study is focusing to the unique needs of health tourism, future expansions could aim to further validate the ontology in order to elevate its trustworthiness and address trust-related issues. This could be achieved by adopting standardized classifications and exploring strategies for data management and protection [19].

4   Example Use Case: Health Tourism Hub Application

In the context of HT, the proposed ontology facilitates the integration of health-care and tourism data to provide a comprehensive and personalized experience for users. For example, a user seeking medical treatment abroad can use the platform to find suitable healthcare providers, book accommodation, and plan wellness activities, all tailored to their medical needs and personal preferences. The proposed HT ontology was integrated within the HealthTourismHub[9] Application ensuring that all relevant information is easily accessible, enhancing the overall user experience and quality of care [20].

This platform allows users to discover and book complete HT packages that include medical appointments, accommodation and recommended tourism activities. Uniquely, HealthTourismHub personalizes these packages based on user needs. Through this application, users seeking HT destinations can explore medical services, schedule trips and arrange their stay with suitable providers, all in the form of a package. Additionally, HealthTourismHub provides detailed information on geolocations, tourist attractions, and destinations, ensuring that health tourists receive a convenient travel experience. Beyond facilitating health tourists, it also serves as a platform for medical experts and accommodation providers, allowing patients to discover and engage with them easily.

The HealthTourismHub Application makes effective use of all three layers of the HT Ontology to provide a personalized experience for users seeking HT services (Fig. 6). The Core HT Ontology Layer underpins the application's ability to organize, classify, and personalize data, thereby facilitating efficient and personalized discovery and access to information. The Domain-Specific Layer extends the core ontology enabling detailed searches for medical services, accommodation, and travel activities. Additionally, The Interoperability Layer is essential in connecting the application through the ontology, translating data and relationships, ensuring that the information is consistent and accurate. By executing SPARQL queries, HealthTourismHub is empowered to offer personalized HT packages, incorporating medical appointments, accommodation, and activities based on user preferences, thus enhancing the overall user experience. Ultimately, the synergistic interaction of these three ontology layers within the HealthTourismHub application creates a dynamic platform that caters to the unique needs of each user, revolutionizing the HT experience.

The HT ontology and the HealthTourismHub application codebase are publicly available on Github[10]. This open-source approach fosters collaboration and community contributions. Developers and domain experts can readily access, modify, and extend the ontology to incorporate new concepts, medical advancements, and evolving user needs.

---

[9] HealthTourismHub.
[10] HealthTourismHub-HT ontology repository.

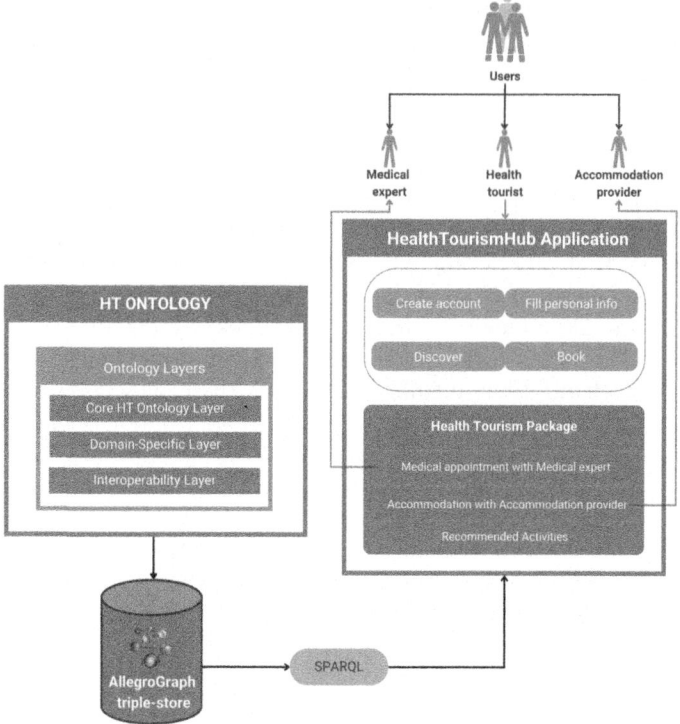

Fig. 6. Example Use Case: Health Tourism Hub Application

5 Conclusions

In conclusion, this manuscript presents a versatile ontology designed to manage and integrate HT data. The proposed design, with its core, domain-specific modules, and interoperability layer, offers a framework that enhances data organization, accessibility, and personalization, ultimately improving functionality across the HT ecosystem. The core ontology layer provides a foundation for organizing and classifying HT data, while domain-specific modules cater to specific healthcare, tourism and location needs. The interoperability layer ensures seamless data exchange between applications and the ontology. This standardized framework promotes reusability and expandability across medical and travel domains, fostering data exchange and interoperability for more coordinated and user-centric health and travel experiences.

The proposed ontology was applied in the creation of the HealthTourismHub Application facilitating the integration of healthcare and tourism data. This platform leverages the ontology to deliver personalized HT packages, incorporating medical appointments, accommodation options, and recommended activities based on individual user preferences.

Acknowledgments. This research has been co-financed by the European Union and Greek national funds through the Operational Program of the Region of Central Macedonia 2021-2027, under the "Innovation Investment Plans" (project code: KMP6-0081778)

References

1. Fensel, D.: Ontology-based knowledge management. Computer **35**(11), 56–59 (2002). http://dx.doi.org/10.1109/MC.2002.1046975
2. Kumbhar, R.: Modern Knowledge Organisation Systems and Interoperability, pp. 95–113. Elsevier (2012). http://dx.doi.org/10.1016/B978-1-84334-660-9.50008-4
3. Li, C., Chen, Y., Shang, Y.: A review of industrial big data for decision making in intelligent manufacturing. Eng. Sci. Technol. Int. J. **29**, 101021 (2022). http://dx.doi.org/10.1016/j.jestch.2021.06.001
4. Ratwani, R.M.: Electronic health records and improved patient care: opportunities for applied psychology. Curr. Dir. Psychol. Sci. **26**(4), 359–365 (2017). http://dx.doi.org/10.1177/0963721417700691
5. Ionescu, A.M., Sârbu, F.A.: Exploring the impact of smart technologies on the tourism industry. Sustainability **16**(8), 3318 (2024). http://dx.doi.org/10.3390/su16083318
6. Kim, H.L., Hyun, S.S.: The future of medical tourism for individuals' health and well-being: a case study of the relationship improvement between the UAE (United Arab Emirates) and South Korea. Int. J. Environ. Res. Public Health **19**(9), 5735 (2022). http://dx.doi.org/10.3390/ijerph19095735
7. Kucukusta, D., Hudson, S., DeMicco, F.J.: Medical tourism: strategies for quality patient/guest experiences. J. Hospitality Tourism Insights **2**(3), 221–223 (2019). http://dx.doi.org/10.1108/JHTI-08-2019-090
8. Vovk, V., Beztelesna, L., Pliashko, O.: Identification of factors for the development of medical tourism in the world. Int. J. Environ. Res. Public Health **18**(21), 11205 (2021). http://dx.doi.org/10.3390/ijerph182111205
9. Roman, M., Roman, M., Wojcieszak-Zbierska, M.: Health tourism-subject of scientific research: a literature review and cluster analysis. Int. J. Environ. Res. Public Health **20**(1), 480 (2022). http://dx.doi.org/10.3390/ijerph20010480
10. Frikha, M., Mhiri, M., Zarai, M., Gargouri, F.: Using TMT ontology in trust based medical tourism recommender system. In: 2016 IEEE/ACS 13th International Conference of Computer Systems and Applications (AICCSA). IEEE (2016). http://dx.doi.org/10.1109/AICCSA.2016.7945768
11. Janchai, W., Bouras, A., Siddoo, V.: An ontology model for medical tourism supply chain knowledge representation. Int. J. Adv. Comput. Sci. Appl. **13**(4) (2022). http://dx.doi.org/10.14569/IJACSA.2022.0130427
12. Chantrapornchai, C., Choksuchat, C.: Ontology construction and application in practice case study of health tourism in Thailand. Springer **5**(1) (2016). http://dx.doi.org/10.1186/s40064-016-3747-3
13. Lee, H.J., Park, S.Y., Jin, H.R., Sohn, M.: A smart orchestrator of ecosystem in medical tourism. In: Proceedings of the 18th Annual International Conference on Electronic Commerce e-Commerce in Smart connected World - ICEC '16. ICEC '16, ACM Press (2016). http://dx.doi.org/10.1145/2971603.2971627

14. Spoladore, D., Pessot, E., Bischof, M., Hartl, A., Sacco, M.: Collaborative design approach for the development of an ontology-based decision support system in health tourism, pp. 632–639. Springer (2021). http://dx.doi.org/10.1007/978-3-030-85969-5_59
15. Musen, M.A.: The protégé project: a look back and a look forward. AI Matters **1**(4), 4–12 (2015). http://dx.doi.org/10.1145/2757001.2757003
16. Glimm, B., Horrocks, I., Motik, B., Stoilos, G., Wang, Z.: HermiT: an OWL 2 reasoner. J. Autom. Reason. **53**(3), 245–269 (2014). http://dx.doi.org/10.1007/s10817-014-9305-1
17. Rahman, H., Hussain, M.I.: A comprehensive survey on semantic interoperability for internet of things: state-of-the-art and research challenges. Trans. Emerg. Telecommun. Technol. **31**(12), e3902 (2020)
18. Pérez, J., Arenas, M., Gutierrez, C.: Semantics and complexity of SPARQL. ACM Trans. Database Syst. **34**(3), 16–45 (2009). http://dx.doi.org/10.1145/1567274.1567278
19. Wilkinson, M.D., et al.: The fair guiding principles for scientific data management and stewardship. Sci. Data **3**(1), 1–9 (2016)
20. Gkevreki, S., Fiska, V., Nikolopoulos, S., Kompatsiaris, I.: Enhancing sustainability in health tourism through an ontology-based booking application for personalized packages. Sustainability **16**(15) (2024). https://www.mdpi.com/2071-1050/16/15/6505

Cross-Referencing Metadata Through an Extension of the MEDFORD Language

Polina Shpilker[1], Benjamin Stubbs[1], Michael Sayers[1], Lenore Cowen[1], Shaun Wallace[2], Alva Couch[1], and Noah M. Daniels[2(✉)]

[1] Department of Computer Science, Tufts University, MEDFORD, MA 02155, USA
`alva.couch@tufts.edu`
[2] Department of Computer Science and Statistics, University of Rhode Island, Kingston, RI 02881, USA
{`shaun.wallace, noah_daniels`}`@uri.edu`

Abstract. Research metadata is difficult to annotate yet critical for research replication and data re-usability. A language called MEDFORD has been previously designed to make the process of writing metadata approachable for non-software focused researchers, but we have identified several flaws that make it difficult to thoroughly and accurately describe research metadata. We propose an extension to the MEDFORD metadata language to support relationships between metadata objects, as well as to reference other MEDFORD files, such that objects can be defined in a singular file and re-used throughout multiple files.

Keywords: Metadata · Research accessibility · FAIR Data

1 Introduction

It is critically important for research to be discoverable, verifiable, and re-usable. The FAIR (Findable, Accessible, Interoperable, and Reusable) data principles, introduced in 2016, define a set of standards that can be used to support research stewardship [8]. Following these FAIR standards ensures that research results can be validated and also allows research pipelines and raw data to be re-used in novel research. FAIR metadata, a crucial part of FAIR data, is increasingly being flagged as a critical ingredient in making published science more reproducible and replicable [3,4]. While many reasonable and successful FAIR metadata standards have been proposed [1,5], annotating research results and pipelines such that they follow FAIR standards is often a second thought, put off until research completion if ever done at all. We believe that this is due to the difficulty of annotating research metadata, as there has been insufficient emphasis on making it easy for scientists to manually enter, access, or correct their metadata.

The MEtaData Format for Open Reef Data (MEDFORD) [6,7] language is our previously-proposed metadata description language designed to help scientists describe their research processes and data in a FAIR manner. MEDFORD makes research Findable and Reusable by providing scientists a vocabulary and

© The Author(s), under exclusive license to Springer Nature Switzerland AG 2025
M. Sfakakis et al. (Eds.): MTSR 2024, CCIS 2331, pp. 153–158, 2025.
https://doi.org/10.1007/978-3-031-81974-2_13

structure to describe their research that can easily be processed by database systems. MEDFORD is a plain-text format with simple syntax rules to describe various research attributes and objects, such as @Software used or @Data generated and analyzed. MEDFORD's simple syntax makes it easy for researchers to describe their research, while its guided format allows automated tools to process and correct the stored metadata.

MEDFORD was designed as a middleware that is simultaneously human-writable and machine-readable while also having been built on top of the BagIt [2] standard to allow users to package their metadata alongside the research data it describes. Consequently, the MEDFORD language assumes that all relevant metadata would be described in its entirety within a single file and that every object could be described independently from all other research objects. For example, although a photo may contain a particular coral species, a researcher using MEDFORD to annotate their metadata cannot easily link the photo file's metadata to the metadata they transcribed of the coral species.

In this work, we extend the MEDFORD language in two ways: First, we allow metadata objects to reference other metadata objects. Second, we implement externally defined metadata in MEDFORD and define syntax such that a researcher may reference an external MEDFORD file's metadata contents. This will improve the usability of MEDFORD and promote adoption, as researchers may describe more complex metadata using cross-object referencing and will not be required to repeat existing metadata described in other MEDFORD files.

2   Metadata Inter-connectivity

Initially, MEDFORD was designed to be entirely composed of independent "blocks", where each block completely explained its metadata object in a separate context from every other MEDFORD block. However, this is insufficient to describe real research data.

When researchers were introduced to MEDFORD and tested the language by describing their current research, they quickly discovered a prime example of this insufficiency. Their research required the description of coral species (@Species) and coral reefs (@Reef). Coral species require a description of information such as their scientific name, the current (at the time of research) genome construction, and the reef at which the species was studied. Reefs required information such as geo-coordinates, the date of study, and the coral species present in the reef. There is a strong dependency between the description of a coral species and a reef: to completely describe one; there must be some description of the other.

This issue could have been resolved by simply making one of the major tokens a minor token of the other token. For example, @Reef could be made an attribute of @Species, and the species would entirely contain all of the reef's metadata:

```
@Species P.Dam
@Species_Reef Reef1
@Species_Reef-Coordinates (coordinates)
```

The first glaring issue with this approach is immediately obvious: what if multiple species are studied in the same reef? The reef metadata would be duplicated in every species block, which increases the chances of errors. There is nothing to enforce that the reef metadata agrees across every species block, and the chance of user error increases with every repetition.

```
@Species P.Dam
@Species_Reef Reef1
@Species_Reef-Coordinates (coordinates)

@Species P.Acuta
@Species_Reef Reef1
@Species_Reef-Coordinates (coordinates, with a typo)
```

Another issue with this approach is the imposed hierarchy on the species and reef metadata. In this example, we arbitrarily chose to make the @Reef a child token of @Species, which makes sense if a researcher is interested in the differences between species in a single reef. However, if the researcher is focused on the differences between multiple reefs, they would prefer if @Species was a child token of @Reef.

Therefore, there must be a concept of relationships between metadata objects that is non-repetitive and non-hierarchical.

3   Naming Metadata Objects

The first issue with implementing inter-connectivity between metadata objects in MEDFORD is a lack of identifiers. MEDFORD does has no way to give a unique identifier to a metadata object, as there was never the necessity to reference a specific metadata object. However, consider the valid MEDFORD text:

```
@Species P. Dam
@Species-Construction Pocillopora damicornis genome v1.0
```

The first line is colloquially called the "description" or desc line of the metadata object in MEDFORD documentation. This line is ignored by the MEDFORD parser and serves as a one-line description of the metadata object described by the following minor token lines. This overlaps with the functionality of the note minor token, which allows users to arbitrarily annotate a given metadata object with text that will not be parsed by the MEDFORD parser, only kept as an annotation for readers. Every block must have a desc line for the file to be considered valid MEDFORD.

Therefore, the solution is obvious: the desc line can be repurposed into a name line. Instead of being a freestyle annotation, the first line of a MEDFORD block will be considered its name. Functionally, this is equivalent – a name can be any combination of ASCII characters and may include standard MEDFORD macros, just like a desc, but the new name provides more clarity on the line's functionality. It prepares the concept of a name for the purposes of cross-object referencing. In the above example, MEDFORD has the concept of a @Species object that is named P. dam. With a name defined, we may now propose a syntax:

```
@Species P.Dam
@Species-Construction Pocillopora damicornis genome v1.0
@Species-Reef Reef1
```

3.1   Object Name Collisions

A major difference between the concept of a name and a desc is quickly apparent: since a name must refer to a single object for inter-object dependencies to be resolvable, name lines must be unique. At first, this appears to possibly add a large burden on the user. Consider the specific case where a researcher is studying two corals and has a singular photo of each coral species.

```
@Species P.Acuta
@Species-Construction NCBI BioProject PRJNA812628

@Photo P.Acuta
@Photo-Type JPEG
```

If a researcher would like to describe that a @Reef contains the coral species P.Acuta, it appears that there would be a name collision. However, MEDFORD's structure offers an easy solution: when a researcher writes a MEDFORD block, that block is immediately associated with a major token. The major token defines the type of object being declared and if a researcher is referencing a block, they have some expectation of the type of metadata they are referencing. Therefore, we adjust the syntax to require the user to declare the major token:

```
@Reef-Species @Species P.Acuta
```

Therefore, name uniqueness in MEDFORD is only required for blocks that share the major token. That is, if the user was to describe a @Species, its name must only be unique compared to the other @Species. We believe that this is a reasonable expectation for users and would be good practice even if the name attribute was not being actively used in MEDFORD logic for readers to be able to quickly differentiate between objects of the same major token.

4   Referencing Metadata from Other Sources

In developing the syntax for internal referencing, other circumstances where a researcher would want to reference data quickly became apparent. The proposed reference syntax is developed solely to reference metadata within the file a researcher is editing, but consider the case where multiple research groups are studying the same set of coral species. It is important to maintain consistent annotation of these coral species across these research groups, but currently, this metadata must be manually copied from the reference MEDFORD file into the researchers' own files. We decided to extend our proposed reference functionality to add the capability to reference metadata stored in external MEDFORD files.

This requires two more additions to the MEDFORD syntax: the capability to declare that referenced metadata exists in a external file, and the capability to declare the location of an external file that will be referenced.

There have been a myriad of approaches to the concept of declaring that an object is imported from an external source. Much like how a user may either use `Import module` or `From module import Function` in Python, MEDFORD must either completely import the external metadata and place all of its objects into the current environment, or allow the user to import particular metadata objects into the current context.

Considering how often a user may want to reference external files, and the relative small size of metadata objects in MEDFORD, we have decided to implement the former. While parsers may optimize to only import relevant metadata for efficiency, requiring researchers to manually import every referenced metadata object would be greatly detrimental to the efficacy of MEDFORD as a user-friendly object and increase the possibility of user error.

However, this causes a new problem: if two separate MEDFORD files both define a `@Species P. dam`, but one references an older genome construction than the other, the MEDFORD language must have a way to deconvolute sources to avoid placing the responsibility on parsers to determine how to handle collisions. This is resolved by a feature we have just introduced: every object in MEDFORD must have a `Name`, and therefore, the syntax to define an external MEDFORD file reference must also include a `Name`.

4.1   External Reference Syntax

We now propose concrete syntax for the two required additions described above. First, the syntax to declare that an attribute is from an external reference is shown below. We imitated Python import syntax, as its plain English syntax made it easier to understand from a quick glance:

```
@Reef Reef1
@Reef-Species from CoralsMFD: @Species P.Dam
```

Even without experience using Python or MEDFORD, a new reader could glean that `@Species P.Dam` comes from some object named `CoralsMFD`.

Next, to provide this nickname `CoralsMFD` as some link to an external source, we propose the following syntax to declare an external MEDFORD metadata source. The example below declares that MEDFORD metadata should be imported from the file `corals_metadata.mfd` to be available for reference anywhere in the MEDFORD file using the nickname `CoralsMFD`.

```
@Import CoralsMFD
@Import-File ~/shared/corals_metadata.mfd
```

5   Conclusion and Future Work

We have proposed an addition to the MEDFORD language that enables metadata objects to reference other objects, such that research data that is intrinsically linked can be accurately documented in MEDFORD. We have also proposed syntax for MEDFORD files to be able to reference other MEDFORD files, such that metadata can be re-used. We are currently implementing these extensions to the MEDFORD parser.

This syntax can be extended to even more powerful functionality. For example, photos taken by modern digital cameras automatically store metadata in a format called EXIF. This metadata could be imported using nearly identical syntax: the Import block will reference the EXIF of the photo file. However, while MEDFORD files can be parsed by any MEDFORD parser, additional work must be done to parse external formats such as EXIF. Once internal and external MEDFORD references have been implemented, we will begin developing methods to add universal plug-ins to MEDFORD parsers to support external formats. The MEDFORD parser and editor is released as an open-source tool on GitHub at https://github.com/TuftsBCB/MEDFORD.

Acknowledgments. The initial development of MEDFORD was supported in part by the National Science Foundation under NSF grants OAC-1939263. OAC-1939795 and OAC-1940233. The current work was supported in part by a seed grant from the Tufts Data Intensive Study Center (DISC).

References

1. Ball, A., Greenberg, J., Jeffery, K., Koskela, R.: RDA metadata standards directory working group: final report, RDA Recommendation, Research Data Alliance (2016)
2. Kunze, J., Littman, J., Madden, E., Scancella, J., Adams, C.: The BagIt file packaging format (V1.0), RFC 8493 (2018)
3. Leipzig, J., Nüst, D., Hoyt, C.T., Soiland-Reyes, S., Ram, K., Greenberg, J.: The role of metadata in reproducible computational research. arXiv preprint arXiv:2006.08589 (2020)
4. Peng, R.D.: Reproducible research in computational science. Science **334**(6060), 1226–1227 (2011)
5. Qin, J., Ball, A., Greenberg, J.: Functional and architectural requirements for metadata: supporting discovery and management of scientific data. In: International Conference on Dublin Core and Metadata Applications, vol. 9, pp. 62–71 (2012)
6. Shpilker, P., et al.: MEDFORD: a human- and machine-readable metadata markup language. Database **2022** 2022
7. Shpilker, P., et al.: MEtaData format for open reef data (MEDFORD). In: Research Conference on Metadata and Semantics Research, pp. 206–211. Springer (2022)
8. Wilkinson, M., Dumontier, M., Aalbersberg, I., et al.: The FAIR guiding principles for scientific data management and stewardship. Sci. Data **3**(1), 03 (2016)

Aligning Data Management Plans with Community Standards Using FAIR Implementation Profiles

Navroop K. Singh[1], Shuai Wang[1(✉)], Angelica Maineri[2(✉)],
Tycho Hofstra[1], Mark Bruyneel[1], Stephanie van de Sandt[1],
Ronald Siebes[1], Jacco van Ossenbruggen[1], and Tobias Kuhn[1]

[1] Vrije Universiteit Amsterdam, De Boelelaan 1105, 1081, HV Amsterdam,
The Netherlands
n.k2.singh@student.vu.nl,
{shuai.wang,t.m.hofstra,m.bruyneel,s.van.de.sandt,r.m.siebes,
jacco.van.ossenbruggen,t.kuhn}@vu.nl
[2] ODISSEI, Erasmus University Rotterdam, 3000, DR Rotterdam, The Netherlands
angelica@odissei-data.nl

Abstract. Data Management Plans (DMPs) are often required by organizations and funding agencies for research projects. One of the goals of DMPs is to capture how researchers plan to comply with some aspects of the Findability, Accessibility, Interoperability, and Reusability (FAIR) principles. When writing DMPs, taking into account community standards for managing and publishing research data can be a challenge for researchers. Community standards are often documented informally or communicated by word of mouth. The introduction of FAIR Implementation Profiles (FIPs) offers a structured way to capture such standards. This paper investigates with a user study, whether FIPs can serve as suggestions for aligning research data management with community standards. Through a customized interface with the related information extracted from FIPs as suggestions, we study whether participants take such suggestions into account when writing DMPs.

Keywords: FAIR Implementation Profile · FAIR Principles · Data Management Plans

1 Introduction

To make research data findable and readily reusable by others, researchers are often mandated by funding organizations and universities to create *Data Management Plans* (DMPs). A DMP is the result of a questionnaire (i.e. DMP template) with each question accompanied by some explanations. When completed, DMPs are formal documents consisting of answers to questions that outline how data is handled throughout and after a research project. Answering these questions, researchers specify the details and methods of data collection, data

M. Sfakakis et al. (Eds.): MTSR 2024, CCIS 2331, pp. 159–171, 2025.
https://doi.org/10.1007/978-3-031-81974-2_14

repositories, responsibility, accessibility, licenses, etc. These answers can be influenced by many factors: the requirements of conferences and publishers, the recommendations by departments and universities, the suggestions by colleagues, the community standards, researchers' willingness to follow the FAIR principles (Findability, Accessibility, Interoperability, and Reusability) [13], etc.[1] Following community standards is a requirement of the FAIR principles (principle R1.3).[2] When uncertain about community standards, many choose to consult data stewards and colleagues. However, not all data stewards and colleagues can be aware of the standards of every community. Moreover, community standards are often in the word of mouth or informally documented (and often inaccessible beyond the community/organization). Adding more complexity to this alignment is when such standards evolve as members of the community adopt new tools, repositories, registries, licenses, etc. Thus, aligning DMPs with community standards remains an unsolved problem.

The introduction of *FAIR Implementation Profiles* (FIPs) offers a structured way to capture community standards [9]. FIPs serve as structured templates about decisions and guidelines by experts and members of communities of practice [9]. Moreover, FIP comes with related tools and metrics that make comparison of community standards and statistical analysis easy [9]. The alignment of DMPs with community standards captured by FIPs has the potential to offer substantial benefits to both researchers and their respective communities. For example, this alignment would make data findable in uniform repositories and promote the standardization of some machine-interpretable format, which makes it easier to integrate into a web framework and automatically compare with other schemas. However, the realization of effective alignment faces several obstacles. The DMP templates universities/institutes use can vary significantly. Some can have multiple versions for faculties and funding agencies. Determining which questions in the template could align with specific community standards can be ambiguous. Moreover, some datasets could be of interest to multiple communities, which further complicates researchers' efforts when selected for reuse.

The idea of using FIPs as suggestions for DMPs was initially proposed by K. Hettne et al. [4]. However, they did not conduct any user study to validate this idea. In this paper, we take an empirical approach and explore the workflow to extract information from FIPs as suggestions on the DMP interface. We study the following research questions. **RQ1:** Which questions in the DMP template can take community standards in FIPs as suggestions? **RQ2:** How can we build a user interface that takes community standards as suggestions? **RQ3:** How do users take advantage of suggestions from FIPs while writing their DMPs?

For RQ1, we first map DMP questions to their corresponding FAIR principles. We then filter out which questions from the mapping can be answered using suggestions from FIPs. For RQ2, we create a knowledge model (KM), a template file that specifies a tree-like structure of the DMP with its questions and some additional information. The KM is then used to generate the DMP interface

---

[1] https://www.go-fair.org/fair-principles/..

[2] The R1.3 principle: https://www.go-fair.org/fair-principles/.

on the FAIR Wizard platform[3] with text-based suggestions. Finally, for RQ3, a user study is conducted followed by a survey to understand how participants take suggestions from FIPs. This paper made the following research contributions[4]: 1) a generic workflow for using FIPs in the interface as suggested in DMPs, 2) a mapping between the chosen DMP template and the FAIR principles, 3) an analysis of the relationship between the DMP questions and the FIP questions, 4) a reusable and extendable knowledge model that is used to generate the interface in the FAIR Wizard platform, and 5) a user study aimed to understand how researchers can effectively use FIPs as suggestions while creating DMPs.

2   Related Work

Despite the potential impact of FAIR community standards on researchers' choices over management and publication of research data, the connection between DMPs and FAIR principles has been empirically examined only in a few studies. Henning et al. [3] analyzed 10 DMP templates and concluded that DMPs fail to capture detailed community-specific implementations, especially the principle of interoperability, and do not cover metadata sufficiently. In a study by Mannheimer, DMPs associated with grant proposals were analyzed along with interviews with the Principal Investigators who wrote them [6]. It was found that the more technical parts of the DMPs (including questions on FAIR) were the least detailed, and that they would need more training and guidance on more specialized concepts such as FAIR and metadata. Likewise, a report by OpenAIRE on the Horizon 2020 template for data management plans highlighted the need to clarify issues and terms around FAIR implementation [2]. Finally, regarding the use of Open Science Framework (OSF) platform for DMPs, Sullivan et al. [11] indicated the importance of referring to best practices applied to different research contexts. These studies suggest that clearer guidance on FAIR implementation and standards can be beneficial to researchers when filling in their DMPs. By following FAIR community standards, for instance, published metadata could also be more easily harvested, refined, or enriched by platforms such as the Data Europa[5], and the ODISSEI portal[6].

To our knowledge, the only attempt that explicitly link the DMPs with the FAIR community standards declared in FIPs used the DMP template of Leiden University. The authors identified seven questions in their DMP template that could be linked to the FIP questions [4].[7] They proposed to develop a knowledge model of the Leiden University DMP template and import answers from a FIP as

---

[3] The FAIR Wizard uses the Jinja template engine: https://fair-wizard.com/.

[4] The DMP template, the knowledge model, the mock DMPs, the survey, Python code, the analytical results, and a demo are in a repository on Zenodo (). The Python scripts for the analysis of survey results are at https://github.com/FAIR-Expertise-Hub/FIP2DMP.

[5] https://data.europa.eu/en.

[6] https://portal.odissei.nl/.

[7] The mapping is at https://osf.io/5jsfp.

pre-filled answers for the DMP, leaving it to the user to select the most relevant ones [8]. A KM is a structured document template with questions, descriptive text accompanying each question, and the type of answers specified. The template includes examples of good data management practices and guidance on how to meet the requirements of various funding agencies and institutions. Our research is inspired by this work. Their proposal takes into account one FIP, while in reality, there could be multiple communities that could be relevant to a research project. They proposed to have imported decisions from the FIP as pre-filled answers in the DMP. However, since the efficacy of using the information captured by FIP has not been evaluated, it remains debatable if such information can be used as pre-filled answers as researchers' data management decisions in their DMPs, not to mention that not all the answers in the FIPs are correct. Moreover, our examination of the FIPs in social science shows that some entries could be missing or incomplete for some FIPs. A question in a selected FIP could correspond to multiple resources. If a user decides to align with a community by taking the resources indicated by its FIP as the answer, then which one should be taken as the pre-filled answer in the DMP? This could lead to confusion. Moreover, they proposed to allow the import of information from a FIP while writing a DMP. This would overwrite the user's answers, which can lead to confusion as the user would have to look into the version history. Thus, their proposed approach could have some lack of consideration in practice. Moreover, they did not include a user study. Our approach is inspired by their work, but differs in the DMP template used, the development of KM, and how (multiple) FIPs are handled as suggestions. In addition, we include a user study and evaluate the efficacy. Details of the user study are in Sect. 6.

3   Workflow

In this section, we provide the details of the workflow of our approach. Given a selected DMP template, to provide suggestions for the right questions in DMP, we need to find the mapping between the questions in DMP and FIPs. To do this, we first associate a list of questions with the FAIR principles. We can further narrow this list by removing questions that do not correspond to any question in the FIP. This results in a mapping from a subset of questions in DMP to a subset of questions in FIP. Note that the mapping is not always one-to-one given that the questions in DMPs are typically developed without considering the correspondence to the FAIR principles, respectively. This mapping is then used to extract community standards captured by the answers to the selected questions in the FIPs.[8] The extracted information can be structured as a table of the communities and their resources for each question (see Sect. 4).

---

[8] In this paper, due to the limited number of FIPs in the domain of social science, we do not filter out any existing FIP in social science. The selection/recommendation of FIP regarding a project could be further explored when there are enough FIPs in social science.

Next, we customize the FAIR Wizard platform to include the extracted information. A knowledge model (KM) of the FAIR Wizard is a customizable template that can be imported into the platform. It is a file of computer readable and actionable statements about questions in chapters with additional information that explains the questions, the specification of API calls, and the expected type of answers (string, yes/no, etc.). A KM can then be loaded into the FAIR Wizard to form a customized interface as specified. For each question in the DMP template, the interface displays the question, additional descriptive information, and suggestions from FIPs. The interface is then used to create DMPs. More details can be found in Sect. 5. To evaluate the efficacy, we perform a user study. Each study participant is asked to create a DMP and complete a survey. The DMP and the survey results are then used for analysis (see Sect. 6).

4   Knowledge Preparation: Connecting DMPs with FIPs

4.1   Data Management Plans

DMPs have become a standard in recent years and are required more and more by funding organizations. Miksa et al. describe them as 'awareness tools', shedding light on data management practices employed in research projects [7]. In practice, they assist researchers in ensuring proper management, documentation, and preservation of data, while also meeting funders' requirements. DMPs are implemented from DMP templates, which consist of questions with specified answer types. DMP templates can be very different from each other, as they are often tailored to best facilitate the data management of researchers and meet the requirements of the funding organizations. Various tools can be used to instantiate such templates with a user interface, such as DMPOnline[9], DMP Tool and Data Stewardship Wizard [10]. For this paper, we use the DMP template by the Vrije Universiteit Amsterdam (VU). The template is hosted on DMPOnline whose strength lies in the convenience for researchers to request feedback from data stewards. Furthermore, DMPOnline dynamically displays or omits questions based on the researcher's responses regarding dealing with personal data. By March 2023 when this project started, the DMP in use at VU was identified as '1 - VU DMP template 2021 (NWO & ZonMW certified) v1.3', which consists of 53 questions. The VU DMP template is used by all faculties except the Medical Faculty. In this study, we focus on researchers in the Faculty of Social Sciences. The questions in the template cover a wide range of topics including authorship, legal and privacy ethics, funding number, etc.

When comparing the VU DMP template with that of Leiden,[10] there are notable differences. The Leiden DMP consists of 48 questions (compared to 53 in the VU template), mostly in multiple-choice format, in contrast to VU's text-based answers. Both address findability, accessibility, and reusability. That of Leiden places more emphasis on privacy concerns and security risks.

---

[9] https://dmponline.vu.nl/.
[10] The Leiden DMP template used is at https://zenodo.org/records/4423065.

4.2 Mapping the DMP Template to the FAIR Principles

Since the FAIR principles are widely endorsed for good data management, most DMPs also include questions on the implementation of FAIR [3]. Hence, to answer RQ1, we begin by analyzing the 53 questions in the chosen VU DMP template and exclude questions that do not correspond to any FAIR principle. After consulting the team at the University Library that develops and maintains the DMP and compare it against the FAIR principles, we identified a total of 17 questions relevant to the FAIR principles.[11] More specifically, 14 of the questions are about the Findability principle, and two questions are related to the Accessibility principle. Three other questions focus on the Reuse principle. Interoperability is not addressed explicitly. Since the template was designed without exactly following the FAIR principles, questions can correspond to multiple principles. For example, Question 5.1 corresponds to both F2 and R1.2 principles. Among all the questions that have to do with the FAIR principles, we observe that 82.4% of the questions are about Findability since a significant amount of questions have to do with persistent identifiers. Question 5.3 can cover much broader topics than one FAIR principle and leads to ambiguity.

4.3 FAIR Implementation Profiles

A FAIR Implementation Profile (FIP) is a set of choices made by a FAIR Implementation Community (FIC) on how to implement the FAIR principles [9]. The community decision in a FIP is collected using a questionnaire[12] in which experts and members of the community collectively indicate their preferred FAIR Enabling Resources (FERs), that include tools, documentation, registries, licenses, standards, and other resources that are needed to achieve a specific aspect of FAIR implementation [9,12].[13] Examples include the REST API, IISG Dataverse[14], CC-BY-NC 2.0[15], etc. Each question corresponds to a FAIR principle. FIPs have been conceptualized to foster convergence of FAIR implementation efforts across communities and domains [9]. FIPs are filled in using the FIP Wizard[16], providing an easy-to-use interface. FIPs can be published in a machine-actionable format as nanopublications.

There are already over a hundred FAIR Implementation Communities covering various domains. For this study, we focus on the six FIPs that pertain to communities in the social sciences [12].[17] The social sciences constitute an interesting use case due to their longstanding tradition of data sharing, showed by the

---

[11] Details are given in the supplementary material.

[12] https://bit.ly/yourFIP.

[13] https://peta-pico.github.io/FAIR-nanopubs/fip/index-en.html#https://w3id.org/fair/fip/terms/FAIR-Enabling-Resource.

[14] https://iisg.amsterdam/nl/data/datasets.

[15] https://creativecommons.org/licenses/by-nc/2.0/.

[16] The FIP Wizard platform is a specified version of the general-purpose FAIR Wizard. It is available online at https://fip-wizard.ds-wizard.org.

[17] These were the only social science FIPs available by the time the project start in spring 2023.

abundant availability of large-scale survey data, yet combined with a large het-
erogeneity in the standards adopted. Among the six FIPs, three come from communities that publish survey data: GESIS social Science Survey Research (GESIS
SSSR), the European Social Survey (ESS), and the Australian correspondent
(AUSSI-ESS). In addition, the Dutch Socio-Economic History (SEH) and the
Media Content Analysis Lab (MCAL) are two communities in the Netherlands.
Lastly, the LGBTQ+ Linked Open Vocabulary (LGBTQVoC) community creates multilingual LGBTQ+ controlled vocabularies for indexing digital records
to represent LGBTQ+ objects in non-English languages. Details about these
communities can be found in [12].

4.4 Assigning FIPs to DMP Questions

Table 1. Mapping of DMP Questions to FIP questions via the FAIR principles.

ID	DMP Question	FAIR principle	FIP Question
4.6	Where will you publish your data assets?	F4 Data	In which search engines are your datasets indexed?
4.8	How will you ensure your data assets get a persistent identifier (e.g. a DOI-code)?	F1 Data	What globally unique, persistent, resolvable identifiers do you use for datasets?
4.9	Will you register your datasets in an online registry other than PURE? If yes, where?	F1 Data	What globally unique, persistent, resolvable identifiers do you use for datasets?
4.13	Please indicate the license and/ or terms of use under which you share your data.	R1.1 Data	Which usage license do you use for your datasets?
5.1	What metadata and documentation will accompany the project?	F2 & R1.2 Data	Which metadata schemas do you use for findability? & Which metadata schemas do you use for describing the provenance of your datasets?
5.2	What metadata and documentation will accompany the data assets?	F2	Which metadata schemas do you use for findability?
5.3	What methods, software or hardware are needed to access and use your data?	R1.2 Data	Which metadata schemas do you use for describing the provenance of your datasets?

Next, we use the mapping in Sect. 4.2 and find the correspondence between questions in FIPs and DMPs. We manually examined questions that correspond to
the same FAIR principle and identified eight DMP questions that may be successfully connected to FIPs. However, one question (Question 6.3) was excluded
due to its ambiguity.[18] Table 1 illustrates the correspondence between these DMP

---

[18] Question 6.3 'For data that are only available upon request, what methods will be
used to handle requests for access and how will data be made available to those
requesting access?' was linked to FAIR principle A1.2 in the previous step.

questions to the FIP questions after manual examination. Question 4.6, 4.8, 4.9, and 4.13 have a clear one-to-one mapping to the corresponding FIP questions.[19] The case of the next section is more complicated. Question 5.2 focuses on meta-data schemas for data assets. Question 5.3 addresses provenance models and methods. Question 5.1 bridges both, encompassing rich metadata and detailed provenance for the entire project, with metadata schemas. Other questions that are nontrivially related to the FAIR principles are 4.2 (F4), 4.3 (F4), 4.10 (A1.2), and 6.3 (A1.2). Thus, around 63.6% of the FAIR-related questions can have suggestions from FIPs.

5   Interface Customization

Recall that RQ2 is about building an interface with extracted community standards as suggestions. Currently, the chosen DMP template is hosted on the DMPOnline platform, which does not support customization of its interface, nor specifying FERs as an answer. Furthermore, the platform cannot convert the resulting DMP to machine-actionable formats and does not support loading content from other datasets using customized queries. Thus, we migrated the template to the FAIR Wizard. In this section, we explain how the knowledge model is constructed and can be used to create the corresponding interface on the FAIR Wizard platform. For a DMP, its KM is a template file based on Jinja[20] (a template engine) that specifies a tree-like structure of the corresponding DMP with its questions, some explanatory text, and the expected type of answer. Additionally, it allows some customized functions to retrieve external information as options for answers.[21] Suggestions extracted from chosen FIPs are included as additional information below the questions. In this paper, we limit our KM to questions chosen in Sect. 4.4. For each question, two types of information are expected: a list of FERs and a string description that explains how the chosen resources will be used as well as some additional information to cover resources not found in the current system. The created KMs can be modified, extended, downloaded, and reused. Finally, the interface is automatically generated when the KM is uploaded. A new DMP project can be initiated for each user.

6   User Study

After reaching out to 31 researchers in the Faculty of Social Sciences of the VU[22], a total of 6 researchers agreed to participate in this study. They have written DMPs or have sufficient knowledge of them. Participants first pick one out of four mock DMP that is closest to their research. These mock DMPs were

---

[19] For a discussion on the mapping of question 4.9, see Sect. 8.

[20] https://palletsprojects.com/p/jinja/.

[21] https://guide.ds-wizard.org/en/latest/about/introduction/knowledge-model.html.

[22] Teaching staff, supporting staff, retired professors, external and visiting researchers were excluded. PhD students were included.

inspired by some ideas of existing DMPs by university researchers. The participants were then asked to complete the DMPs with selected questions by using our customized interface, followed by a small survey about their experiences and the effectiveness of the suggestions. The survey consisted of 12 survey questions (SQs) in two parts (see the supplementary material for the complete list of questions). In Part A (SQ1-SQ7), participants assessed the relevance and usefulness of the suggestions: the relevance of communities for DMPs, decision alignment with communities, and the effectiveness of suggestions for specific DMP questions, along with the ease of locating FERs. Part B (SQ8-SQ11) focused on participants' background and experience with DMPs. Additionally, they were asked to rate the clarity of the study's goals. Finally, the survey ended with a question about how they consider aligning with community standards compared to other stakeholders. The user study was conducted in October 2023.

7   Evaluation

For our analysis, we used the answers of five participants[23]. The participants had a range of 3 to 10 years of experience in academia, counting from the start of their PhD (SQ8). With the exception of one participant, all participants had prior experience in writing DMPs (SQ9). The survey results indicated that participants, on average, found the objective of the study to be moderately clear, with a mean rating of 3.4 out of 5 (see SQ10 in Table 2). Some indicated the lack of knowledge of FIP and FER. Five key survey questions and an analysis of the corresponding results are included in Table 2. In SQ1, participants were asked to rate the relevance of research communities for their DMPs. The mean rating of 3.4 out of 5 suggested that *some* participants found research communities relevant to their DMPs. Responses of SQ2 spans from 2 to 4, with a mean rating of 3.4 and a median of 4, indicating that the participants perceived these suggestions relatively helpful. Regarding SQ3, participants found alignment with community decisions moderate important with a mean of 3.33.

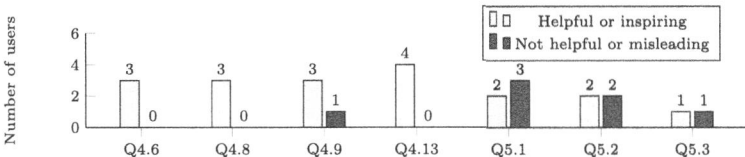

Fig. 1. Comparing the impact of suggestions on DMP questions: helpful or inspiring vs. not helpful or misleading.

Next, we evaluate the effectiveness of the suggestions for each DMP question (corresponding to SQ4 and SQ5). Figure 1 shows that questions 4.6, 4.8, 4.9,

---

[23] The PDF file of one of the mock DMPs downloaded from the DMPOnline had missing pages. This was not reported until the end of the user study. One participant chose that DMP and was therefore excluded from the analysis.

Table 2. Survey questions and their results together the range, mean, median, and standard deviation.

Survey Question ID	Survey question	Mean	Median	Std
Q1	On a scale of 1 to 5, how relevant are communities for this DMP? 1 indicating that no community is relevant and 5 indicating that many communities are relevant.	3.4	3	0.89
Q2	On a scale of 1 to 5, please evaluate whether the suggestions provided in this DMP are helpful for the communities in answering their corresponding questions. 1 indicating that it is not helpful and 5 indicating that it is very helpful.	3.4	4	0.89
Q3	On a scale of 1 to 5, how much would you consider aligning the decisions in this DMP with those made by the relevant community? 1 indicating minimal alignment and 5 indicating complete alignment.	3.4	3	1.14
Q7	On a scale of 1 to 5, how easy was it for you to find the FAIR-Enabling Resource in the search bar? 1 indicating extremely difficult and 5 indicating extremely easy.	3.6	4	1.14
Q10	On a scale of 1 to 5, how clear was the goal of the study to you? 1 indicating not clear at all and 5 indicating very clear.	3.4	4	0.89

and 4.13 in the VU DMP template were perceived by the participants as helpful or inspiring to some extent. However, a closer look reveals varying responses to Question 5.1. This question, which inquired about the types of documentation to be produced during the research project, was frequently perceived as not helpful or misleading. This might be attributed to the inherent ambiguity of the question, but also the weak link with the FIP question, which does not include the documentation part. The DMP question demands descriptions of documentation, including codebooks, lab journals, read-me files, research logs, and protocols. The challenges arise because the FIP question can only provide FERs. Questions 5.2 and 5.3 were less attended with neutral results.

Our survey includes participants' experience with FERs. Although most participants cannot find all the FERs desired through the search bar, they find the search bar easy to use to find resources with only one participant reported successfully finding all the FERs they intended to specify (SQ6) and a mean rating was 3.6 out of 5 when asked to rate how easy it was to find FERs using the search bar. This removed authors' concerns about switching platforms from DMPOnline to the FAIR Wizard. Some further analysis of the resulting DMPs shows that all participants managed to specify at least one FER for Questions 4.6 and 4.13. In Questions 4.9 and 5.1, some users struggled to locate the desired FERs through the search bar. This was reflected in SQ12: some are confused about the terminology; some are not familiar with metadata standards.

8   Discussion

The pilot study, along with the analysis, elicits discussion on the approach. The mapping between the questions in the DMP template and the FIP questions is not unambiguous and can depend on interpretation. This is because the chosen DMP template did not take the FAIR principles into account by design. Our analysis shows that out of the seven identified DMP questions, suggestions from FIPs to three questions (5.1, 5.2, and 5.3) can be unhelpful or misleading. This is because the Questions 5.1 and 5.3 cover multiple issues and are only weakly linked to the FIP questions. 5.1 and 5.3 both correspond to R1.2 where three FIPs lack resources to contribute to the suggestion. Moreover, Question 4.9 is formulated in a way that excludes the PURE system, the default choice required by the university, as an answer[24]. At further inspection, it emerged that principle F4 Data would match this DMP question better, yet this was missed due to the way the FIP question was formulated, mentioning search engines. It is only recently that the FIP question was re-formulated and now focuses on services (registries). This shows that an accurate mapping is crucial for FIP suggestions in DMPs to make sense. For instance, the way FIPs intend 'Accessibility' focuses mostly on machine accessibility. In contrast, DMPs focus more on human accessibility. Thus, a unified vocabulary for DMP and FIP is essential. Another limitation worth noting is that, despite the detailed introduction, some participants expressed that they found it difficult to comprehend certain terminologies and lacked knowledge of metadata standards. This could also be a cause of confusion for Question 5.2. In practice, metadata handling is typically the responsibility of data repositories or data stewards.

Inspired by [5], we included in the survey a question (SQ11) about which stakeholders have the greatest impact on their decision-making. Our participants indicated that the department, faculty, and the university research data management team, as well as the ethics committee, have the most significant influence on their decisions in DMPs (13.95%). That of community shares the second place with the university I.T. team, as well as the data management platform (9.30%). Some other factors could also be taken into account. Despite the scale of the survey, it shows that the decision can be influenced by many factors. However, these suggestions and guidelines from other stakeholders are mostly formatted as textual information in PDF format, which cannot be easily imported into a DMP editing platform.

Finally, the pipeline faces some challenges. Note that FIP is not free from errors. Mistakes from FIP could propagate through the pipeline and eventually end up in the DMP if the suggestion were taken. The pipeline depends on the correct mapping between the DMP questions and FIP questions. Thus, a careful review of the questions in the DMP template and the mapping is essential in future work. As the number of FIPs grows, there could be many resources as suggestions that could be confusing, especially for interdisciplinary projects. Thus, a selection of FIPs could be offered to the user in future work.

---

[24] https://vu.nl/en/employee/research-data-support/research-portal-pure.

9   Conclusion and Future Work

Alignment with FAIR community standards via the DMP, could facilitate the harvesting of metadata of published dataset from Portals[25]. This paper explored how FIPs can be used as suggestions for DMPs and whether researchers can align their DMPs with community decisions through the use of FIPs. To address RQ1, we constructed a mapping between DMP and FIP, and identified 7 DMP questions where community standards captured by FIPs could be used as suggestions. For RQ2, we constructed a KM tailored to the VU DMP template with the information of six distinct research communities' standards integrated into each question. Finally, for RQ3, a pilot user study was conducted, which revealed that, for some questions, some users find the suggestions from FIPs helpful or inspiring. Due to the fixed scope and the limited number of participants, the conclusion still needs to be validated in different research domains and on a larger scale. Moreover, alternative principles exist next to FAIR, such as the CARE principles (Collective Benefit, Authority to Control, Responsibility, and Ethics) [1], calling for an extension of our approach in future work. As a proof-of-concept, our primary focus was on the social science using six FIPs, but we aspire to broaden the scope of our work to include other domains and FIPs in the future.

Acknowledgments. The research for this paper was made possible by the Platform Digitale Infrastructuur SSH. The authors appreciate help from volunteers.

References

1. Carroll, S.R., et al.: The CARE principles for indigenous data governance. Data Sci. J. **1** (2020)
2. Grootveld, M., et al.: OpenAIRE and FAIR Data expert group survey about horizon 2020 template for data management plans (2018). https://doi.org/10.5281/zenodo.1120245
3. Henning, P., et al.: The FAIRness of data management plans: an assessment of some European DMPs. Rev. Eletrônica de Comunicação, Informação e Inovação em Saúde (2021)
4. Hettne, K., et al.: FIP2DMP: linking data management plans with fair implementation profiles. FAIR Connect **1**(1), 23–27 (2023)
5. Kvale, L., et al.: Understanding the data management plan as a boundary object through a multi-stakeholder perspective. Int. J. Digit. Curation **16**, 16 (2021)
6. Mannheimer, S.: Toward a better data management plan: the impact of DMPs on grant funded research practices. J. eSci. Librarianship **7**(3) (2018)
7. Miksa, T., et al.: Ten principles for machine-actionable data management plans. PLoS Comput. Biol. **15**(3), e1006750 (2019)
8. Schoots, F., et al.: Data management plan template Leiden university (4.2). Zenodo (2021). https://doi.org/10.5281/zenodo.4423065

---

[25] See for an example: https://data.europa.eu.

9. Schultes, E., et al.: Reusable FAIR implementation profiles as accelerators of FAIR convergence. In: Advances in Conceptual Modeling. Springer (2020)
10. Spaaks, J.H., et al.: The data stewardship wizard: a tool bringing together researchers, data stewards, and data experts. Int. J. Digital Curation **14**(1) (2019)
11. Sullivan, I., et al.: Open and reproducible research on open science framework. Curr. Protoc. Essent. Lab. Tech. **18** (2019)
12. Wang, S., et al.: FAIR implementation profiles for social science. In: Garoufallou, E., et al. (eds.) Metadata and Semantic Research, pp. 284–290. Springer, Cham (2024)
13. Wilkinson, M.D., et al.: The fair guiding principles for scientific data management and stewardship. Sci. Data **3**(1), 1–9 (2016)

A Greek Music Audiovisual Collections Platform: Presentation of the Open Source ReasonableGraph Platform for Music Collections

Pantelis Brattis[1], Emmanouel Garoufallou[2](✉) ⬤, Eugenios Politis[3],
Niki Maria Chatziefstratiou[2], Petros Vouvaris[3], Evangelia Spyrakou[3],
Thalia Adelfopoulou[3], Giorgos Kokkonis[4], Nikos Ordoulidis[4], Giorgos Evangelou[4],
Aimilios Kampouropoulos[5], Asterios Zacharakis[5], Savvas Kazanis[5], Vera Kriezi[6],
Valia Vraka[6], Mirena Mountzia[6], Kostas Maistrelis[1], Simos Leonidakos[1],
Nikos Papazis[1], and Pavlos Siskos[2]

[1] ReasonableGraph (AltSol), Athens, Greece
[2] «MetaDATA LAB», International Hellenic University, Thessaloniki, Greece
mgarou@ihu.gr
[3] University of Macedonia, Thessaloniki, Greece
[4] University of Ioannina, Ioannina, Greece
[5] Aristotle University of Thessaloniki, Thessaloniki, Greece
[6] The Friends of Music Society, Athens, Greece

Abstract. This article presents the platform developed within the framework of the research project "M.EL.O.S.," co-funded by Greece and the European Union through the Greece 2.0 programme and the Recovery and Resilience Fund. The project aims to create a specialized music ontology with innovative features, allowing the automatic extraction and integration of qualitative attributes from musical scores. By relying on the open-source ReasonableGraph (RG) platform, the project builds a comprehensive tool for managing and semantically organizing digital music collections. The theoretical foundations of the platform rest on ontology management, metadata standards, and linked data principles, which facilitate interoperability and ensure open and interconnected datasets. This approach aligns with current trends in digital humanities and cultural heritage management, promoting standardized, accessible, and reusable data in music and beyond.

At the core of the project is the development of a music ontology that addresses the specific needs of music collections, enabling enhanced cataloging, retrieval, and display of musical documents. These documents range from scores and performances to other archival materials like programs, recordings, and concert posters. Through the adaptation of the ReasonableGraph platform, two key products have been developed: the "Local Music Ontology Repository" (TAMO) for managing local collections, and the "Central Music Authority Repository" (KeMKA) for handling centralized, collaborative repositories. These repositories aim to streamline the management of music collections across multiple institutions, offering a scalable solution for the organization and documentation of cultural content.

On the practical side, the platform supports a variety of innovative features. It incorporates tools for searching, linking, retrieving, and enriching semantically

M. Sfakakis et al. (Eds.): MTSR 2024, CCIS 2331, pp. 172–182, 2025.
https://doi.org/10.1007/978-3-031-81974-2_15

annotated information, while also facilitating the use of social networks and crowd-sourcing for the expansion of collections. Computational music analysis further enhances the platform by automatically extracting qualitative features such as melody, harmony, and timbre from musical works. External data sources, such as Wikidata and VIAF, are also integrated into the system, allowing for automatic updates of information related to musical entities. Moreover, the platform supports user-generated extensions, enabling institutions to customize metadata fields according to local requirements without compromising the integrity of the central repository.

The broader impact of the "M.EL.O.S." project lies in its ambition to fill a significant gap in the international market regarding the availability of repositories that support open and linked data. By fostering collaboration among institutions with music collections, the platform sets a new standard for the management of cultural assets and digital music archives. The platform's unique capabilities, combined with the interdisciplinary research conducted, pave the way for the integration of other institutions and the continuous expansion of the collaborative network. Through workshops, training, and international presentations, the project is gaining recognition as a pivotal tool in the fields of musicology and digital cultural heritage management.

Keywords: Crowdsourcing · Music ontology · Metadata · Repositories · Linked data

1 Introduction

The project "M.EL.O.S." [3] is a research project, co-funded by Greece and the European Union, under the Greece 2.0, Recovery and Resilience Fund. It was initiated with the aim of developing a specialized music ontology that will contain innovative features and allow the incorporation of qualitative features automatically extracted from musical scores. This ontology will address the needs of music collections and will be based on open ontology management platforms and relevant international conceptual schemes. The aim of this action is to give international visibility to the proposed music ontology in order to contribute to the international scientific dialogue on music and cultural documentation in general [4].

Another objective is to create products for the collection of cultural content and to make them available to cultural heritage providers. In particular, the project will develop and adapt the open source ReasonableGraph (RG) platform based on the selected music ontology and the specific needs of music collections. The development of the RG platform will offer two final products: One for the needs of managing local music collection repositories, which we call the "Local Music Ontology Repository" (TAMO) and one for the needs of managing collaborative centralized music repositories, which we call the "Centralized Music Authority Repository" (KeMKA). Based on the above, the promotion of the RG platform in the Greek and international market is facilitated as a repository for the management not only of music collections but also as a general repository for the management of cultural assets, in order to fill the gap that exists in the international market regarding the lack of repositories that support and implement open and interconnected data.

In addition to the development of collaborative repositories, the use of social networks and crowdsourcing is being exploited to enrich and promote music collections and the cultural heritage in general. For this reason, the required support functions will be developed on the RG platform, workshops have been and are still being organized to inform and raise awareness among the music community, in order to participate in the creation and qualitative enrichment of the cultural heritage.

The development of tools and methodologies for the search, interconnection, retrieval, presentation and enrichment of semantically annotated information and knowledge contained in the collections. Part of the study will extend beyond the current scientific benchmarking, as the development of metrics for the combined use of metadata and qualitative attributes of music content in the interconnection and presentation/illustration of repository entities will be thoroughly explored. The use of the tools and information will be made available to scholars, ordinary users and third party organizations that want to exploit metadata for research, entertainment and commercial purposes.

2 Collaborative Network: KeMKA – TAMO

2.1 Central Music Archives (KeMKA)

In order to enable the interconnection of data within the RG platform, it was deemed necessary to create the main pillars, the Central Music Repository and the Local Repositories of Music Ontologies, which would serve the collaborative operation of the network. Each project entity has its own TAMO repository in which it can create the set of entities (general and musical) related to its own metadata and documents, and in addition it has a number of other entities in the relevant tabs that can catalogue any other type of archival or bibliographic material that the M.EL.O.S. entities have.

The next step in making the above work was to establish rules that would define their operation. The first rule stipulated that any established entity, for example, Music Work, Music Person, Music Organization, Music Genre, etc. would be created exclusively in the KeMKA. Entities related to the description of the document in question such as (Score, Performance, Program etc.) would be created in the TAMO. In this way, each part of this collaborative network can perform specific procedures.

More specifically, if an entity is created in the KeMKA environment, it can be viewed and interconnected in any TAMO. In the same way, if an entity is created in a TAMO, it is automatically uploaded to the KeMKA, becomes part of the central repository and can be viewed from there and used by the other TAMOs. In order to limit any problems from this interface, it was also defined that any entity created in the KeMKA, allows its editing by all members of the M.EL.O.S. project who have the relevant access rights to the KeMKA. Similarly, any records created in a TAMO can only be edited by the entity that created them. In parallel with the creation of an entity in the TAMOs, it is possible to create an entity in the KeMKA and transfer it to the TAMOs, provided that this entity is used in even one record in the local TAMO.

The mode of operation mentioned above has helped in collaborative cataloguing between project members, in defining a uniform policy and also in reducing the working time since several established entities found in the KeMKA are relevant to all members.

2.2 The Current TAMO Repositories and Project Participants

There are currently three repositories. The TAMO of the University of Macedonia, via the Department of Music Science and Art, the TAMO of the University of Ioannina, via the department of Music Studies - Music Documentation Laboratory and finally, the TAMO of the "The Friends of Music Society" of the largest Music Library of Greece "Lillian Voudouri". Common to all three members of the M.EL.O.S. project was the open source repositories (Dspace and Vsmart) which they used for the registration of their documents, so that the documents of their collections are available in digital form and available for viewing by their users.

TMET contributed to the project with the documentation and digital display of Professor Evgenios Politis' "Greek Archive of Double Bass". In the Dspace of University of Macedonia, the so-called "PSEPHEDA", there are physical and digital documents related to musical works of Greek composers on the double bass in a specialized Dublin Core format. The documents included were scores, programs, posters, photographs, photographs, clippings, recordings, etc. numbering approximately 109 concertos, chamber music and solo works. Dspace created problems in the recordings of the documents since information from other entities was confused, there was no clear separation of musical works from scores and discography, but there were no established terms that would help in indexing the documents and, by extension, in their more direct retrieval by the individual user.

The University of Ioannina, has developed the "Greek Music Archive", which integrates metadata referred to the traditional and urban folk Greek music. They participate in this project with "Vassilis Tsitsanis Collection of Recordings". The collection, located at Vsmart using MARC21, contained a digital archive of music discs containing recordings of Tsitsanis' works, either in their entirety or individually. The items are estimated at 1,267 recordings on CDs and other items (such as photographs of the album covers). The problems encountered were the inability to describe in detail the physical documents in the archive beyond the discs and recordings, as well as an inadequate separation of the musical works from them.

The "Friends of Music Society" contributes to the project through the documentation and digital display of the "Mikis Theodorakis Archive". The content of the collection corresponds to a physical archive with an archival structure of M. Theodorakis. It consists mainly of scores and other archival documents, which are summarized in 40,000 downloads for 330 works. Until recently they used Dspace using specialized Dublin Core. However, the lack of an archival structure and established terms, the lack of separation of musical works from scores and of general documentation from other entities, were major problems.

The Special Account for Research Funds of the Aristotle University of Thessaloniki via the School of Music Studies and the Faculty of Fine Arts. The members of the TMS research team have research experience in computational models of musicological analysis. Their existing research activity, based on a relevant European Research Project, examines the use of augmented ontologies that utilize semantic content and, at the same time, draw on automatically, using symbolic musical representation data, qualitative characteristics of the musical content.

Finally, an important contribution is made by AltSol, which specializes in the development of applications based on ontologies and conceptual models. The company contributes to the project the integrated open source ontology management platform RG, which will be analyzed in detail below.

3 Functions and Capabilities of the RG Platform

3.1 Extensions

In order for data interconnection to be successful not only within the RG platform but also in a wider context, it was necessary to have the possibility to introduce extensions to the system entities. This feature allows TAMOs to add information and metadata to an entity created in KeMKA or another TAMO. Since earlier versions of the RG, metadata from Wikidata[1] could be imported. For example, if we want to import a Person entity into the platform, information such as place and date of birth, geographic coordinates and even photos, if and when they exist, will be automatically transferred to the relevant entity.

As part of the M.EL.O.S implementation, the above mentioned functionality has been extended. More specifically, for entities located in Wikidata, if the unique url of Wikidata is entered in the corresponding field of the platform, then an extension entity (the Wikidata extension) is automatically created in ReasonableGraph. The metadata of this entity is embedded in the view of the main entity providing the end user with the additional information coming from Wikidata (such as birth and death dates). If, respectively, we have entered in the VIAF[2] field the url of the entity in VIAF an extension entity (the VIAF extension) is created on the platform that interfaces with the main one and in it information from VIAF is transferred and displayed to the end user (such as the establishment of the entity in LC, NLG and BnF[3]).

At the same time, in order to satisfy the needs of crowdsourcing and the possibility for each entity participating in the project to create and present different or more refined metadata for the common established entities, the corresponding interoperability was developed in the platform. This was done by enabling the creation of Extension entities, which are directly linked to the established entity but allow us to add information and/or documentation at central or local level, without having to change the metadata of the original entity.

---

[1] Wikidata is a free, collaborative project that was created in 2012 and is a cognitive database of structured data. The resources available on Wikipedia are directly linked to Wikidata.

[2] The Virtual International Authority File is an international file of established terms. It is common project of several international libraries operated by OCLC. The aim is to to link national standard archives. In this file identical entries from different established records are linked together. An entity existing in different established records, acquires in VIAF a unique VIAF number and a unique URI. VIAF does not assign any unique header to the entity but presents the different versions of the headings based on different policies cataloging policies, different languages, different cultural understandings, etc.

[3] National Library of France acronym for Bibliothèque Nationale de France.

3.2 Multiple Levels of Entity Interface

As mentioned earlier, the problem with the preexisting repositories was the inability to interconnect entities. For example, while it was possible to interface a musician with a musical work he created, at the same time the entity of the musical instrument he used could not be added to the musical work. That is, the interface remained at a simple level of a one-to-one interface.

Within the M.EL.O.S. project, this problem has been solved, as in one field it is possible to interface an entity, several descriptive fields, other musical concepts and genres, such as musical instruments, modality and other musicological concepts. At the same time, taxonomies for musical concepts and genres were created through a tree-like display of terms within the ReasonableGraph platform [4].

More specifically, some basic taxonomies were created with respect to the Concept entity, such as Musical Instruments, families and categories of musical instruments, ethnic groups, axioms, activities. While for the Genre entity, the taxonomies of musical genres and structures and trope were created. Each taxonomy consists of its own subdivisions which are interconnected within the whole platform.

In order to achieve the complete interconnection of the musical works, it was deemed necessary to include the corresponding score and recording files under the Musical Work entity, in order to enable the user to view the scores and generally any kind of documentation associated with the work, providing comprehensive information.

There is a "Linked data LC" field where we enter information related to the Library of Congress' established and interlinked Linked data metadata [1, 8, 9]. The field "National Library of Greece" in which we enter information related to the establishment of the entity by the National Library of Greece (NLG). While this field is also included we record information related to the organization's registration in MusicBrainz[4] [6].

3.3 Taxonomies of Musical Concepts and Genres

Another critical functionality that was implemented in the context of the project is the creation of taxonomies for musical concepts and genres (and more generally), so that the members of the collaborative network can easily locate the relevant information through the tree structure of terms provided by ReasonableGraph [2]. The main taxonomies created in the Concept entity are for:

- Musical instruments
- Families and categories of musical instruments
- Musical activities/properties
- Families and families of musical instruments
- Nationalities
- Ethnic groups
- Axioms
- Activities

---

[4] MusicBrainz is an open music encyclopedia that collects music metadata and makes it.available to the public [7].

The Genre entity is where we enter thematic terms related to forms and types that we want to manage as standalone thematic entities in the RG platform. Genre entities are a more specialized type of the more general thematic terms entered in the Concept entity. A Genre term can consist of more than one word.

For resources related to Genre you can visit relatively established archives such as the established subject terms of the National Library of Greece and the corresponding ones of the Library of Congress [5]. Especially for the M.EL.O.S. project and for the needs of recording genres and forms directly related to music, special Genre music types have been created such as:

- Musical genres
- Musical genres
- Trope

3.4 Interface and Display of Musical Works with Scores and Recordings

The way in which musical works are linked to the scores and/or recordings associated with them was of particular interest to the project's research team. The linking of scores and recordings to the project was designed so that under the Musical Work entity users can directly see which scores, recordings and/or documents are linked to the project.

3.5 Platform Filters

The graphical communication interface of the platform is considered user-friendly since the multitude of metadata entered can be both separated and made more specific by using filters. On the home screen of the repository there are filters (see Fig. 1) by subject category that help the user to be as specific as he wishes in his search until he finds what he wants.

3.6 Automatic Musicological Inferences Through Computational Analysis

Each entry in the M.EL.O.S. project collection is a set of metadata that can be extracted through computational analysis to available sound files. This metadata may relate to elements of the musical work, for example tonality, melody extraction, characteristics of the performance in question such as tempo, or performer attributes, following modern vocal isolation techniques, for example pitch range, timbral characteristics, vibrato, etc. For example, in Fig. 1 below, we can see the practical application on what was mentioned above.

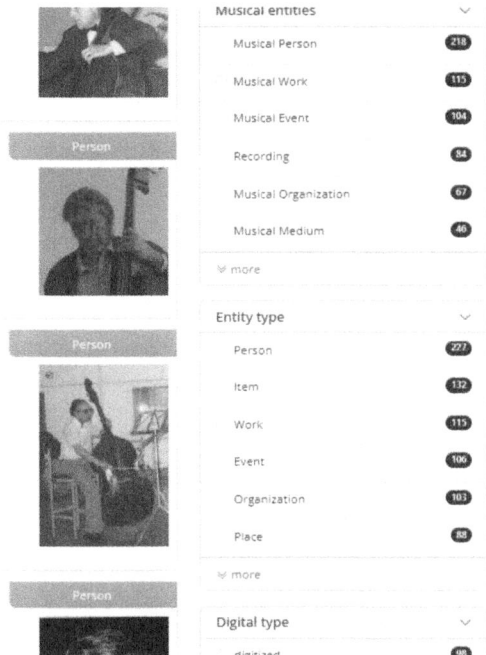

Fig. 1. Platform filters for specific results

The use of the above metadata works in support of the existing recordings, as it highlights features that cannot be extracted otherwise such as vibrato speed and amplitude. In addition, they can link registered works, performances and performers based on sound characteristics. In addition to enabling personalized search according to the extracted features, this feature will also allow for grouping categories that have similar features (Fig. 2).

As a result of the above, users of the ReasonableGraph platform find the system to be highly efficient and user-friendly. In addition to supporting multiple languages, the platform offers useful filters that refine user's searches and improve retrieval results. Recently, workshops have been held to University of Macedonia and the purpose was to inform students and music experts about the platform and also to train them. The feedback has been quite positive, as people using the platform for the first time have been able to enter new records with ease or search some records through search bars and filters.

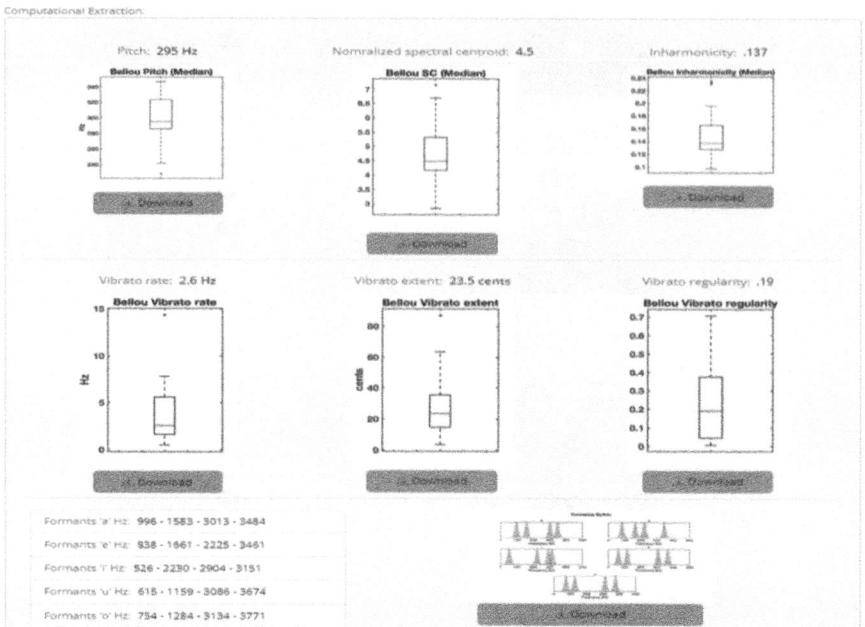

Fig. 2. Display of automatic musicological metadata entry for Sotiria Bellou.

4   Conclusions and Future Directions

The M.EL.O.S. research project has made significant progress in the development of a specialized music ontology and in the adaptation of the RG platform for music collection management. The completion of the development and configuration of the RG platform is a major milestone, with the central KeMKA collaboration system and the three local TAMO systems fully operational. Training in the use of the platform has also been completed, allowing librarians and musicologists to create interlinked music entities in RG for user indexing.

One of the main achievements of the project is the creation of a collaborative network that allows for efficient data interconnection between the central repository and local repositories. This structure facilitates collaborative cataloging, uniform policy definition and reduced work time, as established entities in KeMKA are accessible and useful to all project members. The ability to create extensions to system entities further enhances functionality by allowing information and metadata to be added locally or centrally without modifying the original metadata.

The RG platform has incorporated innovative features that overcome the limitations of pre-existing repositories. The possibility of multiple levels of entity interconnection allows for more complex and comprehensive associations between musical works, performers, instruments and other musicological concepts. The creation of taxonomies for musical concepts and genres offers a structured approach to organizing and retrieving information. In addition, the possibility of automatic musicological inference through computational analysis opens up new avenues for extracting and exploiting metadata from sound files.

The bilingual interface for viewing metadata is an important innovation, making the platform accessible to an international audience. This, combined with the ability to interface with external sources such as Wikidata and VIAF, greatly enhances the usefulness and reach of the system. The platform's filtering features further enhance the user experience, allowing for more targeted and effective searches.

As the project is in full swing, the goal of creating 10,500 music entities is well underway, with the potential for further enrichment of the database. The organization of seminars and presentations at international library and musicology conferences has received positive reviews, indicating the interest and potential impact of the project on the wider scientific community.

M.EL.O.S. aspires to become a model and guide for the development of metadata related to music and music archives in Greece. The new technologies implemented, such as the way the collaborative network in ReasonableGraph is synchronized and operated, the possibilities of extension to entities and the introduction of automated computer-based music inference, provide powerful tools for rapid and correct development of music content.

The successful operation of the collaborative network with common established axes paves the way for the future integration of other institutions with musical cultural resources, even at an international level, into the M.EL.O.S. This could lead to an extensive network of interconnected music data, enhancing collaboration and knowledge sharing between different cultural institutions.

In conclusion, the M.EL.O.S. project is an important step towards the creation of an integrated and interoperable platform for the management of music collections. The continuous development and improvement of the platform, combined with the increasing participation of the scientific community, promises to bring significant developments in the field of digital musicology and cultural heritage management.

References

1. Baker, T., Coyle, K., Petiya, S.: Multi-entity models of resource description in the Semantic Web. Library Hi Tech **32**(4), 562–582 (2014). https://doi.org/10.1108/lht-08-2014-0081
2. Goehr, L.: The imaginary museum of musical works: an essay in the philosophy of music. Oxford University Press, Oxford, UK (1992)
3. M.EL.O.S. (2024). https://melos-project.gr/el
4. IFLA Study Group on the Functional Requirements for Bibliographic Records and International Federation of Library Associations and Institutions. Section on Cataloguing. Standing Committee. (1998). Functional requirements for bibliographic records. Munchen, Germany: K. G. Saur
5. Library of Congress. Encoded Archival Description Official Site (EAD Official Site, Library of Congress) (2015). http://www.loc.gov/ead
6. MusicBrainz. The Open Music Encyclopedia. Musicbrainz.org (n.d.). https://musicbrainz.org/
7. VIAF. Virtual International Authority File. Viaf.org (2024). https://viaf.org/, http://www.springer.com/lncs. Accessed 21 Nov 2016

8. Gaitanou, P., Andreou, I., Sicilia, M.-A., Garoufallou, E.: Linked data for libraries: creating a global knowledge space,a systematic literature review. J. Inf. Sci. **50**(1),204–244 (2024). https://doi.org/10.1177/01655515221084645
9. Alemu, G. , Garoufallou, E.: The future of interlinked, interoperable and scalable metadata. Int. J. Metadata Semant. Ontol. **14**(2), 81–87 (2020). https://doi.org/10.1504/IJMSO.2020.108340

Track on Digital Libraries, Information Retrieval, Big, Linked, Social and Open Data

The Integration of the Pinakes Model to the IFLA Library Reference Model

Ana Carolina Novaes de Mendonça[1,2](✉) ⓘ, Ana Carolina Simionato Arakaki[1,2] ⓘ,
Bruno Costa da Cunha Costa[2,3] ⓘ, Dayane Onaga Ferreira Machado[2] ⓘ,
and Greicy Kely Carla dos Santos[2] ⓘ

[1] Federal University of São Carlos, São Carlos - SP, Brazil
{anamendonca,anaarakaki}@ibict.br
[2] Brazilian Institute of Information in Science and Technology (Ibict), Brasília, Brazil
{brunocosta,dayanemachado,greicysantos}@ibict.br
[3] Federal Institute of Education, Science and Technology of
Rio de Janeiro (IFRJ), Rio de Janeiro, Brazil

Abstract. The Coordination of Bibliographic Services (Cobib/Ibict) has modernized its systems, including the National Collective Catalog of Serial Publications (CCN), in the initiative called Pinakes, with the aim of updating the data generated over decades. This work aims to present the correspondence between the entities of the IFLA Library Reference Model (IFLA LRM) and the classes of the Pinakes domain. From the IFLA LRM diagram, the main entities were identified and defined, mapping them to specific classes of the Pinakes Model, categorized and numbered. The relationships and their cardinalities were established, highlighting the importance of inverse properties for the organization of the data. This mapping provides a robust initial framework for the Pinakes Model, which is essential for the organization and retrieval of bibliographic information. In addition, this work lays a solid foundation for future expansions and refinements of the model, facilitating the development of a comprehensive ontology for the Pinakes catalog.

Keywords: IFLA-LRM · CCN · Pinakes catalog · Ontology

1 Introduction

The main purpose of the National Collective Catalog of Serial Publications (CCN) is to facilitate access to periodicals, both national and international, indicating their location in the main Brazilian libraries. Created in 1954 by the Brazilian Institute of Bibliography and Documentation (IBBD), currently known as the Brazilian Institute of Information in Science and Technology (Ibict), a research unit of the Ministry of Science, Technology and Innovation (MCTI), the CCN began as a catalog in cards.

Initially, catalog information was accessed locally, by phone or mail. In 1968, the catalog was automated, and between 1970 and 1978, the automated system allowed the printed dissemination of the CCN by large areas of knowledge. Due to the increase in new titles and the interconnection between areas, in 1978, Ibict began to disseminate the

M. Sfakakis et al. (Eds.): MTSR 2024, CCIS 2331, pp. 185–196, 2025.
https://doi.org/10.1007/978-3-031-81974-2_16

CCN on microfiche. In 1983, to improve the quality of CCN's services, Ibict developed the Integrated System of Serial Publications (SIPS), compatible with the International Serials Data System (ISDS), optimizing the processing and exchange of data through magnetic tapes. In July 1989, a comparative study was carried out to adapt the catalog to the Collective Catalog of Serial Publications for Latin America and the Caribbean (CAPSALC) and to meet the CCN network. In 1994, access to the CCN was made available online via Telnet, and in 1997, an integrated system in Oracle was developed, allowing access via the web from 1998. Over the years, the CCN has evolved and consolidated itself as one of the main catalogs in Brazil, bringing together thousands of technical and scientific bibliographic records from various Brazilian institutions.

The systems of the Coordination of Bibliographic Services (Cobib/Ibict) have been undergoing a restructuring and modernization of their databases and catalogs, an initiative called Pinakes[1], which aims to update the data accumulated over decades. In ancient times, "Pinakes" referred to a catalog created by Callimachus, a Greek poet and librarian, for the Library of Alexandria. This catalog, known as "Pinakes," aimed to list all the important works in the library. Drawing inspiration from Callimachus, the Pinakes Project seeks to restructure the traditional bibliographic services offered by Ibict, including the National Collective Catalog of Serials (CCN), Bibliodata, and the Bibliographic Communication Program (Comut).

Thus, the objective of this work is to present the clear and functional correspondence between the entities of the IFLA Library Reference Model (IFLA LRM) and the classes of the Pinakes domain.

2 Initial Considerations

2.1 Methodology

The research adopted an exploratory and descriptive approach to integrate the conceptual models IFLA LRM and the Pinakes Model within the context of the National Collective Catalog of Serial Publications (CCN). Initially, a comprehensive literature survey was conducted to gather relevant information on both IFLA LRM and the Pinakes Model. This included an in-depth analysis of existing studies, such as the seminal report by Riva, Bœuf, and Žumer (2017), with the goal of thoroughly understanding the definitions, hierarchies, and roles of entities within the IFLA LRM framework and how they might relate to the bibliographic domain of the CCN. Following the theoretical groundwork, the research progressed to systematically identify the IFLA LRM entities most pertinent to the CCN bibliographic domain. This phase involved critical analysis to ensure the selection of the most relevant entities, thereby aligning theoretical models with the practical needs of the CCN.

Once the pertinent IFLA LRM entities were identified, a detailed mapping process commenced, where each entity was carefully aligned with the corresponding class within the Pinakes Model. The Pinakes Model classes were categorized, numbered, and documented to facilitate easy reference, ensuring a clear and functional correspondence. This

---

[1] https://pinakes.tcti.ibict.br/sobre-O-pinakes/.

mapping required a deep understanding of both models and involved extensive cross-referencing to maintain accuracy. To visually represent and organize the data, Unified Modeling Language (UML) class diagrams were employed. These diagrams detailed the attributes, relationships, and inverse properties of the mapped entities, playing a crucial role in making the system more understandable and accessible, particularly in fostering communication between developers, librarians, and other stakeholders involved in the project.

Throughout the process, qualitative analysis ensured the accuracy and consistency of the mapping, highlighting significant correspondences between IFLA LRM entities and Pinakes Model classes, and identifying any differences in definitions or hierarchies. This analysis refined the integration process, ensuring that the final model was both comprehensive and aligned with the specific context of the CCN. The iterative refinement of the model, incorporating feedback from domain experts and stakeholders, ensured that the final product not only adhered to theoretical frameworks but also met the practical needs of the CCN. This structured approach enabled a thorough examination and integration of the IFLA LRM and Pinakes Model, ultimately contributing to a more robust and effective bibliographic framework for the CCN.

2.2 Theorical Framework

The conceptual structure of the CCN system domain model was developed based on the definition of entities and attributes from the Library Reference Model (LRM), created by the International Federation of Library Associations and Institutions (IFLA). This conceptual framework is based on modeling theories, with the Entity-Relationship Model (MER) being one of the main approaches.

The Entity-Relationship Model (MER), proposed by Peter Pin-Shan Chen in 1976, is a method for describing entities, attributes, and relationships, representing the abstract structure of a database with a focus on aspects of the data. Chen defined the entity as an identifiable "thing", which can be physical or logical, and relationships as associations between these entities. Cardinality, an essential element of MER, indicates the minimum and maximum number of relationships between the entities' instances, which can be one-to-many (1), many-to-many (M), or one-to-one (1:1).

Entity-Relationship (DER) diagrams visually represent entities, relationships, and attributes, using rectangles for entities, rhombuses for relationships, and ellipses for attributes, with cardinality expressed in the lines that connect relationships to entities. This representation facilitates the construction of conceptual models of relational databases (Chen 1976; Elmasri; Weeldreyer; Hevner 1985; Song; Froehlich 1994; Thalheim 1992).

Another essential method is the Unified Modeling Language (UML), developed in the 90s, widely used in information systems engineering to graphically represent concepts and relationships of a system's domain. UML covers several levels of abstraction, including data, software, and processes, and provides a common and standardized language to describe structures and behaviors, facilitating communication and understanding of requirements, resulting in a more efficient development aligned with the expectations of end users.

Among UML diagrams, Class Diagram is widely used in domain modeling, allowing the visualization of classes, properties, and relationships, facilitating communication between developers and stakeholders. In UML, classes are represented by rectangles with the name at the top and the attributes below, and relationships are indicated by lines with cardinality at the ends, similar to MER DERs, but with more detail and flexibility. For example, in a library, you can model classes such as "Book," "Publisher," "Employee," "User," and "Loaner" with their specific attributes and relationships. In addition to the Class Diagram, UML includes other diagrams, such as Use Case, Activity, and Sequence, used at different stages of development to capture aspects and behaviors of the system.

While MER and DER focus on the representation of data and its relationships in databases, UML offers a broader approach to information systems modeling. The combined use of these tools can provide a deeper and more detailed understanding of the domains to be modeled, resulting in more robust and well-structured information systems.

Based on UML, the CCN model is composed of 27 classes. The main concepts are Library, Serial Publishing and Collection. A library, whether central or sectoral, is located at one address and can have several contacts. It can be affiliated to an institution of a public, private administrative nature, etc. (for example: Federal University of Rio de Janeiro) or to a unit (for example: Institute of Mathematics). A unit can have subunits (e.g.: Department of Computer Science).

A serial publication has one or more ISSN codes associated with physical media. Your title can have several complements and it is available in one or several languages, although it is linked to only one country. The model can be made available on the Web by various homepages, and the publication is qualified by controlled subjects, free terms, notes, indexers and areas of knowledge. A serial publication can be related to other publications. It must have at least one publication, made by one and at most one publisher, in one or more cities (linked to a state and this to a region). A library has one or more collections of a serial publication. A collection is a record of the physical availability of the item in question.

The IFLA Library Reference Model (LRM) is a conceptual model for bibliographic resource information, the result of the harmonization and expansion of the IFLA Functional Requirements (FR) family. Started in 1998, this family includes the conceptual models: Functional Requirements for Bibliographic Record (FRBR) for bibliographic records, Functional Requirements for Authority Data (FRAD) for authority records, and Functional Requirements for Subject Authority Data (FRSAD) for subject records. Although developed with different scopes and by different teams, these three models share similar solutions. The guidelines for the creation of the LRM were implemented in a consistent and standardized way, consolidating the ontological commitments outlined in the first FR.

According to Riva, Le Bœuf and Žumer (2017), LRM is a conceptual reference that provides a framework for the analysis of non-administrative metadata related to library resources. Being a high-level conceptual model, it serves as a guide for the formulation of cataloging rules and implementation of bibliographic systems. LRM represents a significant advance for the communication of catalogs with the Web and, especially, with modern users, who demand increasingly faster responses. This initiative also contributes to the direction of study and practice in Cataloguing and Semantic Technologies, integrating guidelines that previously seemed unattainable (Arakaki 2020; Riva; Le Bœuf; Žumer 2017).

Although the formalization of the model is recent, there are already studies discussing the mapping of the entities presented with other metadata standards, as highlighted in the literature (Bianchini 2022; Escolano Rodríguez et al. 2019; Oliveira et al. 2023; Riva; Žumer 2017; Žumer 2018).

The IFLA LRM is essential for the development of taxonomies and ontologies in several specific domains or subareas. However, due to the generic nature of the LRM, there are limitations to the definition of specialized informational resources, such as serial publications. As described by Riva, Le Bœuf, and Žumer (2017), serial publications are complex constructions that combine whole/part relations and aggregation relations. According to the authors, these relationships are difficult to model, "[…] for it is not limited to a description of the past but should also allow end users to make assumptions about the future behavior of the serial work, at least soon." (Riva, Le Bœuf and Žumer 2017, p. 98). Thus, for a better definition of classes and to establish more coherent connections to the domain, it will be necessary to investigate models specialized in this type of informational resource.

The hierarchy of the entities is presented in the table below (Table 1).

Table 1. Hierarchy of the entities IFLA LRM

Top level	Second level	Third level
LRM-E1 Res	–	–
–	LRM-E2 Work	–
–	LRM-E3 Expression	–
–	LRM-E4 Manifestation	–
–	LRM-E5 Item	–
–	LRM-E6 Agent	–
–	–	LRM-E7 Person
–	–	LRM-E8 Collective Agent
–	LRM-E9 Nomen	–
–	LRM-E10 Place	–
–	LRM-E11 Time-span	–

The superclass Res is specialized by the classes Work, Expression, Manifestation, Item, Agent, Nomen, Place, and Time Span. The classes Person and Corporate Body specialize the Agent class. Thus, the attributes and associations of the Res superclass are inherited by the subclasses, just as the subclasses Person and Corporate Body inherit from the Agent superclass. The model defines entities as abstract classes of conceptual objects, called individuals or instances, characterized by specific attributes. The model is hierarchically structured, allowing the creation of subclasses and subproperties that inherit higher-level characteristics. (Riva, Le Bœuf & Žumer 2017). This approach unifies different views of data, standing out for its integration capability.

3 Results

In the process of formalizing a domain, entities are defined conceptually, that is, their meaning is made explicit according to the context. At this stage, the need arises to integrate ontology with already consolidated models and previously established conceptualizations. In this way, the definitions of entities, attributes and relationships are standardized from a common vocabulary, enabling the construction of a solid and understandable foundation, which avoids ambiguities and misinterpretations. Noy and McGuinness (2001) discuss the essential steps for the construction of ontologies, highlighting reuse as one of the main ones. They suggest extending and refining concepts coming from existing sources to create a common conceptual framework that allows for data interoperability. In addition, the reuse of a consolidated model that is widely accepted by the community allows you to save time and effort.

The integration of the models was established from the correlation of the terms defined in the IFLA LRM with the existing terms in the CCN model. It is worth noting that some domain classes were not associated with the LRM entities, as they do not fall within the defined scope. These classes will be analyzed in the future and, if necessary, will be mapped according to specialized ontologies. The classes in question are: Library Type, Contact, Administrative Nature, Homepage, Referrer, Free Term and Printed Publication. To adapt to the reality of the Pinakes Model, the prefix MP refers to the Pinakes Model and the letter C indicates classes, followed by sequential numbering. The definitions of the LRM are generic and applicable to entities in the bibliographic context. In the Pinakes Model, several classes were mapped in relation to the LRM, such as Serial Publication (MP-C2), Related Publication (MP-C3), Language (MP-C4), Physical Medium (MP-C5), Collection (MP-C6), Publisher (MP-C7), among others. Serial Publication and Related Publication were associated with the Work entity (LRM-E2), representing the intellectual content of journals. Language was associated with the Expression entity (LRM-E3) because it is the language of the publications.

In Table 2, the first column presents the entities from the IFLA LRM, while the second shows the Pinakes domain classes related to these entities. The prefix MP refers to the Pinakes Model, and the letter C indicates classes, followed by sequential numbering. The third column details the hierarchy of the entities, with Res at the top level and the others in the subsequent levels. The fourth column provides examples of real entities from the CCN system, and the fifth contains the definitions of the LRM entities associated with the domain model.

Table 2. Extension of the LRM model to the Pinakes Model (MP)

Stage	Sub-stage	Hierarchy	CCN Examples	LRM Definition
LRM-E1: RES	–	Higher level	Res is inherent in the MP-C2, MP-C3, […]	Any entity in the universe of discourse
LRM-E2: Work	MP-C2: Serial Publishing	Second level	{Ciência da Informação} [quarterly serial publication]	The intellectual or artistic content of a specific creation
LRM-E2: Work	MP-C3: Related Publishing	Second level	{Bibliografia Brasileira de Ciência da Informação is a continuation of Bibliografia Brasileira} [Related Publications]	The intellectual or artistic content of a specific creation
LRM-E3: Expression	MP-C4: Language	Second level	{Portuguese} [primary language of serial publication]	A specific combination of signals that convey intellectual or artistic content
LRM-E4: Manifestation	MP-C5: Physical Medium	Second level	{Printed} [physical medium]	A set of all supports that supposedly share the same characteristics of intellectual or artistic content and aspects of physical form. This set is defined by the content
LRM-E5: Item	MP-C6: Collection	Second level	EMBRAPA/CPAF-AC/BT (AC) 1973 2 (1); 1974 3 (2); 1977–79 6-8; 1981–85	One or more objects carrying signs intended to convey intellectual or artistic content

(continued)

Table 2. (*continued*)

Stage	Sub-stage	Hierarchy	CCN Examples	LRM Definition
LRM-E6: Agent	MP-C7: Publisher	Second level	{Brazilian Institute of Information in Science and Technology} [Publisher of the serial publication: Ciência da Informação]	An entity capable of deliberate actions, of assigning rights and of being held accountable for its actions
LRM-E8: Collective Agent	MP-C8: Library	Third level	{Lydia de Queiroz Sambaquy} [Library of the Brazilian Institute of Science and Technology]	A meeting or organization of people with a specific name and capable of acting as a unit
LRM-E8: Collective Agent	MP-C9: Unit	Third level	Brazilian Institute of Science and Technology} [Research Unit of the Ministry of Science, Technology and Innovation]	A meeting or organization of people with a specific name and capable of acting as a unit
LRM-E8: Collective Agent	MP-C10: Institution	Third level	{Brazilian Institute of Information in Science and Technology (IBICT)} [Name of research organization]	A meeting or organization of people with a specific name and capable of acting as a unit
LRM-E9: Nomen	MP-C11: ISSN	Second level	{0100-1965} [ISSN printed from the serial publication: Information Science]	An association between an entity and a designation that refers to it
LRM-E9: Nomen	MP-C12: Complement Title	Second level	{Inf. Science} [Abbreviated title of: Information Science]	An association between an entity and a designation that refers to it
LRM-E9: Nomen	MP-C13: Controlled Subject	Second level	{Distance learning} [Distance learning USE Distance learning—Brazilian Thesaurus of Information Science]	An association between an entity and a designation that refers to it

(*continued*)

Table 2. (*continued*)

Stage	Sub-stage	Hierarchy	CCN Examples	LRM Definition
LRM-E9: Nomen	MP-C14: Knowledge Area	Second level	{Information Retrieval Techniques} [Information Science Area]	An association between an entity and a designation that refers to it
LRM-E9: Nomen	MP-C15: Knowledge Area Table	Second level	{Table of CNPq areas of knowledge} [Penalty area; Area; Sub-area; specialty]	An association between an entity and a designation that refers to it
LRM-E10: Location	MP-C16: Country	Second level	{Brazil} [Country or geographic territory where the Serial Publication was published]	A determined span of space
LRM-E10: Location	MP-C17: Federative Unit	Second level	{Federal District} [Federative Unit where the Lydia de Queiroz Sambaquy Library is located]	A determined span of space
LRM-E10: Location	MP-C18: Region	Second level	{Midwest} [Regional division where the Lydia de Queiroz Sambaquy Library is located]	A determined span of space
LRM-E10: Location	MP-C19: City	Second level	{Brasilia} [City where the Lydia de Queiroz Sambaquy Library is located]	A determined span of space
LRM-E10: Location	MP-C20: Address	Second level	{Sector of Southern Autarchies (SAUS). Quadra 05, lote 06, bloco H 5° andar} [address]	A determined span of space

Physical Medium was associated with the Manifestation entity (LRM-E4), indicating the type of support (physical or digital). The Collection was linked to the Item entity (LRM-E5), representing libraries or institutions with sets of informational resources. Publisher was associated with the entity Agent (LRM-E6), being responsible for informational resources and copyrights. Library, Unit and Institution were associated with Collective Agents (LRM-E8), organizing people with organizational characteristics described by Riva, Le Bœuf and Žumer (2017).

ISSN, Complementary Title, Controlled Subject, Area of Knowledge and Area of Knowledge Table were associated with the Nomen entity (LRM-E9). The ISSN uniquely identifies serial publications. Complementary Title, Controlled Subject and other classes organize terms representative of the entities. Country, Federative Unit, Region, City, and

Address were associated with the Place entity (LRM-E10), representing specific space extensions.

Riva, Le Bœuf and Žumer (2017) highlight that relationships in IFLA LRM are properties that link entity instances, essential in conceptual modeling for organization and information retrieval. The "Time Range" entity has not been mapped due to a lack of proper matching, but future adjustments will be made as the project evolves.

The Fig. 1 is the diagram of the relationships that can exists in the LRM.

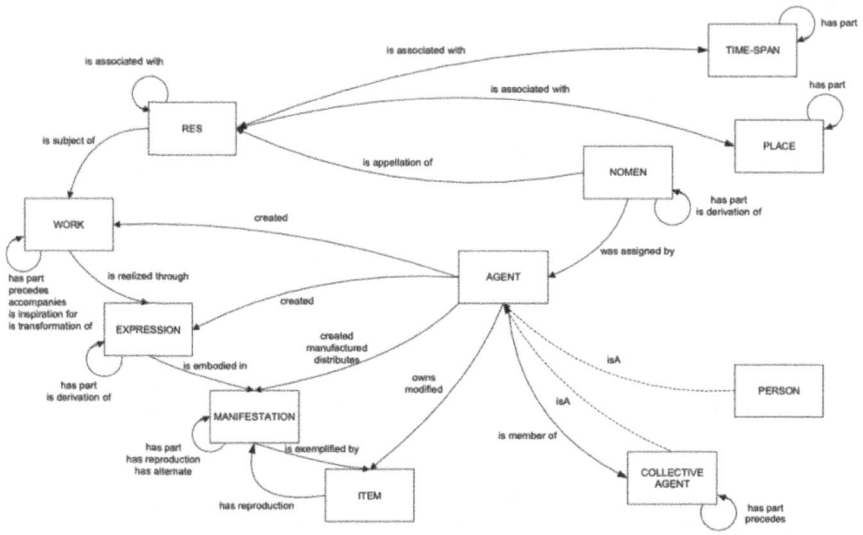

Fig. 1. LRM Relationships

The relationships between the entities in the Pinakes Model, as mapped from the IFLA LRM relationships, which are LRM-R1 to LRM-R36, not all of which were used. These relationships are crucial for defining how entities interact within the framework. As illustrated in Fig. 1 some of the relationships are "is associated with," "has reproduction," "isA," "has part," "is derivation of," "was assigned by", "is appellation of" and "is transformation of" serve to describe both hierarchical and associative connections between entities.

In addition, there are inverse relationships, following the explanation of Riva, Le Bœuf and Žumer (2017, p. 64) about the notation "i" for reciprocal relationships. For example, in the LRM-E1 domain, the Res entity is associated through the LRM-R1 relationship, which has the property "has association with" and its inverse "is associated with", with cardinality M to M. In the LRM-E2: Work domain, the Serial Publication class is associated by the LRM-R2 relationship ("is accomplished through"), with inverse "accomplishes" and cardinality 1 to M, linking works to their expressions.

The class Physical Medium, in the domain LRM-E4: Manifestation, is linked by the relationship LRM-R4 ("is exemplified by"), with inverse "exemplifies" and cardinality 1 for M, relating manifestations to physical items. In the LRM-E5: Expression domain, the Collection class is bound by the LRM-R10 relationship ("is owned by"), with inverse "owns of" and M to M cardinality, binding items to their owners (LRM-E6: Agent).

Library, Unit and Institution, in the LRM-E8 domain: Collective Agent, are associated by the LRM-R31i relationship ("is part of"), with inverse "owns part" and cardinality M to M. On the other hand, the ISSN class, in the LRM-E9 domain: Nomen, is linked by the LRM-R14i relationship ("was assigned by"), with inverse "assigned" and cardinality M to 1, linking names to agents that assigned them.

Classes such as Complementary Title and Controlled Subject in the LRM-E9 domain: Nomen, have the relationship LRM-R15 ("is equivalent to"), with inverse also "is equivalent to" and cardinality M to M, joining equivalent nouns. Country, Federative Unit, Region, City, and Address, in the LRM-E10: Place domain, are connected by the LRM-R33i relationship ("is associated with"), with the inverse "has association with" and M to M cardinality, linking entities to geographic locations.

According to Riva, Le Bœuf and Žumer (2017, p. 60), "The relationships between works, expressions, manifestations and items are considered the structural core of the model." The relationships in IFLA LRM are abstract and generic, allowing for adaptations. Therefore, the Pinakes Model, in its initial phase, aims to establish fundamentals and define an initial implementation strategy, with future refinements to optimize its effectiveness and coherence. This adaptability is particularly valuable as the model evolves, providing a flexible yet structured approach to managing the complex relationships inherent in bibliographic data.

4   Considerations and Future Work

This work, carried out within the scope of the Pinakes/CCN project, is essential for the next steps in the development of a conceptual model that represents the domain of CCN. It will serve as the basis for creating a specific ontology for the catalog. This conceptual basis is crucial not only for the CCN, but also for the future reach of the Pinakes Catalogue, including Bibliodata and Comut.

The complexity involved in establishing relationships between serial publications requires continuous adjustments. The integration of entities from PRESSoo presents itself as a viable solution, providing more detailed and appropriate relationships for these resources. This integration will allow for a more robust and accurate representation, strengthening the structure of the Pinakes Model.

The mapping of the entities of the Pinakes Model with PRESSoo, as well as the detailed analysis of the definitions and hierarchies of the entities, are fundamental steps to ensure integrity, consistency and efficiency in the organization and retrieval of bibliographic information. The modeling of classes in UML complements this process, offering a clear and structured visualization of relationships and attributes, essential for the development of an expandable and comprehensive ontology (Fettke & Loos 2003).

Mapping is not just a direct correspondence of entities, but involves a deep understanding of the characteristics and functions of each entity within the context of the system. This detailed process allows you to identify gaps and specific needs, which are then addressed through accurate modeling and the integration of new concepts as needed. In addition, continuous mapping and periodic review ensure that the model evolves along with user needs and technological innovations.

Thus, this work not only lays a solid foundation for the continued development of the Pinakes Model, but also paves the way for a future ontology that can encompass the entire universe of the Pinakes Catalog. In the future, it is hoped that integration with PRESSoo and detailed modeling will ensure that the system can evolve coherently and efficiently, meeting current and future bibliographic information management needs. With these advances, it is hoped that Pinakes will be better equipped to serve as a comprehensive and effective tool for libraries and other information institutions, promoting easier and more organized access to knowledge.

Acknowledgments. Acknowledgements of support from the Brazilian Institute of Information in Science and Technology (Ibict).

References

Arakaki, A.C.S.: O Modelo IFLA library reference model e o linked data. Informação Informação **25**(3), 163–186 (2020). https://doi.org/10.5433/1981-8920.2020v25n3p163

Bianchini, C.: The entities of the IFLA-LRM, RiC-CM and CIDOC-CRM models in the semantic web. JLIS.it **13**(3), 63–75 (2022)

Chen, P.P.-S.: The entity-relationship model: toward a unified view of data. ACM Trans. Database Syst. **1**(1), 9–36 (1976)

Elmasri, R., Weeldreyer, J., Hevner, A.: The category concept: An extension to the entity-relationship model. Data Knowl. Eng. **1**(1), 75–116 (1985)

Escolano Rodríguez, E., et al.: Mapping from ISBD to IFLA LRM (2019)

Fettke, P., Loos, P.: Ontological evaluation of reference models using the Bunge-Wand-Weber model. In: AMCIS 2003 Proceedings, pp. 384 (2003)

Instituto Brasileiro de Informação em Ciência e Tecnologia.: Catálogo Coletivo Nacional de Publicações Seriadas (CCN). In: Catálogo Coletivo Nacional de Publicações Seriadas (2024). https://novo.ccn.ibict.br/

Instituto Brasileiro de Informação em Ciência e Tecnologia. Sobre o Pinakes. https://pinakes.tcti.ibict.br/sobre-o-pinakes/

Noy, N.F., McGuinness, D.L.: Ontology development 101: a guide to creating your first ontology. Knowl. Syst. Lab. Stanford **32**, 1–25 (2001). https://doi.org/10.48550/arxiv.243772462

Oliveira, R.H.A., Gil, L.C.C., Arakaki, A.C.S., Castro, F.F.: Analysis and correspondence between the entities of the Europeana Data Model, IFLA LRM, and Bibframe conceptual models. Encontros Bibli **28**, e92822 (2023)

Riva, P., Le Bœuf, P., Žumer, M.: IFLA library reference model: a conceptual model for bibliographic information. Netherlands: [s.n.] (2017). https://www.ifla.org/files/assets/cataloguing/frbr-lrm/ifla-lrm-august-2017_rev201712.pdf

Riva, P., Žumer, M.: FRBRoo, the IFLA library reference model, and now LRMoo: a circle of development (2017)

Song, I.-Y., Froehlich, K.: Entity-relationship modeling. IEEE Potentials **13**(5), 29–34 (1994)

Thalheim, B.: Fundamentals of cardinality constraints. In: International Conference on Conceptual Modeling, pp. 7–23. Springer (1992)

Žumer, M.: IFLA library reference model (IFLA LRM)—Harmonisation of the FRBR family. KO Knowl. Organ. **45**(4), 310–318 (2018)

The Convergence of Open Data, Linked Data, Ontologies, and Large Language Models: Enabling Next-Generation Knowledge Systems

Andrea Cigliano[1]([✉])(iD) and Francesca Fallucchi[1,2]([✉])(iD)

[1] Guglielmo Marconi University, Department of Engineering Science,
00193 Rome, Italy
`{a.cigliano,f.fallucchi}@unimarconi.it`
[2] Leibniz Institute for Educational Media, Georg Eckert Institute,
38118 Brunswick, Germany

Abstract. This paper explores the convergence of Open Data initiatives, Linked Data technologies, ontological knowledge representation, and Large Language Models (LLMs) in generative Artificial Intelligence (AI). It examines how these complementary approaches can be integrated to create more powerful, flexible, and context-aware knowledge systems. The paper provides an overview of the open data landscape, the Semantic Web and Linked Data vision, ontologies and knowledge organization systems, and recent advances in LLMs. It then discusses how these technologies can be synergistically combined to enable next-generation knowledge systems that leverage both structured knowledge and natural language understanding. Potential applications in areas such as scientific research, government transparency, and intelligent information retrieval are discussed. The paper also addresses key challenges including scalability, data quality, ethical considerations, and the need for explainable AI. A strategic roadmap for realizing this integration is proposed, emphasizing collaboration between academia, industry, and government. While significant technical and ethical challenges remain, the convergence of these technologies has the potential to fundamentally transform how we interact with and derive insights from information, enabling more intelligent and context-aware knowledge systems to address complex real-world problems.

Keyword: Open Data, Linked Open Data, Artificial Intelligence, Generative Artificial Intelligence, Large Language Model, LLM, Ontologies, SKOS

1 Introduction

The open data movement has its roots in the principles of transparency, accountability, and collaborative innovation. It emerged as a response to the increasing

M. Sfakakis et al. (Eds.): MTSR 2024, CCIS 2331, pp. 197–213, 2025.
https://doi.org/10.1007/978-3-031-81974-2_17

digitization of information and the growing recognition of data as a valuable public resource. The concept of Open Data can be traced back to the 1950s and 1960s, with early initiatives in scientific data sharing, particularly in fields such as geophysics and astronomy. However, the modern open data movement gained significant momentum in the early 2000s, driven by advancements in internet technologies and a growing demand for government transparency [1]. There were the main open data key milestone:

- 2003: The Berlin Declaration on Open Access to Knowledge in the Sciences and Humanities [2]
- 2007: The Sebastopol Meeting, which established eight principles of open government data [3]
- 2009: Launch of Data.gov in the United States, one of the first national open data portals [4]
- 2013: G8 Open Data Charter, committing major economies to open data principles [5]

Open data is typically characterized by the following principles [6]:

- Accessibility: Data should be available as a whole, preferably downloadable over the internet
- Machine-readability: Data should be in formats that can be easily processed by computers
- Described: Open Data are described fully so that consumers of the data have sufficient information to understand their strengths, weaknesses, analytical limitations, security requirements, as well as how to process them. This involves the use of robust, granular metadata (i.e., fields or elements that describe data), thorough documentation of data elements, data dictionaries, and, if applicable, additional descriptions of the purpose of the collection, the population of interest, the characteristics of the sample, and the method of data collection
- Free of charge: There should be no cost barrier to accessing the data;
- Reusable: Data should be provided under terms that permit reuse and redistribution;
- Public: All public data should be made available within the bounds of privacy and security;
- Managed Post-Release: A point of contact must be designated to assist with data use and to respond to complaints about adherence to these open data requirements.

The open data movement has had significant impact across various sectors [7]:

- Government: Enhancing transparency, citizen engagement, and public service delivery;
- Science: Accelerating research through data sharing and collaborative analysis;
- Business: Enabling new products and services based on public data;

– Civil Society: Empowering Non-Governmental Organizations (NGOs) and activists with data for advocacy and decision-making.

From a different point of view than the evolution of Open Data, the evolution of Large Language Models (LLMs) is a fascinating journey that spans several decades of research and development in Natural Language Processing (NLP) and Artificial Intelligence (AI) [8]. This field has its roots in the early days of computational linguistics, which began in the 1950s and 1960s. During this time, researchers were just beginning to explore how computers could be used to process and understand human language. As we moved into the 1970s and 1980s, the focus shifted towards rule-based systems and expert systems. These approaches relied heavily on hand-crafted rules and knowledge bases, attempting to encode human expertise into computer programs. While these systems showed promise in certain narrow domains, they struggled with the complexity and ambiguity inherent in natural language. The 1990s and early 2000s saw a significant shift towards statistical methods in NLP. This approach, leveraging large corpora of text and probabilistic models, began to show more robust performance across a wider range of language tasks. However, it wasn't until the resurgence of neural networks in the broader field of machine learning that we started to see truly transformative advances in NLP. A key moment in this resurgence was the introduction of *word embeddings*, with models like *Word2Vec* and *GloVe* in the early 2010s. These models could represent words as dense vectors in a continuous space, capturing semantic relationships in a way that previous methods couldn't. This was followed by the successful application of Recurrent Neural Networks (RNNs) and Long Short-Term Memory (LSTM) networks to sequence modeling tasks, which are crucial in language processing. The next major breakthrough came with the introduction of *attention mechanisms* [9], culminating in the Transformer architecture in 2017. This architecture, which relies entirely on self-attention, proved to be a game-changer. It allowed for more efficient processing of long-range dependencies in text and opened the door to much larger and more powerful language models. The concept of pre-training LLMs on vast amounts of text data, followed by fine-tuning on specific tasks, began to take hold around this time. Models like BERT, GPT, and T5 demonstrated unprecedented performance across a wide range of NLP tasks. These models grew rapidly in size and capability, with GPT-3 in 2020 showcasing remarkable few-shot learning abilities. As these models have grown, so too have the challenges and ethical considerations surrounding them. Issues of bias, fairness, and the environmental impact of training such large models have come to the forefront of discussions in the AI community. There are also concerns about the potential misuse of these powerful language models, such as generating convincing misinformation or deepfake text. Recent developments have seen a push towards more efficient architectures, such as sparse models and Mixture Of Experts (MoE) approaches. There's also been growing interest in multimodal models that can work with both text and images, as well as models that can follow instructions and perform tasks with minimal additional training. Looking to the future, researchers are exploring ways to make these models more reliable, interpretable, and aligned with human values. There's also ongoing work on integrating external knowledge sources and improving the models' ability to reason and understand context. The field of LLMs continues to evolve at a rapid pace, with new breakthroughs and applications emerging regularly. As these models become more sophisticated and integrated into various aspects of our digital lives, they promise to revolutionize how we interact with information and technology. However, their development also raises important questions about the nature of language, intelligence, and the role of AI in society, ensuring that this will remain an active and critical area of research and debate for years to come.

2   The Semantic Web and Linked Data Vision

The Semantic Web, a term coined by Tim Berners-Lee in 2001, represents an evolution of the World Wide Web where information is given well-defined meaning, enabling computers and people to work in better cooperation [10]. This vision extends beyond mere document retrieval to creating a web of data that can be processed directly and indirectly by machines. At the core of the Semantic Web is the concept of Linked Data, which provides a set of best practices for publishing and connecting structured data on the Web. The primary goals of Linked Data are to: 1. Use URIs (Uniform Resource Identifiers) as names for things: This ensures that each entity or concept has a unique, web-accessible identifier;// 2. Use HTTP URIs: This allows people to look up those names and access more information about the identified entities;// 3. Provide useful information using standard formats (like RDF) when someone looks up a URI: This ensures that the data is in a machine-readable format;// 4. Include links to other URIs: This enables the discovery of related information, creating a web of interconnected data.// The Linked Data paradigm aims to transform the Web from a collection of documents into a global, distributed database.

Significant initiatives have emerged to realize this vision, such as the Linking Open Data project, which aims to create a web of data by identifying existing datasets, converting them to RDF, and publishing them according to Linked Data principles. Notable examples include DBpedia (a structured version of Wikipedia) and the Life Sciences Linked Open Data cloud. The Semantic Web and Linked Data vision has implications across various domains, including:

– Scientific research: Enabling more efficient data sharing and integration across disciplines;
– E-commerce: Facilitating product discovery and comparison;
– Government transparency: Making public data more accessible and interconnected;
– Cultural heritage: Linking and preserving information about artifacts and historical events. Despite the potential, challenges remain in widespread adoption, including the complexity of implementation, the need for data quality standards, and scalability issues. However, as tools and best practices evolve, the Semantic Web and Linked Data continue to play a crucial role in shaping the future of information management and knowledge discovery on the Web.

2.1 Ontologies: Formal Representations of Knowledge Domains

Ontologies serve as formal, explicit specifications of shared conceptualizations within specific domains. They provide a structured way to represent entities, their properties, and the relationships between them. Key aspects of ontologies include:

a) Classes and hierarchies: Ontologies define classes of objects and their hierarchical relationships, allowing for the representation of complex domain structures;
b) Properties and relationships: They specify attributes of objects and the various types of relationships that can exist between entities;
c) Axioms and rules: Ontologies can include logical statements and rules that govern the behavior and interactions of entities within the domain;
d) Reasoning capabilities: The formal structure of ontologies enables automated reasoning, allowing for the inference of new knowledge from existing data.

2.2 Integration of Ontologies and SKOS in Knowledge Ecosystems

Ontologies and the Simple Knowledge Organization System (SKOS) play crucial roles in structuring and organizing knowledge in the digital realm. These frameworks provide the foundation for creating semantic relationships and standardized vocabularies, essential for effective information retrieval and interoperability across diverse data sources. The combination of ontologies and SKOS can create powerful knowledge organization systems:

a) Complementary strengths: Ontologies provide rich, formal representations of domain knowledge, while SKOS offers a simpler way to organize and link concepts across different vocabularies;

b) Bridging formal and informal knowledge structures: This integration allows for the connection of rigorous domain models with more flexible, user-friendly knowledge organization schemes;

c) Enhanced information retrieval: The semantic structures provided by ontologies and SKOS enable more intelligent and context-aware search and retrieval systems;

d) Support for Linked Data: Both ontologies and SKOS are compatible with Linked Data principles, facilitating the creation of interconnected, machine-readable knowledge graphs.

3 Enabling Technologies and Frameworks

The convergence of Open Data, Linked Data, Ontologies, and Large Language Models is made possible by a rich ecosystem of enabling technologies that span multiple domains of computer science and information technology. Enabling technologies and frameworks, can be explained as follows:

1. Enabling Technologies: There are eight key areas of technology that form the foundation for modern knowledge systems:
   - Web Technologies;
   - Database systems;
   - Big Data processing;
   - Cloud Computing;
   - Generative AI and Machine Learning;
   - Data Visualization;
   - APIs and Microservices;
   - Semantic Web Technologies.
2. Integration Frameworks: This is a comprehensive list of frameworks and tools that facilitate the integration of the aforementioned technologies. These include:
   - Semantic Web and Linked Data frameworks (e.g., Apache Jena, RDF4J, Virtuoso);
   - Graph databases (e.g., Blazegraph, GraphDB, Stardog);
   - AI, NLP, Machine Learning libraries (e.g., Hugging Face Transformers, TensorFlow, PyTorch, ChatGPT, Anthopic, Llama);
   - Open data management systems (e.g., CKAN, Socrata, OpenDataSoft);
   - Data visualization and exploration tools (e.g., Apache Superset, Tableau Public).

Each framework is briefly described with its key features and typical use cases, highlighting how they contribute to building scalable, modular approaches for integrating various components of modern knowledge systems. The list covers a wide range of applications, from low-level data handling to high-level AI and visualization tools, emphasizing the interdisciplinary nature of this technological ecosystem.

4   Case Studies

Below are some case studies illustrating the quality of the solutions presented in this work and provide empirical evidence of the feasibility and effectiveness of integrating Open Data, Linked Data, Ontologies, and Large Language Models. They demonstrate how this integration can lead to significant improvements in various fields: In drug discovery (BioMedKG), the integration allowed for faster literature reviews, novel drug-target discoveries, and more efficient clinical trial processes [41]. For smart city management (CityPulse), the system improved traffic flow, reduced energy consumption, and increased citizen engagement through a more accessible and responsive platform [42]. In environmental research (EcoSphere), the integrated approach enabled cross-country data analysis, accelerated climate modeling, and facilitated more informed policy-making [43]. For legal research (LegalMind), the system dramatically reduced research time, improved prediction accuracy, and democratized access to legal insights [44]. Key takeaways from these case studies include: The power of combining structured (Linked Data, ontologies) and unstructured (text processed by

LLMs) data for more comprehensive insights. The importance of domain-specific ontologies in providing context and structure to open data. The role of LLMs in making complex knowledge systems accessible through natural language interfaces. The potential for AI-driven hypothesis generation and predictive modeling when leveraging these integrated systems. The scalability of this approach across different domains, from life sciences to urban planning to environmental research. These case studies validate the theoretical perspectives discussed in these paper by showing concrete, measurable benefits in real-world applications. They demonstrate that the integration of these four components can indeed lead to more powerful, flexible, and context-aware knowledge systems.

5   Open Data Landscape

Open Data has transformed information access, sharing, and utilization across society, driven by principles of transparency, collaboration, and innovation. Government initiatives have been at the forefront, launching portals to make public sector information freely available, aiming to enhance transparency, civic engagement, and economic growth. The scientific community has embraced open data to accelerate research and innovation, promoting reproducibility and global collaboration through initiatives like the European Open Science Cloud. Challenges persist, including:

- Ensuring data quality and interoperability;
- Standardization efforts to manage diverse data formats;
- Improving data literacy among potential users.

The open data landscape represents a fundamental shift in viewing information as a public resource and innovation driver. As it matures, the open data ecosystem has the potential to reshape government-citizen interactions, scientific research practices, and approaches to global challenges. In essence, the open data movement is a dynamic, evolving ecosystem that promises to foster a more informed and engaged global community, despite ongoing challenges in implementation and adoption.

6   Large Language Models in Generative AI

The field of artificial intelligence has been revolutionized in recent years by the development of LLMs, which have demonstrated remarkable capabilities in natural language understanding and generation. These models, built on transformer architectures and trained on vast amounts of text data, have pushed the boundaries of what's possible in areas such as text completion, translation, summarization, and even creative writing [13].

At the core of these models is the ability to capture complex patterns and relationships within language, allowing them to generate coherent and contextually appropriate text. Models like GPT-3, BERT, and their successors have shown an impressive grasp of syntax, semantics, and even some degree of world knowledge, often producing outputs that are difficult to distinguish from human-written text [17].

The training process for these models involves exposure to diverse corpora of text, ranging from books and articles to websites and social media posts. Through this process, the models develop a statistical understanding of language patterns and associations. This allows them to perform a wide range of language tasks without explicit programming for each task, a capability known as few-shot or zero-shot learning.

However, despite their impressive capabilities, LLMs face several significant challenges and limitations. One of the most pressing issues is the phenomenon of "hallucination," where models generate plausible-sounding but factually incorrect information. This highlights the fact that these models are fundamentally pattern matching systems, not repositories of verified knowledge.

Another major concern is the presence of biases in model outputs, reflecting biases present in the training data. These can manifest as gender, racial, or cultural biases, raising ethical concerns about the deployment of these models in real-world applications. Researchers are actively working on techniques to detect and mitigate these biases, but it remains an open challenge.

The immense size of these models also presents practical challenges. Training and running LLMs requires significant computational resources, raising questions about their environmental impact and accessibility. There are ongoing efforts to develop more efficient models and training techniques to address these concerns.

Despite these challenges, the potential of LLMs in advancing AI is immense. Researchers are exploring ways to enhance these models by grounding them in external knowledge sources, such as databases or knowledge graphs. This could help address issues of factual accuracy and provide a path towards more reliable and trustworthy AI systems.

Another promising direction is the development of techniques for injecting domain-specific knowledge into LLMs. This could allow for the creation of specialized models that combine the flexibility of general language understanding with deep expertise in particular fields, opening up new possibilities in areas like scientific research, legal analysis, and medical diagnosis.

As research in this field progresses, we can expect to see LLMs becoming increasingly integrated into a wide range of applications, from intelligent personal assistants to advanced research tools. However, realizing the full potential of these models will require ongoing work to address their limitations and ensure their responsible and ethical deployment.

The intersection of LLMs with other AI technologies, such as computer vision and speech recognition, is also an area of active research. These multimodal models promise to deliver even more sophisticated and human-like AI capabilities, further blurring the lines between human and machine intelligence.

While challenges remain, the ongoing research and development in this field suggest a future where AI systems can engage in increasingly sophisticated and helpful interactions with humans across a wide range of domains [18].

7   Integrating Open Data, Linked Data, Ontologies, and LLMs

The convergence of open data initiatives, Linked Data technologies, ontological knowledge representation, and LLMs presents a unique opportunity to create next-generation knowledge systems that are more powerful, flexible, and context-aware than ever before. This integration leverages the strengths of each approach while mitigating their individual limitations [19, 20].

One promising direction is the use of LLMs to generate Linked Data from unstructured sources. Traditional methods of creating Linked Data often require significant manual effort or complex rule-based systems. LLMs, with their advanced natural language understanding capabilities, can potentially automate much of this process. For example, an LLM could be trained to extract structured triples from scientific papers or government reports, converting them into RDF format. This would greatly accelerate the growth of the Linked Data ecosystem, making more information available in a machine-readable format.

Conversely, ontologies and knowledge graphs can be used to improve the outputs of LLMs through ontology-based prompting. By incorporating domain-specific ontologies into the prompting process, we can guide LLMs to produce more accurate and contextually relevant responses. For instance, when querying about medical conditions, an LLM could be prompted with relevant sections of a medical ontology, ensuring that its responses align with established medical knowledge and terminology.

The combination of symbolic and neural approaches for reasoning is another exciting area of integration. While LLMs excel at handling natural language and fuzzy concepts, they often struggle with precise logical reasoning. On the other hand, ontology-based systems are adept at formal logic but can be brittle when dealing with ambiguous or incomplete information. By combining these approaches, we can create hybrid systems that leverage the strengths of both. For example, an LLM could be used to interpret a natural language query, which is then translated into a formal SPARQL query to retrieve information from a knowledge graph. The results could then be passed back to the LLM for natural language generation of the response.

LLMs also show promise as natural language interfaces to knowledge graphs. Traditional interfaces to Linked Data, such as SPARQL endpoints, require specialized knowledge and are not accessible to most users. An LLM could act as an intermediary, interpreting natural language queries from users and translating them into appropriate queries for the knowledge graph. This would make the wealth of information in Linked Data sources accessible to a much wider audience.

The integration of these technologies also opens up new possibilities for knowledge discovery and inference. LLMs could be used to generate hypotheses based on patterns in Linked Data, which could then be verified against formal ontologies. This could lead to the discovery of new relationships or insights that might not be apparent through traditional analysis methods.

However, this integration also presents challenges. Ensuring the consistency and accuracy of LLM-generated Linked Data is crucial, as errors could propagate through the knowledge ecosystem. Similarly, when using Linked Data to ground LLMs, care must be taken to avoid reinforcing biases present in the data. Balancing the computational requirements of these complex integrated systems with the need for real-time performance is another significant challenge.

Despite these challenges, the potential benefits of integrating open data, Linked Data, ontologies, and LLMs are immense. As research in this area progresses, we can expect to see increasingly sophisticated knowledge systems that combine the breadth and flexibility of LLMs with the precision and structure of Linked Data and ontologies, all built on a foundation of open, accessible data.

8   Ethical Considerations

A comprehensive analysis highlights the complex ethical landscape needs to addressing issues is crucial for the responsible development and deployment of technologies that integrate open data, linked data, ontologies, and LLMs. Ethical analysis covers a wide range of important considerations that must be addressed in the development and deployment of AI-driven knowledge systems. Here are some key points to emphasize. Data Privacy and Security: As we integrate vast amounts of data from various sources, protecting individual privacy becomes increasingly challenging. The risk of re-identification in anonymized datasets is a significant concern, especially when combining multiple data sources. Robust security measures and clear data governance policies are essential. Bias and Fairness: The potential for bias in these systems is multifaceted. It can stem from biased training data for LLMs, historical biases in open datasets, or biases introduced during the creation of ontologies and knowledge graphs. Continuous monitoring and correction of biases is crucial to ensure fair and equitable outcomes. Transparency and Explainability: The complexity of integrated knowledge systems, especially those involving LLMs, poses significant challenges for transparency. Developing methods to explain system outputs in a way that is understandable to users is essential for building trust and accountability. Societal Impact: These systems have the potential to greatly impact society, from reshaping labor markets to influencing public discourse. Careful consideration must be given to ensuring equitable access and preventing the exacerbation of existing societal inequalities. Environmental Considerations: The environmental impact of large-scale AI systems is an often overlooked ethical concern. As these systems grow in complexity and scale, their energy consumption and carbon footprint become significant issues that need to be addressed. Ethical Governance and Policy: Developing appropriate regulatory frameworks and ethical guidelines is crucial. This should involve a wide range of stakeholders and consider both current and potential future impacts of these technologies. Long-term Considerations: As AI systems become more advanced, we must consider their long-term implications on human society, including the potential development of Artificial General Intelligence (AGI) and its alignment with human values.

9   Potential Applications

The convergence of open data, Linked Data, ontologies, and LLMs opens up a wide range of exciting applications across various domains. This integration of technologies has the potential to revolutionize how we interact with and derive value from vast amounts of structured and unstructured information [21, 22]. In the realm of scientific research, this synergy could significantly enhance the literature review process and accelerate hypothesis generation. Researchers could leverage LLMs trained on extensive open datasets and guided by domain-specific ontologies to quickly synthesize findings from thousands of papers across multiple disciplines. This would not only save time but also potentially uncover non-obvious connections that human researchers might overlook. For instance, a biomedical researcher studying a rare disease could use such a system to identify potential drug candidates by analyzing patterns in seemingly unrelated chemical, genomic, and clinical trial datasets [23]. Government services and transparency could also be dramatically improved through these integrated technologies. By combining open government data with Linked Data principles and natural language interfaces powered by LLMs, citizens could access and understand complex public information more easily. Imagine a system where a citizen could ask natural language questions about local budget allocations, environmental policies, or public health statistics, and receive clear, contextualized answers drawing from multiple government datasets. This could foster greater civic engagement and enable more informed public discourse on policy issues. In the realm of personal productivity and information management, we could see the emergence of more intelligent and context-aware personal assistants. These assistants would go beyond simple task management and information retrieval, leveraging vast knowledge graphs and the natural language understanding capabilities of LLMs to provide deeper, more nuanced assistance. For example, when planning a trip, such an assistant could not only book flights and hotels but also provide culturally relevant advice, health precautions, and personalized activity suggestions based on a rich understanding of the destination and the user's preferences. Perhaps one of the most exciting potential applications is in cross-domain knowledge discovery and innovation. By breaking down silos between different fields of knowledge, this integrated approach could catalyze breakthroughs at the intersection of disciplines. For instance, an entrepreneur looking to develop sustainable energy solutions could use such a system to explore connections between cutting-edge materials science, energy policy data, and climate models. The system could suggest novel approaches by identifying patterns and possibilities that might not be apparent when these domains are considered in isolation. In education, these technologies could power adaptive learning systems that tailor content and learning paths to individual students' needs and interests. By drawing on vast educational resources structured as Linked Data and interpreting student interactions using LLMs, these systems could offer personalized explanations, generate relevant examples, and even create custom exercises that bridge a student's current knowledge to new concepts they're trying to master. The legal and compliance sectors could also benefit greatly from this technological convergence. Legal professionals could use advanced systems to navigate complex regulatory landscapes, drawing insights from case law, statutes, and regulatory guidelines. These systems could assist in contract analysis, risk assessment, and even predictive modeling of legal outcomes based on historical data and current case factors. In each of these applications, the key advantage lies in the ability to combine the structured, interlinked nature of Linked Data and ontologies with the flexible, natural language capabilities of LLMs, all built on a foundation of open, accessible data. This combination promises to make vast amounts of information more accessible, understandable, and actionable for both specialists and general users alike, potentially democratizing access to knowledge and insights in unprecedented ways. However, as we explore these exciting possibilities, it's crucial to remain mindful of the challenges and ethical considerations that come with such powerful information systems. Issues of privacy, data quality, bias, and the potential for misinformation must be carefully addressed to ensure that these applications truly serve the public good [24].

10   A Comprehensive Strategic Roadmap

A comprehensive strategic roadmap for achieving the integration of Open Data, Linked Data, Ontologies, and Large Language Models (LLMs) will outline specific milestones, partnerships, and collaborations necessary to realize this vision. It emphasizes collaboration, ethical considerations, and progressive development, guiding stakeholders in academia, industry, and government on how to contribute to and benefit from this transformative initiative. Here are some key points to highlight:

1. Phased Approach: The roadmap is divided into four phases, each building on the achievements of the previous one. This allows for a gradual, systematic development of the necessary technologies, standards, and practices;// 2. Cross-sector Collaboration: Throughout all phases, there's a strong emphasis on collaboration between academia, industry, and government. This is crucial for ensuring that the developed systems meet diverse needs and leverage expertise from various domains;// 3. Ethical Considerations: The roadmap incorporates ethical considerations from the very beginning, with ongoing initiatives for responsible AI development. This proactive approach to ethics is essential for building trust and ensuring the long-term sustainability of these systems;// 4. Technical Development: The plan includes specific milestones for developing necessary tools, frameworks, and infrastructures. This ranges from creating standardized frameworks for data sharing to developing advanced AI models that can reason across diverse knowledge domains;// 5. Pilot Projects and Scaling: The roadmap emphasizes the importance of real-world implementation, starting with pilot projects in key sectors and gradually scaling to widespread adoption. This approach allows for iterative improvement based on practical feedback;// 6. Education and Skill Development: There's a strong focus on developing the necessary workforce skills, including updating curricula and creating professional certification programs. This is crucial for ensuring that there are enough skilled

professionals to implement and manage these complex systems;// 7. Ongoing Research and Innovation: The plan doesn't end with implementation but includes continuous research and development initiatives to push the boundaries of what's possible with these integrated systems;// 8. Global Perspective: The roadmap takes a global view, emphasizing international collaboration and the need for cross-border agreements on data sharing and governance.//

To make this roadmap actionable, stakeholders can:

- Academia: Focus on research in areas like ontology development, ethical AI, and advanced reasoning systems. Develop and update relevant curricula;//
- Industry: Participate in pilot projects, contribute to open-source tool development, and work on creating user-friendly interfaces for these complex systems;//
- Government: Support open data initiatives, work on developing supportive legislation, and participate in international collaborations for data sharing and governance.// By following this roadmap, we can work towards creating a powerful, integrated knowledge ecosystem that leverages the strengths of open data, linked data, ontologies, and large language models to address complex challenges across various domains.

11   Challenges and Future Directions

The integration of open data, Linked Data, Ontologies, and LLMs presents a promising frontier for advanced knowledge systems. However, this convergence also brings forth significant challenges that must be addressed to fully realize its potential.

One of the primary challenges lies in the realm of scalability and computational requirements. As we amalgamate vast amounts of open data with the intricate structures of Linked Data and ontologies, the computational demands grow exponentially. LLMs, already resource-intensive in their training and deployment, add another layer of complexity. Future research must focus on developing more efficient algorithms and hardware solutions to handle these increased computational loads. Distributed computing and edge processing may offer avenues to mitigate these challenges, allowing for more localized processing of data and reducing the strain on centralized systems [25–27].

Maintaining data freshness and consistency presents another significant hurdle. The dynamic nature of open data sources means that information is constantly being updated, added, or removed. Ensuring that Linked Data structures and ontologies reflect these changes in real-time is a formidable task [36]. Moreover, when this ever-changing data is used to fine-tune or query LLMs, there's a risk of inconsistencies or outdated information creeping into the system's outputs. Developing robust mechanisms for real-time data synchronization and versioning will be crucial in addressing this challenge [28].

The issue of explainability and trust in AI-assisted knowledge systems cannot be overstated. As these systems become more complex, understanding how they arrive at certain conclusions or generate specific outputs becomes increasingly difficult. This "black box" problem is particularly pronounced with LLMs.

Future research must focus on developing methods to make these systems more transparent, allowing users to trace the provenance of information and understand the reasoning behind AI-generated content. This transparency is not just a technical challenge but also a societal one, as it directly impacts the trustworthiness and adoption of these systems in critical domains such as healthcare, legal systems, and scientific research [29, 30].

Ethical considerations in large-scale knowledge integration represent a multifaceted challenge. As we combine data from diverse sources and use AI to generate new insights, questions of data privacy, consent, and potential misuse come to the fore. There's also the risk of perpetuating or amplifying biases present in the original data or embedded in the AI models. Addressing these ethical challenges will require a multidisciplinary approach, bringing together technologists, ethicists, policymakers, and domain experts to develop guidelines and safeguards for responsible development and deployment of these integrated knowledge systems [31, 32].

Looking to the future, we can anticipate exciting developments in this field. Advancements in Quantum Computing may provide the computational power needed to handle increasingly complex knowledge structures and AI models [33, 34]. We might see the emergence of more sophisticated hybrid systems that seamlessly blend symbolic reasoning (based on ontologies and Linked Data) with the pattern recognition capabilities of neural networks [35]. There's also potential for these integrated systems to play a crucial role in addressing global challenges, from climate change to pandemic response, by enabling more effective cross-domain knowledge sharing and discovery.

As we move forward, it's clear that the path to fully realizing the potential of this technological convergence is not without obstacles. However, the promise of creating more intelligent, context-aware, and ethically sound knowledge systems makes this a worthy endeavor. The future directions of this field will likely be shaped by ongoing dialogues between researchers, practitioners, and society at large, ensuring that these powerful technologies are developed and deployed in ways that benefit humanity while mitigating potential risks.

12   Conclusion

The convergence of open data initiatives, Linked Data technologies, ontological knowledge representation, and LLMs represents a significant leap forward in our ability to organize, access, and generate knowledge. This integration has the potential to revolutionize how we interact with and derive insights from the vast amounts of information available in our increasingly digital world.

As we have explored throughout this paper, each of these components brings unique strengths to the table. Open data initiatives have dramatically increased the availability of valuable information across various domains, from government operations to scientific research. Linked Data technologies provide a standardized framework for connecting and querying this diverse data, enabling unprecedented levels of interoperability and discovery. Ontologies and knowledge organization systems like SKOS offer structured representations of domain knowledge, providing essential context and relationships. LLMs, with their remarkable ability to understand and generate natural language, offer a powerful interface for interacting with these complex knowledge structures.

The synergy between these approaches addresses many of the limitations each faces individually. For instance, while LLMs excel at processing natural language, they often struggle with factual accuracy and consistency. By grounding these models in the structured, verified information provided by Linked Data and ontologies, we can significantly enhance their reliability and usefulness. Conversely, the natural language capabilities of LLMs can make the often abstruse world of semantic technologies more accessible to a broader audience, potentially accelerating their adoption and impact.

However, as we move forward in developing these integrated knowledge systems, we must remain mindful of the challenges and ethical considerations involved. Issues of data quality, privacy, and bias become even more critical when working at this scale and level of integration. The potential for misuse or unintended consequences grows alongside the power of these systems. Therefore, it is crucial that development in this field proceeds with careful consideration of its societal impacts and with robust safeguards in place.

Looking ahead, the potential applications of these integrated knowledge systems are vast and exciting. From accelerating scientific discovery to enhancing government transparency and enabling more intelligent and context-aware personal assistants, the possibilities are limited only by our imagination and our ability to address the technical and ethical challenges involved.

In conclusion, the integration of open data, Linked Data, ontologies, and LLMs represents a promising frontier in knowledge management and artificial intelligence. As research in this field progresses, we can anticipate increasingly sophisticated systems that not only store and retrieve information but also understand, reason about, and generate new knowledge in ways that were previously unimaginable. This convergence has the potential to fundamentally transform how we interact with information, paving the way for more intelligent, responsive, and insightful knowledge systems that can help address some of the most complex challenges facing our world today.

References

1. Terzic, R., Majstorovic, M.: Open data concept its application and experiences (2019). https://doi.org/10.5937/vojtehg67-19935
2. https://openaccess.mpg.de/67605/berlideclarationengl.pdf
3. https://opengovdata.org/
4. https://data.gov/
5. https://www.gov.uk/government/publications/open-data-charter/g8-open-datacharter-and-technical-annex
6. https://resources.data.gov/PoD/principles/
7. Young, A., Verhulst, S.: The Global Impact of Open Data. O'Reilly Media, Inc. (2016)

8. Lange, R., Tian, Y., Tang, Y.: Large language models as evolution strategies (2024)
9. Liu, T., Xu, C., Qiao, Y., Jiang, C., Chen, W.: News recommendation with attention mechanism. arXiv preprint arXiv:2402.07422 (2024)
10. https://www.w3.org/RDF/Metalog/docs/sw-easy
11. Ranaldi, F., et al.: Investigating the impact of data contamination of large language models in text-to-SQL translation. arXiv preprint arXiv:2402.08100 (2024)
12. Sjöström, J., Cronholm, S.: Meta-requirements for LLM-based knowledge exploration tools in information systems research. Springer (2024)
13. Chang, Y., et al.: A survey on evaluation of large language models. arXiv preprint arxiv:2307.03109 (2023)
14. Charalabidis, Y., Zuiderwijk, A., Alexopoulos, C., Janssen, M., Lampoltshammer, T.J., Ferro, E.: The open data landscape: concepts, methods, tools and experiences. In: The World of Open Data (2018)
15. Machado, L.M.O.: Ontologies in Knowledge Organization. MDPI (2021)
16. Samani, Z.R., Shamsfard, M.: The state of the art in developing fuzzy ontologies: a survey. arXiv preprint arXiv:1805.02290 (2018)
17. Hadi, M.U., et al.: Large language models: a comprehensive survey of its applications, challenges, limitations, and future prospects. TechRxiv (2023)
18. Jiang, D., et al.: GenAI arena: an open evaluation platform for generative models arXiv preprint arXiv:2406.04485 (2024)
19. Doumanas, D., Soularidis, A., Kotis, K., Vouros, G.: Integrating LLMs in the Engineering of a SAR Ontology. Springer (2024)
20. Nahhas, S., Bamasag, O., Khemakhem, M., Bajnaid, N.: Linked data approach to mutually enrich traditional education resources with global open education. IEEE (2018)
21. Buchmann, R., et al.: Large language models: expectations for semantics-driven systems engineering. Data Knowl. Eng. **152**, 102324 (2024)
22. Boparai, N.K., Aggarwal, H., Rani, R.: Analyzing fuzzy semantics of reviews for multi-criteria recommendations. Data Knowl. Eng. **152**, 102314 (2024)
23. Karagiannis, D., Buchmann, R.A.: Linked open models: extending linked open data with conceptual model information. Inf. Syst. **56**, 174–197 (2016)
24. Shen, L., et al.: The language barrier: dissecting safety challenges of LLMs in multilingual contexts. arXiv preprint arXiv:2401.13136 (2024)
25. Babaei Giglou, H., D'Souza, J., Auer, S.: LLMs4OL: large language models for ontology learning. Springer (2023)
26. Zhai, C.X.: Large language models and future of information retrieval: opportunities and challenges. ACM (2024)
27. Iga, V.I.R., Silaghi, G.C.: LLMS for knowledge-graphs enhanced task-oriented dialogue systems: challenges and opportunities. Springer (2024)
28. Patil, R., Gudivada, V.: A Review of Current Trends, Techniques, and Challenges in Large Language Models (LLMs). MDPI (2024)
29. Pesl, R.D., Stötzner, M., Georgievski, I., Aiello, M.: Uncovering LLMs for service-composition: challenges and opportunities. Springer (2024)
30. Ding, B., et al.: Data augmentation using large language models: data perspectives, learning paradigms and challenges. arXiv preprint arXiv:2403.02990 (2024)
31. Bender, E.M., Gebru, T., McMillan-Major, A., Shmitchell, S.: On the dangers of stochastic parrots: can language models be too big?. In: Proceedings of the 2021 ACM Conference on Fairness, Accountability, and Transparency, pp. 610–623. ACM (2021)

32. Bostrom, N., Yudkowsky, E.: The ethics of artificial intelligence. In: Frankish, K., Ramsey, W.M. (eds.) The Cambridge Handbook of Artificial Intelligence, pp. 316–334. Cambridge University Press, Cambridge (2014)
33. Liang, Z., et al.: Unleashing the potential of LLMs for quantum computing: a study in quantum architecture design. arXiv preprint arXiv:2307.08191 (2023)
34. Liao, Y., Ferrie, C.: GPT on a quantum computer. arXiv preprint arXiv:2403.09418 (2024)
35. Hohenecker, P, Lukasiewicz, T.: Ontology reasoning with deep neural networks (2020). https://doi.org/10.1613/jair.1.11661
36. Herron, D., Jiménez-Ruiz, E. , Weyde, T.: On the potential of logic and reasoning in neurosymbolic systems using OWL-based knowledge graphs (2024). https://openaccess.city.ac.uk/id/eprint/32688/
37. Rubiolo, M., Caliusco, M.L., Stegmayer, G., Coronel, M., Gareli Fabrizi, M.: Knowledge discovery through ontology matching: an approach based on an artificial neural network model. Inf. Sci. **194**, 107–119 (2012)
38. Shvaiko, P., Euzenat, J.: Ontology matching: state of the art and future challenges. IEEE (2011)
39. Pascala, H., Federicob, B., Monireha, E., Kamruzzamana, S.M.: Neural-symbolic integration and the semantic web. Semantic Web **11**(1), 3–11 (2020)
40. Adegun, A.A, Fonou-Dombeu, J.V., Viriri, S., Odindi, J.: Ontology-Based Deep Learning Model for Object Detection and Image Classification in Smart City Concepts. MDPI (2024)
41. Bang, D., Lim, S., Lee, S., Kim, S.: Biomedical knowledge graph learning for drug repurposing by extending guilt-by association to multiple layers. Nat. Commun. (2023). https://www.nature.com/articles/s41467-023-39301-y
42. Puiu, D., et al.: CityPulse: large scale data analytics framework for smart cities. IEEE Access **4**, 1086–1108 (2016). https://doi.org/10.1109/ACCESS.2016.2541999
43. Halpern, B.S., et al.: Priorities for synthesis research in ecology and environmental science. Ecosphere **14**(1), e4342 (2023). https://doi.org/10.1002/ecs2.4342
44. Brozek, B.: The Legal Mind: A New Introduction to Legal Epistemology. Cambridge University Press (2019)

Semantic Enrichment of Metadata in the Bibliodata Network

Ana Carolina Novaes de Mendonça[1,2]([✉]) [iD] and Ana Carolina Simionato Arakaki[1,2] [iD]

[1] Federal University of São Carlos, São Carlos - SP, Brazil
anamendonca@ibict.br
[2] Brazilian Institute of Information in Science and Technology (Ibict), Brasília, Brazil
anaarakaki@ibict.br

Abstract. Technology reflects the values of its developers, which reinforces the need for ethical and responsible development in digital solutions. Awareness of gender equality in Information Science is reflected in United Nations Resolution 62/10 and the Sustainable Development Goals (SDGs), which promote gender equality. The aim of this research is to promote advances in the representation of women and girls in the Bibliodata Network, based on the use of sources such as the Virtual International Authority File (VIAF) and Wikidata for the semantic enrichment of metadata, as well as the importance of inclusive terminology to achieve this end. Although the study focuses mainly on enriching the records of people who identify as female, it is hoped in the future that the methodology employed will be adaptable for all genders. The expected results aim to promote significant advances in the representation of women and girls in the Bibliodata Network, improve the quality and accuracy of metadata, and create more robust information networks, with an ongoing commitment to equity and inclusion. Currently, the main challenge of the research is the migration and reorganization of data within the network to align with updated standards, ensuring data preservation and preventing potential loss.

Keywords: Bibliodata · Semantic enrichment · metadata

1 Introduction

Technology reflects the values and knowledge of its creators, which highlights the importance of ethical and responsible development in digital solutions [1]. This is evident, for example, in the division of male and female authors into separate categories at the National Library of Spain (BNE), which demonstrates a commitment to gender equity and inclusion in the organization of knowledge [8].

Extraordinary women and girls have always been present as artists, scientists and politicians. However, due to institutional and social barriers, they have often been limited in their talents, under-represented and forgotten. The active participation of women in political and socio-cultural spheres is a recent historical achievement that deserves recognition and prominence in contemporary society. This is evidenced by the growing

M. Sfakakis et al. (Eds.): MTSR 2024, CCIS 2331, pp. 214–219, 2025.
https://doi.org/10.1007/978-3-031-81974-2_18

interest in recent years in the works of Spanish women authors who, until then, had been largely forgotten [2].

Adequate and inclusive representation is fundamental to achieving gender equality and promoting equity in the various areas of society. However, data collection, descriptions and metadata related to the female gender are often insufficient, leading to a significant loss of information. Information retrieval, considered a well-developed solution by Information Science (IS), is still in the process of being improved [5]. In this context, knowledge organization, inclusive terminology and information retrieval emerge as closely related fields, especially in improving the accessibility and accuracy of data retrieval, contributing to a more inclusive and equitable representation.

In recent years, there has been a growing awareness of the importance of gender equality in various areas of society. This awareness prompted the creation of United Nations Resolution 62/10 [3], which promotes principles of social justice, defending gender equality and the rights of indigenous peoples and migrants. This resolution is reflected in the Sustainable Development Goals (SDGs), which highlight the need to achieve gender equality and empower all women and girls [4].

The underrepresentation of women in Wikipedia is evident, with only 19.80% of biographies in English are dedicated to women. To address this disparity, the WikiProject Women initiative focuses on improving existing records and creating new biographies of notable women. By advocating for gender-inclusive language and eliminating biases, WikiProject Women aims to create a more balanced and inclusive representation of women on one of the world's most widely used information platforms [25].

Basic information such as publication date, author and language, although essential, does not meet all the information needs of researchers [6]. To overcome this limitation, three different sources were used to enrich the metadata, resulting in a genre identification rate of 78.9% of the authors present in a specific digital library. These results demonstrate the potential of this approach to improve the representation and retrieval of information.

Thus, this study presents ongoing research, which aims to use external sources such as the Virtual International Authority File (VIAF) and Wikidata to enrich the metadata, in order to improve the records of names and subjects related to the female gender within the Bibliodata Network catalog. It also highlights the importance of inclusive terminology to achieve fairer and more accurate representation.

2   Methodology

The approach of this research, considering the objectives and the analysis of similar studies, is outlined as qualitative research, which will address the following themes: metadata, gender, gender metadata, inclusive terminology, and semantic enrichment. A literature review was carried out as an integrative review of the proposed topic [26], enabling the construction of theoretical knowledge on the new perspectives for recognizing data sets, verifying the possibilities of informational treatment to make it possible to obtain information.

The research is exploratory in nature, given the originality of the research in aligning gender metadata under the semantic enrichment approach. As a theoretical study, the research will begin with a documentary study of reports and publications on female gender representation from the main cataloging institutions and good practices, such as the International Federation of Library Associations and Institutions (IFLA) and the publications of the World Wide Web Consortium (W3C).

Primary, secondary and tertiary sources were consulted in Information Science databases, such as the Reference Database of Journal Articles in Information Science (BRAPCI), Library and Information Science Abstracts (LISA), as well as journals in the field of Information Science on the CAPES Journal Portal. In addition, the international databases Web of Science, Scopus and Scientific Electronic Library Online (SciELO) will be consulted.

The inclusion criteria are articles available in full, languages (Portuguese, English and Spanish), works indexed by scientific databases, works that are within the time frame of 2013 to 2023. The exclusion criteria could be texts with languages other than Portuguese, English and Spanish, no mention of the terms in the title, keywords or abstract, the work is a reference to the article (only a citation), non-academic works, works that do not adhere to the research theme, works that only describe the bibliographic context and repeated works.

3   Theoretical Foundation and Related Work

The term "enrichment" refers to the process of applying an enrichment tool, which can result in the creation of new metadata at the end of the procedure or the enrichment of existing metadata with more contextualized meanings [9, 13]. It also increases the richness of the data by adding context and semantic relationships that go beyond the explicit information present in the basic metadata [9]. Thus, the main objective of semantic enrichment is to make data more interoperable and accessible, making it possible to connect to other databases and make information available that was previously isolated or disconnected.

To carry out semantic enrichment, there are various methods and approaches that can be applied [9, 12]. These methods allow structured, semi-structured and unstructured data [14] to be enriched in a way that improves its quality and discoverability. When data [15] is structured and standardized, it represents the fundamental attributes of a bibliographic item and can be widely accessed and made available. By identifying the context in which the data is inserted, it becomes possible to understand the meaning and make a correct interpretation of the information transmitted. This is especially important considering the linguistic elements since the meaning can vary depending on the context in which it is used.

Data also takes on the role of characterizing other data and is called metadata. The definition of data on data is not a useful definition [16], metadata encapsulates information that describes any document or object in digital and traditional formats [17]. The use of metadata to describe information resources is essential for good retrieval and interoperability between systems, as well as being essential for characterizing and identifying bibliographic records.

In the context of this research, authority data, which is structured data, and the use of VIAF and Wikidata sources were chosen for enrichment. One of the main objectives of VIAF is to reduce costs and increase the usefulness of library authority files [11], which makes cataloging more efficient and contributes to improving the quality of bibliographic data, as well as supporting interoperability between different bibliographic systems and promoting the use of Linked Data [19], which allows data to be more easily linked and used on the Semantic Web. In addition to these, Wikidata.

[10] is an integral part of the Linked Open Data movement [18], which promotes the significant interconnection of data sets on the web.

In addition, it is important to use inclusive terminology [20] that reflects diversity and promotes equity in the representation of information, since each language is a constantly changing social product that accumulates and expresses the stereotypes and values marked by each society, passed down from one generation to the next [21]. Furthermore, the use of knowledge organization systems (KOS) and the adoption of Linked Open Data (LOD) are fundamental strategies in the semantic enrichment process, since KOS, which include controlled vocabularies, thesauruses and ontologies, provide the necessary structure for the effective organization and retrieval of information [9].

In some studies, the implementation of these techniques has yielded significant results for the enrichment of bibliographic metadata. In the context of SearchCulture.gr, 77 collections were enriched, totaling 177,986 cultural heritage objects (CHO), representing 20% of the content [24]. Similarly, in the Virtual Library Miguel de Cervantes (BVMC), the process created 2,000 external links, achieving a disambiguation accuracy of 73% overall, with a rate of 95.8% for identifying the most frequent country [23].

But the enrichment process poses challenges like data heterogeneity, linguistic variations, and limitations of external knowledge bases, requiring a balance between automation and manual review. Additional difficulties include selecting suitable ontologies, maintaining enriched data, and integrating external datasets [23]. For example, in Greek history and culture, name disambiguation was complex due to varied forms of personal names and limited biographical metadata [24].

With the tools established, this research aims to enrich authority data within the Brazilian initiative CALCO (Computer-Readable Cataloging) stands out, a project that gave rise to the largest national collective catalog, called Bibliodata/CALCO [7]. The Bibliodata Network, created in 1942, established a cooperative cataloging network between libraries, and its purpose is to promote the dissemination of Brazil's bibliographic collections, with more than 2,000,000 titles and an extensive list of authorities with more than 250,000 records of names and subjects [22]. This network was designed to facilitate the shared cataloging of bibliographic materials, thereby enhancing the accessibility and organization of library collections across the country. The primary aim of Bibliodata Network is to support the comprehensive dissemination of Brazil's bibliographic holdings, making them more accessible to researchers, librarians, and the general public.

The impact of Bibliodata/CALCO extends beyond national borders, as it represents a model of cooperative bibliographic management that could inspire similar initiatives in other countries. By centralizing and standardizing bibliographic data, Bibliodata Network not only enhances the efficiency of library operations within Brazil but also contributes to the global exchange of bibliographic information.

4   Discussion and Conclusion

The future goal of this research is to drive significant advancements and changes in the records and representation of women and girls within the Bibliodata Network. As highlighted, there is a notable underrepresentation of women, which is reflected in the records [25]. For instance, this involves enriching metadata related to name variations across different languages and gender metadata, using sources like VIAF and Wikidata, which contain such data.

The use of sources such as VIAF and Wikidata for the semantic enrichment of metadata is a well- established practice [6, 9] that generates numerous benefits for the description and retrieval of information. By implementing these sources, it becomes possible to connect previously isolated data, and this process is especially beneficial for the representation of historically under-represented groups, such as women and girls, which ensures that their contributions and presence are more visible and valued in bibliographic collections.

In addition, the inclusion of terminology that is increasingly inclusive and sensitive to cultural and social diversity contributes to building an information environment that reflects, respects and values human diversity. The adoption of semantic enrichment methodologies, combined with the use of inclusive terminology and knowledge organization systems, contributes to better structuring and access to data. In this way, the Bibliodata Network will be able to fulfill its purpose of promoting the cooperation of bibliographic collections in Brazil and be a reference model in terms of equity and inclusion in the organization and retrieval of information.

Currently, one of the challenges faced is the migration of the Bibliodata Network and the reorganization of its data according to updated standards. This process ensures data preservation and prevents potential data loss.

The continuation of this study offers promising prospects for the future of female gender representation in the representation and organization of information. With the successful implementation of semantic enrichment techniques, a continuous improvement in the quality and accessibility of bibliographic data is expected. Although the study focuses mainly on enriching the records of people who identify as female, it is hoped that the methodology employed will be adaptable for all genders and the application of these practices can serve as a model to be followed by other bibliographic networks and institutions, both in Brazil and internationally.

References

1. European Commission. Directorate-General for Communications Networks, Content and Technology: Women in the Digital Age: Executive Summary. Publications Office (2018)
2. Bde Bibliográfica, S.I.: LibGuides: autoras españolas en la BNE: Autoras desde el siglo XIX hasta 1941. Guias.bne.es (n.d.). https://guias.bne.es/guiaautoras/XIXyXX
3. United Nations Development Programme: UN General Assembly, World Day of Social Justice, A/RES/62/10, Resolution. United Nations (2007). https://documents.un.org/doc/undoc/gen/n07/464/37/pdf/n0746437.pdf?token=HIHPqfcdFMIehgrBMO&fe=true
4. United Nations: Transforming our World: The 2030 Agenda for Sustainable Development. Department of Economic and Social Affairs, United Nations, New York (2015)

5. Saracevic, T.: Empty: Ciência da Informação: Origem, Evolução e Relações. Perspectivas em Ciência da Informação **1**(1) (1996)
6. Peng, Z., Chen, M., Kowalczyk, S., Plale, B.: Author gender metadata augmentation of HathiTrust digital library. Proc. Am. Soc. Inform. Sci. Technol. **51**(1), 1–4 (2014). https://doi.org/10.1002/meet.2014.1450510109
7. Barbosa, A.P.: Novos Rumos da Catalogação. BNG / Brasilart, Rio de Janeiro (1978)
8. Listado de Autores en la BNE. Biblioteca Nacional de España (2024)
9. Zeng, M.L.: Semantic Enrichment for Enhancing LAM Data and Supporting Digital Humanities. Profesional De La Información **28**(1) (2019). https://doi.org/10.3145/epi.2019.ene.03
10. Wikidata: Linked Open Data Workflow - Wikidata. www.wikidata.org (n.d.)
11. VIAF. Viaf.org (n.d.). https://viaf.org/
12. de Lira, M.A.B.: Uma Abordagem para Enriquecimento Semântico de Metadados para Publicação de Dados Abertos. Centro de Informática, Universidade Federal de Pernambuco, Recife, Dissertação de Mestrado (2014)
13. Isaac, A., Manguinhas, H., Stiller, J., Charles, V.: Report on Enrichment and Evaluation. Europeana Task Force on Enrichment and Evaluation, The Hague, Netherlands (2015)
14. Schöch, C.: Big? Smart? Clean? Messy? data in the humanities. J. Dig. Human. **2**(3), 2–13 (2013)
15. Santos, P.L.V.A.C., Santana, R.C.G.: Dado e Granularidade na Perspectiva da Informação e Tecnologia: Uma Interpretação pela Ciência da Informação. Ciência da Informação **42**(2) (2013)
16. Pomerantz, J.: Metadata. The MIT Press (2015)
17. Zeng, M.L., Qin, J.: Metadata. Neal-Schuman Publishers, New York, NY (2008)
18. Bizer, C., Heath, T., Berners-Lee, T.: Linked data: the story so far. Int. J. Semant. Web Inf. Syst. **5**(3), 1–22 (2009)
19. Linked Data - Design Issues. W3.org (2009). https://www.w3.org/DesignIssues/LinkedData.html
20. A Guide for Inclusive Language (n.d.). https://www.edi.uwo.ca/resources/reports/Inclusive-Language-Guide.pdf
21. Cordo, A.: Lenguaje Inclusivo: ¿Por Qué? ¿Para Qué? ¿Para Quiénes? MIDES, Montevideo (2013)
22. Ibict: Bibliodata. Instituto Brasileiro de Informação Em Ciência E Tecnologia (2024). https://www.gov.br/ibict/pt-br/servicos/informacao-cientifica/bibliodata
23. Candela, G., Escobar, P., Carrasco, R.C., Marco-Such, M.: A linked open data framework to enhance the discoverability and impact of cultural heritage. J. Inf. Sci. **45**(6), 756–766 (2019)
24. Georgiadis, H., et al.: Enriching the Greek national cultural aggregator with key figures in Greek history and culture: challenges, methodology, tools and outputs. In: Silvello, G., et al. (eds.) Linking Theory and Practice of Digital Libraries. TPDL 2022. Lecture Notes in Computer Science, vol. 13541, pp. 42–54. Springer, Cham (2022). https://doi.org/10.1007/978-3-031-16802-4_4
25. Wikipedia: WikiProject Women. https://en.wikipedia.org/wiki/Wikipedia:WikiProject_Women
26. Grant, M.J., Booth, A.: A typology of reviews: an analysis of 14 review types and associated methodologies. Health Inf. Libr. J. **26**(2), 91–108 (2009)

Track on Cultural Collections and Application

On the Interoperability Between Archival and Library Authorities

Aggeliki Drakopoulou[1], Leonidas Papachristopoulos[1],
and Christos Papatheodorou[2]([⊠])

[1] Department of Archives, Library Science and Museology, Ionian University,
Corfu, Greece
{l19drak,lpapachr}@ionio.gr
[2] Department of History and Philosophy of Science, National and Kapodistrian
University of Athens, Athens, Greece
papatheodor@phs.uoa.gr

Abstract. The interoperability of the data models that describe authority data is an important requirement for exchanging the data of Memory
Organizations in the World Wide Web. In this paper we focus on the
semantic interoperability between archival and library authorities. Initially we mapped EAC-CPF to MARC21 Authority standard and then
we mapped EAC-CPF to CIDOC Conceptual Reference Model, which is
an ontology for the cultural heritage. The study of the models and the
methodologies for the development of the proposed mappings revealed
the differences of information needs each model addresses.

Keywords: metadata interoperability · EAC-CPF · MARC21
Authority · mappings · CIDOC-CRM

1 Introduction

Cultural heritage institutions manage heterogeneous resources and use metadata
standards according to the diversity of their material and its description needs
[9]. The problem which has emerged is how these standards can be interoperable
so as the exchange of data and the integration of information to be feasible.
Interoperability is the compatibility of two or more systems enabling data and
information exchange without any loss [2].

In this paper we focus on the interoperability of archival authorities. These
authorities describe entities, persons, corporate bodies or families, that are creators of archives. ISAAR standard [7] provides a structured framework for the
documentation of the archive creators, their roles, their activities and in general
the historical and biographical data about them. ISAAR has been implemented
as an XML schema, the Encoded Archival Context for Corporate bodies, Persons
and Families (EAC-CPF) [5].

It is important for researchers to access information about the creator of an
archive, the historical context, the events and the circumstances under which

the archive was generated. This information is an access point for the archives they produced. By preserving archival authorities several relationships between archival organizations and also between libraries, museums and other memory organizations and other administration structures can be revealed [1]. For example, the real name of the Greek nobelist poet George Seferis was George Seferiadis, who was also a diplomat in the Greek Ministry of Foreign Affairs. The poet in some of his poems signs as Seferis and in others as Seferiadis but in the archival material of the Ministry of Foreign Affairs he is registered with his real surname. Thus, if in the archive of one institution Seferis is registered with his pen name and in the archive of another institution with the real one, then these two records should be connected, because they concern the same person (entity).

In the context of the World Wide Web, the question that arises is how archival authorities will be interlinked with other authority data. To address this issue, this paper presents a mapping of EAC-CPF standard to MARC21 Authorities [8]. Then, EAC-CPF is mapped to CIDOC - CRM (CIDOC- Conceptual Reference Model) [4], a domain ontology for the formal description of events related to cultural heritage. These standards were chosen because, MARC21 Authorities covers the area of Library data, while CIDOC - CRM the wider area of cultural heritage. Therefore, the proposed mappings will enable the archival authorities to be accessible not only by the archival community, but also by the wider community of cultural heritage data management.

2   Archival Authorities

The main objective of EAC-CPF [5] is to standardize the encoding of the creators' descriptions and to enable this information to be shared in an electronic environment. The standard is based on ISAAR [7] and supports the connection of information of a record creator with other creators, highlights their relationships and links the records descriptions with the related entities.

Each EAC-CPF document contains two mandatory elements, <control> and <cpfDescription> or <multipleIdentities>. The element <control> contains metadata about the authority record per se (the EAC-CPF instance and not the entity), such as identifiers, information about the creation and maintenance of the authority record (dates, used rules, etc.), its status, its language, etc. Thus, it may enclose the elements <recordId> or <otherRecordId> , whose values are identifiers. Moreover, it contains the elements <maintenanceAgency>, <maintenanceStatus> and <maintenanceHistory>. <maintenanceAgency> provides information about the agency that is responsible for the creation of an EAC-CPF instance, <maintenanceStatus> records the most recent status of an EAC-CPF instance and <maintenanceHistory> includes details about the history of the creation and the maintenance of an EAC-CPF instance. In addition, there are three elements to be declared for languages, rules and conventions used in the EAC-CPF instance: <languageDeclaration>, <conventionDeclaration> and <localTypeDeclaration>.

The element `<cpfDescription>` provides information about the names of the archive creators, their descriptions and relationships. It contains the elements `<alternativeSet>`, `<description>`, `<identity>`, `<relations>`. `<alternativeSet>` is used when two or more authority records coming from two or more authority systems are referred within a unique EAC-CPF instance. `<description>` is a wrapper element for the information regarding the description of the CPF entity described in the EAC-CPF instance. `<identity>` is a wrapper element for the name or names relevant to the identity being described within the element `<cpfDescription>`, while the element `<relations>` defines the relations with other corporate bodies, persons, families, resources, and functions.

There are two alternatives for the semantics of `<multipleIdentities>`: It denotes either two or more separate `<cpfDescription>` elements for the same entity (e.g. Seferis as poet and Seferiadis as diplomat, as mentioned) or multiple individuals operating with a common identity (e.g. the Ministry of Education, renamed to the Ministry of Education and Research at a particular time) [6]. In Listing 1 a fragment of an EAC-CFP document is given.

Listing 1. A fragment of an EAC-CPF document

```
<eac-cpf>
<control>
 <recordId>cpf.brown723</recordId>
 <languageDeclaration>
   <language languageCode="eng">English</language>
   <script scriptCode="Latin">Latin Alphabet</script>
 </languageDeclaration>
</control>
<cpfDescription>
<identity>
   <entityId localType="eadwg">CLU-SC-000008</entityId>
   <entityType>person</entityType>
   <nameEntry><part>Brown, Bob, 1886-1959</part></nameEntry>
</identity>
<description>
   <biogHist>
     <p>Robert Carlton Brown (1886-1959) was a writer</p>
   </biogHist>
</description>
<relations>
   <resourceRelation resourceRelationType="creatorOf"
   xlink:href="brown723.xml" xlink:role="archivalRecords">
   <relationEntry>Bob Brown papers, 1844-1960</relationEntry>
   </resourceRelation>
</relations>
</cpfDescription>
</eac-cpf>
```

3   MARC21 Authorities

The MARC21 Authorities is designed to provide information regarding the forms of names for persons, organisations, conferences, titles and themes as well as their thematic subdivisions. It is used to create access points to MARC records that describe documents. A MARC21 Authority record includes fields with (a) record identification codes, (b) the standard forms of names or subjects (1XX fields), (c) information about the gender or status of the described entity (3XX fields), as well as references to non-authorised forms of a name or subject (fields 4XX) and finally references to sources related to the described entity or subject (field 6XX). Table 1 presents a part of the Authority Record for the Greek poet George Seferis hosted by the Library of Congress. The symbol "|" denotes a MARC21 subfield of a field e.g. the subfield |a of the field 400, while the first two places are the indicators of a field with values (_ , 0, 1, ..., 9).

Table 1. A fragment of George Seferis' Authority record (source: Library of Congress).

MARC21 fields	Values (Metadata)
LC control no.:	n 82037877
LCCN Permalink:	https://lccn.loc.gov/n82037877
HEADING:	Seferis, George, 1900-1971
000	03963cz a2200781n 450
100	1_ |a Seferis, George, |d 1900-1971
368	_ _ |c Nobel Prize winners
370	_ _ |a Izmir (Turkey) |b Athens (Greece)
374	_ _ |a Poets |a Diplomats
375	_ _ |a Males
377	_ _ |a gre
400	1_ |a Seferiadis, George, |d 1900-1971
400	1_ |a Sepheris, Giorgos, |d 1900-1971
400	1_ |a ÎčÎţÏΕÎŋÏÄĮÎůÏĆ, ÎŞÎžÏÕÏĄÎŞÎ£ÎĆ , |d 1900-1971
670	_ _ |a Wikipedia, |b (George Seferis a Greek poet-diplomat.)
670	_ _ |a Encycl. Brit. |b (George Seferis)

4   CIDOC CRM

CIDOC-CRM (CIDOC Conceptual Reference Model, ISO 211127) [4] is an ontology intended to facilitate the integration, mediation and interchange of heterogeneous cultural heritage information. It was developed by a interdisciplinary team of experts, coming from fields such as computer science, archaeology, museum documentation, history of arts, natural history, library science, physics and philosophy, under the aegis of the International Committee for Documentation (CIDOC) of the International Council of Museums (ICOM). The model is event centric, that is, actors, places and objects are connected through events.

CIDOC-CRM is composed of a hierarchy of 86 classes (or entities) and 137 properties. A class is a category of objects that have one or many common characteristics. A class can be the domain or the range of properties. Properties are used to define relationships between two classes. An instance of a property is a relation between an instance of its domain and an instance of its range. A chain of one or more triples *domain class - property - range class* define a *CIDOC-CRM path*, where the *domain class*, *range class* and *property*, are the domain and range classes of a given property of CIDOC-CRM. Actually *CIDOC-CRM paths* are statements that express the semantics regarding a cultural heritage object, event, activity, or person, or organization, etc.

5   The Mappings

This section presents the following mappings:

- The mapping between the EAC-CPF and MARC21 Authority standard. This mapping is implemented as a mapping table between the two standards.
- The mapping between the EAC-CPF and CIDOC-CRM standard. For this mapping the XPATHs paths of the EAC-CPF are mapped to *CIDOC-CRM paths*. As mentioned, a *CIDOC-CRM path* is defined as a chain of triples *domain class - property - range class*.

5.1   The Mapping of EAC-CPF to MARC21 Authorities

According to the EAC-CPF syntax, several elements could be associated as subelements of other elements. Due to this syntactic complexity of EAC-CPF and the large number of its element, as well as the syntax of MARC 21 Athority fileds, we organize the EAC-CPF elements to following categories:

The first category includes the elements <identity> and <multipleIdentities> that document the identity of the archive creator. The subelements <entityId>, <otherRecordId> of the element <identity> hold identifiers that are relevant to the entity described. Moreover, the element <nameEntry> and its subelement <part> contain information about the name, surname and the family name of an agent.

The element <multipleIdentities> is used in two cases: in the first case it represents more than one identities identifying the same entity. For example, Peškov Aleksej Maksimovič was a novelist and used the name Maksim Gorki as a pseudonym, so there exist two entities for the same person. The second case describes one collective entity with multiple individuals who operate cooperatively and are subordinates to this identity. For instance, the Greek Ministry of

Spatial Planning Settlement and Environment renamed the Ministry of Spatial Planning and Energy; however, the archive of this entity remained the same.

The second category of EAC-CPF elements includes information about the dates and events related to the agent. The elements <date> and <event> and the XPATHs they appear in, define the dates of birth or death of a person or dates of start or end of an organization.

The third category includes elements about the places related to the agent. The element <placeEntry> provides information about where the EAC-CPF entity was based and lived. The element <placeRole> declares the role of a place (e.g. place of birth or residence).

The fourth category includes information about the language used for the cataloging (such as the XPATH eac-cpf/languageDeclaration/language and the language used by the described entity (such as the XPATH eac-cpf/languagesUsed/language). The fifth category includes information about citations relevant to the entity. The citations refer to information such as occupation, biographical history, the place or controlled vocabularies.

The sixth category includes information about the script used for the cataloging (XPATH: eac-cpf/languageDeclaration/script) and the script used by the described entity (XPATH: eac-cpf/languagesUsed/script). The seventh category includes descriptions about the profession and the functions of the described entity (e.g. its function, its occupation, its legal status, biographical or historical information, the structure of a corporate body or the genealogy of a family). The eighth category groups together one or more relation elements expressed by <cpfRelation>, <resourceRelation> or <functionRelation> denoting the relations of the agent with other agents. The relationship between agents and archives are given by the element <resourceRelation>. The final category includes the element <control> which records information about the EAC-CPF document itself as well as the agency that is responsible for the creation of the authority document (e.g. the name or the code of the agency, maintenance, status and also rights details). Additionally, this category provides information about the description of sources (e.g. bibliographic sources).

After the organization of the information that EAC-CPF provides, a vocabulary is needed to express the semantic relationships between the EAC-CPF elements and the corresponding MARC21 Authority fields. Therefore, the following properties from the SKOS vocabulary [12] were utilized:

- exact Match: matches concepts that have the same meaning;
- close Match: denotes two sufficiently similar concepts that can be used interchangeably;
- narrow Match: denotes a hierarchy in the match between two concepts. It is used when an EAC-CPF element has a semantically narrower meaning of a MARC21 Authority field.

Table 2 presents the mapping between the two standards. In the first column the elements of the EAC-CPF are analytically listed, organized to the mentioned categories; the second column presents the corresponding XPATHs that these elements can be found, according to the EAC-CPF syntax; in the third column the semantic relationship between EAC-CPF XPATHs and the corresponding MARC21 Authority fields is given, based on the SKOS properties, while in the last column the corresponding fields of the MARC21 Authority are listed.

5.2   The Mapping of EAC-CPF to CIDOC-CRM

The next step is to align the EAC-CPF standard to a conceptual schema that represents the semantics of cultural heritage information, such as CIDOC-CRM. This mapping will enable the publication of the archival authorities to the Semantic Web. For this purpose, the semantics of an archival authority record, such as an EAC-CPF document, is needed to be represented and expressed by the terms of CIDOC-CRM, which is an international standard and a reference model for the representation of the cultural heritage objects, events, activities and agents. As mentioned, the desired representation of the semantics of EAC-CPF to CIDOC-CRM will be implemented by mapping the XPATHs generated by the syntax of the EAC-CPF schema to *CIDOC-CRM paths*.

Thus, an archival authority record (included in the element `<eac-cpf>`) is a document describing textually the creator of an archive. Hence an archival authority record is a document that documents an entity and is also a textual object. In CIDOC-CRM terms, the element `<eac-cpf>` is mapped to both the classes *E31 Document* and *E33 Linguistic Object*, which are correlated by the property *P106 is composed of*, expressing the statement that an instance of the class *E31 Document* is composed by text (an instance of the class *E33 Linguistic Object*). This mapping is shown by the blue boxes and arrow of the Fig. 1.

Moreover, the creator of the archive is represented by the CIDOC-CRM class *E39 Actor*. Thus, the XPATH `/eac/cpfDescription/identity` that provides the main information of the creator is mapped to the CIDOC-CRM path *E31 Document - P70 documents - E39 Actor*, meaning that an instance of the class *E31 Document* documents an instance of the class *E39 Actor* who is the creator of an archive. This mapping is shown by the orange boxes and arrow of the Fig. 1. In detail, the creator's type is indicated by the EAC-CPF path `/eac-cpf/identity/entityType`; if the creator is a Person, then it is mapped to the CIDOC-CRM class *E21 Person*, while if the creator is a corporate body or family, then it is represented by the class *E74 Group*. Both the classes *E21 Person* and *E74 Group* are subclasses of the class *E39 Actor* and therefore they both inherit the properties of their parent class *E39 Actor*.

The full mapping of all the EAC-CPF XPATHs to *CIDOC-CRM paths* is given at http://users.uoa.gr/~papatheodor/eac-cpf.html; due to space limitations at this section we present some core EAC-CPF elements for the description of a creator of an archive and their mapping to CIDOC-CRM.

The name of the archive creator is provided by the XPATH `/eac-cpf /Identity/nameEntry/part @localType`, which corresponds to the CIDOC-CRM path *E39 Actor - P1 is identified by - E41 Appellation*. The values of the attribute `@localType` could be `surname`, `forname`, or `familyname`. This information is represented by the CIDOC-CRM path *E41 Appellation - P2*

Table 2. The mapping of EAC-CPF to MARC21 Authorities.

EAC-CPF elements	EAC-CPF Xpaths	Relation	MARC21 Authorities
entityId	eac-cpf/cpfDescription/identity/ entityId	exactMatch	001
otherRecordId	eac-cpf/ control/otherRecordId	exactMatch	024
nameEntry	eac-cpf/cpfDescription/identity /nameEntryParallel/nameEntry	exactMatch	100-500|wr|i
	eac-cpf/multipleIdentities/ cpfDescription/identity/nameEntry	exactMatch	100 and 373
part	eac-cpf/cpfDescription/identity/ nameEntryParallel/nameEntry/- part@localType=surname/ forname/familyname	exactMatch	378|q
date	Eac-cpf/ cpfDescription/description/ existDates/date	exactMatch	100|d or 110|d
event	eac-cpf/cpfDescription/description/ biogHist/chronList/chronItem/ event	exactMatch	678|a
placeEntry	Eac-cpf/cpfDescription/description/ place/placeEntry	narrowMatch	370|a|b|c|e|f
placeRole	eac-cpf/cpfDescription/description/ place/placeRole	narrowMatch	370|a |b |e
language	eac-cpf/control/ languageDeclaration/language	exactMatch	040|b
	eac-cpf/cpfDescription/ description/languagesUsed/language	exactMatch	377|a
Citation	eac-cpf/cpfDescription/description/ biogHist/citation	narrowMatch	678|u
	eac-cpf/cpfDescription/description/ occupation/citation	narrowMatch	374|u
	eac-cpf/cpfDescription/description/ place/citation	narrowMatch	370|u |a |b |e
script	eac-cpf/control/languageDeclaration /script	exactMatch	040|b
	eac-cpf/cpfDescription/description/ languageUsed/script	exactMatch	377|a
biogHist	eac-cpf/cpfDescription/description /biogHist	exactMatch	678|a
function	eac-cpf/cpfDescription/ description/function	exactMatch	100|c|e and 372|a|s|t
occupation	eac-cpf/cpfDescription/ description/occupation	exactMatch	374|a
cpfRelation	eac-cpf/cpfDescription /relations/cpfRelation	exactMatch	373|a|s|t
functionRelation	eac-cpf/cpfDescription /relations/functionRelation	exactMatch	372|a|s|t
resourceRelation	eac-cpf/cpfDescription/relations/ resourceRelation	exactMatch	700|t

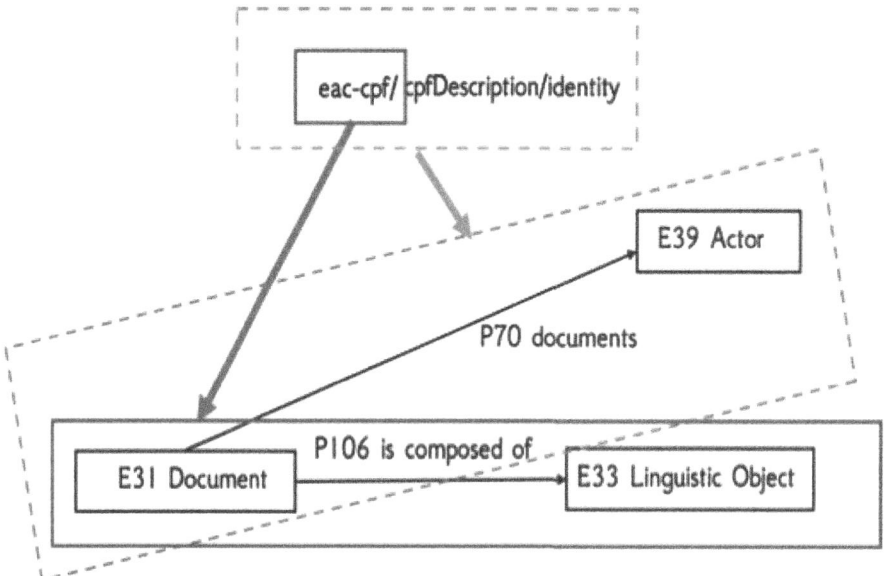

Fig. 1. The mapping of the XPATHs /eac/cpf and /eac/cpf/cpfDescription/identity to CIDOC-CRM paths.

has type -E55 Type, while the instances of the *class E55* Type belong to the vocabulary *surname, forname, familyname*.

The creator's place(s) are represented by /eac-cpf/description/ places /place/placeEntry, which is mapped to the CIDOC-CRM path *E39 Actor - P74 has current or former residence - E53 Place - P87 is identified by - E44 Place Appellation*. Similarly, the XPATH /eac-cpf/place/placeRole provides information about the place of residence or registered office (for organizations) of a creator of an archive and is mapped to the path *E39 Actor - P74 has current or former residence - E53 Place - P87 is identified by - E44 Place Appellation - P2 has type - E55 Type*, where the instances of the class *E55 Type* are either the value residence or registered office.

The language of an EAC record is indicated by the <language> element to which the EAC path /eac/LanguageDeclaration/language ends. The corresponding CIDOC-CRM path is: *E33 Linguistic object - P72 has language - E56 Language*. The script of the EAC document is declared by the path: /eac/LanguageDeclaration/script. However, CIDOC-CRM does not provide a path with the same semantics. This issue could be overcome by two paths starting from the class *E33 Linguistic object*: *E33 Linguistic object - P72 has language - E56 Language* and *E33 Linguistic object - P3 has note - E62 String P2 has type - E55 Type*.

Regarding identifiers, the EAC-CPF XPATH /eac-cpf/identity/ entityId corresponds to the CIDOC-CRM path *E39 Actor - P1 is identified by - E41 Appellation - P48 has preferred identifier - E42 Identifier*. This

CIDOC-CRM path is used for any identifier related to an archive creator e.g. number, symbol, code, etc. Furthermore, the /eac-cpf/control/ other-RecordId, provides information for alternative EAC-CPF document identifiers associated with the given archive creator. These identifiers are represented by the CIDOC-CRM path *E31 Document - P1 is identified by - E41 Appellation - P48 has preferred identifier - E42 Identifier.*

EAC-CPF provides several elements regarding the dates that signify particular states of the lifecycle of an archive creator. For instance, the paths /eac-cpf/existDates/date, /eac-cpf/description /existDates/date-Set and /eac-cpf/description/existDates/dateRange/toDate denote the range from the birth date to the death date of an individual or the range of the dates of establishment and dissolution of an organization. CIDOC-CRM provides two different events for the birth and the death. Thus, the birth date of a person or the establishment date of a corporate body is mapped to the path *E39 Actor - P92 brought into existence - E63 Beginning of Existence - P4 has time-span - E52 Time Span,* while the death date, or the dissolution date of a corporate body is mapped to the path *E39 Actor - P92 took out of existence - E63 End of Existence - P4 has time-span - E52 Time Span.* It should be noted that the class *E52 Time Span* means either a date range, or a particular date. In detail if the creator of an archive is a person then the dates of its birth and death are represented by the paths *E21 Person - P98 brought into life - E67 Birth - P4 has time-span - E52 Time Span* and *E21 Person - P100 was death of - E69 Death - P4 has time-span - E52 Time Span* respectively. If the creator is a corporate body then the date of its formation is represented by the path *E74 Group - P95 has formed - E66 Formation - P4 has time-span - E52 Time Span,* while the date of its dissolution is represented by *E74 Group - P99 dissolved - E68 Dissolution - P4 has time-span - E52 Time Span.* Additionally, the path /eac-cpf/description/existDates/dateSet/eac-cpf/biogHist/ChronList/ChronItem/event denotes that the creator participates in an event at a particular time and is mapped to the generic path *E39 Actor - P11 had participant - E5 Event - P4 has time span - E52 Time Span.*

The XPATH /eac-cpf/cpfDescription /alternativeSet/set-Component has the meaning that the creator of an archive has been also described by other EAC-CPF documents or other documents based on other archival authority systems. This path could be represented by CIDOC-CRM in two parallel steps. The first one focuses on the description of the activities of an agent. Thus the XPATH /eac-cpf/cpfDescription is expressed in CIDOC-CRM terms by the *E39 Actor - P14 carried out by (performed) - E7 Activity - P70 - documents (is documented in) - E31 Document,* while the rest path cpfDescription/alternativeSet/setComponent denoting that there is another document with a name or an identifier that documents also a creator of an archive could be expressed by the path starting from the class *E39 Actor: E39 Actor - P67 refers to (is referred to by) - E31 Document - P1 is identified by (identifies) - E41 Appellation.*

6   Discussion and Conclusions

The advent of web technologies triggered the development of powerful methods for the management of documents in digital format. Various metadata schemes were created to address the needs of memory organizations to describe, manage and preserve such objects. However, there is still the difficulty in searching - retrieving information due to the plethora of heterogeneous metadata schemes. Thus, the need for "communication" between these schemes arose and therefore interoperability methods are needed so as the entities that are creators of either bibliographic or archival material to be identified and treated seamlessly.

In this paper, an attempt was made to align two standards for encoding authority records, the EAC-CPF XML Schema and MARC21 format for Authority Data. After examining the semantic relationships (exact, narrow, close match) between the elements of these two models, Table 2 was created, presenting their mapping table. Furthermore, the EAC-CPF paths were expressed as CIDOC-CRM paths, establishing a mapping between the standard for archival authority and the well-known CIDOC-CRM, which is a reference model for the semantic interoperability between cultural heritage metadata.

The mappings revealed the following remarks: In EAC-CPF the entities corporate bodies, persons and families are represented and described by the same set of elements, while in CIDOC-CRM there is a distinction between the class *Person* and *Group*; the latter does not discriminates between organizations and families. Similarly, MARC21 Authority treats these entity types differently since persons and corporate bodies are declared in separate fields (field 100 for persons or families and field 110 for the corporate bodies).

An important issue is the handling of multiple identities. The representation of multiple entities is a usual case in archives and in name authority files in general. MARC21 Authority provides a set of elements for denoting such relationships, e.g. the combination of the fields 1XX and 5XX|a with the utilization of the pair of subfields 500|wi and 500|i or the utilization of the vocabulary of the subfield 500|e for the declaration of the real and alternate entities. However, CIDOC-CRM does not provide a direct way for their identification and discrimination.

Another observation concerns dates and time periods. The EAC-CPF standard provides elements that facilitate the detailed description of time and place. Furthermore, MARC21 Authority standard is even more expressive as it combines time and place in field 370. CIDOC-CRM provides a generic class *E52 Time Span* for the representation of dates and time periods, while the representation of place is defined by the class *E53 Place* as well as the classes for the declaration of geographical coordinates. In general, the event orientation of CIDOC-CRM generates expressive statements with clear semantics for events of any type. Both EAC-CPF and MARC21 Authorities provide elements that encode and describe events, but they do not semantically correlate events with other events, or persons, or materials, or objects as explicitly as CIDOC-CRM does. However it should be mentioned that the event-oriented character of CIDOC - CRM sometimes generates complex paths, e.g. the representation of a simple bibliographic reference.

The proposed mapping from EAC-CPF to MARC21 Authority does not exhibit a serious degree of information loss, although 47 from the 91, elements of EAC-CPF, almost half, were mapped to the MARC21 Authority. Thus the elements `<objectXMLWrap>`, which include data encoded in other XML schema than EAC-CPF, `<objectBinWrap>`, for a base64-encoded binary representation of a resource [10], are not mapped to MARC21 Authority. Moreover, the elements `<abbreviation>`, an abbreviation of a thesaurus, controlled vocabulary, or other standard to formulate the EAC-CPF description, `<otherAgencyCode>`, an alternate code representing the institution responsible for the creation, maintenance or dissemination of the EAC-CPF instance and `<chronItem>` are not mapped to MARC21 Authority elements. However, these elements are of secondary importance, and therefore the lack of mappings does not signify any significant information loss. Additionally it should be mentioned that although for some EAC-CPF elements that it seems there is not any MARC21 Authority element with the same meaning to be mapped to, actually, their semantics are included in combinations of MARC21 Authority elements. Thus the meaning of the element `<agentType>`, is incorporated into the field 1XX, where the field 100 describes persons and the field 110 describes families and corporate bodies, while their discrimination is inferred by its subfields.

An EAC-CPF element that should be discussed is `<structureOrGenealogy>` which holds information about the internal administrative structure of a corporate body or the genealogy of a family. In particular its subelement `<level>` holds textual information about the hierarchical level of a person in a genealogy or the level of an administrative structure in the hierarchy of a corporate body (e.g. 'first level', 'second level', etc.) For its mapping to the MARC21 Authority there are the following cases: If the `<entityType>` concerns a Corporate Body, then the mapping is directly to 110|b that holds the subordinate units of a corporate body. Alternatively, the mapping could be realized as a combination of the following fields: In the field 110|a the name of the Corporate body could be inserted while in the field 510|a the name of the related unit could be mentioned and in the subfield 510|e the relator term (the term of the relationship) should be inserted.

In the case the `<entityType>` concerns a Family, then it is mapped to the field 100|a with indicators 3_; additionally (a) in the subfield 500|a the name of the related member of the family (person) in referred, (b) in the subfield 500|w the code r should be inserted denoting that the generation of a tag related reference instruction phrase in a cross reference display should be suppressed, (c) in the subfield 500|i the type of the relationship in the genealogy (e.g. member of family, or progenitor, etc.) should be referred. Alternatively to (b) and (c), the subfield 500|e could be used which provides a vocabulary describing the types of the relationships of two related persons in a Family.

It should be remarked that the relationships represented by MARC21 Authority are binary, they can represent relationships between two entities (Persons, Corporate Bodies, Families and their members). Hence, the genealogies as well as the hierarchical structures of the corporate bodies are inferred from the mutual binary relationships between the members/departments/branches, etc. of the described entities.

CIDOC-CRM represents genealogy and administrative hierarchy indirectly by the property P107 has current or former member. In conclusion, MARC21 Authority is more flexible and more expressive than EAC-CPF and CIDOC-CRM in defining complex hierarchical relationships by using the combination of 1XX and 5XX fields, their corresponding subfields as well as the terms of the vocabulary given in the subfield 500|e.

Another significant point is that there are several relationships between an entity (corporate body, person, or family) with other entities or resources (archives and archival descriptions). CIDOC-CRM reveals the semantics of these relationships more accurately than the other standards, although its paths are complex. EAC-CPF provides particular elements to denote relationships between an entity and either a function of a corporate body or an archive. MARC21 Authority also provides particular 3XX and 6XX fields that are combined with the 1XX fields in order to provide clear information about the relationships between roles and functions, as well as between existing bibliographic works.

Regarding the field EAC-CPF <control>, which provides information about the creation and the maintenance of a record, the MARC21 Authority standard is more expressive and clearer than the EAC-CPF. Certainly, the family of MARC standards provide clear semantics regarding the creation and management of records and XML documents. In CIDOC-CRM such crucial information is represented by long and complex paths concerning the description of instances of the class E73 Information Object.

One more remark refers to the element <legal status>, which needs particular vocabularies for its definition in both EAC-CPF and CIDOC-CRM. On the contrary, MARC21 Authority provides a rich vocabulary for legal characterizations. Finally, regarding the authorized form of names is provided by the element <preferredForm> in EAC-CPF standard. This concept is not defined by CIDOC-CRM, while the MARC21 Authority provides fields to establish and keep the preferred form of the name of an entity.

Concluding, this paper recommends two alternatives for the incorporation of archival authorities in the environment of the semantic web. Either the transformation of EAC-CPF data to the CIDOC-CRM model, or their transformation to MARC21 Authorities, which then can be transformed as RDF triples utilizing either RDA vocabulary [11] or BIBFRAME model [3]. Regarding the first approach, CIDOC-CRM is a model of wide acceptance by the cultural heritage community and therefore the archival authorities could be interlinked to several other metadata schemas that are based or mapped to CIDOC-CRM. Moreover, the proposed mapping to CIDOC-CRM, although complex enough, reveals precisely the semantics of archival authorities and the processes for the creation of archives and archival metadata. On the other hand, the disadvantage is that there is not a large number of implemented applications that use CIDOC-CRM semantics as the core component of a mediator for the integration of cultural heritage data. Hence there is still the demand for implementations of the mappings of cultural heritage data to CIDOC-CRM and the publishing of CIDOC-CRM based metadata as linked data.

Concerning the second approach, the existing powerful tools for authority management, as well as for the incorporation of authority data into the semantic web should be considered a significant advantage. Nevertheless, as mentioned, there exist issues in the semantic precision of the mapping of EAC-CRPF to MARC21 authorities. Some of the EAC-CPF elements are not mapped and some others are mapped to MARC21 Authority fields of wider or even narrower semantics, generating probably ambiguity and misunderstandings in the reasoning mechanisms of the information agents operating in the linked data environment.

References

1. Bountouri, L., Gergatsoulis, M.: The semantic mapping of archival metadata to the CIDOC CRM ontology. J. Archi. Organ. **9**(3–4), 174–207 (2011). https://doi.org/10.1080/15332748.2011.650124
2. Chungoora, N., Canciglieri, O., Young, R.I.: Towards expressive ontology-based approaches to manufacturing knowledge representation and sharing. Int. J. Comput. Integr. Manuf. **23**(12), 1059–1070 (2010). https://doi.org/10.1080/0951192x.2010.518976
3. Library of Congress: Overview of the BIBFRAME 2.0 Model (BIBFRAME - Bibliographic Framework Initiative). https://www.loc.gov/bibframe/docs/bibframe2-model
4. CIDOC-CRM, version v.7.3. https://www.cidoc-crm.org
5. EAC-CPF - Encoded Archival Context for Corporate Bodies, Persons, and Families. https://eac.staatsbibliothek-berlin.de/
6. EAC-CPF Tag Library. https://eac.staatsbibliothek-berlin.de/schema/taglibrary/cpfTagLibrary2019_EN.html
7. ISAAR (CPF) - International Standard Archival Authority Record for Corporate Bodies, Persons and Families, 2nd Edition, International Council on Archives. https://www.ica.org/en/isaar-cpf-international-standard-archival-authority-record-corporate-bodies-persons-and-families-2nd
8. MARC21 Format for Authority data, Library of Congress. https://www.loc.gov/marc/authority/
9. Haynes, D.: Metadata for Information Management and Retrieval: Understanding Metadata and Its Use, 2nd edn. Facet Publishing, London (2018)
10. Noy, N.F.: Semantic integration. ACM SIGMOD Record **33**(4), 65–70 (2004). https://doi.org/10.1145/1041410.1041421
11. RDA Toolkit. https://access.rdatoolkit.org/
12. Simple Knowledge Organization System, SKOS. https://www.w3.org/TR/skos-primer/

Applying New Standards to Legacy Data for Semantic Interoperability and Multilingualism: A Case Study at the National Library of Greece

Sofia Zapounidou[1]([✉]) [iD], Michalis Gerolimos[1] [iD], Eftychia Koufakou[1] [iD], and Giorgos Veranis[2] [iD]

[1] National Library of Greece, Athens, Greece
{szapounidou,m.gerolimos,koufakou}@nlg.gr
[2] Dataly Tech, Thessaloniki, Greece
gveranis@datalytech.gr

Abstract. The National Library of Greece (NLG) adopted new cataloguing standards, namely IFLA LRM and RDA, two international standards which adhere to linked data principles. Even though newly created metadata is linked data compliant, the legacy data is not. Considering the objective of publishing the data of the NLG to the linked data cloud, interoperability in terms of technology, standards, and language is essential. Towards this goal, workflows have changed, corrections and enrichments were made, new system functionalities were developed, and new tools were used. This paper presents the implemented approach.

Keywords: bibliographic data · interoperability · National Library of Greece · MARC21 · RDA · IFLA LRM

1 Introduction

Nowadays, advanced information technologies based on the representation of information using machine-understandable semantics and relationships are used on a global scale. Structured library data (especially authority records) was considered a "low-hanging fruit" [1], and, indeed, libraries worldwide initiated projects to convert their data using new conceptual models and machine-understandable representations. A major obstacle to this process is the use of the legacy MARC format by Integrated Library Systems (ILSs). The structure of the information remains flat and record-based rendering difficult to represent information using semantic conceptualizations defined in the International Cataloguing Principles [2] and the new bibliographic models, e.g., IFLA Library Reference Model (IFLA-LRM) [3], Resource Description and Access (RDA) [4]. Thus, despite that i) core tools in terms of bibliographic models, rules, vocabularies, and mappings exist [5], and ii) there is some experience in implementing entity-based cataloguing principles in the everyday workflow [6–8], there are not any mature commercial and open-source systems that could be used for native linked data production

© The Author(s), under exclusive license to Springer Nature Switzerland AG 2025
M. Sfakakis et al. (Eds.): MTSR 2024, CCIS 2331, pp. 237–242, 2025.
https://doi.org/10.1007/978-3-031-81974-2_20

[9]. Libraries continue to engage with the linked data community despite the lack of tools. A main concern is to render their data "linked-data ready". In this context, NLG adopted in 2022 the new bibliographic models (IFLA-LRM, and official RDA) updating its policies, workflows, systems, and data.

2   Status Quo and Research Questions

The NLG Catalogue (koha.nlg.gr) includes more than 650.000 bibliographic records and more than 330.000 authority records. These records were created in various contexts in terms of people, standards, processes, completeness, and consistency. The Cataloguing Department consists of two teams: a team of 9 cataloguers, and a team of 3 system librarians. In 2022, when the IFLA-LRM and the official RDA rules were adopted, cataloguers had to learn new cataloguing rules and adapt. Additionally, the mindset had to change; data is to be created for human and machine consumption alike. Given that today's ILSs cannot deliver advanced search services consuming structured information, a linked data prototype was envisioned [10]. Towards the goal of publishing NLG data as linked data, the following research questions were posed:

1) Besides the mapping algorithm, are there any other ways to further facilitate the transformation process of both structured and unstructured data residing in MARC21 records?
2) Is there a way to increase the reusability of legacy data in terms of interoperability and multilingualism?

This paper reports on the methodology used by the NLG towards delivering interoperable and multilingual data.

3   Methodology

The transition from record-based cataloguing to entity-based cataloguing, using IFLA-LRM conceptualizations as implemented in RDA, is not a straightforward process. It demands changes regarding staff's mindset and knowledge, workflows, systems, and quality control.

One of the first attitude changes was to familiarize the NLG cataloguers with the notion that different people may create and update metadata. Traditionally, and due to staff shortage, each record describing either a publication or another bibliographic entity, e.g., a Person or a Work, was created by the same person and in rare cases updated by another. A newly introduced perspective was that the data must be available for both human and machine consumption, meaning that bibliographic information needs to be represented in ways that enable its reuse equally by humans and machines. The net result is that interoperability becomes a core goal in the cataloguing process.

Following these ideas and the adoption of new bibliographic models in the everyday business, the cataloguing team formulated the following core principles: i) transition from record-based cataloguing to entity-based cataloguing using structured information (controlled vocabularies) as much as possible, and ii) extensive use of identifiers, recording semantics of properties, relationships and values using URIs in the MARC21 records. The use of URIs in MARC is known in the literature as 'linky MARC approach' [11].

The implementation of the aforementioned principles framed a new workflow that consists of phases and enrichments performed by different teams, namely:

 i) acquisition metadata with core info about publications, e.g., title, publisher is sent by the Acquisition Department.
 ii) enrichment of the acquisition metadata by a system librarian who adds or edits data in MARC21 fields to fulfil NLG minimum requirements.
iii) further enrichment by cataloguing staff implementing the official RDA rules. In this context, cataloguers correct the bibliographic records according to the official RDA rules, add subjects and Dewey class numbers. Moreover, they create all the needed authority records to describe entities involved in the publication, e.g., author of the work, translators of the expression, monographic series, concepts as subjects, etc.
 iv) quality control by the system librarians, plus batch record edit (if possible) and enrichments of both new and legacy data based either on findings from the quality control or on cataloguing decisions made, e.g., add $0 to the main field in all authority records, add the $7 subfield for translated terms.
 v) dissemination of bibliographic and authority records through the online catalogue.
 vi) conversion to RDA/RDF and publication as linked data in the local Wikibase instance (data.nlg.gr).

Along with the workflow, the ILS needed to adapt. The NLG uses the open-source system Koha, allowing for customizations and newly developed functionalities tailored to the workflow and the new standards. All Koha templates (known as frameworks) were adapted to include new MARC21 fields that could be used for the accommodation of structured information. In addition, constraints were added to the frameworks to avoid mistakes during data entry. Several new lists with authorized values were, also, created and linked to the proper MARC21 fields/subfields. Considering that linked data is all about identifiers, an NBN identifier generator was created and integrated into the NLG Koha installation to produce unique and permanent identifiers. Tables 1 and 2 present the new MARC21 fields and subfields that are currently used by the NLG. The added value of using these MARC21 fields/subfields is discussed in the next section of the paper.

4   Discussion and Conclusions

The new workflow has enabled better management of the cataloguing process overcoming the difficulties arisen from the lack of staff in conjunction with the lack of familiarity with the new rules, the ever-increasing number of publications to be catalogued, and the obligation for timely delivery of the national bibliography. In the context of the new workflow, a small number of subfields and fields have been added in the NLG records (see Tables 1 and 2) to ease the transformation process of MARC21 records to RDA/RDF for the NLG Wikibase project [10], and especially to enhance the NLG data in terms of interoperability, multilingualism, and reusability.

A major facilitator for the transformation of authority records has been the use of the 075 field (Table 2). The MARC21 format for authority records allows the description

Table 1. New MARC21 subfields used in all records

Field	Scope	Example
$0	NLG identifier	100 1# $aΜέσκος, Μάρκος,$d1935-2019 **$0** urn:nbn:gr:nlg:01-A009930
$1	URI of value	334 ## $aπολυμερής μονάδα$b1005$2rdami **$1** http://rdareg istry.info/termList/ModeIssue/1005
$4	URI of relationship property	500 1#wriΦυσικό πρόσωπο. Σχετικό φυσικό πρόσωπο:$aΚαζαντζάκη, Γαλάτεια,$d1881-1962$0 urn:nbn:gr:nlg:01-A005274 **$4** http://rdareg istry.info/Elements/a/object/P50316
$7	Data provenance, e.g. transliteration standard or English translation	400 1# $aMeskos, Markos,$d1935-2019 **$7** ALA-LC romanization:Greek:2010 450 ## $aAgritourism **$7** eng

Table 2. New MARC21 fields used in authority or bibliographic records

Field	Auth	Bib	Scope	Note
024	x		Identifiers in other datasets	Identifiers associated with the entity described in the authority record
046	x		Dates in EDTF format	Standardized format of dates
075	x		Type of RDA entity being described in the record	Instantiation of entities in RDA/RDF
33X		x	Categorizations (e.g., media type)	Values from controlled vocabularies expressed in Greek and with URIs
37X	x		Contextual information (e.g., associated country, profession)	
1XX		x	$i & $4 Relationships with other entities	RDA relationships expressed in Greek and with URIs
5XX	x			
7XX		x		

of different entities using the same set of fields. What differentiates the type of entity being described is the existence of specific subfields in the basic field of the record. As an example, the basic field for personal names is 100, but if 100$t is used then the record does not describe the name of a person, but a work written by the person. Thus, to avoid complex algorithms checking the existence of specific subfields to determine the type of entity described, NLG has added the field 075 to all authority records holding the proper RDA class as value, e.g., code C1004 and URI http://rdaregistry.info/Elements/ c/C10004 for the RDA Person entity.

Linked data is about providing information for identified resources. The development of the NBN identifier generator supports easy assignment of identifiers to the bibliographic entities in the NLG catalog (see Table 1, subfield $0). These identifiers are to be used as basis for the construction of permanent URIs. Most important, the use of identifiers within the legacy ILS has increased the data independence. Data can be exported from one system to another retaining relationships and linkages expressed in a system-agnostic way. These relationships are retained during transformation of MARC21 records to RDA/RDF, and even when NLG records are shared with other libraries. Due to the use of the relationship property URI in the $4 subfield, the semantics of these relationships are also retained in a system and language-agnostic manner. A good illustration of this is the example for subfield $4 in Table 1. The MARC21 sample is from an authority record describing an RDA Person. The example presents the relationship between this Person and another one. The identifier of the second Person is recorded in $0, while the exact nature of their relationship is expressed as a URI in $4. Since identifiers and relationships are major enablers for linked data and data exploration, identifiers as URIs from third-party datasets are also added in authority records to ease the linking of the NLG data to Wikidata and other datasets in the linked data cloud (see field 024 in Table 2).

URIs are also used in fields when a value has been taken from a third-party vocabulary or dataset. The subfield holding the URI is $1. The example in Table 1 shows that a value from an RDA controlled vocabulary is used. The term is recorded as a string in Greek in subfield $a, while the URI of the term is in $1. Considering that both linked data and RDA rules necessitate structured information, the NLG has selected many controlled vocabularies to be used in authority and bibliographic records (see 075, 37X, and 33X fields in Table 2). In these fields, the approach of using Greek terms and their semantic equivalent as URI in $1 is implemented. The same approach is used in subfields describing relationships. The text describing a relationship is written in Greek (subfield $i) and the URI of the relationship is recorded in $4 (see Table 2, fields 1XX, 5XX, 7XX). Thus, Greek users can understand the semantics of a term or a relationship (subfields $a and $i respectively), while international audience and/or machines can understand the semantics of the value considering the URIs in subfields $1 and $4.

To further support multilingualism, English translations and equivalents from the Library of Congress Subject Headings (LCSH) are recorded as variant access points in the NLG authority records describing topics. The English language is explicitly noted in subfield $7 (see example in Table 1). Subfield $7 is also used to present the standard used for transliterating Greek characters to Latin ones. Transliterations can be used by developers to match Greek names with names in third systems. The NLG uses two standards, ALA-LC romanization tables and the ELOT743 (Greek translation of ISO843). Both standards are selected for interoperability reasons; US libraries use the ALA-LC romanization tables, while European ones mostly use the ISO 843.

Structured information of data was also achieved using the EDTF standard for the recording of dates. Cataloguers have always used dates for recording birth and death dates, event dates, etc. Yet, these dates were recorded as strings, while now with the use of the EDTF standard in the 046 field (Table 2), dates can be consumed by humans and machines equally, they can be easily calculated and further support timespan-oriented searches.

To conclude, the NLG has changed the cataloguing workflow and managed to bring structured information, consistency, interoperability, support for multilingualism, and system independent data, by adding a limited number of fields and subfields in both bibliographic and authority records. Continuous efforts for the interoperability of data and for further support of multilingualism are needed. In this context, the NLG will examine the use of more fields/subfields and controlled vocabularies, as well as the use of AI for further enrichments.

References

1. Library Linked Data Incubator Group Final Report. https://www.w3.org/2005/Incubator/lld/XGR-lld-20111025. Accessed 19 July 2024
2. Statement of International Cataloguing Principles (ICP) 2016. https://repository.ifla.org/handle/123456789/80. Accessed 19 July 2024
3. IFLA Library Reference Model: A Conceptual Model for Bibliographic Information. https://repository.ifla.org/handle/123456789/40. Accessed 19 July 2024
4. RDA Toolkit. https://www.rdatoolkit.org. Accessed 19 July 2024
5. Gaitanou, P., Andreou, I., Sicilia, M.-A., Garoufallou, E.: Linked data for libraries: creating a global knowledge space, a systematic literature review. J. Inf. Sci. **50**(1), 204–244 (2024)
6. Cagnazzo, L.: Linked data: implementation, use, and perceptions across European National Libraries. University of Strathclyde Glasgow Computer and Information Sciences, Glasgow (2017)
7. KB becomes the first national library to fully transition to Linked Data. https://www.mynewsdesk.com/se/kungliga_biblioteket/pressreleases/kb-becomes-the-first-national-library-to-fully-transition-to-linked-data-2573975. Accessed 19 July 2024
8. Program for Cooperative Cataloging. PCC (Program for Cooperative Cataloging) Strategic Directions January 2018-December (2019). https://www.loc.gov/aba/pcc/about/PCC-Strategic-Directions-2018-2021.pdf. Accessed 19 July 2024
9. Moi, A.: When Linked Data Is (not) Enough. Cataloguing Tools Between Obsolescence and Innovation. JLIS. It **11**(2):1–19 (2020)
10. Zapounidou, S., Ioannidis, L., Gerolimos, M., Koufakou, E., Bratsas, C.: Entity management using RDA and Wikibase: a case study at the national library of Greece. J. Libr. Metadata **24**(2), 111–131 (2024)
11. Wallis, R.: MARC and beyond: our three Linked Data choices. In: IFLA WLIC 2018 – Kuala Lumpur, Malaysia – Transform Libraries, Transform Societies, Session 113 - Information Technology. IFLA, Hague (2018)

CTP Ontology: An Ontology for Creating and Structuring Cultural Thematic Paths

Tiziana Pasciuto[1,2](✉)[iD], Riccardo Albertoni[1][iD], and Roberta Maggi[1]

[1] Institute for Applied Mathematics and Information Technologies "Enrico Magenes"
National Research Council, Genoa 16149, Italy
{riccardo.albertoni,roberta.maggi}@ge.imati.cnr.it
[2] Department of Modern Languages and Cultures, University of Genoa,
Genoa 16124, Italy
tiziana.pasciuto@ge.imati.cnr.it

Abstract. A thematic path is a tool for the enjoyment of cultural heritage that allows the connection of cultural objects of different nature through the identification of common themes. This study aims to develop the Cultural Thematic Path (CTP) Ontology, an ontology for the creation and structuring of cultural thematic paths, in order to support the linked data publishing and managing for the enjoyment of cultural heritage in the GLAM (Galleries, Libraries, Archives, and Museums) domain. Despite the literature revealing that numerous ontologies deal with managing and describing cultural resources related to the GLAM domain, the absence of a schema capable of fully depicting and representing thematic paths is highlighted. In this work, all the phases of ontology development are presented, from design assumptions to the ontology requirements specifications, from the implementation activity to the description of the ontology's defined entities and properties.

Keywords: Thematic Path · Cultural Thematic Path · Ontology · GLAM · Cultural Heritage Domain

1 Introduction

A thematic path is "a tool for the enjoyment of cultural heritage that allows connecting cultural objects of different nature (tangible and intangible) through identifying common themes. The chosen theme, which may concern specific topics, contexts, events, places, historical periods or characters, and so on, is expressed synthetically by a title and in-depth with a written descriptive text; it can be further identified through the use of keywords. The thematic path could be structured either as a collector of cultural objects, without establishing an order of priority, or present a predetermined order. The development and use of this enjoyment strategy can be profitable to convey messages and cultural, ethical, and social values." [17] These paths serve to organize and present cultural content coherently and engagingly, facilitating meaningful connections and

© The Author(s), under exclusive license to Springer Nature Switzerland AG 2025
M. Sfakakis et al. (Eds.): MTSR 2024, CCIS 2331, pp. 243–255, 2025.
https://doi.org/10.1007/978-3-031-81974-2_21

interpretations for users. However, despite the existence of numerous examples of thematic paths, there is currently no universally recognized pattern for their structural organization, in addition to the numerous definitions and nuances of meaning associated with the same concept [17]. To address this current gap in the GLAM (Galleries, Libraries, Archives, and Museums) domain, this study aims to develop an ontology for the creation and structuring of cultural thematic paths, named **Cultural Thematic Path (CTP) Ontology**, in order to support the linked data publishing and managing for the enjoyment of cultural heritage in the GLAM domain.

2   Related Works

Literature reveals that numerous ontologies manage and describe cultural resources related to the GLAM domain [4,9,10,24]. However, the comparison of ontologies across all different sub-domains highlights the absence of a schema capable of fully describing and representing thematic paths. While these standards offer solutions for delineating relationships between objects (such as the hierarchical structure of an archival collection, a museum collection, or a library book collection) and provide methods for organizing these objects into a superstructure, thus forming a collection, this terminology falls short in capturing certain specificities inherent in a thematic path. At a first survey, concepts that could be assimilated to the thematic path are *Collection* (e.g. adopted by BIBFRAME, Record in Context (RiC), ArCo Ontology), *Dataset* (Europeana Data Model (EDM)), *Curated Holding* (CIDOC-CRM), *Work* connected with *Conceptual Object* through the property *R10 is member of* (LRMoo).

However, equating these concepts to a thematic path can be simplistic. In fact, a *Collection* or a *Dataset* represents a set of objects, elements, or information grouped by a common characteristic or specific purpose. Additionally, a *Curated Holding* indicates that these collected objects are managed by one or more agents. Instead, a thematic path, in addition to incorporating the above definitions, is a way of presenting such objects, elements, or information that share a common theme or topic. In the related work, the organization of resources within a collection is based on logical criteria or practical needs, and this information can only be realized through the use of notes and text strings (e.g. *CollectionArrangement* Class in BIBFRAME). In contrast, a thematic path adopts a narrative or logical structure that guides the user through a series of interconnected objects, often sourced from different collections, arranged in a specific order to illustrate or explore a particular concept or topic; this approach may include narratives, illustrations, or other forms of support to communicate the main message or idea. Furthermore, relationships can be created not only between thematic paths and cultural resources but also between agents with specific roles, temporal entities, and places. This allows for the indication of who or what inspired a thematic path through the use of object properties, rather than just datatype properties. Finally, the main aim of a collection is to organize resources according to practical and/or logical criteria, while a thematic path aims to tell, educate, or inform people about a specific topic.

3   Methodology

To develop the ontology, the Linked Open Terms (LOT) Methodology was followed [20]. This methodology is specifically designed for building ontology, drawing on existing methods, and oriented towards the development and technologies of the semantic web. The LOT Methodology was chosen due to its foundation in years of practical industrial application experience and strong academic credibility. It is based on a workflow comprising four activities: ontology requirements specification, implementation, publication, and maintenance. In this paper, to outline the foundations upon which the ontology is built, to delve into the adopted design assumptions and the proposed modeling, all four activities of the workflow will be illustrated, but the primary focus will be on the first two, the Ontology Requirements Specification and the Ontology Implementation.

4   Design Assumptions

For the development of the CTP Ontology, the decision was made to create new classes and properties to model the domain. This approach aimed to establish an autonomous model, independent of the constraints and axioms that would typically be assumed when importing reused ontologies (hard reuse) or referencing URIs of reused ontology elements (soft reuse) [18,20].

Presutti et al. [21] identify and classify the main operations that can be conducted on Content Patterns (CP), which are "special kind of ontologies", and highlight how these operations are useful in the creation and modeling of ontologies. In this case, the adopted solution combines two of the operations proposed by Presutti's work: *Cloning* and *Specialization*. The operation of *Cloning* involves duplicating ontology entities into new namespaces, allowing them to be reused in a Content Pattern or serve as a prototype for defining a new ontology entity within a CP, while *Specialization* involves creating a new ontology by refining and elaborating on the entities of an existing one. This choice enables tracking the consulted ontologies used as models for CTP ontology modeling, facilitating potential future alignments with domain-specific and relevant ontologies for defining specific aspects (e.g. time modeling). The ontologies from which classes and properties have been derived are specified in the CTP Ontology Description (Sect. 6.1) and in Fig. 1. Ontology Design Patterns (ODPs) were also considered, which are reusable modeling solutions that encode best practices in modeling, providing a standardized approach to solving common ontology design issues. [11,21]. The chosen ODPs were taken from the online catalog of CPs.

In the following, we describe the CTP ontological design, providing insight into the **Ontology Requirements Specification** (Sect. 5) and **Ontology Implementation** (Sect. 6), two of the activities foreseen by the LOT Methodology. **Ontology Publication** and **Maintenance** are briefly discussed in Sect. 7.

5   Ontology Requirements Specification

This first activity involves gathering the ontology's requirements to satisfy [26]. It consists of several sub-activities, three of which will be examined in detail: **Use Case Specification, Purpose and Scope Identification**, and **Functional Ontological Requirements Proposal**.

The **Use Case Specification** sub-activity involves identifying scenarios, that are situations in which the ontology can be utilized and indicating the target audience. Three scenarios were selected: the first two are mainly aimed at enhancing movable and musealized cultural heritage, while the third one concerns cultural itineraries, thus focusing on immovable and intangible cultural heritage. To read a brief description of the selected scenarios see Table 1.

Table 1. Description of selected scenarios for the CTP Ontology development.

Scenarios
***Exhibition "Transitions	Enterprise - Work - Society"***- The scenario's purpose is to preserve the memory of the exhibition "Transitions	enterprise - work - society," organized by the Ansaldo Foundation and held at the Falcone Theater of the Royal Palace of Genoa from 02/22/2023 to 04/25/2023 [5]. The exhibition narrated the evolution of three interconnected sub-thematic paths (enterprise, work, and society) associated with the development of the Ansaldo Company, spanning from its inception in the early 1850s to the present day.
Target audience: Genoese citizens, tourists, and scholars.
Novum Corpus Fontanianum - This scenario aims to celebrate the legacy of the scientist Felice Fontana by compiling his professional works into a comprehensive "opera omnia" accessible to both the scientific community and the general public [16]. As a prominent figure in the Italian and European scientific research community during the 18th and 19th centuries, Fontana studied various fields of natural science, pioneering cutting-edge methods, models, and analytical tools.
Target audience: Scholars (especially those specializing in the history of science), and tourists.
Cultural Routes - Camino de Santiago - This scenario aims to promote the fundamental principles and foundational values of European culture through the establishment of cultural itineraries. These itineraries are not merely physical routes but genuine channels for intercultural dialogue, serving as a means to overcome geographic barriers and historical differences. Cultural itineraries become a vehicle for a deeper understanding of European history, creating a bridge between the past and the present. This itinerary considers the Italian Way to Santiago de Compostela [23].
Target audience: Tourists, and citizens.

To make clear to the community why an ontology is being developed, decisive is the **Purpose and Scope Identification** sub-activity. Regarding the ontology's purpose, the development of an ontology for thematic paths aims not only to provide a clear and comprehensive definition of the concept but also to specify its main and basic requirements and the organization of content. The main purpose is to ease the enhancement of cultural heritage by facilitating user navigation through a series of described and interconnected information and resources. This achievement can be attained through the development of an ontology that serves as a tool for the organization, management, exchange, and enjoyment of online information. About the scope, although the structuring of thematic paths can be related to any sector, in this study the attention will be focused on the GLAM domain. Therefore, the reference scope will be related to the cultural heritage.

The **Functional Ontological Requirements Proposal** sub-activity involves defining a set of functional requirements, which can be represented in different ways. To realize the CTP Ontology, the requirements were materialized both through the definition of **Competency Questions** and through the tabular structuring of information (**Tabular Information**). Regarding **Competency Questions**, these are a set of questions that the ontology must address, and for this initial version of the ontology, 29 have been formulated and are reported in Table 2.

Table 2. Competency Questions that the CTP Ontology has to address.

N.	Competency Question
01	What is a thematic path?
02	What is the theme/What are the themes of the path X?
02bis	What is the theme/What are the themes of the paths that contain a certain keyword?
03	Where are cultural objects connected to thematic path X usually kept?
04	To which historical period does thematic path X refer?
05	By whom were the objects of the thematic path X made?
05bis	Who is involved in the production of the objects in the thematic path X and what is their role?
06	By whom and when were the objects belonging to the thematic path X made?
07	When were the objects linked to the thematic path X made?
08	To which agent is the thematic path X inspired by?
09	Which cultural resources are part of more than one thematic path?
10	Which thematic paths have been created and by who?
11	Which thematic paths have been funded and by who?
12	Which types of cultural heritage are present in the thematic path X?
13	Which thematic paths can be identified through the subject "XYZ"?
14	Which are the places related to the thematic path X?
15	Which cultural, ethical, and social values does the thematic path X aim to convey?
16	Which cultural resources are in the thematic path X and in which order?
17	The thematic path X is realized in one or more events (e.g. virtual or physical exhibition)? Which one/s?
18	Which thematic path is composed by one or more sub-thematic paths (e.g. exhibitions' sub-paths)?
19	How is it possible to access the thematic path X?
20	Where can cultural resources related to the thematic path X be viewed?
21	Which cultural resources are linked to the thematic path X?
22	Where is it possible to buy products related to the thematic path X?
23	Which is the identification code associated with the cultural resource X by holder Y?
24	Which is the internal identifier of the resource X in the XY catalog?
25	Which thematic paths have been created in the year YYYY?
26	What are the thematic paths that can be associated with a specific range of time?
27	Who or what inspired the thematic path X?

The **Tabular Information**, instead, involves the creation of three distinct types of tables: *Concepts*, representing the main entities/classes of the ontology, *Relations*, denoting the properties between concepts, and *Attributes*, indicating the relationships between entities and data values. To assess whether the defined requirements were comprehensive for modeling the thematic path domain, they were proposed and discussed with GLAM domain experts from the Ansaldo Foundation, an Italian cultural institution that provided one of the three outlined scenarios. The definition of classes and properties and their hierarchy was achieved through a combined development, mixing top-down and bottom-up approaches [14]. Initially, the most general concepts and relationships were established; subsequently, these were refined based on specific reference scenarios and competency questions to provide further specialization.

6   Ontology Implementation

The main purpose of this activity is to develop the ontology in a formal language, guided by the ontological requirements defined in the previous Sect. 5. Below will briefly explain three main sub-activities of this phase, which are **Ontology Conceptualization**, **Ontology Encoding**, and **Ontology Evaluation**, and will indicate which tools were used in their development. Then, in Subsect. 6.1, a description of the modeled ontology will be provided.

In the **Ontology Conceptualization** sub-activity, a model representing the ontology's domain is created. This model is rendered through a diagram, which, along with the previously defined requirements, aims to explain how the knowledge of that domain has been structured. The model created for the conceptualization of Cultural Thematic Path Ontology can be seen in Fig. 1. For each equivalent class and property in the CTP Ontology, it is possible to find the reference in the aforementioned image. The namespaces depicted in the image are defined in prefix.cc.

During the **Ontology Encoding** sub-activity, it is necessary to produce the ontology in an implementation language, and the open-source editor Protégé was used. The OWL/RDF encoding has been defined in the namespace https://w3id.org/ctp.

The last phase of this activity involves the **Ontology Evaluation**, which refers to checking the technical quality of the ontology. Ontology validation was approached from two perspectives: **technological** and **methodological**.

From a technological point of view, evaluation is conducted using OOPS! (OntOlogy Pitfall Scanner!) [19], a web service for diagnosing ontologies that automatically identifies the most common pitfalls encountered during ontology development. Additionally, a further technical test involved defining SPARQL queries, derived from the Competency Questions, to verify if the ontology can satisfy them. Indeed, the current ontology modeling successfully meets all the 29 Competency Questions that were provided (SPARQL query for CQ {num}: https://w3id.org/ctp/cq/CQXX).

On the other hand, from a methodological point of view, the logical consistency checking and validation of the ontology are conducted not only by instantiating the scenarios in Protégé but also through the discussion and interaction of the Ansaldo Foundation GLAM domain experts. On a GitHub repository, the instantiated scenarios are available as examples, specifically Exhibition "Transitions | Enterprise - Work - Society", Novum Corpus Fontanianum, and Cultural Routes - Camino de Santiago.

6.1   CTP Ontology Description

In this section, we describe the main ontology entities and will indicate relevant references to some of the CQs, pointed out in Table 2. When cloning terms from existing ontology (e.g. OWL-Time, FOAF, PROV, etc.), we have minted equivalent terms in CTP Ontology. In the below discussion, for brevity, we use the terms in their original namespace, specifying only when we have extended or varied the original terms.

The entity that serves as the central hub of the conceptualization is the *ctp:ThematicPath* (see also Table 2, CQ01): indeed, from it stems all the relationships that characterize the domain. The *ctp:ThematicPath*, which can be characterized by various elements (such as a title, a description, an identifier, a URL (CQ19) and so on), has a self-loop through the *ctp:includes* property and its inverse *ctp:isIncludedIn*, indicating that a thematic path may include sub-thematic paths. Therefore, they can be used to deepen the topics dealt with previously (CQ18). Through the *ctp:conveys* datatype property, the thematic path can convey cultural, ethical, and social values (CQ15). The *ctp:ThematicPath* can also serve as a means to sell items (CQ22). For instance, when it is used to preserve the memory of a temporary exhibition, it can facilitate the online sale of specific types of items, such as an exhibition catalog. The property that enables this is *ctp:allowsTheSaleOf*, and it can indicate not only the URL that leads the user to purchase the *ctp:Product* through the *ctp:isSelledBy* datatype property but also the type of item sold, through the *ctp:Type* entity.

Every thematic path, to qualify as such, can be defined by at least one theme, identified by *ctp:Theme* (CQ02, CQ02bis): through this entity, defined by a title and detailed written text, the theme upon which the thematic path is based is explicitly stated, serving as a common thread that connects all relevant cultural resources. Both the *ctp:ThematicPath* and the *ctp:Theme* can be described by one or more *ctp:Subject* (CQ13), which are concepts that can be drawn from thesauri and controlled vocabularies (e.g. Library of Congress Subject Headings (LCSH) and Getty's Art & Architecture Thesaurus).

Interconnected cultural resources therefore define a thematic path. The *ctp:CulturalResource* entity is a tangible or intangible resource, movable or immovable, realized by nature or man-made that has been identified as possessing artistic, historical, archaeological, or ethno-anthropological significance. In addition to being identified by various elements such as a URI, URLs (CQ20), a title, a description, etc., the cultural resource is categorized according to its *ctp:Type* (CQ12), that can be excerpt from thesauri and controlled vocabularies (e.g. Library of Congress Subject Headings (LCSH) and Getty's Art & Architecture Thesaurus). To characterize the relationship between *ctp:ThematicPath* and a *ctp:CulturalResource*, the **ODP PartOf**, employed to represent entities and their parts, has been reused, through the *ctp:hasPart* (CQ21) and *ctp:isPartOf* (CQ09) object properties.

As indicated in the definition of thematic path, it can be structured as a collector of cultural objects or present an undetermined or predetermined order. In the latter case, cultural resources can be sorted according to a certain criterion (e.g. alphabetical, chronological, in order of author, curator decided order, etc.). To allow this, the *ctp:OrderedListSlot* is required, which indicates the slot in an ordered list with a fixed index (CQ16). For sorting resources in the CTP ontology, we utilized the cloning operation of certain classes and properties from the **OLO ontology** [15] and the specialization operation of elements from the **ODP List**. This approach enables the determination of an order in the resource sequence (e.g. *ctp:previousItem* / *ctp:nextItem*). The cultural resource is not directly linked to the order of the path but rather to the *ctp:OrderedListSlot* entity that manages it, allowing it to be included in multiple thematic paths. Sorting classes and properties serve as an alternative to *ctp:hasPart* and *ctp:isPartOf* object properties, allowing the cultural resources to be organized either without a predetermined order or according to specific sorting criteria.

For **time modeling** of the domain (CQ04, CQ06, CQ07, CQ25, CQ26, CQ27), a cloning operation of some classes and properties of the **OWL-Time Ontology** [27] was conducted. In detail, the *time:TemporalEntity*, *time:Instant* and *time:Interval* entities, related *time:hasTime*, *time:hasBeginning*, *time:hasEnd* object properties and *time:inXSDDate* (corresponding to *ctp:hasDate*) datatype property were considered. In order to evaluate the use of ODPs, the ODP TimeInterval had been proposed, but the need to express an interval as a temporal space between two dates (e.g. start and end date) is already provided by the Owl Time Ontology, with *time:TemporalEntity* as superclass of Interval, linked to *time:Instant* with the properties *time:hasBeginning* and *time:hasEnd*. Dates are expressed with the ISO 8601 International Standard [12] in the extended form (e.g. 2024-07-18T12:33).

Cloning of some **FOAF Ontology** [8] classes and properties was also done for **agent modeling**. Specifically, *foaf:Agent* and their subclasses *foaf:Person*, *foaf:Group* and *foaf:Organization* were considered. However, the necessity arose to create a new superclass, *ctp:GroupsOfPeople*, to generically represent a collection of individual agents and to indicate that both an *ctp:Organization* and a *ctp:Group*, subclasses of *ctp:GroupsOfPeople*, can be members of a *ctp:Agent*. In the current FOAF model, the property *foaf:member* has as range *foaf:Agent*, while as domain only *foaf:Group*, which is not comprehensive enough to meet CTP domain requirements. For example, in the FOAF model, it is not possible to indicate that an organization can have groups as members. Each agent can assume a specific responsibility towards a cultural resource and/or a thematic path: indeed, the person who created an artifact becomes its creator (CQ05), while the one who funded a particular project becomes its sponsor (CQ11). From a modeling perspective, it would have been possible to identify qualified relations, such as by creating triples of this type: *ctp:CulturalResource - ctp:isCreatedBy - ctp:Person*. However, this modeling is limiting, as it can be complex and time-consuming to model a large number of qualified relations, with the risk of inevitably overlooking some. To overcome this issue, it was decided to assign a **role** to each agent involved in a relationship with a thematic path or cultural resource. However, with the aim of not strictly characterizing an agent by assigning them a "predefined" role, and wanting to maintain their independence to potentially assume a different role regardless of the number of relationships it has, a decision was made to create a class called ***ctp:RelationToAgent***. This class allows associating a specific *ctp:Agent* with the *ctp:Role* defined for that type of relation (CQs involving agents in a particular role: CQ05, CQ05bis, CQ06, CQ08, CQ10, CQ11, CQ27). In this case, cloning operation was performed from the **PROV Ontology** [22], specifically for *prov:AgentInfluence* and *prov:Role* entities and *prov:hasRole* object property. Similarly to what was mentioned regarding *ctp:Subject*, the terms characterizing the *ctp:Role* can be taken from thesauri and controlled vocabularies (e.g. Library of Congress Subject Headings (LCSH) and Getty's Art & Architecture Thesaurus).

Another entity described in the ontology is **Place**, which identifies a specific location in physical space. It can denote a precise point in space (e.g., geographic coordinates) or a broader area (e.g., geographical region). It can be linked to other entities in various ways, conveying diverse types of information: if connected through the *ctp:isLocationOf* property to a *ctp:CulturalResource*, it can indicate the location of immovable resources (e.g. landscape assets, historical buildings, churches, etc.) (CQ14, CQ27)). This modeling approach was suggested by the **ODP Place**, alongside the cloning of selected classes and properties from the DCMI Metadata Terms (DCTerms) [7], the Data Catalog (DCAT) [1,6], and ISA Programme Location Core (LOCN) [13] vocabularies. This entity can also be used to collocate mobile and musealized cultural artifacts: in fact, the *ctp:isPreservedBy* property indicates the relation between a *ctp:CulturalResource* and a *ctp:Agent* that has "Holder" *ctp:Role* and the "Holder" is located in a *ctp:Place*, that is a museum, a library, and so on (CQ03).

A thematic path can be linked to one **ctp:CulturalEvent** or more, such as a temporary exhibition held at a specific *ctp:Place* and *ctp:TemporalEntity*, organized and funded by *ctp:Agent* (CQ17).

Every entity within the domain of the CTP ontology can be associated with two types of identifiers. The **Primary Identifier** (CQ24) refers to a unique identifier of the entity, namely the URI of the resource. This is used, for example, to uniquely identify the cultural resource linked to the thematic path, as well as URIs related to *ctp:Type*, *ctp:Subject*, and *ctp:Role*, which reference controlled vocabularies and thesauri. The primary identifier is therefore a string that defines any entity through the *ctp:hasPrimaryIdentifier* datatype property. On the other hand, the **Secondary Identifier** (*ctp:Identifier*) is a sequence of characters or symbols that serves to uniquely distinguish an entity or object within a specific system or context. Unlike the primary identifier, the secondary allows indicating the *ctp:Agent* who generated it through the *ctp:hasCreator* object property (CQ23). For example, it can represent the catalog code associated with a specific cultural resource. Cloning operations were performed for the *ctp:Identifier* entity from Asset Description Metadata Schema (ADMS) [2], and for the *ctp:hasNotation* datatype property from SKOS [25].

7   Ontology Publication and Maintenance

The goal of the **Ontology Publication** activity is to make the ontology available online, ensuring it is accessible as both human-readable documentation and

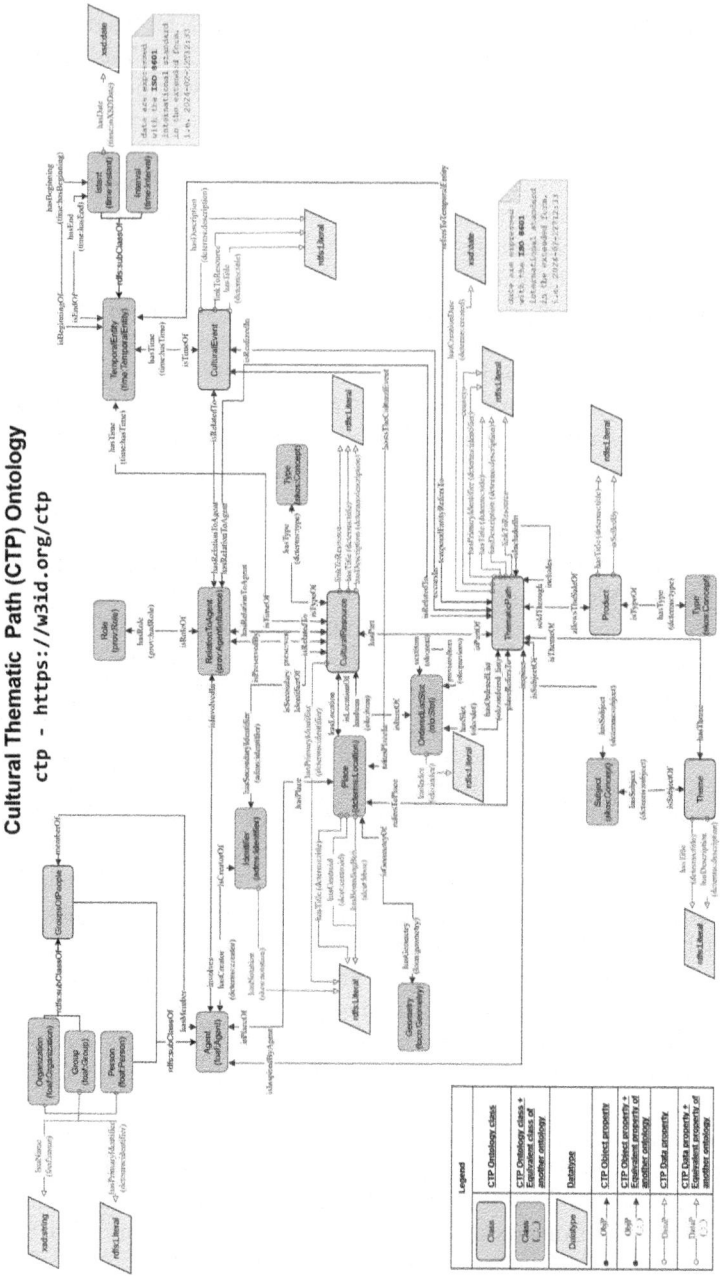

Fig. 1. Conceptualization of the CTP Ontology. The yellow boxes show the native classes of the ontology, the blue boxes are the classes with an equivalent class in another ontology, and the green ones are the datatypes. All the diagram terms are minted in https://w3id.org/ctp. When not indicated in the classes and properties, the *ctp* namespace is implied. The other namespaces are defined in prefix.cc. (Color figure online)

a machine-readable file via its URI. The ontology is made available on the Web following W3C guidelines for publishing vocabularies [3]. This ensures that it can be accessed through its URI both as a file in a formal language and as human-readable documentation through content negotiation. It is possible to consult the CTP Ontology, covered by the CC-BY-4.0 license, on the dedicated GitHub repository. It is accompanied by human-readable documentation created with WIzard for DOCumenting Ontology (WIDOCO), which is a tool designed to facilitate ontology documentation by guiding users through the required steps and identifying any missing metadata that needs to be included.

Instead, the objective of the **Ontology Maintenance** is to revise and update the ontology throughout its lifecycle. It mainly consists of detecting bugs and identifying new requirements. Since the ontology is available on a GitHub repository and is open to the community, these activities will be encouraged mainly by interaction with other domain experts and/or ontology developers.

8   Conclusion and Future Works

This paper introduces the first version of the Cultural Thematic Path (CTP) Ontology, designed to create and structure cultural thematic paths. The ontology aims to support the publication and management of linked data to enhance the enjoyment of cultural heritage within the GLAM domain. The ontology was validated technologically by resolving the 29 Competency Questions through SPARQL queries and methodologically through the discussion and interaction of the Ansaldo Foundation GLAM domain experts. The CTP Ontology and scenarios instantiations are available in a GitHub repository. Future developments will focus on aligning the CTP ontology with other cultural domain ontologies (e.g. CIDOC-CRM, EDM) to ensure interoperability and facilitate data exchange. Ontology maintenance activity will also continue, involving bug identification and the acquisition of new requirements. These aspects may emerge not only from the development of new scenarios and implementation projects but also from interactions with users in the web community.

Acknowledgements. This work is developed under the Ph.D. Research Project in Digital Humanities, supported by PON "Ricerca e Innovazione" 2014-2020, Asse IV "Istruzione e ricerca per il recupero", Azione IV.5 "Dottorati su tematiche Green" DM 1061/2021. Thanks to the DigitXL Project and the Ansaldo Foundation for providing case studies and insights.

References

1. Albertoni, R., Browning, D., Cox, S., Gonzalez-Beltran, A.N., Perego, A., Winstanley, P.: The W3C data catalog vocabulary, version 2: rationale, design principles, and uptake. Data Intell. **6**(2), 457–487 (2024)

2. Asset description metadata schema (ADMS). https://www.w3.org/TR/vocab-adms/. Accessed 22 July 2024
3. Best practice recipes for publishing RDF vocabularies. https://www.w3.org/TR/swbp-vocab-pub/. Accessed 22 July 2024
4. Biagetti, M.T.: An ontological model for the integration of cultural heritage information: CIDOC-CRM. JLIS **7**(3), 43–77 (2016)
5. Carabelli, B., Cerioli, C., Fiori, L., Repetto, P.: Transitions - Enterprise, Work. Society, Erga Edizioni (2023)
6. Data catalog vocabulary (DCAT). https://www.w3.org/TR/vocab-dcat-2/. Accessed 22 July 2024
7. DCMI metadata terms. https://www.dublincore.org/specifications/dublin-core/dcmi-terms/. Accessed 22 July 2024
8. FOAF ontology. http://xmlns.com/foaf/spec/. Accessed 22 July 2024
9. Freire, N., Voorburg, R., Cornelissen, R., de Valk, S., Meijers, E., Isaac, A.: Aggregation of linked data in the cultural heritage domain: a case study in the Europeana network. Information **10**(8) (2019)
10. Gaitanou, P., Andreou, I., Sicilia, M.-A., Garoufallou, E.: Linked data for libraries: creating a global knowledge space, a systematic literature review. J. Inf. Sci. **50**(1), 204–244 (2024)
11. Gangemi, A., Presutti, V.: Ontology design patterns. In: Staab, S., Studer, R. (eds.) Handbook on Ontologies. IHIS, pp. 221–243. Springer, Heidelberg (2009). https://doi.org/10.1007/978-3-540-92673-3_10
12. International Organization for Standardization: ISO 8601-1:2019. Date and time - Representations for information interchange. 1st edn. (2019)
13. ISA programme location core vocabulary. https://www.w3.org/ns/legacy_locn. Accessed 22 July 2024
14. Noy, N.F., McGuinness, D.L.: Ontology development 101: a guide to creating your first ontology. Knowl. Syst. Lab. **32**, 1–25 (2001)
15. Ordered list ontology. https://smiy.sourceforge.net/olo/spec/orderedlistontology.html. Accessed 22 July 2024
16. Pasciuto, T., Albertoni, R., Maggi, R., Artese, M.T., Gagliardi, I., Gentilini, M.: Travelling Culture: Define, Implement, Enrich and Disseminate the Digital Cultural Heritage. The "DigitXL Project" Case Study. In: Towards Smart and Inclusive Learning Ecosystem, EDEN Research Workshop Proceedings, pp. 134–139. EDEN Digital learning Europe (2022)
17. Pasciuto, T., Albertoni, R., Maggi, R.: Travelling Culture - The Enjoyment of Cultural Heritage Through a Conceptualization of Thematic Path: A Preliminary Characterization. In: Garoufallou, E., Sartori, F. (eds.) Metadata and Semantic Research 17th Research Conference, MTSR 2023, Milan, Italy, 25-27 October 2023, Revised Selected Papers, CCIS 2048, pp. 213–219 (2024)
18. Poveda-Villalón, M., Suárez-Figueroa, M.C., Gómez-Pérez, A.: The landscape of ontology reuse in linked data. In: Proceedings Ontology Engineering in a Data-driven World (OEDW 2012), pp. 1–11. (2012)
19. Poveda-Villalón, M., Gómez-Pérez, A., Suárez-Figueroa, M.C.: OOPS! (OntOlogy Pitfall Scanner!): an on-line tool for ontology evaluation. IJSWIS **10**(2), 7–34 (2014)
20. Poveda-Villalón, M., Fernández-Izquierdo, A., Fernández-López, M., García-Castro, R.: LOT: an industrial oriented ontology engineering framework. Eng. Appl. Artif. Intell. **111**, 1–22 (2022)

21. Presutti, V., Blomqvist, E., Daga, E., Gangemi, A.: Pattern-Based Ontology Design. In: Suárez-Figueroa, M.C., Gómez-Pérez, A., Motta, E., Gangemi, A. (eds.) Ontology Engineering in a Networked World, pp. 35–64. Springer, Heidelberg (2012). https://doi.org/10.1007/978-3-642-24794-1_3

22. PROV-O: The PROV Ontology. https://www.w3.org/TR/prov-o/. Accessed 22 July 2024

23. Saint James Way, Italy Itinerary. https://saintjamesway.eu/blog/portfolios/it_itine/. Accessed 22 July 2024

24. Salse, M., Guallar-Delgado, J., Jornet-Benito, N., Mateo Bretos, M.P., Silvestre-Canut, J.O.: GLAM metadata in museums and university collections: a state-of-the-art (Spain and other European countries). Global Knowl. Memory Commun. **73**(4/5), 477–495 (2024)

25. SKOS schema overview. https://www.w3.org/2009/08/skos-reference/skos.html. Accessed 22 July 2024

26. Suárez-Figueroa, M.C., Gómez-Pérez, A., Fernández-López, M.: The NeOn methodology framework: a scenario-based methodology for ontology development. Appl. Ontol. **10**(2), 107–145 (2015)

27. Time Ontology in OWL. https://www.w3.org/TR/owl-time/. Accessed 22 July 2024

Ontological Patterns for Modeling Art Exhibitions: An Initial Investigation

Nicola Carboni[✉][iD]

University of Geneva, Geneva, Switzerland
`nicola.carboni@unige.ch`

Abstract. Exhibitions play a crucial role in shaping art history by defining artistic movements and promoting visual canons. However, current models fail to capture their complex dynamics, especially in terms of contingency and participation. This study proposes a framework for modeling catalog-derived and database-derived exhibition data, by employing a bottom-up approach based on two major datasets: the Artl@s BasArt project (catalog-derived) and the MoMA Exhibition Index (database-derived). Developed using CIDOC-CRM, a de-facto standard ontology in the heritage domain, the model specifies ontological patterns for documenting key aspects of exhibitions, such as their temporal duration, spatial extension, mereological structures, source of knowledge, the role of its participants and the function of the artwork exposed. The adoption of the proposed model facilitates the integration and analysis of diverse exhibition data, enabling a comprehensive and richer understanding of the spatial, temporal, and participatory dimensions of each exhibition, helping to contextualize their reach and impact within the global artistic milieu, and enabling better data-driven studies in digital art history and cultural analytics.

Keywords: Ontology · CIDOC-CRM · Exhibitions · Cultural Heritage · Digital Art History

1 Introduction

With the increasing availability of digital museum resources researchers can now potentially explore the circulation of art and artists across the globe. Catalogues raisonnés and exhibition catalogs provide crucial information on what has been produced by an artist as well as where and when it was exhibited. However, studying exhibitions reveals more than just what was exhibited and by whom. Exhibitions have also played an important role in shaping art. They have mediated the history of forms through the circulation of ideas, images, and works. They are a primary medium for the construction [30] and reinforcement [1,2] of the artistic canon. They bear witness to developments in the artistic field, and "highlights the connections between art and other realms, such as commerce, and they reveal politics and policies of an institution" [8]. The datafication of exhibition information opens the door to novel methodologies (e.g., distant reading)

© The Author(s), under exclusive license to Springer Nature Switzerland AG 2025
M. Sfakakis et al. (Eds.): MTSR 2024, CCIS 2331, pp. 256–267, 2025.
https://doi.org/10.1007/978-3-031-81974-2_22

to study exhibitions, overcoming the limitations of the single case study, and helping investigate at global scale phenomena such as the (i) geography of art, (ii) the development of the artistic milieu, (iii) the process of patrimonialization, and (iv) the impact of the curatorial discourse. However, the integration of exhibition datasets presents complex ontological challenges that heavily restrict the possibilities for transversal studies of exhibition history. Interconnecting scattered collections through a shared conceptualization is, therefore, a matter of urgency, specifically given the rise of data-driven studies in fields such as Digital Art History and Cultural Analytics [16, 22]. This contribution focuses on the development of an initial ontological model for integrating and analyzing different types of exhibition data (catalog-derived and database-derived). The article investigates the ontological nature of exhibitions, and how to express and/or harmonize its diverse characteristics, specifically with respect to the expression of contingency and participation patterns. The purpose is to create a framework, based on CIDOC-CRM, for the conceptualization and formalization of key aspects found in exhibition data. After an initial literature review (Sect. 2), the article expands on the identity criteria and ontological requirements for modeling exhibitions, listing in 3.2 seven important characteristics to consider: Objects in events, Participation, Temporal duration, Spatial extension, Contingency relationships, Mereological structure, Knowledge Source. Section 4.1 introduces the strategy used and the two datasets employed for guiding the development of the model (Artl@s BasArt and MoMA). Finally, Sect. 4.2 discusses challenges and limits of current ontological patterns and presents the results.

2   Literature Review

Linked data have been used in the cultural heritage sector [9] to provide access to museum catalogs [10, 28], architectural reconstructions [17, 23], photo archives [14], or iconographical objects [3, 6]. Even if the use of computational data for studying exhibitions has widely been recognized [15], and numerous exhibition datasets have recently become available via *ad-hoc* interfaces[1] or data export[2], not much work has been done to develop ontological models for exhibition documentation. Rodríguez-Ortega and her team have developed a new ontology for the description of art exhibitions [27], specifically focusing on the annotation of their discursive and social layers.

---

[1] To cite a few: Artl@s (https://artlas.huma-num.fr/en/artlas-bases-de-donnees-en-acces-public/), Database of Modern Exhibitions (https://exhibitions.univie.ac.at/), Salons (https://salons.musee-orsay.fr/).

[2] To cite a few, the MoMA dataset mentioned in the article, the Zürich Kunsthaus (https://github.com/KunsthausZuerich/exhibitions), the Cooper Hewitt, Smithsonian Design Museum (https://github.com/cooperhewitt/collection).

3   Functional Requirements

3.1   Information Analysis

Exhibition information typically originates from two primary sources: catalogs and databases. Catalog-derived data generally result from the automatic or manual extraction of the content of an exhibition catalog, a publication aimed to describe and document the exhibition for the general public. Catalogs record the title of the exhibition, when it was held, where it was held, who participated, and with which artworks. Additional information may pertain to the presence of a committee, of illustrations representing a specific work, the address where to contact the artist, his availability to sell the presented artwork, a small artist biography, and his relation to existing and affirmed artists. Database-derived data generally result from the extraction of a selection of records from an internal database or database-like application. These records document the exhibition for management purposes, serving the institution's internal audience. For this reason, the focus is on the organizational machine behind the exhibition itself. These records tend to describe in detail who organized the exhibition and in which role.

3.2   On the Nature of Exhibition

We can define a few characteristics that a model for documenting exhibitions must consider.

Objects in Events. The objects exhibited may be present for the complete duration of the exhibition, or just for a smaller temporal segment (temporary presence). The role of the object in the exhibition may be generic or specific. An example of the latter is the use of a specific object to promote the exhibition itself. Objects may be owned by the organizers of the exhibition or by an external entity (e.g., a private owner, or another institution). An exhibition may display material objects, digital/virtual representations as well as host performances.

Participation. Exhibitions can be collaboratively developed within an institution. A model should differentiate between the degree of involvement of the various agents (e.g., constant/temporal), as well as be capable of formalizing their role (e.g., artist, curator, arranger) within the exhibition (e.g., direct/mediated).

Temporal Duration. Exhibitions always comprise a temporal component (start/end date) which may be known/unknown or precise/imprecise. Temporal relationships should be able to express our knowledge about the event no matter the granularity of information available (year, day, decade, century). We should be able to order exhibitions based on absolute and relative temporal information (e.g., before, after).

Spatial Extension. Exhibitions unfold in space, such as in specific museums or galleries. They may take place in a room within an institution or within multiple rooms. The same exhibition can be held at multiple places (different institutions) at the same time (e.g., virtual exhibitions) or at different times (e.g., traveling exhibitions). Multiple exhibitions can occur in the same space, for example in the same room at the same museum/gallery.

Contingency Relationships. The model should differentiate between activities performed prior to the exhibition, which are directly linked (CAUSE) to the creation of the exhibition itself (e.g., curation), and activities that are key to its development, hence they aid (ENABLE) its creation (e.g., loans) [31].

Mereological Structure. Exhibitions may be documented as having multiple parts/stages. It is the case of traveling exhibitions, which are designed to be moved and displayed at multiple locations at different times or, at the same time. Each identified stage of a traveling exhibition may have its own starting and ending date.

Knowledge Source. Exhibitions are documented through internal database-archival records or using one or more media, such as catalogs, videos, images, and advertisements.

4 Data Modeling

4.1 Strategy

To provide a model able to sustain documentation and analysis of catalog-derived and database-derived exhibition information, it is paramount to analyze the characteristics of an exhibition and how they can be documented. Generally, the source used for answering such a query can be retrieved by studying a domain (top-down) or by analyzing how exhibitions are described in existing information structures (bottom-up). Both methods have their advantages/disadvantages. Bottom-up approaches adhere to the concreteness of the data and encourage a culture of reuse, but result in the proliferation of details that make it difficult to integrate datasets. Top-down approaches help create artifacts reusable across diverse application scenarios but restricted in scope [12]. This contribution integrates the two approaches, developing a set of requirements and characteristics (see 3.2) based on the domain and its source, while at the same time iteratively refining and comparing the theoretical requirements with information present in two major exhibitions datasets: BasArt[3] and the MoMA Exhibition Index[4].

   BasArt is a collaborative database of exhibition catalogs [20]. At the time of this writing, it documents 5653 exhibitions from the 19th century to the

---

[3] https://artlas.huma-num.fr/map/.
[4] https://github.com/MuseumofModernArt/exhibitions.

present day. Part of the Artl@s project, BasArt provides researchers access to a wealth of information beyond the traditional European and North American sources. Every exhibition in the database is recorded using a comprehensive set of descriptors including temporal information about the exhibition, artwork exhibited and by whom, as well as many details of the artists involved. The recorded data focus mainly on four entities, the exhibition itself, its participants (artists), the artwork exhibited, and the source used for the description (catalog). The diversity of the catalogs recorded in BasArt, and its global reach make it the perfect use case for developing a model for catalog-derived exhibition information.

MoMA Exhibition Index Dataset documents 1.788 exhibitions held at the Museum of Modern Art in New York from 1929 to 1989. The dataset, released in 2016, has been compiled as part of the Exhibition History, a project of the Museum of Modern Art Archives. For every exhibition held during the documented period at MoMA, we may retrieve a series of descriptors focusing on who organized (and in which role) and who participated in the exhibition. The focus on the dataset on the recording and documentation of the internal activities of a single modern and exemplary memory institute makes it the perfect use case for developing a model for database-derived exhibition information.

The work presented here not only provides mappings of the data described in these two sources but also analyzes the underlying characteristics of the information (a summary of how the characteristics in 3.2 apply to each analyzed dataset is available in Table 1). These information requirements will then be mapped onto CIDOC-CRM ontological structures, illustrating deficiencies and pinpointing aspects that need to be enhanced or integrated into the ontology to better fulfill the described use case. Additionally, this analysis aims to lay the informational groundwork for potential future expansions of the model by incorporating new requirements that are presently unaddressed because of limitations in data extraction technologies.

4.2   Model and Analysis

We model exhibitions as perduring entities, i.e. they happen or occur in time. Thus, they exist as temporal entities, the same as events or activities. Their identity is not linked with a fixed list of artworks, as the works of art exposed at the beginning of an exhibition may differ from the ones exposed at its end. While this may appear ontologically odd at first, it is not that very different from describing a fighting army that moved from point A to point B. It is clear to every reader that such a statement does not imply that all the participants moved, or all the participants indeed survived [24]. What is clear is that the identity of the army does not change from A to B. The spatial coordinates where an exhibition took place cannot be used as identity criteria either, as an event may occur in several places at different times. Similarly, several temporal events can occur in the same place. Space is not a criterion of identity for events, because events have a spatial projection but no spatial dimension [18]. The identity of an Exhibition is temporal and it may be composed of several shorter segments or phases $(p_1, p_2...p_n)$

temporally defined in that they can occur parallelly or sequentially and at different locations [11]. Exhibitions result from extensive work by diverse actors in different roles. This type of work starts to take place prior to the starting date of the exhibition and may last until the exhibition is finished. These activities can be modeled as part of the exhibition itself or as a separate part. Choosing one approach over the other is highly contingent on the available data and the aims of the modeling process. The proposed modeling presents the exhibition as composed of two parts: (x) the exhibition itself (identified by the opening/closing temporal boundaries) and the (y) exhibition management, which involves all the coordination, design, and implementation activities that bootstrap the exhibition and, in some cases, continue until the exhibition end. Using this modeling we can precisely document the agency, work, and role of each of the exhibition participants. Different ontologies can sustain these modeling choices, including DOLCE, Event-Model-F, and FARO [4,25,26,29]. Due to its popularity within memory institutions, the data has been modeled using CIDOC-CRM, a standard ontology developed under the aegis of ICOM (International Council of Museums) to aggregate information about cultural objects and activities. CRM is actively developed, and it features several official/unofficial extensions that help formalize a diversity of statements about cultural heritage objects and practices [5]. CRM has the advantages of being an event-centric model and information is represented through events. As mentioned above, exhibitions are perdurant, therefore we can model them in CRM as a single activity (`crm:E7_Activity`). Among the formalized classes and properties in CRM (and its extensions), there are a few particularly interesting ones for the documentation of exhibitions, specifically with respect to the requirements outlined in Sect. 3.2.

Table 1. Summary of the diverse information characteristics present in the model and how they are reflected in the analyzed datasets.

Model Characteristics	BasArt	MoMA
Objects in events	Tangible objects	Tangible objects
Participation	Full involvement	Full and partial involvement
Temporal duration	Precise temporal information	Precise temporal information
Spatial extension	Address or city information	N/A
Contingency relationships	During	Pior and during
Mereological structure	Travelling exhibitions and pavillions	N/A
Knowledge Source	Catalog	Associated documents

Objects in Events. Exhibitions can display tangible objects, born-digital artworks, and host performances. We can link each of these exhibited items to their respective owner using the property `crm:P52_has_current_owner`. It is possible to document the display of a material object using `crm:P16_used_specific_object`. Using the CIDOC-CRM extensions LRMoo[5] (formerly FRBRoo) and CRMDig[6], it is also possible to document the presence of performances (lrmoo:F31_Performance) as well as digital objects (crmdig:D1_Digital_Obje ct). We can even define the specific role each of these items/performances plays within the exhibition, for instance, documenting that "a photo of the artwork β was used for advertising the exhibition x". It is possible to formalize such a statement using the n-ary constructs available in the CRM properties of properties (.1 pc extension). However, this solution is only partially satisfactory, as the resulting pattern is quite complex (a total of five triples, and three of them are used only for the n-ary construct).

Mereological Structure. The ontology does not formalize explicitly the notion of phase. However, each activity can be composed (crm:P9_consists_of) by different temporal segments. We can use this pattern to model traveling exhibitions, where each move/stage can be modeled as a single segment of a larger activity (Fig. 1). We can use the same pattern to document the temporary presence of artworks within the exhibition. This parthood relationship makes it possible to record the different stages of the exhibited collection, instantiating multiple crm:E7_Activity as the number of documented stages. Therefore, if fifty artworks are present across the whole exhibition, but twenty are present for only half the time, we can instantiate two (crm:E7_Activity) sub-activities, one representing the temporal segment where fifty artworks are exhibited, and a second one representing the segment when seventy are present.

Temporal Duration. Temporal relationships between the documented exhibition segments can be specified using time and time-relationships properties. The latter are extensively documented in CRM (e.g., crm:P183_ends_before_ the_start_of), and the scope note of the properties do specify their equivalences to Allen operators. One of the advantages of using CRM is the availability of both precise and imprecise temporal properties. While a larger discussion on how to model precision is surely needed [7], the ontology features two types of temporal statements, P81a/P81b and P82a/P82b, that help define the level of precision of the recorded temporal statements.

Spatial Extension. The level of detail in the spatial information linked to an exhibition is a matter of encoding rather than modeling. CRM leaves to the user the specifications of the exact type of place where an activity occurred. This information can be encoded using reference resources (e.g., a vocabulary entry) or using WKT (crm:P168_place_is_defined_by). The use of WKT is particularly beneficial as it defines the precise point or polygon that represents the geographical area where the exhibition took place. These approaches can be combined using an external vocabulary to qualify the status of the WKT coordinates (e.g., city/address/building).

Contingency. CRM includes two properties that express contingency relationships between events: crm:P17_was_motivated_by and crm:P20_had_speci

---

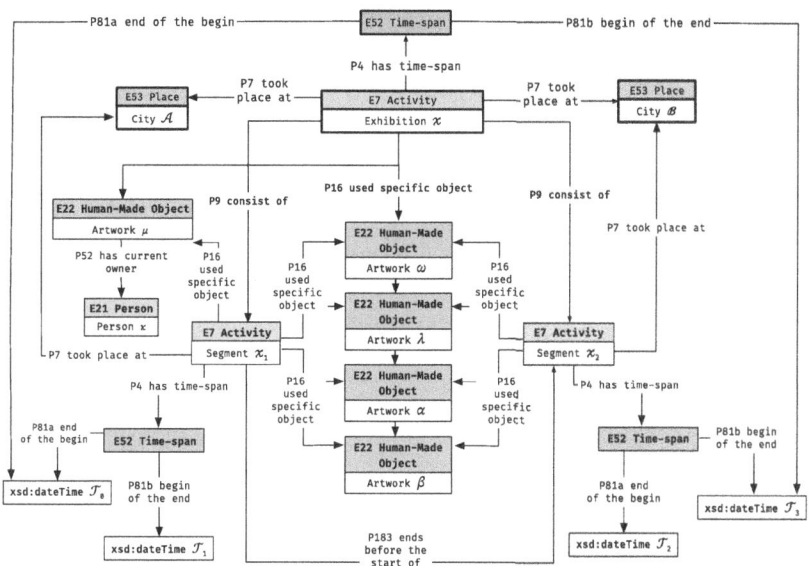

Fig. 1. Graphical Representation of the modeling of a travel exhibition. We can document the exhibitions in City $\mathcal{A}$ and City $\mathcal{B}$ as two distinct (but linked) stages (called x_1 and x_2) of the same exhibition x occurring in different places and at different times. The modeling showcases the possibility of documenting the diverse artworks displayed at the different stages of the exhibition. In the example, segment x_1 is linked with artwork μ while segment x_2 is not. The two exhibition stages have specific and different temporal boundaries and are further linked together by a relative temporal statement (crm:P183_ends_before_the_start_of).

fic_purpose, with P17 being the closest property for indicating causation. However, the scope note of the latter does mention that it describes "items that are regarded as a reason for carrying out the instance of E7 Activity", which does not express exactly that the outcome of one activity leads to the occurrence of another. P20 instead expresses the "relationship between a preparatory activity" and a subsequent event. While there is no direct causation, this property expresses a type of temporal dependency [13]. Quality change dependencies in events [19,21] are not yet present in CRM at the moment of this writing. Due to this reason, the final modeling can only rely on P20 to express the causal relationship between the management activity ($E7_y$) and the resulting exhibition ($E7_x$). Additionally, some activities may have been conducted prior to the exhibition that, even if unsuccessful, do not change the existence of the exhibition itself (DESPITE according to [31]). It is the case of refused loans, which are recorded internally. Negative actions are quite difficult to translate into CRM. Recently, the CRM-SIG worked on the development of an extension for the formalization of plans: CRMAct[7]. Currently under development, and not yet formalized in

---

[7] https://www.cidoc-crm.org/crmact/.

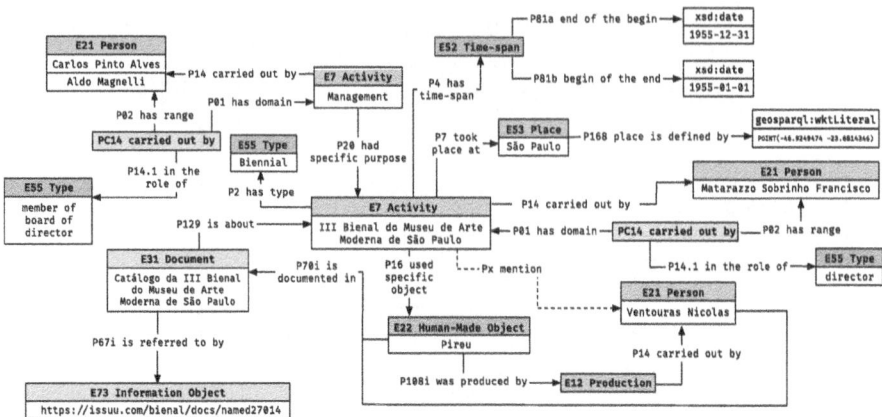

Fig. 2. Graphical Representation of the modeling of the III Bienal do Museu de Arte Moderna de São Paulo. By separating the management stage from the exhibition itself, it becomes easier to classify the contributions of different agents, specifically preparation and direction. The roles of the different agents in each event are expressed using a combination of .1 properties and internal vocabularies. The catalog is modeled as the primary source of historical knowledge, documenting the presence of artworks (and their authors) in the catalog

RDF, the extension uses the concept of Activity Plan and Event Template to define "not yet happened" activities, such as proposals for conservation work. However, CRMAct is about future activities and plans and, therefore, cannot be used to document unsuccessful past plans.

Knowledge Source. The source of the recorded information can be annotated in CRM by linking (`crm:P70_documents`) an entity with the source or document (`crm:E31_Document`) that attests its existence and accuracy. In the context of exhibitions, the catalog usually serves as the main source, and it is linked to the location where it can be retrieved (e.g., URL; archive).

Participation. Currently, CIDOC-CRM lists only two properties for defining types of participation: `crm:P11_had_participant` (involvement in the event) and `crm:P14_carried_out_by` (implies causal or legal responsibility). Differentiating involvement from responsibility is crucial, but participation can be specified with a few new sub-properties. For example, the nature of a curator's participation in the creation of an exhibition differs from that of an arranger, particularly in terms of directness and causality. However, in CRM we would use the same property, leaving the comprehension of the differences in participation a matter of external knowledge, as such distinctions are not captured within the property's semantics. This problem arises also in the case of agents who act indirectly upon an exhibition, by approving it or making it financially possible. In this instance, the use of P14 does not tell us very much about the action. To specify this type of information we would have to create a specific sub-activity documenting it. While possible, the most effective solution would be to use directed/mediated participation properties, such as the ones formalized in BFO. Moreover, the properties used by DOLCE of constant participation (participation during the whole temporal extension of the activity), and temporary participation (participation only during a segment of temporal extension of the activity) [4, 26] should also be considered, as they help specify the type of participation of an agent in an activity. Each of these novel participation properties may be formalized as sub-properties of P14 or P11. There is another important problem linked with participation, and it relates to artists. Do artists participate in the exhibition? Some of the exposed artwork may not have a living creator, thus we may say that artists are only present and involved through their artworks and are not direct participants. Using CRM, we can document that an artwork, created in a production event by an artist, is used by an exhibition. However, theoretical accuracy can sometimes obscure the work's practical objectives. This is not a very pragmatic solution, specifically because analyses of exhibitions tend to focus first and foremost on the artists who participated. The absence of a direct property to list them is quite inconvenient. While it is possible to use P11, it may suggest that a deceased individual is involved in events taking place after his death, potentially leading to significant issues if automatic data enrichment processes are in use. If participation in an exhibition does not involve presence, surely it involves a type of mediated or indirect contribution or at least a direct reference.

The requirements outlined above have been mapped into a CIDOC-CRM model[8] (illustrated using an example in Fig. 2). The proposed framework, while rooted in established CRM patterns, provide a pragmatic solution that balance the existing capabilities of the ontology and the nuanced demands of exhibition representation.

5   Conclusion

This paper presents an initial investigation of the ontological requirements for modeling art exhibitions, addressing both catalog-derived and database-derived information. Leveraging CIDOC-CRM, the study develops a model that accommodates the complex nature of exhibitions, including their temporal, spatial, and participatory dimensions. The research underscores the limitation in expressions of current ontologies, specifically with respect to contingency and participation patterns, and advocates for the improvements of ontological models to better capture the multifaceted nature of exhibitions. The proposed model formalizes the established requirements using core concepts and relationships of CIDOC-CRM while illustrating their deficiencies and pinpointing the aspects that need to be enhanced to better match the intended meaning of the data.

Despite the identified limitations in capturing the data nuances by CRM's class and properties, the proposed model was successfully used to (i) transform

---

[8] Given the limitation of the paper a full version of the model is available on GitHub:https://github.com/ncarboni/Exhibitions.

a large subset of information from the BasArt database, as well as (ii) transform the MoMA Exhibition dataset in RDF. This work made it possible to query and analyze two major sources of exhibition information, enabling the use of distant reading methods for analyzing artistic exchanges across the Atlantic in the 20th century. These practical applications highlight the model's potential, particularly as a flexible foundation for the further ontological developments required in order to attain a comprehensive documentation of exhibitions.

Disclosure of Interests. The author has no competing interests.

References

1. Altshuler, B.: Salon to Biennial - Exhibitions that Made Art History, Volume 1: 1863–1959. Phaidon Press, London ; New York (2007)
2. Altshuler, B.: Biennials and Beyond: Exhibitions that Made Art History: 1962–2002. Phaidon Press Ltd., London New York, 1st edn. (2013)
3. Baroncini, S., Sartini, B., Van Erp, M., Tomasi, F., Gangemi, A.: Is dc:subject enough? A landscape on iconography and iconology statements of knowledge graphs in the semantic web. J. Documentation **79**(7), 115–136 (2023). https://doi.org/10.1108/JD-09-2022-0207
4. Borgo, S., et al.: DOLCE: a descriptive ontology for linguistic and cognitive engineering. Appl. Ontol. **17**(1), 45–69 (2022). https://doi.org/10.3233/AO-210259
5. Bruseker, G., Carboni, N., Guillem, A.: Cultural heritage data management: the role of formal ontology and CIDOC CRM. In: Vincent, M.L., López-Menchero Bendicho, V.M., Ioannides, M., Levy, T.E. (eds.) Heritage and Archaeology in the Digital Age. QMHSS, pp. 93–131. Springer, Cham (2017). https://doi.org/10.1007/978-3-319-65370-9_6
6. Carboni, N., de Luca, L.: An ontological approach to the description of visual and iconographical representations. Heritage **2**(2), 1191–1210 (2019)
7. Carboni, N., Usel, T., Joyeux-Prunel, B.: Intégrer des données historiques spatio-temporelles. In: Recueil Des Communications Du 4e Colloque Humanistica. Association francophone des humanités numériques, Geneva (2023)
8. Collicelli Cagol, S.: Exhibition History and the Institution as a Medium. Stedelijk Stud. J. (2) (2015). https://doi.org/10.54533/StedStud.vol002.art03
9. Davis, E., Heravi, B.: Linked data and cultural heritage: a systematic review of participation, collaboration, and motivation. J. Comput. Cult. Heritage **14**(2) (2021). https://doi.org/10.1145/3429458
10. Dijkshoorn, C., Aroyo, L., van Ossenbruggen, J., Schreiber, G.: Modeling cultural heritage data for online publication. Appl. Ontol. **13**(4), 255–271 (2018). https://doi.org/10.3233/AO-180201
11. Dretske, F.I.: Can events move? Mind **76**(304), 479–492 (1967)
12. Francesconi, E., Montemagni, S., Peters, W., Tiscornia, D.: Integrating a Bottom–Up and Top–Down Methodology for Building Semantic Resources for the Multilingual Legal Domain. In: Francesconi, E., Montemagni, S., Peters, W., Tiscornia, D. (eds.) Semantic Processing of Legal Texts: Where the Language of Law Meets the Law of Language, pp. 95–121. Springer, Berlin, Heidelberg (2010). https://doi.org/10.1007/978-3-642-12837-0_6
13. Galton, A.P.: States, processes and events, and the ontology of causal relations. IOS Press (2012). https://doi.org/10.3233/978-1-61499-084-0-279

14. Gonano, C.M., Tomasi, F., Mambelli, F., Vitali, F., Peroni, S.: Zeri e LODE. Extracting the Zeri photo archive to linked open data - formalizing the conceptual model. In: IEEE/ACM Joint Conference on Digital Libraries, pp. 289–298 (2014). https://doi.org/10.1109/JCDL.2014.6970182
15. Goodyear, A.C.: The Art-Historical Catalogue in the Digital Era. In: The Routledge Companion to Digital Humanities and Art History. Routledge, New York (2020)
16. Greenwald, D.S.: Painting by Numbers: Data-driven Histories of Nineteenth-Century Art. Princeton University Press, Princeton (2021)
17. Guillem, A., Bruseker, G., Ronzino, P.: Process, concept or thing? Some initial considerations in the ontological modelling of architecture. Int. J. Digit. Libr. **18**(4), 289–299 (2016). https://doi.org/10.1007/s00799-016-0188-0
18. Hacker, P.M.S.: Events and objects in space and time. Mind **91**(361), 1–19 (1982)
19. Jaimini, U., Henson, C., Sheth, A.: An ontology design pattern for representing causality. In: Proceedings of the 14th Workshop on Ontology Design and Patterns. CEUR-WS.org, Athens (2023)
20. Joyeux-Prunel, B., Marcel, O.: Exhibition catalogues in the globalization of art. A source for social and spatial art history. Artl@s Bull. **4**(2), 8 (2015)
21. Lehmann, J., Borgo, S., Masolo, C., Gangemi, A.: Causality and Causation in DOLCE. In: Proceedings of the International Conference on Formal Ontology in Information Systems FOIS 2004. IOS Press, Amsterdam (2004)
22. Manovich, L.: Cultural Analytics. MIT Press, Cambridge, Massachusetts (2020)
23. Nevola, F., Cooper, D., Capulli, C., Brunke, L.: Immersive renaissance florence: research-based 3-D modeling in digital art and architectural history. Getty Res. J. **15**, 203–227 (2022)
24. Quinton, A.: Objects and Events. Mind **88**(350), 197–214 (1979)
25. Rebboud, Y., Lisena, P., Troncy, R.: Beyond Causality: representing Event Relations in Knowledge Graphs. In: Corcho, O., Hollink, L., Kutz, O., Troquard, N., Ekaputra, F.J. (eds.) Knowledge Engineering and Knowledge Management, pp. 121–135. Springer International Publishing, Cham (2022). https://doi.org/10.1007/978-3-031-17105-5_9
26. Rodrigues, F.H., Abel, M.: What to consider about events: a survey on the ontology of occurrents. Appl. Ontol. **14**(4), 343–378 (2019). https://doi.org/10.3233/AO-190217
27. Rodríguez-Ortega, N., Roldán-García, M.d.M., Díez Platas, M., Salvachúa, M.: OntoExhibit: Una ontología para el modelado del ámbito de las exposiciones artísticas y sus expansiones semántico-discursivas (2023)
28. Sanderson, R.: Implementing linked art in a multi-modal database for cross-collection discovery. Open Lib. Human. **10**(2) (2024). https://doi.org/10.16995/olh.15407
29. Scherp, A., Franz, T., Saathoff, C., Staab, S.: F–a model of events based on the foundational ontology dolce+DnS ultralight. In: Proceedings of the Fifth International Conference on Knowledge Capture, pp. 137–144. K-CAP 2009, Association for Computing Machinery, New York, NY, USA (2009). https://doi.org/10.1145/1597735.1597760
30. Vogel, F.: On the canon of exhibition history. In: Re-Envisioning the Contemporary Art Canon, pp. 205–218. Routledge, London (2016)
31. Wolff, P.: Representing causation. J. Exp. Psychol. Gen. **136**(1), 82–111 (2007). https://doi.org/10.1037/0096-3445.136.1.82

Building a Transliteration Tool to Enhance the Exchange of Metadata About Greek Authors

Charalampos Bratsas[1,2] , Lazaros Ioannidis[1,2] , Ilias Tsitsilegkas[1] ,
Michalis Gerolimos[3] , Eftychia Koufakou[3] , and Sofia Zapounidou[3(✉)]

[1] Department of Information and Electronic Engineering, International Hellenic University,
Sindos, Greece
cbratsas@iee.ihu.gr, larjohn@okfn.gr, it185301@it.teithe.gr
[2] Open Knowledge Greece, Thessaloniki, Greece
[3] National Library of Greece, Athens, Greece
{m.gerolimos,koufakou,szapounidou}@nlg.gr

Abstract. The National Library of Greece (NLG) transliterates Greek authors'
and corporate bodies' names to Latin characters, and integrates the transliterated text into authority records. Submitting data to the Virtual Authority File
(VIAF) revealed that transliterations help cluster the Greek version of names under
the proper cluster. To further enhance shareability and matching potential of the
NLG data, it was decided to enrich name authority records with transliterations
under two standards: ALA-LC Romanization tables, and ELOT743 (equivalent
to ISO843). The NLG collaborated with the International Hellenic University,
Department of Information and Electronic Engineering, and the Open Knowledge
Foundation Greece to build a transliterator tool. This paper presents the development of the tool, along with the challenges in applying the rules that each standard
determines. The tool was evaluated against a Gold Dataset created by the NLG
staff.

Keywords: transliteration · interoperability · Romanization tables · ISO 843 ·
National Library of Greece

1 Introduction

Libraries have always created metadata that could be shared and re-used by other
libraries. The MAchine-Readable Cataloging (MARC) format, a data format created
in the 1960s is still used in library catalogs worldwide. Bibliographic metadata are
entered in fields of flat MARC21 records according to a predefined set of rules. The
most common set of rules has been the Anglo-American Cataloging Rules (AACR)
that require libraries to select a language of cataloging for metadata not copied from
the publication itself, e.g., notes, subject terms, etc. For names and text that need to be
copied from the publication, such as author names, titles, etc., and are in a non-preferred
language, a transliteration standard must be selected.

Transliteration is the process of representing the characters of one script using the
characters of another script [1]. It is based on converting the characters and does not

© The Author(s), under exclusive license to Springer Nature Switzerland AG 2025
M. Sfakakis et al. (Eds.): MTSR 2024, CCIS 2331, pp. 268–273, 2025.
https://doi.org/10.1007/978-3-031-81974-2_23

consider phonetics, contrary to the transcription method. Thus, it can be easily used by anyone without prior knowledge of either the source script or the target one. The focus on the conversion of characters guarantees that reverse transliteration, also known as retransliteration [1], is feasible without uncertainties. Transliteration has been used by libraries to catalog materials published in foreign languages [2]. It has also enabled the exchange of records between libraries even when the libraries involved have selected different languages as the preferred language of cataloging. In aggregations of metadata or union catalogs, transliteration has helped match names of entities written in different languages/scripts [3], e.g., names of authors, while inconsistent transliterations have proven to hinder information retrieval [4].

There are several international or local transliteration standards. Regarding the transliteration of Greek, libraries in the US, as well as libraries participating in the Program for Cooperative Cataloging (PCC) use the Romanization table for Greek [5] created by the American Library Association and the Library of Congress. Another international standard used worldwide is the ISO 843 [1]. There are important differences between these two standards. The ALA-LC Romanization table for Greek provides slightly different rules for the conversion of Ancient or Medieval Greek texts (written before 1453), and of Modern Greek texts (written after 1453). The ALA-LC table also considers the origin of a word during transliteration while the ISO 843 does not. As an example, if a modern Greek word originates from an ancient Greek word that had a 'rough breathing' diacritic (known as daseîa), then the transliteration retains the rough breathing and uses the character H. The ALA-LC Romanization table for Greek ignores all other diacritics, but considers diphthongs 'αυ', 'ευ', 'ηυ', 'ου', 'υι', and 'ωυ', as well as the position (start, middle, or end) of specific diphthongs in a word, namely 'γγ', 'γκ', 'μπ', and 'ντ'. The ISO 843 standard determines the same rules for Ancient and Modern Greek, but it additionally provides the option to implement the rules using either the polytonic or the monotonic system. The only special rule pertains to the transliteration of the diphthongs: 'αυ', 'ευ', and 'ου'.

The National Library of Greece (NLG) has adopted in 2022 new bibliographic models that adhere to linked data principles with the aim to provide interoperable and usable data. Considering that records describing Greek literary works exist in library catalogs worldwide, and that 81% of these records include transliterated text only and not the original script [2], the NLG decided to systematically include the transliterated names of Greek authors and corporate bodies in authority records. Furthermore, to facilitate the matching of entities for Virtual Authority File (VIAF) [6] clusters or for information retrieval purposes, the NLG decided to implement the two aforementioned transliteration standards: the ALA-LC Romanization table for Greek, and the ISO 843 standard. Cataloguers implementing this cataloging policy decision struggle to deliver two different transliterations, especially when each one of them requires the use of special characters that cannot not be typed using the keyboard. The need for a transliteration tool becomes apparent and the following research question emerges:

Can a software handle transliteration of Greek characters considering the differences between Ancient and Modern Greek, as well as the origin of words and the diacritics of monotonic or polytonic orthography, without degenerating into an exhaustive dictionary?

2 Methods and Results

To determine if a software can transliterate Greek characters to Latin ones according to the two selected standards, the NLG staff experimented with Artificial Intelligence (AI). Transliteration is a rule-based problem where Large Language Models do not fit well. Yet, it was decided to experiment with ChatGPT 4.0 hoping that its model (trained with many texts) would heuristically recognize the root words of Modern Greek ones appearing in any grammatical case, conjugated or compound form. The standards were uploaded, and three prompts were used. In detail, two prompts were used for the Romanization of Ancient and Modern Greek, and the third prompt was used for the ISO 843 standard. To evaluate the results, a gold dataset was created with 385 Greek names and short phrases[1]. The list was created to include all cases and exceptions described in both standards' rules. ChatGPT correctly transliterated 59,7% of the list (230 out of 385) using the ALA-LC Romanization table. Most common errors related to the following Greek characters: vita (B, β), ita (H, η), phi (Φ, φ), chi (X, χ), and the diphthongs 'Aυ', 'Eυ', 'Oυ', 'Nτ', 'Γκ', 'Mπ'. Another common error was the transliteration of Modern Greek words that originate from Ancient Greek words with a rough breathing ('daseîa'). Using the ISO 843:1997 standard, ChatGPT correctly transliterated 31,2% of the names (120 out of 385). It failed to transliterate the acute accent ('), as well as the Greek characters ita (H, η), omega (Ω, ω), and the diphthongs 'αυ', 'ευ', 'ου'.

Following the ChatGPT experiment and the relatively low success rate in the transliteration of Greek words, the team decided to proceed with the development of a transliterator tool that could be later integrated as an online service by the NLG to be used by anyone freely. The requirements for this tool were defined as follows: deliver simultaneous transliterations under two different standards, namely the ISO 843 and ALA-LC Romanization table for Greek (Ancient and Modern). Regarding the ISO 843 standard, the requirement for transliteration using the monotonic system was set. Dictionaries cannot be integrated into the tool due to copyright, and the use of open technologies is preferred. Regarding the technologies and the conversion method to be used in the tool, Javascript was selected as the programming language owing to its speed, versatility, and interoperability. HTML and CSS were selected for the graphic user interface (GUI) (see Fig. 1).

Regarding the conversion method, the mapping method was selected as it accelerates similarity search, while also supporting scalability, and computer memory efficiency [7]. Most importantly, the mapping tables used in the method may support, with the appropriate coding, reverse conversion, known as retransliteration. Two mapping tables were created including all the Greek characters that must be recognized by the tool, along with all Latin characters that will be used as the tool's output. Given that there are many variations of the Greek characters owing to the use of different orthographies, polytonic versus monotonic, more than 620 Unicode codes were used for capital and small letters, as well as for all their combinations with diacritics (see Fig. 2). As an example, for the first letter of the Greek alphabet, Alpha (A), 33 variations were included in the table. Some of the variations include the capital or small Alpha character accentuated or not, with or without smooth and rough breathings (psilí and daseîa), etc. Similarly, Latin

---

[1] The dataset is available via Zenodo repository: https://doi.org/10.5281/zenodo.13318809.

characters with accentuation (needed for the ISO 843 transliteration) or other special diacritics (needed for the ALA-LC Romanization transliteration) were identified and integrated into the tool.

Fig. 1. The transliteration tool. The name of author Nikos Kazantzakis is transliterated using the ALA-LC Romanization and the ISO 843 standard.

```
//Perispomeni ( ˜ )
    //Uppercase
        'Ἆ':'A','Ἦ':'Ê','Ἶ':'I','Ὦ':'Ô',//+Apostrofos
        'Ἆ':'A','Ἦ':'Ê',            'Ὦ':'Ô',//+Apostrofos +iota
        'Ἇ':'A','Ἧ':'Ê','Ἷ':'I','Ὗ':'Y','Ὧ':'Ô',//+Daseia
        'Ἇ':'A','Ἧ':'Ê',            'Ὧ':'Ô',//+Daseia +
    //Lowercase
        'ᾶ':'a','ῆ':'ē','ῖ':'i','ῦ':'y','ῶ':'ō',
        'ἆ':'a','ἦ':'ē','ἶ':'i','ὖ':'y','ὦ':'ō',
        'ἇ':'a','ἧ':'ē','ἷ':'i','ὗ':'y','ὧ':'ō',//+Apostorofos
        'ἆ':'a','ἦ':'ē',            'ὦ':'ō',//+Apostorofos+
        'ἇ':'a','ἧ':'ē','ἷ':'i','ὗ':'y','ὧ':'ō',//+Daseia
```

Fig. 2. Part of the transliteration function that recognizes Ancient Greek vowels with the 'perispomeni' (~) diacritic alone or in combination with other diacritics.

Besides the mapping tables, additional code and mapping tables were developed to handle special rules. The ALA-LC romanization standard provides different rules for Ancient and Modern Greek, and additionally respects the origin of a word and the position of specific diphthongs in a word, namely 'γγ', 'γκ', 'μπ', and 'ντ'. According to the 'origin of the word' rule, the 'rough breathing' (daseîa) must be considered during transliteration regardless if it is Ancient or Modern Greek, or if it is written on the text or not. This means that Modern Greek words that originate from Ancient Greek words with 'rough breathing', must be transliterated as if the 'rough breathing' appears in the Modern Greek word. As an example, the Modern Greek name 'Ελένη' is transliterated as 'Helenē', because it originates from the Ancient Greek name 'Ἑλένη', the first letter of which is the capital letter 'Epsilon' with a 'rough breathing'. To include root words into a separate mapping table, a list of almost 800 root words that take the 'rough breathing' diacritic was prepared. All root words are 3–5 characters, and some of them are accentuated. The list was prepared after consulting Greek dictionaries [8, 9] and a Wiktionary list of 112.371 Modern Greek last names [10]. After integration of the root words in the separate mapping table, Modern Greek words that match the root word are transliterated as if they have a 'rough breathing', thus taking the Latin character 'H' as the first letter. Regarding the position of the diphthongs 'γγ', 'γκ', 'μπ', and 'ντ', special functions with variables were created. Depending on the value of the variable (if diphthongs are at the start or middle or end of a word) a different mapping table is implemented (Fig. 3).

```
//5 letters
  //Uppercase
    'Άλατα':'Ha','Άλατά':'Ha','Άλατό':'Ha','Άλιεύ':'Ha','Άμαρτ':'Ha','Απαλό':'Ha',
    'Εβραι':'He','Ειμαρ':'He','Εκάβη':'He','Εκάτη':'He','Εκτωρ':'He','Ελικώ':'He',
    'Ελλάδ':'He','Ελλάν':'He','Ελλάς':'He','Ελλην':'He',
    'Ερμής':'He','Ερμιό':'He','Ερμιο':'He','Εσπερ':'He','Εσπέρ':'He','Εστία':'He',
    'Εταιρ':'He','Εκατό':'He','Εκατα':'He','Εκατο':'He','Εξηντ':'He',
    'Ηγουμ':'Hē','Ηρακλ':'Hē','Ηράκλ':'Hē','Ηρόστ':'Hē','Ησαία':'Hē','Ησίοδ':'Hē',
    'Ησαία':'Hē','Ηραιο':'Hē','Ηραιο':'Hē',
    'Ιερου':'Hi','Ιστορ':'Hi','Ιδρώς':'Hi',
```

Fig. 3. Part of the mapping table with root words originating from Ancient Greek words taking the rough breathing.

To evaluate the transliteration output produced by the tool, the same gold dataset was used. The transliteration tool correctly transliterated 97,9% of names (377 out of 385) using the ALA-LC Romanization table for Greek characters. False transliterations involve words that originate from Ancient Greek words with 'rough breathing', and the identification of articles 'o', 'η' when they are preceded by a parenthesis '(' or a quotation mark '«'. The transliteration according to the ISO 843 standard delivered no errors. All 385 were transliterated correctly.

3 Discussion and Conclusions

The primary aim of this study was to evaluate the effectiveness of utilizing a custom-developed software to accurately transliterate Greek characters into Latin script, considering the specific rules outlined by the chosen standards, ALA-LC Romanization and ISO 843.

The transliterator tool uses open technologies (Javascript) and mapping tables enabling smooth updates even by people with little expertise in coding. Moreover, the tool's code can easily be integrated into any website, thus significantly increasing its use and value by anyone involved in Greek text transliteration from any trade and profession. To further support the reuse of the code, many comments were used for clarity in explaining mapping tables and functions. Special functions with variables were developed to handle the transliteration of diphthongs in both standards. Besides the mapping tables, a special code was developed to handle challenging rules like the 'origin of words rule' in ALA-LC Romanization.

The Greek language poses significant challenges owing to its extensive history and complex etymological structures, as well as the different orthographies (monotonic and polytonic) and the application of diacritical marks. The ALA-LC Romanization table considers different rules for Ancient and Modern Greek, the origin of words, and the position of specific diphthongs in words, while the ISO843 respects the accentuation and all other diacritics. Each standard uses its own special characters. Finding and integrating all Ancient and Modern Greek characters with their variations depending on accentuation and breathing, and combinations of them has been a challenging task. A similar task was demanded for the integration of all special characters used in the transliteration output. The ones needed for the ALA-LC Romanization standard were easy to find, as they are included in the standard itself. Finding the output characters for the ISO 843 standard proved challenging because the standard uses special characters for accentuated vowels and for vowels with combined diacritics, e.g., small ypsilon letter with accent (´) and diaeresis (¨) combined (ΰ). Respecting the origin of words related to the ALA-LC Romanization required extensive investigations about the etymology of words and names and was managed with specialized mapping tables that eventually increased the complexity of the mapping algorithm. Both standards include special rules about the conversion of diphthongs. These rules were handled with special functions further adding to the intricacy of the code. In general, applying the ALA-LC Romanization standard proved to be more challenging than ISO 843.

As the evaluation exercise has demonstrated, the transliteration tool can provide accurate transliterations. Yet, it must be highlighted that despite the extensive list of root words, all derivations of words due to conjugation or composition cannot be identified by the tool. Thus, the tool may demonstrate better results for Greek names than extended texts. Extra updates to cover more cases have been set for future releases of the tool. Another prospect that will be investigated in the future is the integration of the tool in Koha [11], the open-source Integrated Library System that the NLG uses. Even though ChatGPT did not deliver high percentages of accurate transliterations, NLG will continue experimenting with AI tools by training them to further simplify repetitive tasks.

References

1. ISO 843. Information and documentation - Conversion of Greek characters into Latin characters. ISO, Genève (1997)
2. Smith-Yoshumira, K., Coombs, K.: Transcription vs. Transliteration. Hanging Together, OCLC research blog (2015). https://hangingtogether.org/transcription-vs-transliteration/. Accessed 19 July 2024
3. Hickey, T.B, Toves, J.A.: Managing ambiguity in VIAF. D-Lib Magaz. 20(7/8) (2014)
4. Kaveh, M., Mirzabeigi, M., Sotudeh, H., Moloodi, A.: The effects of the challenges in the transliteration of Persian names into English on the recall of retrieved results in the web of science. Scientometrics 127, 1099–1128 (2022)
5. ALA-LC Romanization Tables. www.loc.gov/catdir/cpso/roman.html. Accessed 19 July 2024
6. Virtual Authority File. https://viaf.org/en. Accessed 19 July 2024
7. Stein, B.: Principles of hash-based text retrieval. In: Proceedings of the 30th annual international ACM SIGIR conference on Research and development in information retrieval (SIGIR 2007), pp. 527–534. Association for Computing Machinery, New York, NY, USA (2007)
8. Liddell, G., Scott, R.: Intermediate Greek-English Lexicon. Thessaloniki, Center for the Greek Language (c2012). www.greek-language.gr/digitalResources/ancient_greek/tools/liddell-scott/index.html. Accessed 19 July 2024
9. Babiniotis, G.: Dictionary of modern Greek [in Greek]. Lexicology Center, Athens (2012)
10. Male last names (Modern Greek). el.wiktionary.org/w/index.php?title=Κατηγορία:Ανδρικά_επώνυμα_(νέα_ελληνικά)
11. Koha, https://koha-community.org/. Accessed 19 July 2024

Track on European and National Projects; and 8th DOAbLE - Papers for Libraries, Archives, Museums

Creation of a Music Ontology in the Framework of the Project Greek Music Audiovisual Collections (M.EL.O.S.)

Pantelis Brattis[1], Emmanouel Garoufallou[2]([⊠]) [iD], Eugenios Politis[3], Pavlos Siskos[2], Petros Vouvaris[3], Evangelia Spyrakou[3], Thalia Adelfopoulou[3], Giorgos Kokkonis[4], Nikos Ordoulidis[4], Giorgos Evangelou[4], Aimilios Kampouropoulos[5], Asterios Zacharakis[5], Savvas Kazanis[5], Vera Kriezi[6], Valia Vraka[6], Mirena Mountzia[6], Kostas Maistrelis[1], Simos Leonidakos[1], Nikos Papazis[1], and Niki-Maria Chatziefstratiou[2]

[1] ReasonableGraph (AltSol), Athens, Greece
[2] «MetaDATA LAB», International Hellenic University, Thessaloniki, Greece
mgarou@ihu.gr
[3] University of Macedonia, Thessaloniki, Greece
[4] University of Ioannina, Ioannina, Greece
[5] Aristotle University of Thessaloniki, Thessaloniki, Greece
[6] The Friends of Music Society, Athens, Greece

Abstract. Music ontology is a framework that is used to publish structured data related to music and became available on the Semantic Web through data interfaces. This process is articulated in this article through the analysis of the Musical Greek Audiovisual Collections (M.EL.O.S.) project and its ontology. Specifically, the project involves the integration of three different types of music collections, gathered on a common platform, Reasonable Graph (RG), while retaining the autonomy of the participating institutions.

The suggested ontology was initially based on the international conceptual models FRBR, FRBRoo, FRAD and FRSAD and their WEMI (Work, Expression, Manifestation, Item) ontologies, while their structure and role in the formation of the musical ontology of the M.EL.O.S. project was also analysed. Being evident that the original ontology could not cover the description needs of the music ontology, the already existing music ontology "MUSIC ONTOLOGY" was additionally utilized, adding the established type of entities "Agent" (Person, Organization, Family) and "Subject" (Concept, Place, Event, Object, Genre and Subject Chain). Thus, additional fields specialized metadata descriptions appeared.

The Reasonable Graph platform is the one that eventually supported music ontology, data interconnection, and the ability to access and research music data with a focus on interoperability and the detailed descriptions of the music materials. Thus, through visualisation examples of the final product, the connection between metadata, entities and conceptual models is explained, while the processes and findings of the analyses within the M.EL.O.S. project opened new paths in data interconnection and the importance of abundance in it.

Thus, this paper goes beyond the common presentation of basic elements of music ontology and focuses on its development, the steps and logic it followed,

© The Author(s), under exclusive license to Springer Nature Switzerland AG 2025
M. Sfakakis et al. (Eds.): MTSR 2024, CCIS 2331, pp. 277–287, 2025.
https://doi.org/10.1007/978-3-031-81974-2_24

the specializations, and its enrichment, providing a basis for future references and approaches to organizing and managing complex musical information. It also covers the key outcomes of the project and its ontology, which contribute to the development of an appropriate music ontology as a result of the M.EL.O.S. project outcomes. This includes processes such as discussions about project and ontology needs, the automated extraction of music content from participating institutions, the crowdsourcing procedures, and the development of collaborative operations. These efforts were implemented on the Reasonable Graph system, alongside the transfer of metadata and digital/digitized documents.

Keywords: Music ontology · FRBR · Entities · Repositories · Linked Data · Metadata

1   Introduction

Ontology, in the context of information science, is a formal system of knowledge representation that describes concepts, relationships and properties within a particular domain. In the case of music ontology, this system is applied to the field of music, allowing for the organization and categorization of information related to musical works, artists, genres, and other related items. The utility of a music ontology lies in its ability to facilitate the efficient search, retrieval, and management of musical information, thus supporting research, education, and preservation of musical heritage. Furthermore, it allows interoperability between different systems and databases, enhancing collaboration and information exchange in the music sector. In this context, the "M.EL.O.S." is an innovative approach to the development of an integrated music ontology.

Our goal is to develop a specialized music ontology with innovative features, as it will allow the integration of qualitative data that will be automatically extracted from recordings and scores. The aim of this action is to promote the proposed music ontology internationally in order to contribute to the scientific dialogue on the documentation of musical and, more generally, cultural works. While the aim is to create technological products for the registration and documentation of cultural content and its dissemination to cultural heritage providers. In particular, through the project, the open source ReasonableGraph (RG) platform has been adapted to the selected music ontology and the specific needs of music collections. The development of the RG platform offers two end products. One for the needs of managing local music collection repositories, called the Local Music Ontology Repository (TAMO). And secondly for the needs of managing collaborative central music repositories, called the Central Music Authority Repository (KeMKA).

In addition, the creation of national collaborative networks for the joint management and creation of cultural collections by institutions with similar cultural collections. In the M.EL.O.S. project, this cooperation will be highlighted through the National Archive of Musical Entities (EAMO), in which entities like musical works and their performances, musicians, or their discography that are related to Greek music will be created and established cooperatively by the project members. These unique entities will be managed by the Central Music Authority Archive (KeMKA). Our goal is to adopt KeMKA as a hub for the creation of established entities for music at the national level, with the integration of other institutions into it.

The project is about integrating three different types of music collections into a common platform, while maintaining the autonomy of the different participating institutions. The project platform had to be able to manage simultaneously the art music works of Theodorakis, the classical music from the double bass archive and the folk - rebetiko music from the Tsitsanis archive. It also had to manage different types of items per collection as the Theodorakis Archive contains mainly printed scores, the Tsitsanis Archive contains discography and the double bass archive, containing materials such as scores, recordings, posters, photographs.

For the music ontology "M.EL.O.S.", we first focused on the diversity of collections and documents, distinguishing between types of collaborative repositories and their specific materials. We then laid the foundations based on international models such as Functional Requirements for Bibliographic Records (FRBR), Functional Requirements for Authority Data (FRAD), Functional Requirements for Subject Data (FRSAD), which provide a powerful framework for organizing bibliographic and other information and examined the existing "Music Ontology".

We also aim to develop tools and methodologies for the search, interconnection, retrieval, presentation/representation and enrichment of semantically annotated information. Part of the study will extend beyond the current scientific benchmarking, as the development of metrics for the combined use of metadata and qualitative attributes of music content in the interconnection and presentation/illustration of repository entities will be thoroughly explored. The use of the tools and information will be made available to scholars, ordinary users and third-party organizations that want to exploit metadata for research, entertainment and commercial purposes. The promotion of the project's outputs on the domestic and international markets through participation in exhibitions.

The process was divided into application sections. Priority was given to the creation of a basic ontology, followed by enrichment with specific entities to cover all descriptive needs. Thus, the ontology of "M.EL.O.S." covered all of the project requirements that been set based on the project participants materials and archives. The following sections describe all the domains covered by the M.EL.O.S. ontology.

2 The Ontology of "M.EL.O.S."

The creation of the M.EL.O.S. Music ontology (MELOS Project, 2024) was based on the FRBR, FRAD and FRSAD models, as well as on "MUSIC ONTOLOGY" and the Reasonable Graph platform which hosts it, fully supports the conceptual model Functional Requirements for Bibliographic Records (FRBR). The basic FRBR entities (Work, Expression, Manifestation, Item) were adapted to the needs of the project and were formulated based on international standards in the field of music, librarianship and archives.

Thus, specialized entities such as "Musical Work", "Musical Expression" and "Musical Manifestation", "Musical Poster" and "Musical Programme" were added, in addition to the existing categories, namely "Bibliographic Works", "Periodical Works", "Archives", "Physical, Digital and Digitized Documents". The specialized entities essentially acted as specializations - sub-entities - sub-entities, on the basis of the FRBR, specializing the descriptions of music documents. This separation upgraded the music ontology at the level of description as well as at the level of relationships and properties of the entities, enriching the original entity schema of the M.EL.O.S.

2.1   FRBR in the Framework of the Project "M.EL.O.S."

There were about two ways available to create either a Work or an Expression or Manifestation entity that would be based on the FRBR model. Creating entities that could stand alone in the RG platform was the one of them; During this way, user of the platform had to link these entities together by using relevant fields that would connect the main Work to its Expression and the Expression to a Manifestation of it.

On the other hand, creating entities through forms of a higher hierarchical entity that would allow the system user to create an expression through a Work record and a Manifestation one inside of an expression of it, surely been preferred for common policy reasons, as this way helped users to avoid create non-linked connections among the entities of theirs.

Depending on the type of material, entities derived from corresponding shapes had to be created. More specifically, bibliographic works should be adapted to the proposed FRBR entities, namely Work, Expression, Manifestation and Item. Second, journal-type publications to entities derived from FRBRoo, namely entities such as Serial Work and Issue (Bekiari et al., 2015, Library of Congress, 2024, Baker, 2014). Third, archival material with physical classification to EAD entities such as Fonds, Series and Files. Fourth, the entities of the documents based on their type. For example, Photo entity for photographs, Poster entity for posters, etc. (International Council on Archives, 2000) However, as the above entities as a whole could not cope with the requirements of the specific musical material of the project, the following additional musical entities were created that are directly related to the musical works and musical documents:

- Musical Work
- Musical Expression, με εξειδίκευση σε Score και Performance/Recording
- Musical Manifestation, με εξειδίκευση σε Disc, Magnetic Medium και Digital Medium.
- Musical Poster
- Musical Programme

At the same time, the standard entities, such as the Creator entities (Person, Organization, Family) and the Subject entities (Concept, Place, Event, Object, Genre and Subject Chain) that existed in the platform should be supported. In addition to these, the following specialized entities were added for the needs of the project:

- Music Person
- Music Organization
- Musical Event
- Musical Medium
- Musical Genre/Form

2.2 FRBR Work

In the FRBR Work entity we create records related to the intellectual or artistic creations of human activity. The entity contains a large number of fields in which the full details of a Work are recorded as well as its links to other Works and other entities (such as Person, Expression and Manifestation). Most of the fields in the FRBR Work entity correspond to MARC21/Authorities and UNIMARC/Authorities fields. Some fields, however, are derived from the corresponding bibliographic formats.

3   Conceptual Models

FRBR and FRAD

The first crucial step was to use material from the collaborating organisations, initially using IFLA's "FRBR" conceptual model. This model created ten entities in three groups, with the first group including "Work", "Expression", "Manifestation" and "Item" (the latter with sub-entities "Digital" and "Physical Item"). The remaining entities were presented using the "FRAD" model, which includes "Person", "Corporate Body", "Concept", "Object", "Event" and "Place". "Work" can have two sub-entities: original language and translation expressions. Each expression may have a unique manifestation with physical or digital copies. The entities "work", "expression", "manifestation" and "object" are related to the entities "agent" (creator) and "subject" (IFLA, 1998).

These links form a tree-like structure with a logical hierarchy, showing how Record Entities interact with Creators and Subjects. In FRBR, Work manifests through Expression, Expression embeds in Manifestation, and Manifestation reproduces in Item. The Item entity is subdivided into "Physical Item" and "Digital Item". "FRAD", another IFLA conceptual model, stands for "The Functional Requirements for Authority Data" and is used in "M.EL.O.S." as the Reasonable Graph platform supports it.

FRBRoo

The "M.EL.O.S." ontology used "FRBRoo" to organize entities describing "serial publications" from collaborating organizations. This enabled accurate metadata capture and relationship mapping between serial works and issues. A "serial work" can have multiple issues that exist as physical or digital objects. Issues relate to articles (bibliographic works) or "clippings", maintaining author and subject relationships. (Bekiari et al., 2015).

Articles can have subjective relationships with subject entities such as "concept", "object", "place", "genre", "event" and "subject chains". These subject entities may also have relationships with document entities such as "serial work", "issue" and their "physical" or "digital" items.

Archival Record Entities (EAD)

In order to incorporate archival material from collaborative digital music repositories, entities were incorporated using the EAD-based archival structure or independently. EAD added entities such as "Fond", "Series", "File", their subcategories and ISAD(G) descriptive rules. Records with archival links acquired specialized metadata (Library of

Congress, 2015) The "File" entity could include physical documents such as "pamphlet", "photograph", "letter", etc. (International Council on Archives, 2000).

In this structure, a photograph in an archival folder links to the archival tree at its level. Books can be catalogued under appropriate archival units and levels. Physical documents in the "M.EL.O.S." ontology included various types such as "Photo", "Negative", "Document", "Leaflet", "Poster", "Postcard", "Drawing", "Stamp", "Programme", "Letter", "Envelope", "Correspondence", "Object", "Artwork 3D" and "Generic Item" for unassigned records. These physical documents belong to EAD entities, while 'Book' comes from the FRBR model and "Magazine" from the FRBRoo model.

No Archival Structure

For archival entities without structure, we added them independently to manage and display materials in both physical and digital forms. This allowed management of "Physical Photo", "Physical Negative", and their "Born-Digital" and "Digitized" forms. Each physical document without archival structure may have a digital copy.

4   Authority Entities

Authority, "Agent" Entities (FRAD)

Technically, entities such as 'Work,' 'Expression,' 'Manifestation,' and 'Item' are both inevitably and directly related to their creators and to the 'subject' they represent (IFLA, 1998; Alemu & Garoufallou, 2020). For this reason, the inclusion of 'Agent' entities in the ontology of the "M.EL.O.S." project could not be omitted. Their role is revealed through the relationships they have with the relevant records, as they link records that have been created and exist to the entities (i.e. their names) of their creators. The inclusion of 'Agent' entities was of particular importance in the semantic representation of the subject content of the records (Gaitanou et al. 2024).

For their creation, the conceptual model "FRAD" was used under its international descriptive rules of Resource Description and Access (RDA). Thus, the music ontology "M.EL.O.S." included entities related to the creation and ownership of records: "Person", "Organization", and "Family". "Person" referred to those involved in the process of creation or ownership of records, while "Organization" and "Family" followed the same principle. These entities also represented relationships that followed their logical order. For example, this could mean a relationship linking the foundation of an organization with the "Person" or "Family" entities that matched. It could even link two families under a common family relationship.

Authority, "Subject" Entities (FRAD)

For the thematic representation of the content of the documents and the organization of the information, established entities of the FRAD conceptual model were used. These included "Concept", "Place", "Event", "Object" and "Genre", which contain metadata for generic concepts associated with the documents. The "Place" entity allows metadata to be entered for locations, "Event" for events and time periods, "Object" for objects as concepts, and "Genre" for concepts related to types and formats of the described material, such as conferences and discography. In this way, documents acquired descriptions for the concepts to which they related, the places and events to which they corresponded, and the objects and genres to which they assigned subject headings and types.

Subject Headings Entity (FRSAD)

The "Subject Chain" entity is essentially an entity that managed the subject headings in the "M.EL.O.S." project. Based on IFLA's FRSAD and using RDA, MARC21, UNI-MARC, LCSH and the subject headings of the National Library of Greece, it managed both individual terms and sequences of terms. Entering a simple entity such as "Concept", "Person" or "Work" in the Subject Headings field allowed the platform to recognize it as a subject heading. For multi-term subject headings, the subject chain contained additional entities beyond the main term, which determined the type of entity.

Collections and Sub-Collections Entities

To complete the first part of the music ontology, an important addition was the collection and sub-collection entities for the Reasonable Graph platform. These improved the management of digital library metadata with descriptive fields and hierarchy within collections. Thus, the user can easily create and prioritize items at different levels, viewing the collections and sub-collections of the M.EL.O.S. project in a tree-like format with search filters.

Musical (Work / Expression / Manifestation) and Musical (Poster / Programme)

Concerning the entity "Musical work", it includes fields and relations describing various types of musical works and is related to specialized musical entities such as "Musical expression" (e.g. Musical expression, recordings or scores of works), "Musical event" (publications of musical works), "Musical person", and "Musical organization" (creators of works), "Musical event" (related musical events), "Musical instrument" (means of performance) and "Musical genre/form" (form of musical work) (IFLA, 1998).

Similarly, "Musical Expression" describes musical expressions (e.g. recordings, scores) and is associated with corresponding entities: the originating musical work, the containing "Musical Expression", the associated "Musical Person" and "Musical Organization", the performing "Musical Event" and the definition of "Musical Genre/Form". Similarly, the "Musical Event" details musical publications containing musical scores or recordings of musical works. This is interlinked with the specialized musical entities "Musical Work" from which the expressions contained in a publication are derived, the "Musical Expression" contained in the publication, the "Music Person" and "Music Organization" associated with the realization of the publication.

In addition, "musical work" was linked to thematic entities to describe the thematic headings of its musical works, and to taxonomies and information related to the form and type, time and place of the musical works it describes, while specialized descriptive fields ensured the possibility of describing the tonality, the explanation of the arrangement or the lyrics of the musical works. In addition, "musical expression" was linked to corresponding thematic units to describe the thematic headings of its musical expressions, and includes specialized fields for the scope and context of the expression, the type of score, the medium of its performance, the dates of the creation of the expressions of the works, the languages, and others.

The "musical expression" entity was linked to generic entities relating to the places of publication or release of a work's expression, the recording of geographical names belonging to the generic entity "place", while specialized fields provided space for the recording of data such as title or edition number, publisher number, publication and release dates, series, ISMN number, "media" and "carrier" type or country of production of a work's expression.

In addition, all three of the above entities were linked to the international, general or musically established archives "VIAF[1]" (VIAF, 2024) and "MusicBrainz[2]" (MusicBrainz, n.d.), but also to a series of fields concerning the relationships of the entities with other works, expressions and versions, and to records of sets or parts of relationships, derivative or descriptive, accompanying or sequential. Finally, for a better semantic association of documents related to musical works, expressions and their versions, the entities "Musical Poster" and "Musical Programme" have also been created, providing important information such as about musical publications, record labels, concerts and programs of performances, events, and meetings.

Agent Entities (Music Person – Music Organization)

As with the Work, Expression and Manifestation entities, the Agent entities were designed to deal with the large accumulation of entities. For this reason, both Person and Organization entities were given specializations, 'Music Person' and 'Music Organization'. Music Person included all persons related to music and contained all the previous fields of the Person entity (place, date of birth/death, place of activity, biographical data, etc.), but also specialized fields such as composer, arranger, conductor, singer, instrumentalist, etc., along with the instruments and genres he/she played, years of active practice, studies, etc.

The corresponding specialized unit formed for the unit "Organization" is the "Music Organization" and with it the members of "M.EL.O.S." define in a more semantic approach the bodies for the production, distribution and education of music. In addition, the fields of recording the type of music organizations and their relations with the entities "Music Person", "Musical Event", etc., as well as taxonomies related to them, precisely defined fields and relations of the now special entity "Music Organization", which were combined with the corresponding, more simplified elements of the entity "Organization", in order to cover both simple and complex records.

Subject Entities (Music Event, Musical Medium, Musical Genre)

The subject entities, in turn, also contributed to the higher quality semantic capture of the entities they represent. This group consists of the subject entities Concept, Place, Event,

---

[1] The Virtual International Authority File is an international file of authority terms. It is a cooperative project of several international libraries, hosted by OCLC. Its purpose is to link national authority records. The file links identical records from different authority records. An entity that exists in different established records is assigned a unique VIAF number and a unique URI in VIAF. VIAF does not assign a unique header to the entity, but presents the different versions of headers based on different cataloguing policies, different languages, different cultural understandings, etc.

[2] MusicBrainz is an open music encyclopedia that collects music metadata and makes it available to the public.

Object, Genre and Subject Chain, and three more have been added. Musical Event, a subclass of Event, best describes the musical events (concerts, performances, etc.) of the M.EL.O.S. documents. It still contains specialized fields of musical events, their place and time, the musicians or ensembles that participated, their works or recordings.

Musical Medium, as a subclass of Object, defines the hierarchy of musical instruments for the performance of musical works. In it we find instruments, alternative forms of their names, definitions of instruments and hierarchical relationships with other instruments (narrower, broader, relative and equivalent terms), and are assigned as multilingual and based on (LCMPT[3]). Finally, Musical Genre/Form, as a subclass of the Genre entity, defines a specific hierarchical scheme of terms, the musical genres/forms of material (sonatas, concertos, etc.). This records genres, forms, alternative names, definitions and hierarchical relationships with narrower, broader, relative and equivalent terms and is mapped to the thesaurus (LCGFT[4]).

5   Challenges Faced During the Project

Throughout the project's implementation, several significant challenges emerged. Among the most critical was the creation of the ontology itself. This required all project partners to thoroughly study and discuss the fields of music and library science to ensure that the music ontology would meet the specific needs of the specialized entities being created. Another key challenge was the unification of the three distinct types of music collections under a common platform while preserving the autonomy of the collaborating institutions. KeMKA, the Central Music Authority Archive, made this unification possible and served as a central hub for the creation of the ontology entities. Thus, users utilized the Local Music Repositories (TAMO) to effectively enrich KeMKA by linking entities that ultimately formed the ontology known today, while maintaining the institutions' independence. Furthermore, the project relied on international conceptual models such as FRBR, FRAD, FRSAD, and the Music Ontology, adapting and customizing them to meet the project's requirements for the specialized music ontology.

6   Results and Conclusion

All of the above has already been implemented in three repositories of music collections, the so-called Local Repositories of Music Ontologies (TAMO) and a central music archive, the "KeMKA". The TAMOs present the metadata and digital items of the collaborating institutions which are the "Greek Archive of Double bass", "Vassilis Tsitsanis Collection of Recordings", "Music Library of Greece Lilian Voudouri" and their music collections; Conversely, KeMKA is the central music archive that contains the unified metadata and digital items from the whole project. TAMOs followed both the general ontology and the later specialized one, whilst maintaining their autonomous function and the music collections they included. Thus, today they display them through the ReasonableGraph platform. On the other hand, the KeMKA supports the "National Archive of Musical Entities" and provides consolidated information on the established musical entities of the project ontology.

---

[3] Library of Congress Medium of Performance Thesaurus for Music.

[4] Library of Congress Genre/Form Terms for Library and Archival.

A point of reference was the transfer of existing metadata, automatically, from the systems of the collaborating institutions to the new, Reasonable Graph's TAMOs, the ones for the "M.EL.O.S." project. Together there was also curation of the Musical Work and their interfaces with the Digital items, while a similar treatment was given to the intermediate entities, which were also developed and enriched, in order to fulfil the initial goal of the project, which was to establish 10.500 established musical entities.

The development of the music ontology in the framework of the "Hellenic Music Audiovisual Collections (M.EL.O.S.)" project is an important step towards the organization and management of complex music collections. The approach adopted, based on the international standards FRBR, FRAD and FRSAD, as well as the specialized "MUSIC ONTOLOGY", has allowed the creation of a flexible and comprehensive framework for the description of musical works, expressions and events. The inclusion of specialized entities such as "musical work", "musical expression" and "musical manifestation" has allowed the specificities of musical documents to be accurately captured, while maintaining compatibility with established bibliographic standards.

The integration of three different types of music collections into a common platform, while maintaining the autonomy of the participating institutions, is a major achievement of the project. The ability to manage a variety of material types, from printed scores and discography to recordings and photographs, highlights the flexibility and adaptability of the ontology developed. In addition, the creation of specialized entities to describe musical people, organizations, events and media has enhanced the system's ability to capture in detail the rich context of music collections.

The implementation of the ontology in the three Local Music Ontology Repositories (TAMO) and the Central Music Authority Archive (KeMKA) demonstrates the practical value and applicability of the system.

The successful transfer and curation of existing metadata, as well as the development and enrichment of intermediate entities, brought us closer to achieve the initial goal of creating 10.500 established music entities, demonstrating the ontology's ability to efficiently manage large volumes of complex music data. Although formal quantitative evaluation metrics such as accuracy or system's efficiency and effectiveness are not available at this time, the past usage and the system's live presentations under seminar's purpose, ended to report positive and valuable feedbacks, indicating high levels of user engagement and interest, particularly regarding the system's adaptability and ease of use. These qualitative insights reflect the success of the ontology in practical terms, even in the temporary absence of specific numerical data.

In conclusion, the development of the music ontology "M.EL.O.S." is an important contribution to the field of organization and management of music information. It provides a powerful tool to facilitate access to and research on music data, ensuring high quality, interoperability and data interconnection. The approach taken opens up new ways of linking data at all levels, providing new ways of analyzing and exploiting music collections. As the field of music informatics continues to evolve, the "M.EL.O.S." ontology provides an important reference point for future efforts in organizing and managing complex music information.

References

Alemu, G., Garoufallou, E.: The future of interlinked, interoperable and scalable metadata. Int. J. Metadata Semant. Ontol. **14**(2), 81–87 (2020). https://doi.org/10.1504/IJMSO.2020.108340

Baker, T., Coyle, K., Petiya, S.: Multientity models of resource description in the semantic Web. Libr. Hi Tech **32**(4), 562–582 (2014). https://doi.org/10.1108/LHT-08-2014-0081

Bekiari, C., et al.: Definition of FRBR OO A Conceptual Model for Bibliographic Information in Object-Oriented Formalism (2015). https://www.ifla.org/wp-content/uploads/2019/05/assets/cataloguing/FRBRoo/frbroo_v_2.4.pdf

Gaitanou, P., Andreou, I., Sicilia, M.-A., Garoufallou, E.: Linked data for libraries: creating a global knowledge space, a systematic literature review. J. Inf. Sci. **50**(1), 204–244 (2024). https://doi.org/10.1177/01655515221084645

IFLA Study Group on the Functional Requirements for Bibliographic Records and International Federation of Library Associations and Institutions. Section on Cataloguing. Standing Committee. Functional requirements for bibliographic records. K. G. Saur, Munchen, Germany (1998)

International Council on Archives: ISAD (G): general international standard archival description: adopted by the Committee on Descriptive Standards, Stockholm, Sweden, 19–22 September 1999 (2nd ed.). International Council on Archives, Ottawa (2000)

Library of Congress: EAD: Encoded Archival Description (EAD Official Site, Library of Congress), 22 January 2024. https://www.loc.gov/ead/

MELOS Project (2024). https://melos-project.gr/el

MusicBrainz. (n.d.). The Open Music Encyclopedia. Musicbrainz.org. https://musicbrainz.org/

VIAF: Virtual International Authority File, 2 July 2024. Viaf.org. https://viaf.org/

Metadata-Driven Cross-Infrastructure Integration Between Solid Earth and Marine Sciences in the GEO-INQUIRE Project

Kety Giuliacci[1]([⊠]) [iD], Daniele Bailo[1] [iD], Rossana Paciello[1] [iD], Jan Michalek[2] [iD],
Valerio Vinciarelli[3] [iD], Manuela Sbarra[1] [iD], Marco Salvi[1] [iD], and Enoc Martinez[4] [iD]

[1] Istituto Nazionale di Geofisica e Vulcanologia, Rome, Italy
kety.giuliacci@ingv.it
[2] University of Bergen, Bergen, Norway
[3] EPOS ERIC, European Plate Observying System, Rome, Italy
[4] Universitat Politècnica de Catalunya SARTI-MAR, Barcelona, Spain

Abstract. This paper describes the integration of cross-disciplinary data from Solid Earth and Marine sciences through a metadata-driven approach within the Geo-INQUIRE project. It highlights the importance of Research Infrastructures (RIs) in managing and providing open access to scientific data, addressing challenges faced by distributed RIs in ensuring multidisciplinary data access. It also highlights the implementation of Virtual Access and Physical or TransNational Access in line with European Union regulations. Additionally, it discusses the successful implementation of a proof of concept between EPOS and EMSO RIs, showcasing the potential of cross-infrastructure metadata-driven integration for supporting comprehensive and multidisciplinary research.

Keywords: Metadata · EPOS-DCAT-AP · Research Infrastructure ·
Geo-INQUIRE · Interoperability

1 Introduction

Over the last few decades, data has become a fundamental asset in nearly all research disciplines. In fields such as space and weather sciences, vast volumes of data are continuously collected by remote sensing technologies and satellite instruments to monitor atmospheric and terrestrial phenomena, analyze climate change patterns, and forecast weather events [1]. Similarly, in the Earth and Marine domains, sensors gather extensive data on ground motion and other geological processes to study plate tectonics and assess climate change impacts on marine environments [2]. This abundance of data, combined with outputs from human-machine interactions (e.g., social networks [3]) and computer simulations, has ushered in the era of data-intensive science, known as the Fourth Paradigm [4]. Consequently, there is an urgent need for effective management of this complex and heterogeneous data to fully realize its potential for scientific discovery and economic value.

© The Author(s), under exclusive license to Springer Nature Switzerland AG 2025
M. Sfakakis et al. (Eds.): MTSR 2024, CCIS 2331, pp. 288–300, 2025.
https://doi.org/10.1007/978-3-031-81974-2_25

Recognizing the societal and scientific importance of data, the European Union (EU) has enacted policies to enhance data accessibility and utility [5], emphasizing the role of Research Infrastructures (RIs) as essential facilities for high-level research [6–8]. Forums like the European Forum on Research Infrastructures (ESFRI) [9, 10] further support these initiatives by integrating data management practices across Europe. Through the Research Data Management (RDM) process [11], RIs facilitate Open Access and adhere to FAIR principles (Findability, Accessibility, Interoperability, and Reusability) [12]. However, distributed RIs face significant challenges in providing multidisciplinary data access due to the complexities of managing diverse data sources and formats.

Metadata is crucial in overcoming these challenges, as it provides context and documentation that enhance data integration and accessibility [13]. The use of semantics through ontologies [14] and data models further clarifies relationships between data elements, making integration across disciplines more coherent. To address the varied requirements of data integration, several architectural approaches such as microservices [15], Linked Open Data [16], and event-driven architectures [17] can be employed. Managing this complex landscape, which involves different data types, metadata standards, ontologies, and architectures, requires coordinated efforts and shared expertise.

The Geo-INQUIRE project addresses these challenges by implementing a metadata-driven approach to improve access to critical data, products, and services through both Virtual Access (VA) and TransNational Access (TNA) [18]. Virtual Access provides remote, digital access to data and services, enabling widespread use without the need for physical presence, while TransNational Access allows researchers to utilize facilities and resources across different member states, fostering international collaboration. By leveraging advanced data management techniques within existing RIs, Geo-INQUIRE aims to enhance the monitoring and modeling of dynamic geosphere processes, support research on geohazards and georesources, and tackle interdisciplinary challenges in land-sea-atmosphere environments.

This paper outlines the four-phased approach used in the Geo-INQUIRE project, encompassing comprehensive landscape analysis, detailed metadata examination, consensus building on integration strategies, and the implementation of a proof of concept between EPOS and EMSO RIs. The objective is to demonstrate how cross-infrastructure, metadata-driven integration can support comprehensive, multidisciplinary research, thereby increasing the accessibility and utility of scientific data across diverse research domains.

2 Background

The context of this work is the Geo-INQUIRE [19] (Geosphere INfrastructures for QUestions into Integrated REsearch) project, which was launched on October 1, 2022. The project aims to enhance access to crucial data, products, and services through both Virtual Access and TransNational Access. This initiative focuses on improving the monitoring and modeling of dynamic geosphere processes with high spatial and temporal precision. It emphasizes efficient data provision to support curiosity-driven research on geohazards and georesources and addresses interdisciplinary challenges in land-sea-atmosphere environments by leveraging advanced data management techniques and relying on existing data infrastructures. A key objective is the integration of various Research Infrastructures (RIs) by cataloging, analyzing, and assessing their maturity for FAIR (Findable, Accessible, Interoperable, and Reusable) data integration.

Among the consortium of 51 partners, there are five key European Research Infrastructures: EPOS ERIC (solid Earth) [20], EMSO ERIC (marine) [21], ARISE (atmosphere) [22], ECCSEL ERIC (carbon capture and storage) [23], and ChEESE (computational seismology) [24]. These infrastructures facilitate both Virtual Access to digital resources and services and TransNational Access to physical facilities, promoting huge collaboration and resource sharing across Europe.

The specific goals of Geo-INQUIRE to implement Virtual Access and TransNational Access include a) achieving data and services integration within the reference infrastructures and b) achieving cross-infrastructure integration to provide users with multi-disciplinary, FAIR access to data, services, and facilities.

Integration within the reference infrastructures involves creating harmonised metadata descriptions for data, data products, software, and services to ensure that new assets comply with existing standards. Such description should adhere to the reference RI standards. For instance, in the case of EMSO ERIC, the datasets are managed according to the NetCDF standard, while the infrastructure portal for data stewardship adopts the ERDDAP technology[1]. In the case of EPOS ERIC [25], data providers belonging to one of the 10 Solid Earth communities encompassed by EPOS have to comply with the already existing community standards (e.g., FDSN services [26, 27] in seismology), and the EPOS central catalog [28] is populated using the EPOS-DCAT-AP standard [29, 30].

Cross-infrastructure integration of RI assets requires addressing the challenge of interfacing with diverse metadata schemes and developing mappings and converters enabling different standards and platforms to interoperate. The approach proposed to achieve this goal combines metadata, semantic interoperability and web services for data access as already described in a previous work [31] and validated in the framework of the European Plate Observing System (EPOS), a comprehensive, multidisciplinary research infrastructure that facilitates the integrated use of data, data products, and services across the solid Earth science community in Europe [20] through a multidisciplinary platform [32].

In addition to data and services-related metadata, such an approach can also support descriptions of equipment and facilities, thus going beyond the Virtual Access and tackling the TransNational Access as required in the framework of GEO-INQUIRE.

3 Metadata-Driven Integration

To achieve interoperability within and across the Research Infrastructures (RIs) involved in the GEO-INQUIRE project, the work underwent four different phases, summarised in Table 1.

---

[1] ERDDAP is a data server that gives you a simple, consistent way to download subsets of scientific datasets in common file formats and make graphs and maps. This particular EMSO ERDDAP installation has oceanographic data (for example, data from satellites and buoys). https://erddap.emso.eu/erddap/index.html accessed on 27/06/2024

Table 1. Overview of the Four Phases for the cross-infrastructure integration.

Phase	Description
Landscaping Exercise	Comprehensive landscape analysis of existing installations and services provided by the GEO-INQUIRE data providers, using the "Implementation Level Matrix". This analysis aimed to identify the types of data services, their integration status, and the metadata standards they followed
Metadata Analysis	The metadata for each identified installation or service was thoroughly analyzed to understand the varying standards and practices across different RIs. This analysis was crucial for identifying the commonalities and differences necessary to achieve interoperability
Consensus Building Towards a Common Approach	Stakeholders reached a consensus on using the EPOS blueprint architecture due to its robust metadata management and semantic interoperability, making it the best solution for the diverse needs of the GEO-INQUIRE project
Proof of Concept	A proof of concept was developed to validate the solution, selecting EPOS ERIC and EMSO ERIC for testing due to their advanced data management practices and readiness to adopt the EPOS metadata model. The proof of concept included the following main activities: **Metadata Mapping and Ingestion** A mapping procedure was created to translate metadata descriptions from EMSO metadata standard to the EPOS-DCAT-AP standard, ensuring accurate capture and seamless integration into the central data catalog. This enabled the harmonization of metadata across the two different RIs, facilitating interoperability and data integration **Testing and Validation of the Prototype** The prototype of the integrated system was tested and validated to ensure it met interoperability requirements and handled diverse data formats and standards. This process confirmed the system's ability to manage and query data effectively, providing consistent and accurate responses across marine (EMSO) and solid Earth (EPOS) data sources

3.1 Landscaping Exercise

As highlighted in the EPOS model approach [31], simply having robust and efficient Web APIs does not ensure interoperability: detailed metadata descriptions, aligned with FAIR principles, are essential and crucial. Thus, the methodology involves data integration through a combination of web services, comprehensive metadata, and semantics. These three critical components are monitored and assessed using a set of criteria divided into three levels, which are compiled into an Implementation Level Matrix (ILM) to evaluate the service provision landscape [33]. The ILM acts as a tool to capture the evolving maturity of installations/services and to monitor their readiness for interoperable integration into RIs. Interoperability begins at the data provider level, necessitating domain-specific coordination and collaborative development efforts.

In the Geo-INQUIRE context, an 'installation' can comprise multiple assets of various types. The assets belong to various scientific domains, including solid Earth, marine, and atmospheric sciences. These assets range from software, time series, to georeferenced and non-georeferenced data, using various metadata standards for integration and description. We focus on assets provided through Virtual Access (VA), such as services. The initial task was to assess the readiness status of VAs/services for implementation. Several criteria were developed and subsequently collected through an online shared spreadsheet, referred to as the Implementation Level Matrix. The status in the ILM within the Geo-INQUIRE project is assessed at three levels:

- Level 1 - Service accessibility and standards
- Level 2 - Data provision and basic functionality
- Level 3 - Advanced functionality and documentation quality

This analysis aimed to identify various service details, such as: (a) the type of data provided by the service (e.g., georeferenced, non-georeferenced, time-series), (b) the response format of the service, (c) whether the API structure is based on a standard (e.g., OGC), (d) the availability of documentation for the service, (e) the accessibility of quality provenance documentation for the provided data, (f) information regarding the license and data policy, (g) metadata standards describing the service at the RI integration level.

3.2 Metadata Analysis

For each identified service in the ILM, the metadata used for integration within the reference RIs was thoroughly analyzed. This step was crucial for understanding the heterogeneity of metadata standards and practices across different RIs and to identify the commonalities and differences that would need to be addressed to achieve interoperability. The analysis showed a high variability in the adoption of metadata standards,. With 61% of the services using EPOS-DCAT-AP (the metadata standard for the European Plate Observing System). Other metadata standards in use include the CF Convention (for climate and forecast data), EUDAT Extended Schema (for research data), in-house standards specific to organizations or projects, ISO-19115 (for geographic information metadata), NRML (for seismic hazard assessment), and OPeNDAP (for data access and sharing). Many of the assets (72%) are georeferenced, using data formats such as JSON,

NetCDF, CSV, GeoJSON, MiniSeed, StationXML, OGC, INSPIRE, QuakeML, HDF5, SRF, and FDSNWS., while software representations account for 16%. Additionally, 13% of the data are non-georeferenced, using formats such as JSON, NRML, OpenQuake-engine, ASCII, Dublin Core XML, RDF, BibTex, and in-house formats. More than half of the assets have already been integrated into their respective RIs, and this percentage continues to increase. Most assets are provided under a CC-BY 4.0 license, aligning with the FAIR principles. Over 60% of the assets are openly shared, with 20% subject to restrictions and embargoes. Authentication patterns reflect a similar trend, indicating that open data is freely accessible [33].

3.3   Consensus Building Towards a Common Approach

A key part of the methodology was building consensus among the stakeholders towards a common integration approach. After evaluating various methodologies, the EPOS blueprint architecture and its metadata-driven approach were identified as the best state-of-the-art solution. The methodologies were selected using a hybrid approach that considered both the existing architectures used within domain-specific RIs and potential new architectural paradigms that could facilitate interoperability and integration across RIs. Among the existing architectures, only two out of five RIs (EPOS ERIC, EMSO ERIC, ECCSEL, ARISE, and ChEESE) have operational e-infrastructures with established architectures namely EPOS ERIC and EMSO ERIC. ARISE was still working on data provision through services and was therefore not considered mature enough. Similarly ECCSEL ERIC focused on TransNational Access in the framework of GEO-INQUIRE, and similarly to ARISE was still at the stage of service design. ChEESE, which is more focused on computational aspects, was not expected to be integrated into the data provision dimension. Potential new architectural paradigms needed to meet a fundamental but challenging requirement: the ability to interoperate across different data and metadata standards provided through a variety of service approaches (e.g., RESTful, SOAP). The option of imposing a single overarching standard, such as OGC, SPARQL, or other semantic web technologies, was discussed but deemed impractical. This would have required rethinking decades of established technical practices and de-facto standards developed by domain-specific communities within the RIs (e.g., Seismology in EPOS). On the other hand, viable architectural approaches that handle the integration of diverse data and service formats are typically based on the microservices paradigm, which the methodological approach used within EPOS.

Considering these factors, the EPOS approach, known for its robust metadata management and semantic interoperability, provided a scalable and adaptable framework suitable for the diverse needs of the GEO-INQUIRE project. Therefore, there was a convergence towards the decision to implement a proof of concept (PoC) of the cross-infrastructure integration of Solid Earth (EPOS) and Marine (EMSO) domains, to be potentially extended to ARISE (atmosphere) and ECCSEL ERIC (carbon capture and storage) when these infrastructures will be technically more mature.

A sketch of the common approach architecture is shown in Fig. 1, which also shows the data flow within the GEO-INQUIRE project, showcasing how heterogeneous datasets are harmonized and accessed. At the bottom of the image, various GEO-INQUIRE services are depicted, including those from EPOS (e.g., Seismology, Near Fault Observatories and others) and EMSO. These services represent the diverse data sources integrated within the project. The core of the integration process is the Cross-Infrastructure Integration System, which includes a Metadata Catalogue essential for harmonizing metadata across various services. The EPOS-DCAT-AP mappings procedures are used to translate and harmonize metadata from different research infrastructures into a common model. Above this integration layer is the Common GEO-INQUIRE Data Platform, based on the EPOS approach, which provides harmonized access to datasets for human users. Additionally, Web APIs facilitate programmatic access to datasets, enabling software applications, such as Jupyter notebooks [34], to retrieve and use data. This integrated system ensures that metadata-driven interoperability is achieved, allowing for consistent and accurate data access and visualization across different research domains.

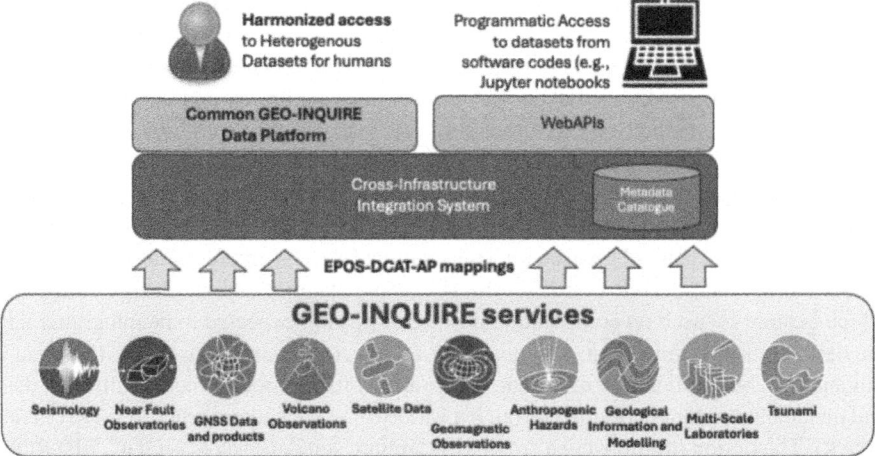

Fig. 1. GEO-INQUIRE integration architecture, showcasing how heterogeneous datasets from services like Seismology, GNSS Data, Volcano Observations, and more are harmonized and accessed. It highlights the Cross-Infrastructure Integration System, which uses a Metadata Catalogue and EPOS-DCAT-AP mappings to ensure metadata-driven interoperability. The Common GEO-INQUIRE Data Platform provides harmonized access for users, while Web APIs facilitate programmatic access, supporting both Virtual Access and TransNational Access across various research domains.

3.4 Proof of Concept (PoC)

To validate the proposed solution, a proof of concept was developed with the goal of demonstrating cross-infrastructure integration of EPOS and EMSO. The proof of concept included Metadata Mapping and Prototype testing.

Metadata Mapping and Ingestion. EMSO adopts metadata specifications detailed in a document listing all necessary metadata terms for a dataset to comply with the

EMSO Metadata Specifications. This format, adapted from the OceanSITES Data Format Reference Manual v1.4 [35], meets the needs of EMSO and its federated data service based on ERDDAP [36]. The EMSO specifications provide a list of terms (both mandatory and optional), define data types, and establish rules for the values (e.g., controlled vocabulary). These definitions are written in a structured language to facilitate machine-to-machine interaction and validation [37].

EPOS developed and implemented an extension of the DCAT Application Profile [38] specifically for Research Infrastructures in the Environmental and solid-Earth domains. This extension, named EPOS-DCAT-AP [29, 30], aims to describe the diverse assets offered by the EPOS community, accessible through its EPOS Platform[2]. EPOS-DCAT-AP introduces new classes, properties, relationships, and roles that cover key assets and resources relevant in the environmental context. Due to its maturity, EPOS-DCAT-AP can be adopted by other initiatives and applied in various contexts.

Following the initial study, a detailed analysis was performed on the metadata fields used by both EMSO and EPOS-DCAT-AP to identify similarities and differences. The analysis revealed that EPOS-DCAT-AP could accurately describe EMSO datasets, enabling the mapping of EMSO metadata fields to EPOS-DCAT-AP entities and properties. A mapping procedure was developed to create the metadata descriptions of RIs services in the EPOS-DCAT-AP format. In the case of the EPOS services, this procedure was not necessary as EPOS Thematic Services are already described in EPOS-DCAT-AP.

In the case of EMSO, a python script was developed to automate the metadata generation process. This script automatically retrieves and collects metadata for each EMSO dataset using ERDDAP's RESTful Web Services[3]. The tool translates the EMSO dataset information into the format and structure required by EPOS-DCAT-AP, ensuring consistent and uniform descriptions. The mapping is described in Fig. 2.

After generating metadata in EPOS-DCAT-AP RDF/Turtle format, a first syntactic validation was performed by means of a Turtle Web editor [42]. Then, a semantic validation was done with a SHACL validator [43]. In case both validations were passed, an ingestion procedure was run to ingest the metadata into the integrated system. This step involved setting up a prototype environment, based on the EPOS open-source system [39], which included a rich metadata catalogue for storing, managing, and integrating heterogeneous asset descriptions, making both the EPOS and EMSO datasets accessible through a single access point.

Prototype Testing and Validation. Finally, the prototype of the integrated system was deployed, tested and validated, as shown in Fig. 3. This critical step, in this initial phase of the project, ensured that the system met the requirements for interoperability and could manage the diverse data formats and standards used by the various RIs, particularly EMSO and EPOS. The testing phase involved evaluating the system's capability to effectively manage and query data, ensuring consistent and accurate responses from marine (EMSO) and solid Earth (EPOS) data sources. Tests were performed by executing the platform API endpoints that triggered the system access to the resources of the

---

[2] EPOS Platform: https://www.epos-eu.org/dataportal.

[3] ERDDAP's RESTful Web Services: https://erddap.emso.eu/erddap/tabledap/index.html?page=1&itemsPerPage=1000.

Global Attributes	Compliance test		dcat:Dataset property	Range
geospatial_lat_min	coordinate#latitude		dct:description	rdfs:Literal
geospatial_lat_max	coordinate#latitude		dct:title	rdfs:Literal
geospatial_lon_min	coordinate#longitude		dcat:keyword	rdfs:Literal
geospatial_lon_max	coordinate#longitude		dct:spatial	dct:Location
time_coverage_start	data_type#datetime		dct:temporal	dct:PeriodOfTime
time_coverage_end	data_type#datetime			
title	data_type#str			
summary	data_type#str			
keywords	data_type#str			

Fig. 2. Mappings from EMSO dataset information to EPOS-DCAT-AP properties.. Such procedure is automated by means of python scripts written on purpose to generate turtle files on the basis of the metadata collected programmatically by the data providers endpoint (from the ERDDAP server)

providers with a given identifier. Namely, the "/resources/details/{instance_id}" endpoint, with the appropriate service instance identifier, was called to get the data from the data provider services. Documentation of the APIs is available at [44]. In case the response was different from what expected, an error detection and bug fixing procedure were done. Validation was also conducted systematically from the GUI: GEO-INQUIRE WP6 participants were asked to access the portal and assess dataset availability from the reference RIs (EMSO and EPOS). Any technical issues identified were promptly addressed.

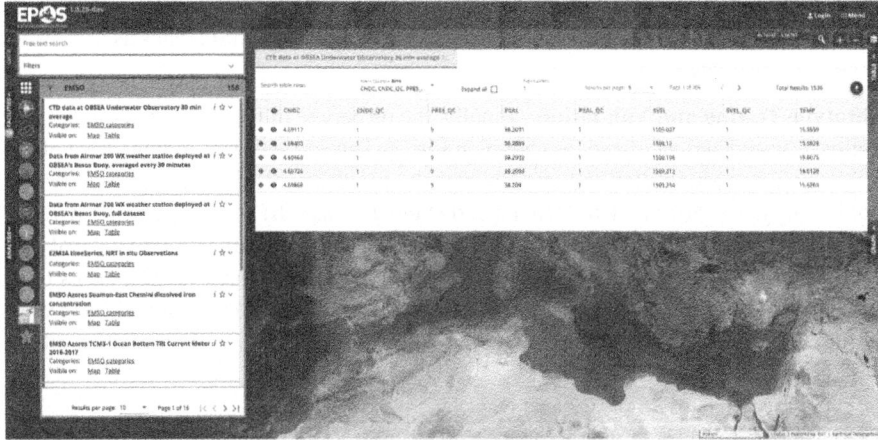

Fig. 3. Common GEO-INQUIRE Data Platform demonstrating the EPOS EMSO cross-infrastructure integration.

4 Metadata-Driven Facility Management

While Virtual Access enables remote access to digital resources, TransNational Access (TNA) allows researchers to use facilities and equipment located in different member states, either physically or remotely, promoting international collaboration and knowledge exchange. Effective management of these facilities is crucial to maximize their utility and accessibility. RIs need to provide detailed information to researchers seeking to apply for TNA opportunities provided by various European organizations, such as those involved in programs like the EPOS TNA [40]. However, existing metadata schemas, like DCAT-AP, lack specific entities tailored for this purpose. To address this gap, the EPOS-DCAT-AP metadata schema introduces two new entities: "epos:Equipment" and "epos:Facility" [41]. These entities encompass a defined set of properties established through collaborative efforts within the EPOS community to specify essential information, rendering them highly suitable for describing diverse research infrastructures such as observatories, laboratories, stations, platforms, research vessels, equipment, resources, and services.

In the EPOS context, once the entities and properties were defined on the metadata side, a dedicated area was created on the EPOS Platform. This area, called "Facilities", allows users to discover the information stored in the metadata catalog and visualize the physical location of each facility on a map. By providing this functionality, the EPOS Platform not only ensures FAIR Virtual Access to data and products but also offers TransNational Access to experimental laboratory facilities.

Within the "Facilities" area, users can find a comprehensive list of facilities. Each facility is accompanied by a detailed description that includes technical details, facility type, location, and the organization involved. Furthermore, if available, users can also access a list of equipment associated with each facility. This list provides specific information about each item, allowing users to gain a better understanding of the resources available. The implementation of these features in EPOS demonstrates how it effectively meets the needs of scientific endeavors such as the Geo-INQUIRE project. By ensuring that both VA and TNA are well-supported through comprehensive metadata management, the EPOS approach, based on the EPOS-DCAT-AP extension, enhances the ability of researchers to access, utilize, and benefit from the huge facilities and equipment available within and across different research infrastructures. This integrated approach not only facilitates better data management and accessibility but also promotes greater collaboration and innovation in scientific research, aligning with the broader goals of the GEO-INQUIRE initiative.

5 Conclusion and Future Work

The GEO-INQUIRE project promotes the integration of cross-disciplinary data from several infrastructures, including Solid Earth and Marine sciences through a metadata-driven approach. By leveraging the EPOS-DCAT-AP model and enhancing it to support both Virtual Access and TransNational Access, the project has provided a robust framework for data interoperability and facility management. This approach enables researchers to access, utilize, and benefit from a wide range of data and facilities, promoting collaboration and innovation across different scientific domains. The successful implementation of the proof of concept between EPOS and EMSO showcases the potential of a cross-infrastructure metadata-driven integration to support comprehensive and multidisciplinary research. On the same page, the extension of the EPOS-DCAT-AP metadata schema with additional entities demonstrates the suitability of this approach for supporting metadata-driven, integrated TransNational Access services.

One of the future directions for the GEO-INQUIRE project involves the development of workflow management systems integrated with Software Data Lakes. These are metadata-based repositories providing access to simulations in the form of data or workflows and are included in the GEO-INQUIRE agenda in Work Package 5. First steps in this direction have already been carried out, as demonstrated in the project deliverables, and would be vital to enhance the model for supporting also workflows, ensuring that researchers have the tools necessary to conduct complex analyses and derive meaningful insights from their data.

Another important area of future work is the potential extension of the EPOS-DCAT-AP model. This extension would explore the feasibility and benefits of adapting the model to comply with the Machine Learning (ML) DCAT-AP standards (e.g., MLDCAT-AP[4]). As EPOS is already committed to advancing machine learning capabilities through its Sponsored Research Activities, extending the EPOS-DCAT-AP model to include support for ML algorithms, models, and ML-ready datasets could significantly enhance its utility. Such an extension would provide a standardized framework for managing and integrating machine learning resources, enabling researchers to leverage advanced AI and ML techniques in their scientific endeavors.

The GEO-INQUIRE project has laid a strong foundation for cross-disciplinary data integration and facility management. The continued development of workflow management systems and the extension of the EPOS-DCAT-AP model will further enhance the project's capabilities, supporting cutting-edge research and fostering greater collaboration within the scientific community.

References

1. What is Remote Sensing? Tutorial on remotely-sensed data, from sensor characteristics, to different types of resolution, to data processing and analysis. https://www.earthdata.nasa.gov/learn/backgrounders/remote-sensing. Accessed 27 Jun 2024
2. Havskov, J., Alguacil, G.: Seismic sensors. In: Havskov, J., Alguacil, G. (eds.) Instrumentation in Earthquake Seismology. Modern Approaches in Geophysics, vol. 22. Springer, Dordrecht (2004). https://doi.org/10.1007/978-1-4020-2969-1_2
3. Clissa, L., Lassnig, M., Rinaldi, L.: How big is big data? a comprehensive survey of data production, storage, and streaming in science and industry. Front. Big Data 6, 1271639 (2023). https://doi.org/10.3389/FDATA.2023.1271639/BIBTEX
4. Hey, T., Tansley, S., Tolle, K.: The fourth paradigm. Data-Intensive scientific discovery. Microsoft Res. (2009). https://doi.org/10.1007/978-3-642-33299-9_1
5. Murray-Rust, P.: Open data in science. Nature Proc. 1–1 (2008). https://doi.org/10.1038/npre.2008.1526.1

---

[4] MLDCAT-AP (Machine Learning DCAT-AP) is an application profile that extends DCAT-AP in the field of machine learning. https://semiceu.github.io/MLDCAT-AP/releases/2.0.0/

6. Cramer, K.C., Hallonsten, O., Bolliger, I.K., Griffiths, A.: Big science and research infras-tructures in Europe: history and current trends. Big Sci. Res. Infrastruct. Europe, 1–26 (2020). https://doi.org/10.4337/9781839100017.00007

7. EU commission. (n.d.). EU Regulation No 1291/2013. Establishing Horizon 2020 – the Framework Programme for Research and Innovation (2014- 2020). Article 2 (6) 11 December 2013. https://eur-lex.europa.eu/LexUriServ/LexUriServ.do?uri=OJ:L:2013:347:0104:0173:EN:PDF. Accessed 2 July 2024

8. European Commission. (n.d.). COUNCIL REGULATION (EC) No 723/2009 of 25 June 2009 on the Community legal framework for a European Research Infrastructure Consor-tium (ERIC). https://eur-lex.europa.eu/legal-content/EN/TXT/?uri=CELEX%3A02009R0723-20131226. Accessed 27 June 2024

9. European Strategy Forum on Research Infrastructures. https://www.esfri.eu/. Accessed 27 June 2004

10. Comm, RTD, & Esfri. (n.d.). ESFRI European Roadmap for Research Infrastructures - Report 2006

11. Surkis, A., Read, K.: Research data management. J. Med. Libr. Assoc. JMLA 103(3), 154 (2015). https://doi.org/10.3163/1536-5050.103.3.011

12. Wilkinson, M. D., et al.: The FAIR guiding principles for scientific data management and stewardship. Sci. Data 3, 160018 (2016). https://doi.org/10.1038/sdata.2016.18

13. Paul, N., et al.: Science friction: data, metadata, and collaboration. Soc. Stud. Sci. 41(5), 667–690 (2011)

14. Poveda-Villalón, M., Espinoza-Arias, P., Garijo, D., Corcho, O.: Coming to terms with FAIR ontologies. In: Keet, C.M., Dumontier, M. (eds.) Knowledge Engineering and Knowledge Management. EKAW 2020. Lecture Notes in Computer Science(), vol. 12387. Springer, Cham (2020). https://doi.org/10.1007/978-3-030-61244-3_18

15. Newman, S. (n.d.).: Building Microservices. O'Reilly Media

16. Bauer, F., Kaltenböck, M. (n.d.).: Linked Open Data: The Essentials A Quick Start Guide for Decision Makers

17. Helmer, S., Poulovassilis, A., Xhafa, F.: Introduction to reasoning in event-based distributed systems. In: Helmer, S., Poulovassilis, A., Xhafa, F. (eds.) Reasoning in Event-Based Dis-tributed Systems. Studies in Computational Intelligence, vol. 347. Springer, Heidelberg (2011). https://doi.org/10.1007/978-3-642-19724-6_1

18. ESFRI EU.: MAKING SCIENCE HAPPEN A new ambition for Research Infrastructures in the European Research Area - ESFRI white paper (2020). www.ec.europa.eu/research/infrastructures

19. GEO-INQUIRE project website. https://www.geo-inquire.eu/. Accessed 27 June 2024

20. Cocco, M., et al.: The EPOS research infrastructure: a federated approach to integrate solid earth science data and services. Ann. Geophys. 65(2), 1–15 (2022). https://doi.org/10.4401/ag-8756

21. Best, M.M.R., et al.: The EMSO-ERIC pan-European consortium: data benefits and lessons learned as the legal entity forms. Mar. Technol. Soc. J. 50(3), 8–15 (2016). https://doi.org/10.4031/MTSJ.50.3.13

22. Blanc, E., et al.: Toward an improved representation of middle atmospheric dynamics thanks to the ARISE project. Surv. Geophys. 39(2), 171–225 (2017)

23. Quale, S., Rohling, V.: The European carbon dioxide capture and storage laboratory infrastructure (ECCSEL). Green Ener. Environ. 1(3), 180–194 (2016)

24. Folch, A., et al.: The EU Center of Excellence for Exascale in Solid Earth (ChEESE): imple-mentation, results, and roadmap for the second phase. Futur. Gener. Comput. Syst. 146, 47–61 (2023)

25. Bailo, D., et al.: Data integration and FAIR data management in solid earth science. Ann. Geophys. 65(2), DM210 (2022). https://doi.org/10.4401/ag-8742

26. Suárez, G., van Eck, T., Giardini, D., Ahern, T., Butler, R., Tsuboi, S.: The international Federation of Digital Seismograph Networks (FDSN): an integrated system of seismological observatories. IEEE Syst. J. **2**(3), 431–438 (2008)
27. Strollo, A., et al.: EIDA: the European integrated data archive and service infrastructure within ORFEUS. Seismolog. Res. Lett. **92**(3), 1788–1795 (2021)
28. Jeffery, K.G., Bailo, D.: EPOS: using metadata in geoscience. In: Closs, S., Studer, R., Garoufallou, E., Sicilia, MA. (eds.) Metadata and Semantics Research. MTSR 2014. Communications in Computer and Information Science, vol. 478. Springer, Cham (2014). https://doi.org/10.1007/978-3-319-13674-5_17
29. Paciello, R., Trani, L., Bailo, D., Sbarra, M.: EPOS-DCAT-AP 2.0 – state of play on the application profile for metadata exchange in the EPOS RI. In: Garoufallou, E., Vlachidis, A. (eds.) Metadata and Semantic Research. MTSR 2022. Communications in Computer and Information Science, vol. 1789. Springer, Cham (2023). https://doi.org/10.1007/978-3-031-39141-5_21
30. EPOS DCAT-AP: An extension of the DCAT Application Profile for Research Infrastructures in the solid-Earth domain, Github repository. https://github.com/epos-eu/EPOS-DCAT-AP. Accessed 27 June 2024
31. Bailo, D., et al.: Integrated access to multidisciplinary data through semantically interoperable services in a metadata-driven platform for Solid Earth Science. In: Garoufallou, E., Vlachidis, A. (Eds.), Metadata and Semantic Research (MTSR 2022): 16th International Conference on Metadata and Semantics Research, London, UK, 7–11 November 2022, Proceedings. Communications in Computer and Information Science, vol. 1789, pp. 1–14 (2022)
32. Bailo, D., et al.: The EPOS multi-disciplinary Data Portal for integrated access to solid Earth science datasets. Sci. Data **10**(1), 1–10 (2023). https://doi.org/10.1038/s41597-023-02697-9
33. Michalek, J., et al.: Geo-INQUIRE project team: methodology for building interoperable Research Infrastructures: Example from Geo-INQUIRE project. EGU General Assembly 2024, Vienna, Austria, 14–19 April 2024, EGU24-11538 (2024)
34. Kluyver, T., et al.: Jupyter Notebooks – a publishing format for reproducible computational workflows. Positioning and Power in Academic Publishing: Players, Agents and Agendas - Proceedings of the 20th International Conference on Electronic Publishing, ELPUB 2016, pp. 87–90 (2016)
35. OceanSITES Data Format Reference Manual NetCDF Conventions and Reference Tables. Version 1.4, 16 July 2020. [GOOS ENDORSED PRACTICE] (2020). https://doi.org/10.25607/OBP-421.2
36. ERDDAP Metadata Specifications. https://github.com/emso-eric/emso-metadata-specifications/blob/develop/EMSO_metadata.md. Accessed 28 June 2024
37. EMSO Metadata Specifications v0.4. https://doi.org/10.5281/zenodo.10669878. Accessed 28 June 2024
38. DCAT-AP 3.0. https://semiceu.github.io/DCAT-AP/releases/3.0.0/
39. Vinciarelli, V., et al.: Advancing open data portals: learnings from the EPOS open-source solution, EGU General Assembly 2024, Vienna, Austria, 14–19 April 2024. EGU24-7931 (2024). https://doi.org/10.5194/egusphere-egu24-7931
40. Wessels, R., et al.: Transnational access to research facilities: an EPOS service to promote multi-domain solid earth sciences in Europe. Ann. Geophys. **65**(2), DM214 (2022). https://doi.org/10.4401/ag-8768
41. Paciello, R., et al.: Representing TransNational access to research facilities using EPOS-DCAT application profile. In: American Geophysical Union (AGU)
42. Turtle Web Editor. https://felixlohmeier.github.io/turtle-web-editor/. Accessed 28 June 2024
43. SHACL Playground. https://shacl.org/playground/. Accessed 28 June 2024
44. API Gateway Documentation. https://www.ics-c.epos-eu.org/api/v1/ui/. Accessed 28 June 2024

Public Libraries - Aggregators of New and Reusable Knowledge Resources for Users' Creative Development

Ioana Cornelia Cristina Crihană[1,2(✉)] (iD)

[1] The National Association of Public Librarians and Libraries in Romania, 30, Tudor Arghezi Street, District 2, Bucharest, Romania

[2] POLITEHNICA Bucharest National University of Science and Technology, Bucharest, Romania

Abstract. After a winding development path full of challenges throughout history, thanks to the intervention of technology, public libraries have evolved in the last decades from traditional libraries to true ecosystems of operational services grafted on the current needs of users. Being perceived rather as conservative institutions, in order to remain relevant, public libraries have been forced to innovate, especially in terms of service-related aspects. Gradually, under the pressure of users, they have integrated various applications and technologies which today allow for a better connection with the audience and a better solution to the specific needs of library service beneficiaries. This paper explores the different understandings of the concept of "renewable knowledge" in the context of public libraries, positioning these institutions as essential spaces for the creation, transfer and long-term capitalization of this knowledge. Through a systematic clarification of terminology, the study analyzes in depth the dynamics of generating and preserving renewable knowledge, emphasizing their role as a universal public good that encourages creativity, co-creation and transformative learning. This research provides a future-oriented perspective on understanding and modeling "renewable knowledge" in libraries and the impact of this transformation on the knowledge assets of learning communities. The author investigates and critically evaluates how the generation of knowledge - understood as the result of interpersonal interactions - makes libraries become nodal centers for conservation, valorization and reuse of renewable knowledge elements. By analyzing the complex process of aggregating renewable knowledge and its distinctive features compared to other knowledge typologies, the present research attempts to clarify how foundational knowledge can be transformed into renewable knowledge. Current work highlights the potential of libraries to serve as critical facilitators in this process of transforming collective knowledge into renewable knowledge assets, leveraging the unique and privileged position of libraries within communities. This article investigates the interest of library and information science professionals in identifying reusable facets of knowledge from the value-added perspective of modern technology-based library services. Using a mix consisting of a Questionnaire and a Structured Interview, this paper explores the role of public libraries as catalysts in the complex process of renewable knowledge development. Highlighting the dynamic and adaptive nature of the acquisition and dissemination

M. Sfakakis et al. (Eds.): MTSR 2024, CCIS 2331, pp. 301–316, 2025.
https://doi.org/10.1007/978-3-031-81974-2_26

of renewable knowledge, this article examines the potential of public libraries to creatively engage with communities, integrate technology, and propagate knowledge in a coherent and sustainable manner. The findings attest to the idea that public libraries have the ability to adapt to the changing information landscape, strengthening their democratic role in the contemporary knowledge society and contributing to the development of intelligent, inclusive and connected communities. In supporting the research results, the author offers as an example a concrete case of application of the concept of renewable knowledge in libraries, carried out within the Horizon project SHIFT: MetamorphoSis of cultural Heritage Into augmented hypermedia assets For enhanced accessibiliTy and inclusion. Being a use study based on the recent practice of libraries in Romania, the practical example refers to the empowerment of pre-existing digital stories with new values based on elements of renewable knowledge. This use case demonstrates once more that the integration of advanced digital technologies can substantially revive the preservation and accessibility of cultural heritage, making it accessible even for users belonging to vulnerable groups.

Keywords: Renewable Knowledge · Library Ecosystem · Knowledge Assets · Co-Creation · Creative Development · Knowledge Generating Process · Library Use Case · Text-to-Speech · NLP Modeling · Digital Stories

1 Introduction

In contemporary society, the lack of continuity and consistency in the storage and management of knowledge poses significant risks to societal progress, which can lead to the depletion and obsolescence of valuable knowledge. This is why public libraries, through the responsible data exchange, management and reuse, are key actors in addressing these challenges, ensuring the continuity and renewal of knowledge as a fundamental asset for the evolution and competitiveness of society. By exploring how technology empowers societies to collect, disseminate and reinterpret knowledge, this study aims to identify solutions that combat the fragmentation of knowledge storage and data management. Also, through this work, the author tries to clarify and enrich the understanding of "renewable knowledge" (R.K.), the term "renewable" being a specific attribute of knowledge, which reflects its capacity for continuous reuse and recomposing. In supporting the foundation of this conceptual article, a comprehensive literature review was conducted to examine how existing science uses the semantics of "renewable knowledge". The author also assessed its value and relevance in relation to the principles of the socio-technical agenda. Practically, the present work explores the application of the "renewable" concept in knowledge management, evaluating its significance as a socio-technical construct that supports the sustainable development of society. Knowledge, seen as a form of human capital, is produced and consumed simultaneously, being considered a collective good, which is renewable and essential for social and economic progress.

2 Theoretical Acceptance and Meanings

The study identifies two major contexts in which "renewable knowledge" plays a critical role: societal development and economic and business performance. In the context of societal development, renewable knowledge underpins education, literacy skills, social interaction, sustainability and disaster preparedness. In the context of business, it contributes to competitiveness, sustainable economic development and the advancement of knowledge. "Renewable knowledge" facilitates the formalization of knowledge bases for common data and has the potential to transform the knowledge base into a renewable resource that catalyzes social development. The present paper argues that knowledgeable individuals who are adept at discovering and generating renewed or recombined knowledge are more likely to achieve success, solve complex problems, and make informed decisions throughout life.

3 Research Methodology

Using the "Action Research" methodology, this study explores the current perception of "renewable knowledge" in public libraries and tests the applicability of the concept in library environments in Romania and five other European countries. Data were collected by applying a Questionnaire addressed to top and middle management in the library sector. The analysis of this data aims to identify ways in which public libraries can generate positive changes in the processes of creating, storing and preserving renewable knowledge. As the main data collection tool, the author used a comprehensive Questionnaire on modern library services and their accessibility, addressed to library managers in Romania and 15 other European countries. The collected data were centralized, evaluated and interpreted using comparative methods and also integrating the observations and findings provided by several reports and official databases of European library organizations. This comparative analysis aims to elucidate the varied practices and understandings of 'renewable knowledge' in different cultural and regional contexts. By synthesizing the collected data, the paper aims to assess the extent to which the concept of "renewable knowledge" has been adopted by library professionals and to encourage a paradigm shift in how libraries contribute to the creation, storage and preservation of renewable knowledge. This study also reviews the existing literature to identify theoretical and methodological frameworks related to the concept, noting the lack of a unified terminology in the field. To address this gap, the paper analyzes "renewable knowledge" in relation to common goods and shared knowledge, taking into account the role of the human factor, interpersonal interactions, but also personal and organizational knowledge. Finally, the paper discusses the evolution of renewable knowledge in libraries, highlighting the importance and challenges of sharing and preserving it. The author explores the properties and benefits of preserving and multiplying renewable knowledge through the active participation of libraries, proposing strategies for improving the role of libraries in supporting lifelong learning and knowledge sustainability. Although the current study focused on libraries in Romania and Europe, it is not without relevance that libraries from various regions outside of Europe are not strangers to the concept of R.K. and its various operational derivations. The exploration of initiatives in Africa, Latin America and Asia provides data which can complete the global picture of challenges and opportunities for cultural and creative institutions in the field of R.K. In Africa, despite the financial difficulties they faced, some African libraries have adopted R.K. principles, providing open access to educational and informational resources. For example, the African Digital Library (A.D.L.) provides free access to academic resources for users across Africa. In this way, A.D.L. supports personal and community development through digital resources and contributes to the elimination of economic barriers to education and science by offering books and scientific articles freely. Another telling example comes from Kenya, where the Kenya National Library Service (K.N.L.S.) developed the "Mobile Library Services" program, using mobile libraries to bring educational resources to rural areas. This program includes access to digital books and education about the use of the Internet, with the aim of developing technological skills and supporting renewable knowledge among disadvantaged youth. On the other hand, in Brazil, the Biblioteca Nacional do Brasil started an extensive program of digitization and open access to cultural resources, especially through the Brasiliana USP platform. This portal provides free access to literary works and historical resources from digital collections, thus supporting renewable knowledge. In addition, Brazil has developed a specific legislative framework to promote open access, which encourages libraries to adopt transparent knowledge sharing policies.

4 A Socio-Technical Perspective on Public Libraries

The socio-technical theory accredits the idea that in any work environment two organically interconnected components can be identified: the technical subsystem, which includes the equipment and technologies used to perform tasks, and the social subsystem, which includes the individuals who operate these tools. The essential purpose of this approach is to harmonize these two dimensions, so that the system as a whole function optimally. In the case of public libraries, the socio-technical framework provides a valuable lens through which to examine the interaction between technology and the human factor. As public libraries evolve into dynamic spaces for the creation, dissemination and reuse of knowledge, the two components, technical and social, interact more and more symbiotically with the aim of optimizing library services and improving user experience. Applying the socio-technical approach in the field of public libraries suggests that the successful integration of new technologies should not only focus on the technical efficiency of these systems, but also consider the social dynamics of the library environment, including user involvement, staff training and interaction with the community.

5 The Role of Public Libraries in Knowledge Creation and Reuse

Public libraries have all the data to fully engage in the creation and recombination of renewable knowledge [1, 2]. In addition, by leveraging socio-technical systems, libraries can become vital resource centers for creative and lifelong learning, where users access, generate and reuse knowledge in innovative ways. In order to fulfill their mission as vibrant hubs of knowledge, libraries are interested in harmonizing the technological tools they use and the social processes that lead to the creation of knowledge [3]. This involves not only providing access to digital resources, but also facilitating and promoting a collaborative environment where users can engage with these resources in meaningful ways. For example, digital platforms that make user-generated content accessible, collaborative learning and knowledge sharing are crucial in transforming libraries into active resource centers for knowledge co-creation. Applying socio-technical principles usually leads to a better understanding of how human, social and organizational factors influence work practices and technical systems [4, 5]. By humanizing processes, work systems in libraries based on both technical and social subsystems become more fluid and reliable. Technical subsystems include the tools and processes needed to create products and services, while social subsystems refer to the work structure that connects people to the technical subsystem and to each other [6].

6   Renewable Knowledge and Data Commons: Empowering Public Libraries as Hubs for Creative Development

Amid the background of rapid technological and societal changes, public libraries are uniquely positioned as the main curators of "renewable knowledge" in the interest of communities, by "renewable knowledge" understanding a collection of dynamic, continuously updated knowledge artifacts that can be harnessed for creative development [1]. The concept of "renewable knowledge" is closely related to the notion of "common data", which refers to the aggregation and open accessibility of data and information resources [1, 2]. By embracing this paradigm, public libraries can play a crucial role in fostering innovation and empowering users to thrive in the ever-changing job market. Once the quasi-general understanding of the concept of R.K. and its relationship with Data Commons through which the knowledge and data in the wide circuit of use can be recombined, adapted and redistributed with enriched meanings for educational, cultural and social purposes, it opens a very promising perspective for the repositioning of public libraries, as key factors in the creative development of users. This new lens of interpretation of R.K provides a strong foundation for new practical strategies for library professionals regarding the implementation of renewable knowledge systems in libraries. These strategies generally aim to transition libraries to a more active role in supporting innovation, education and civic participation and may include.

6.1   Encouraging Cohabitation Between R.K. and Data Commons

Libraries can support this process by creating open collections and ensuring democratic access to materials and knowledge resources that can be used repeatedly and creatively, while respecting copyright regulations. On the other hand, libraries have a mission to support Data Commons collections, understood as complex data sets collected and openly managed to support innovation, research and education. Understanding the importance of sharing and managing these resources in a way that is useful and sustainable for users is an essential condition for the long-term sustainability of this approach. In this way, libraries can support the democratization of access to knowledge and cultivate closer collaboration. Between local, regional and global knowledge communities.

6.2 Consolidation of Open Platforms and Collections

Another possible strategy for library practitioners could be to develop digital infrastructures to support renewable knowledge. In support of this mission, public libraries can be involved in the creation of open access platforms, which contain digital collections available to the general public (open access e-books, research articles available under open access regime, local data sets and global useful for different community projects, learning resources for different age and professional categories etc.). To ensure the long-term sustainability of these collections, they should be easily accessible and provide multiple opportunities for interaction and collaboration between users.

6.3 Lifelong Learning for Librarians

To facilitate the transition to the R.K. librarian-curator model, it is necessary to constantly invest in modern skills and lifelong education for library professionals. In order to increase the performance of libraries as aggregators of R.K., a special emphasis should be placed on the continuous training of librarians in areas such as data management, digital curation, combating fake news, management of collaborative platforms, knowledge and compliance with copyright policies.

6.4 Collaborating with Local Communities and Encouraging Open Innovation

In order to support the creative development of users, libraries are called to engage in long-term partnerships with different local actors – schools, universities, cultural centers, etc. These collaborations have the potential to lead to the development of joint projects, based on the heterogeneous collections of the libraries, recombined and renewed in the process of R.K. and amplified through open innovation. For example, by organizing hackathons, coding workshops or debate competitions, libraries can support users in developing creative solutions to problems specific to local communities.

7 Overcoming Challenges in Preserving Renewable Knowledge

One of the key challenges in effectively managing renewable knowledge is the difficulty of upgrading and maintaining its relevance over time. Changes in technology, industry demands, and societal trends can quickly make certain knowledge artifacts obsolete or insufficient, requiring an ongoing process of reviewing, updating, and disseminating [7]. To meet these challenges, public libraries can leverage their extensive experience in information management and community engagement to create dynamic, interactive platforms that facilitate the continuous renewal and dissemination of knowledge. This may involve integrating user-generated content, collaborating with local businesses and organizations, and continually monitoring emerging trends and needs within the community. (Zelenika & Pearce, 2014).

7.1   Rapid Technological Development and Digital Obsolescence

Accelerated technological development can cause certain digital formats and platforms to quickly become obsolete. In order for the data and information stored on digital platforms to remain updated and accessible, libraries must implement digital archiving policies based on open and interoperable standards, which ensure the transition between technologies and their long-term accessibility. This desideratum can be achieved by cultivating partnerships with institutions specialized in digital preservation, such as national archives or centers of excellence in digitalization, to ensure the migration of data to updated platforms and formats, as well as by creating backup copies on multiple media (physical and cloud).

7.2   Insufficient Financial and Human Resources

Public libraries often operate on limited budgets, which affects their ability to maintain and renew their collections up-to-date or to attract and motivate qualified staff. To combat this shortcoming, libraries should diversify their sources of funding by attracting external funds, government grants or private sources, and optimize the way they use resources by calling on open-source solutions and working in shared networks with other libraries.

7.3   Designing Flexible and Scalable System

R.K. conservation involves a dynamic approach to the collection, organization and provision of resources. Many times, knowledge management systems are rigid, making it difficult to adapt to the changing needs of users and ever-increasing volumes of data. To improve this situation, the implementation of data and knowledge management systems based on flexible and scalable principles, the adoption of modular and interoperable architectures for the easy exchange of data and resources between institutions and the use of open data standards to facilitate access and reuse of information is required together with developing clear internal procedures for updating and periodically reviewing, archiving and preserving policies.

8   Harnessing Renewable Knowledge for Economic and Creative Development

By positioning themselves as hubs for renewable knowledge and shared data, public libraries can play a vital role in supporting economic and creative development within their communities. This can be achieved by providing tailored resources, training and collaboration opportunities that enable users to successfully navigate the rapidly changing workforce landscape and capitalize on emerging opportunities. For example, public libraries have the capacity to organize and disseminate knowledge related to growing creative industries which encompasses domains and professions that rely on creativity, innovation, and problem solving [2]. By providing access to relevant data, tools, and learning resources, libraries can enable members of their community to develop the skills and knowledge needed to thrive in these dynamic fields. On the other hand, public libraries can support independent economic activities and growing entrepreneurial initiatives by providing resources and guidance on topics such as freelancing, small business development and digital marketing.

9 Promoting Connectivity, Collaboration and Capacity Building

A key aspect of the renewable knowledge and shared data paradigm is the emphasis on promoting connectivity, collaboration and capacity building within the wider knowledge sharing ecosystem. Public libraries play a critical role in this, facilitating partnerships and knowledge sharing initiatives between local businesses, educational institutions and community organizations. Through these collaborative efforts, public libraries can help address the major barriers of connectivity, collaboration, content, and capacity that often impede the effective dissemination and use of renewable knowledge [8, 9]. R.K. and the Data Commons have revolutionized the way libraries fulfill their role of storing, curating and distributing information. By promoting open access and collaboration between users and cultural institutions, these concepts have had a significant impact on the creative development of users. Public libraries are not only spaces where knowledge is consumed, but also spaces where knowledge is created. With the modernization of libraries, the focus is increasingly on promoting connectivity, collaboration and capacity building and on turning users into active participants in the processes of collaborative learning, skills development and innovation.

9.1 Public Libraries - Connectivity Triggers

Libraries promote democratic access to informational and cultural resources, while enabling users to access knowledge from a wide range of fields and geographic regions. In India, for example, the National Digital Library of India (N.D.L.I.) provides free access to millions of books and scholarly articles in multiple languages, democratizing access to education and knowledge. In a country with such great cultural and linguistic diversity, this initiative has connected millions of users, allowing them to collaborate and develop their creative skills in an innovative way. The connectivity promoted by the libraries operating with R.K. is not limited only to access to resources, but also to the creation of global networks of collaboration between users and institutions. This opens up new opportunities for creative development through the exchange of ideas and expertise at international level. For example, La Referencia, a Latin American platform connecting academic libraries in Brazil, Argentina and Chile, facilitates the exchange of data and resources. By accessing the common database, researchers and students can collaborate on international projects, using shared knowledge and contributing to the development of innovative solutions to global problems. This cross-border collaboration has led to the development of new perspectives and creative solutions for the personal and professional development of users.

9.2 Creating Innovation Centers in Libraries

Libraries have begun to become hubs for innovation and creative development by providing spaces and resources for user experimentation. These innovation centers provide access to advanced technology such as 3D printers, virtual reality labs and creative workshops that encourage users to explore new ways of creative expression. Libraries in the United States, for example, organize "Makercamps" type events where young people can learn to create objects and different applications using digital technology and Do-it-Yourself (D.I.Y.) tools. Thus, young users have the opportunity to collaborate to develop common projects, such as building robots, creating software or D.I.Y. projects.

10 Methodology for Surveying Public Library Services and Accessibility

The study is based on the design and distribution of a comprehensive Questionnaire on modern library services addressed to a diverse sample of public library managers from Romania and from several European countries. The questionnaire consisted of 14 questions focused on exploring the range of modern library services offered, as well as the degree of accessibility of these services to library users. The data collected through this survey was then integrated and analyzed, making comparisons between the landscape of public libraries in Romania and that of the participating European countries. The research also included a review of relevant reports and official databases maintained by European library organizations, providing a wider context for understanding the current state of public library services and accessibility. This multi-layered approach allowed for a more nuanced understanding of the specific practices and conceptual frameworks surrounding the notion of "renewable knowledge" within different library environments and cultural contexts. Starting from the essential role that public libraries play in promoting the sustainable development of the community by providing personalized services, the Questionnaire explored the most widespread categories of services available in public libraries in Romania. By classifying these services into broader, generic families, the author asked respondents to confirm or deny the availability of these types of services within their library systems.

11 The Process of Analyzing the Data Revealed by the Questionnaire

The data collected through this Questionnaire was classified, analyzed and graphed using statistical methods and software. Both quantitative and qualitative tools were used during the data analysis process. In order to better target and adapt this type of survey to understand the role of libraries in providing modern services to users, the author addressed 100 representatives from the upper and middle management of public libraries in Romania and 60 representatives of libraries and library associations in Europe. Among them, 46 respondents from Romania and 14 respondents at European level participated.

By applying this Questionnaire, the author proposed to achieve the following objectives:

- To investigate the views of senior and middle management representatives from public libraries in Romania and Europe regarding "renewable knowledge".
- To determine the main typologies of modern library services and how they contribute to the preservation of "renewable knowledge".

- To analyze the adequacy and degree of accessibility of modern library services.
- To assess the level of awareness and use of the main categories of modern services.
- Determine to what extent existing services meet real and current needs from the point of view of "renewable knowledge".
- To establish the relationship between technology - modern services - "renewable knowledge".
- To analyze the extent to which physical and software facilities in libraries can be transformed into hubs of "renewable knowledge".

The 46 respondents who accepted the invitation to answer to the thematic Questionnaire come from 22 counties in Romania (Figs. 1 and 2).

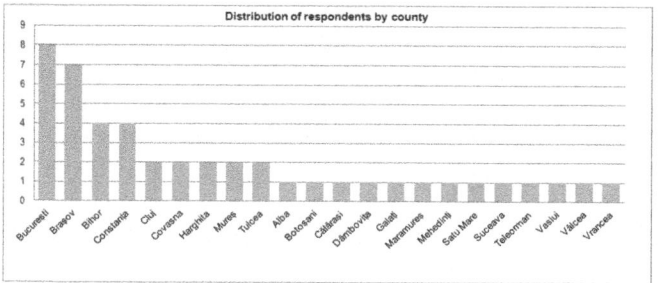

Fig. 1. Distribution of respondents by county

Regarding the professional profile of respondents, they are in leadership positions in different types of libraries in the Romanian public system. According to the position occupied within the organization, the respondents are divided into the following categories: Librarian (23), Manager (7), Head of Service (4), Director (3), Head of Office (3), Deputy Director (2), Project Coordinator (1), Methodologist (1), Editor (1), and Library Responsible (1).

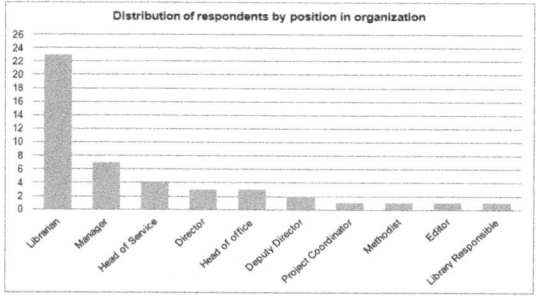

Fig. 2. Distribution of respondents according to position in the organization (Romania)

Regarding the membership of relevant organizations for the library field, the respondents who accepted the invitation to complete the Questionnaire come from different types of libraries and respectively from a representative professional association, namely: County Library (26), City Library (6), Communal Library (4), Metropolitan Library (4), National Library (3), Municipal Library (1), Professional Association (1), and Scholar Library (1) (Figs. 3 and 4).

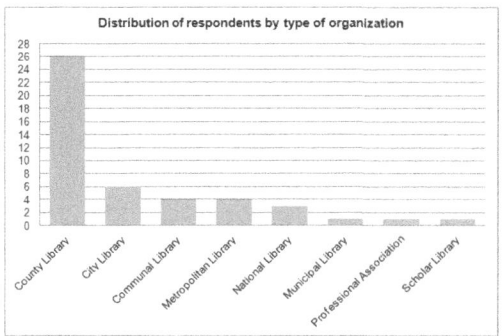

Fig. 3. Distribution of respondents according to type of organization

The Questionnaire regarding the offer of modern library services and the degree of their accessibility among the services users from the public libraries was also applied to a base of over 60 library leaders in libraries in Europe. A number of 14 persons accepted the invitation to answer the 14 questions of the Questionnaire in English. The distribution of the 14 respondents who accepted the invitation to answer to the thematic Questionnaire come from 5 countries in Europe, namely Lithuania (9), Slovenia (2), Bulgaria (1), Germany (1), and Portugal (1), as follows:

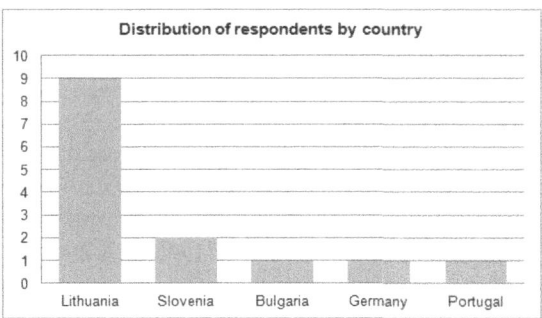

Fig. 4. Distribution of respondents according to country

In terms of their position in the organization, the respondents are divided into the following categories: Librarian (5), Director (3), Head of Department (2), Cultural project manager (1), Deputy Director (1), Assistant Director (1), and Coordinator of cultural activities (1) (Fig. 5).

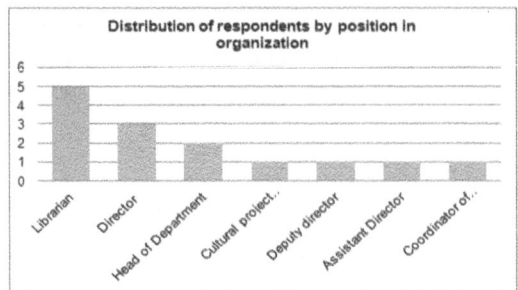

Fig. 5. Distribution of respondents according to position in the organization (Europe)

12   From Library 2.0 to Persistent Infrastructures for Knowledge Curation

The transition from traditional libraries to the Library 2.0 paradigm has marked a significant change in the way libraries interact and serve their users. Initially, libraries could be seen as two-dimensional platforms that provide users with a static collection of resources, allowing them to engage in limited activities such as borrowing books or accessing information. Once Library 2.0 occurred - characterized by improved interactivity, user participation and co-creation - libraries gained a new level of depth and complexity. This evolution has transformed them into ubiquitous and persistent infrastructures capable of integrating and curating a multitude of interconnected networks, both "messy and rich" [10].

13   Understanding Renewable Knowledge: Perspectives from Romanian Respondents

Romanian respondents who participated in the Questionnaire demonstrated a comprehensive understanding of library services and key operational concepts in the field of knowledge management. A significant majority recognized that the librarian profession is constantly changing and adapting, requiring continuous updating of professional knowledge. This aligns with broader trends in the field, where digital literacy and technological fluency are increasingly seen as essential competencies for librarians [11]. The general acceptance of "renewable knowledge" among Romanian respondents was reflected in its definition as inexhaustible knowledge that generates added value and which can be capitalized on through the use of Information and Communication Technologies (ICT). This perspective emphasizes the potential of renewable knowledge to continuously evolve and contribute to the development of new knowledge assets, echoing the concept of knowledge as a renewable resource [12]. Another segment of respondents saw renewable knowledge as the use of existing knowledge to design new knowledge, highlighting the coexistence of traditional and modern library services. This duality reflects the continued integration of digital technologies into library practices, which has been described as a key factor in the evolution of libraries into hybrid institutions which combine physical and digital resources [13].

14   Renewable Knowledge as a Driver of Continuous Learning

Romanian respondents also associated renewable knowledge with the concept of continuous learning and continuous improvement of skills. They pointed out that without renewable knowledge, librarians could not create modern services which require the perpetual renewal of skills. This understanding aligns with the notion that libraries are not static repositories of information but active sites of learning and knowledge production [14] (Fig. 6).

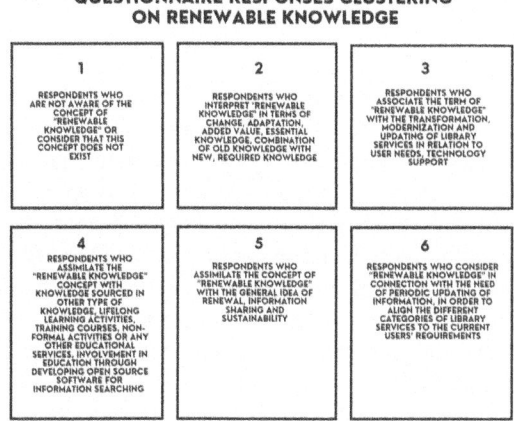

Fig. 6. Questionnaire Responses Clustering on Renewable Knowledge

Furthermore, renewable knowledge has been linked to improving the skills of library staff in line with modern library services. Depending on their personal context, respondents defined renewable knowledge as reinventing library services to meet current demands, particularly in relation to technological upgrading. This reflects the wider trend of libraries to adapt to the digital age by adopting new tools and platforms that facilitate access to information and knowledge [15].

15   European Perspectives on Renewable Knowledge

European respondents, demonstrating a more nuanced and multifaceted understanding of cognitive processes, considered (in the majority) that knowledge encompasses the scope of available facts and skills, while information encompasses facts and components of knowledge that exist independently of a person and can be acquired in certain circumstances. This distinction between information and knowledge reflects the knowledge hierarchy model, where data becomes information, information becomes knowledge, and knowledge can lead to wisdom [16]. According to the answers collected from European respondents, knowledge is perceived as meaningful and tested information that has been understood. Such information becomes part of an individual's mindset and influences behavior, suggesting that knowledge is more meaningful than information. On the other hand, knowledge is created based on information and could not be generated without it. This view is consistent with the idea that information serves as the building blocks of knowledge, a sine qua non for its generation. Incorporating their professional experience in librarianship and leadership, European respondents concluded that knowledge is considerably more important to individuals, representing information acquired by a person, transformed, processed and adapted to that person's cognitive needs. This perspective emphasizes the personalized nature of knowledge and its centrality in individual and collective learning processes [17].

16   SHIFT Project – A Recent Use Case of Renewable Knowledge in Libraries

For a better consolidation of the research results, the author offers an eloquent example of the application of renewable knowledge in libraries, developed in the context of the Horizon SHIFT project: MetamorphoSis of cultural Heritage Into augmented hypermedia assets For enhanced accessibiliTy and inclusion. Based on the partnership between 13 partners from 8 countries, this research-innovation project proposes the integration of advanced digital technologies in the preservation and accessibility of cultural heritage, especially for visually impaired people. This use case from Romania brings to the fore a transformative approach to pre-existing digital stories and how these narratives can become more accessible and emotionally resonant for visually impaired people with the support of technology applications based on AI.

17   Digital Storytelling as a Tool to Make Cultural Content Accessible

Knowing the complex values of the digital story technique for encapsulating and preserving the cultural heritage of communities, the National Association of Public Librarians and Libraries in Romania (ANBPR) and SHIFT partners intervened with the means of technology on a complex database of pre-existing digital stories in order to makes them more inclusive and accessible for people belonging to vulnerable groups. Focusing on the semantic and emotional decoding of valuable cultural heritage content, the SHIFT partners engaged in an extensive process of technological upgrading of the digital stories in the ANBPR portfolio, in an attempt to make them more accessible to a wider audience, especially to people with special needs. The transformative power of digital storytelling lies in its ability to synthesize complex cultural artifacts into compelling narratives. Through the use of modern technologies such as affective speech synthesis and natural language processing (NLP), the cultural heritage artifacts in the ANBPR portfolio - as a provider of use cases from the perspective of libraries - are transformed into vibrant, emotionally expressive stories that resonate deeply with different audiences. This process not only revitalizes pre-existing digital stories, but also ensures that they are more accessible to the visually impaired, thus promoting wider inclusion. The implementation of advanced technologies, such as Text-to-Speech (TTS) systems and NLP modeling with which SHIFT operates, plays a crucial role in improving the accessibility of cultural heritage assets. The TTS technology, for example, enables the conversion of written text into spoken words, providing an auditory experience of cultural narratives that is crucial for the visually impaired. This listening experience is further enriched by the use of affective speech synthesis, which adds an emotional layer to the spoken content, making it more engaging and easier to decode. This innovation-oriented approach allows SHIFT partners to give new life to pre-existing digital stories by enriching them with elements of renewable knowledge, which gives them an addition of significance from a cultural point of view, thus increasing their impact on the audience. One of the key objectives of the SHIFT project is to create strong emotional connections between the audience and the various cultural heritage assets in library and museum collections. By using the techniques of transferring style or adding emotions, the project aims to evoke imagination and create powerful and inspirational experiences for users. The emotional resonance of digital stories is especially important for visually impaired people, for whom auditory cues are a primary means of experiencing the world. Practically, through the mediation of technology, the emotional expressiveness of the digital stories in the ANBPR portfolio is improved by modulating and adapting the tone of the narrator's voice, the rhythm and the inflection, which are critical elements in conveying the subtle nuances of the digital stories with which the SHIFT project operates. This approach not only makes digital stories more engaging, but also ensures that they are accessible to a diverse audience, beyond any possible physical or other limitations. The pioneering approach of the SHIFT project once again underlines the potential of advanced technological solutions in facilitating the inclusion of visually impaired people as full beneficiaries of cultural heritage from library and museum collections. By reconsidering and empowering pre-existing digital stories, the SHIFT project demonstrates that modern technological solutions can create a more engaging, inclusive and impactful cultural experience. So, the use of TTS, NLP and affective speech synthesis revitalizes cultural narratives and transforms them into emotionally resonant cultural assets accessible to all.

18 Conclusion

Perceptions of renewable knowledge among library professionals in Romania and Europe reveal a nuanced understanding of the concept as it applies to modern library practice. Renewable knowledge is seen as an inexhaustible resource, vital for the continuous development of library services and the professional development of librarians. As libraries continue to evolve in response to technological advances and changing user needs, the ability to harness renewable knowledge will be crucial in supporting their role as dynamic and adaptable institutions. The findings of this study contribute to supporting the role of libraries in the digital age, emphasizing the importance of continuous learning and the integration of technology into knowledge management. As public libraries increasingly serve as curators of traditional and digital knowledge, understanding and applying the principles of renewable knowledge will be key to their success in promoting lifelong learning and their commitment to serving communities. By capitalizing on the insights gained from this study, the authors aim to contribute to a broader understanding of how public libraries can continue to evolve as critical infrastructures for knowledge preservation. This includes exploring new models of library services that integrate advanced digital tools with user-centered design principles, fostering an environment conducive to user creativity, learning and creative development. The findings of this study align with previous research on the evaluation of user-oriented library services [18] and the importance of libraries in building communities [19]. Finally, this research highlights the importance of public libraries in fostering the creation, storage and dissemination of renewable knowledge, thus contributing to society's resilience and adaptability in the face of ever-evolving challenges.

References

1. Houghton, K., Foth, M., Miller, E.: The local library across the digital and physical city: opportunities for economic development. In: UTS ePRESS, pp. 39–60, 23 July 2014. https://doi.org/10.5130/cjlg.v0i0.4062
2. Barbakoff, A.: Building a future-ready workforce: the role of public libraries in creating equitable, resilient, and entrepreneurial communities. Taylor & Francis, **40**(2), 167–181, 13 December 2019. https://doi.org/10.1080/01616846.2019.1688094
3. Jain, P., Mutula, S.M.: Libraries as learning organisations: implications for knowledge management. Library Hi Tech News **25**, 10–14 (2008)
4. Okoh, P., Haugen, S.: Improving the robustness and resilience properties of maintenance. Process. Saf. Environ. Prot. **94**, 212–226 (2015)
5. Bass, B.M.: Continuity and change in the evolution of work and human resource management. Hum. Resour. Manage. **33**, 3–31 (1994)
6. Davis, M.C., Challenger, R., Jayewardene, D., Clegg, C.W.: Advancing socio-technical systems thinking: a call for bravery. Appl. Ergon. **45**(2), 171–180 (2014)
7. Zelenika, I., Pearce, J M.: Innovation through collaboration: scaling up solutions for sustainable development. Springer Science+Business Media, **16**(6), 1299–1316, 27 March 2014. https://doi.org/10.1007/s10668-014-9528-7
8. Thiele, J.: Information Access in Rural Areas of the United States: the Public Library's Role in the Digital Divide and the Implications of Differing State Funding Models, 1 January 2016. https://dc.uwm.edu/cgi/viewcontent.cgi?article=2217&context=etd
9. Serholt, S., Eriksson, E., Dalsgaard, P., Bats, R., Ducros, A.: Opportunities and challenges for technology development and adoption in public libraries, 29 September 2018. https://doi.org/10.1145/3240167.3240198
10. Weinberger, D.: Everything Is Miscellaneous: The Power of the New Digital Disorder. Times Books (2007)
11. Bawden, D., Robinson, L.: Introduction to Information Science (2012)
12. Nonaka, I., Takeuchi, H.: The Knowledge-Creating Company: How Japanese Companies Create the Dynamics of Innovation. Oxford University Press (1995)
13. Mattern, S.: Library as Infrastructure. Places Journal (2014). https://placesjournal.org/article/library-as-infrastructure/
14. Lankes, R.D.: The Atlas of New Librarianship (2011)
15. Miller, C.A.: The enriching indigenous southeast asian collections in libraries conference (e-iseacol). Library Hi Tech News **22**, 14–15 (2005)
16. Ackoff, R.L.: From data to wisdom. J. Appl. Syst. Anal. **16**, 3–9 (1989)
17. Polanyi, M.: The Tacit Dimension. Routledge & Kegan Paul (1966)
18. Prakashe, V A., & Patle, B V.: Evaluation of User Oriented Library Services in Select NIT Libraries, 1 February 2018. https://doi.org/10.1109/ettlis.2018.8485236
19. Rosenfeldt, D.: Libraries Building Communities. Emerald Publishing Limited, **7**(3), 185–192, 1 September 2006. https://doi.org/10.1108/14678040610713147

Track on Agriculture, Food
and Environment (AgroSEM'24)

Vector Spaces Model: A Knowledge Integration Method for Research on Linkage Relationships in Agricultural Science and Technology

Chai Miaoling[1,2] , Zhang Xian[1,2(✉)] , Tang Yawei[3,4] , and Dawazhuoma[5]

[1] National Science Library (Chengdu), Chinese Academy of Sciences, Chengdu, China
{chaiml,zhangx}@clas.ac.cn

[2] Department of Information Resources Management, School of Economics and Management, University of Chinese Academy of Sciences, Beijing, China

[3] Agricultural Research Institute, Tibet Academy of Agricultural and Animal Husbandry Science, Lhasa, China

[4] State Key Laboratory of Barley and Yak Germplasm Resources and Genetic Improvement, Lhasa, China

[5] Tibet Autonomous Region Institute of Science and Technology Information, Lhasa, China

Abstract. This study proposed an integration model that utilizes vector space features of multimodal data to address deficiencies in knowledge integration and logic within Science and Technology linkage research, and facilitate it in agricultural field. The research constructs a Vector Spaces Model (VSM) from three aspects: spatial direction, spatial matrix, and spatial topics. First, based on the social structure of multimodal data, an interactive merging method was used to integrate the linear model and the chain model to construct an Innovation Ecological Chain (IEC) from scientific research to the market. Second, a distance matrix was constructed based on classification of data processing depth and technology maturity to measure the semantic distance on the ecological chain. Third, combined metadata and ontology with Latent Dirichlet Allocation (LDA) to construct the spatial topic model, furthermore, the Large Language Model (LLM) utilizes in multimode data topic extraction. The experiments have shown that, 12 types of data from 1953 to 2023 in the Chinese highland barley can be obtained. Under the landscape of enterprise knowledge discovery, the 65 records topics in the corporate annual reports (2011–2022) spans across 5 sectors in VSM, 6 types of data could integrate in VSM and distribute in 6 sectors of it, and 17 key stakeholders identified from 5 types of data, and the Fund is important to distinguish the identity. Overall, the work verified that multimodal data could integrate under the VSM, while metadata and ontology can quantify the spatial vectors in semantics.

Keywords: Knowledge Integration · Vector Space · Ontology · Multimodal Data · Semantic · Highland Barley

M. Sfakakis et al. (Eds.): MTSR 2024, CCIS 2331, pp. 319–333, 2025.
https://doi.org/10.1007/978-3-031-81974-2_27

1 Introduction

Integrating scientific and technological knowledge helps understand the conversion of scientific research into market, providing methodological paths for research on key technology identification, outcome evaluation, and industrial development etc. Library and information science primarily explores the relationships between science and technology through classification [1, 2] and topic [3], with citations [4–7], social networks [8–11], geographical aggregation [12–14], and temporal relationships [15] based on academic papers and patent. Recently, the rise of information technology has led to additional types of data such as conference papers, dissertations, reports, news, monographs, and fund to join in information analysis [16, 17]. The basic idea of analysis is internal and external features of events in textual data, including metadata analysis, and text mining. However, there are still some issues that need to be addressed. Firstly, researchers seldom discussed the rationality, comprehensiveness, and applicability of data selection, and the logic of data usage still unclear. Second, communication within the research community is insufficient, with library and information science focusing mainly on papers and patents, and other types of data are seldom utilized. Third, the value of papers is not fully realized.

Based on this background, the study introduces multimodal data, which is widely distributed in the agricultural field, to establish a comprehensive data chain for scientific and technological research. Multimodal data encompasses diverse data forms in terms of structure, format, features, and storage [16]. From a perspective of social structure, it belongs to different entities and includes formats such as video, images, audio, numerical data, text, and datasets. Semantically, it includes multiple dimensions with macro, meso and micro expressions, and demonstrating complementarity and synergy of the metadata. Multimodal data enables comprehensive, multi-dimensional observation but its hierarchical and complex structure challenges it application in scientific and technological linkage research. Therefore, this study aims to explore the spatial vector features of multimodal data in agriculture, and ontology utilizes in the study in order to integrate knowledge, structured data sematic and support heterogeneous data analysis. And metadata, social structure, data form and format of multimodal data are considered. The advancement of LLM has facilitated participation in topic extraction, knowledge fusion.

2 Related Work

2.1 Linkage Models of Science and Technology

The relationship between science and technology mainly refers to the structural relationship that links and connects the two systems of science and technology. The academic community has mainly explored the correlation, direction, measurement, and model between the two. Vannevar Bush [18] was the first to propose a linear model, which suggests that the landscape of science to the market develops in a linear manner. This model is based on the perspective of foundation and application, here we introduce three main models under this logic:

Linear Model. Proposed by Vannevar Bush [18], it posits that "basic research is the pioneer of technological progress." In his essay "Science: The Endless Frontier," described the pathway from scientific research to technological development, which was later termed the linear model by Derek de Solla Price [19]. The model suggests that science and technology are relatively independent and develop linearly rather than interactively. In the 1970s, the linear paradigm was preliminarily formed, but by the late 1990s, the academic consensus was that the linear model did not fully reflect the complexity of the innovation process, ignoring the reverse influence of technology on science. Zhang Huiqin [20] argued that under the constraint of total resource input, the linear model could still be effective.

Chain-Linked Model. Proposed by Stephen J. Kline in 1985 [21], it extends the research chain from science-technology to market, suggesting that long-term basic scientific research can stimulate product innovation, and market demand can stimulate significant research, creating a positive interaction in the technological innovation chain that can improve innovation efficiency. This model not only analyzes the path of technological innovation, but also discusses the interactive relationship between each link and Research.

Two-Dimensional Model. Donald E. Stokes [22] introduced a two-dimensional model with "consideration of application" and "pursuit of basic understanding" as axes, categorizing scientific research into four quadrants. He later proposed a dynamic model analyzing the transition among pure basic research, applied research, use-inspired basic research and skill training and experience. Stokes' model has been applied to research programs such as those funded by DARPA, which have led to the development of internet, robots, the 3D printing of kidney organoids, etc. [23–25]. The model has also been used in the research projects selection at Pasteur Institute's in France [26], and in China for technological innovation in research institutions [27].

2.2 Social Structures of Science and Technology

Science and technology and social structure influence mutual and human activities form networks in an environment of technological language and common problem-solving, which can achieve the knowledge transfer through institutional activities. Grant, Robert M. [28] believes that knowledge can be externally integrated through cross organizational relationship networks. R. S. Cowan [29]examines the vast social implications of recent technological developments such as atomic energy, birth control, genetic engineering and personal computers, and the ways in which they are causing changes in America's political, social and economic structure. Wright G. [30] suggests technological progress was a network phenomenon, emerging from interactions among numerous individuals, and not necessarily in formally structured institutions of coordination. From the perspective of result transformation, the interaction among subjects forms the pathway for result transformation. Lander, B., et al. [31] viewed transformation as a process that moves dynamically and recursively between scientific discovery and utility, forming diverse transformation pathways through interactions among academic, commercial, medical, government, and other institutions. Zeng, Zhimin., et al. [32] classified research institutions into three types based on the research activities and core missions: knowledge creation, industrial transformation, and strategic frontier.

2.3 Application of Knowledge Organization System

Knowledge Organization System (KOS), including classification scheme, ontology, Subject headings, thesauri and taxonomy, is a general term for information organization methods. [33] KOS can be used for multiple purposes: firstly, in the early stages, it assists knowledge management and information retrieval through the classification of prior knowledge. [34] It also used for website architecture and network database interfaces. [35] Secondly, KOS utilizes structured information to organize and express stored information. And ontology has gradually become a core component of domain knowledge representation, knowledge management systems, decision support systems, and other intelligent systems. Thirdly, KOS can facilitate knowledge mining and discovery through terminology extraction, text mining, etc. Wu, Q. et al. [36] use the KOS and LDA in cancer field to label biomedical to discovery frontier knowledge. All these effectively facilitate knowledge integration. However, Goldstein, A., et al. [37] also believe that the lack of evaluation process in most proposed agricultural ontologies affects their effectiveness in use. In addition, since ontology is built on prior knowledge, there is insufficient extraction of new knowledge in unexpected events when used for knowledge mining. [36] In addition, metadata plays an important role in the fusion of multi-source data, and metadata standardization is beneficial for data reuse and reduces interoperability costs. For example, Diamantopoulos, N. [38] proposed VOA3R with the aim of integrating existing agricultural and aquaculture repositories by reusing mature metadata standards and defining domain specific metadata configuration files.

3 Research Methodology

To integrate agricultural science and technology knowledge, this study establishes association logic for multimodal data, identifies the data vector space, and measures the semantic distance of the data. This is discussed in three key aspects: spatial direction, spatial vector, and spatial topics.

Firstly, the spatial direction of scientific and technological development is defined using an interactive fusion method, combining linear model and chain linked model, integrating the social structure characteristics of multimodal data to construct an innovation ecological chain, defining the path from science to market based on the interactive characteristics of subjects. Secondly, the spatial distance is constructed by creating a matrix that identifies and describes the distribution of multimodal data within the ecological chain. This distance matrix is based on the classification features of library data and technology maturity. Lastly, a spatial topic model is constructed using an optimized LDA method, incorporating Chinese Library Classification, AGROVOC, National Industries Classification of China and metadata to establish a spatial topic model, achieving the feature extraction of multimodal data (see Fig. 1).

The study adopts the perspective of librarians to discover, understand, and analyze multimodal data, leveraging the accuracy and peer review advantages of paper data to form data anchors that determine the semantic relationships of multimodal data within the ecological chain.

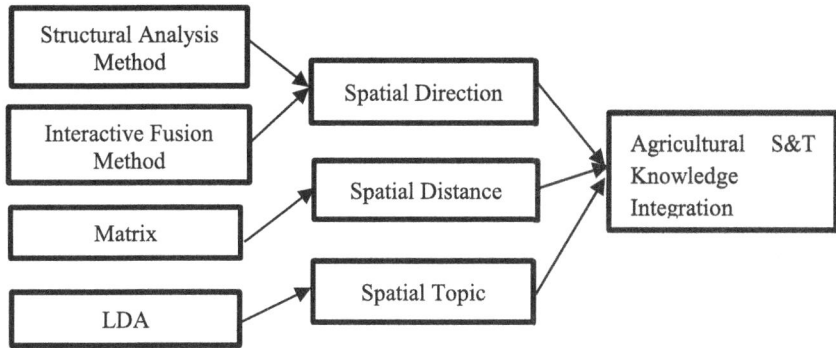

Fig. 1. Methods and Content of Agricultural S&T Knowledge Integration

4   Integration Process

4.1   Spatial Direction of Multimodal Data

This part establishes a scientific and technological innovation ecological chain (hereinafter referred to as the ecological chain) based on the spatial sequence characteristics of scientific and technological innovation activities, the spatial direction, sequence, and data scope of the chain.

First, analyze Social Structure of Agriculture Multimodal Data. The purpose is to reveal its internal composition and the interrelationships. Firstly, from the librarian's perspective and guided by the spatial direction of the linear model, after consulting with agricultural experts, 31 types of multimodal data have been identified, including observation data, graphs, audio, video, specimens, maps, experimental data, etc. [39, 40] Secondly, 12 types of data related to highland barley have been obtained. (See 5.1.) These data can be categorized into four types of institutions: individuals, scientific institutions, enterprises, and organizations related to technology, service, and promotion, which are led or served by governments, research institutes, and enterprises. Thirdly, by analyzing the social structure and characteristics from multimodal data, it is discovered that the landscape of scientific research to market aligns with spatial changes.

Second, construct the stages of IEC. The IEC builds upon the Linear Model and Chain-linked Model, incorporating two principles. First, the journey from scientific discovery to market development progresses in a linear manner. Secondly, to extends the "Research" and "Innovation" stages in the chain-linked model. (see Fig. 2). The research sectors are defined as natural observation and laboratory observation, distinguished by the degree of human participation in the activities. For the innovation part, the author added an incubation platform before "redesign and production," based on the characteristics of the organizational structure of highland barley.

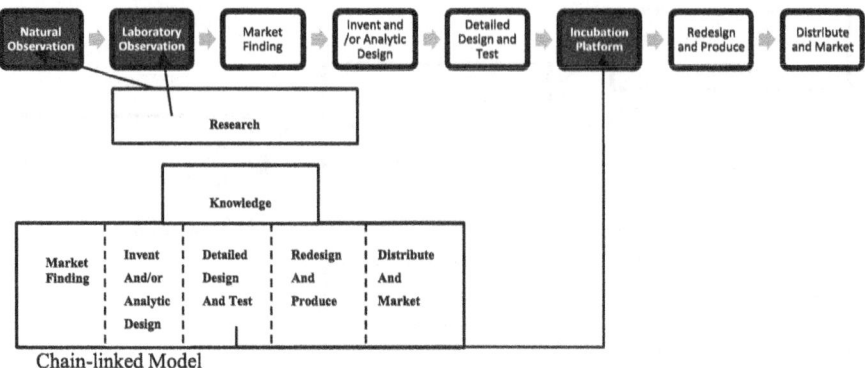

Chain-linked Model

Fig. 2. Innovation Ecological Chain

4.2 Spatial Distance Matrix Construction

The spatial distance matrix for multimodal data reflects the semantic distance between data points within the Innovation Ecological Chain. The basic criteria for measuring distance are based on depth of data processing and technology maturity. The process of generating is comprised of 3 steps.

Step1, construct a existence matrix of Multimodal data. Construct the matrix to discover and describe the multimodal data distribution characteristics in the IEC. Firstly, define the multimodal dataset is D and IEC is S. Let D be the union of the subsets of the multimodal dataset, There is $D=D_1 \cup D_2 \cup D_3 \cup \cdots D_n$, where n $\geq$ 1. Secondly, let S be the IEC, $S = O1 \cup O2 \cup S1 \cdots S6$, and $O1$ is natural observation, $O2$ is experimental observation, $S1$ is potential market analysis, $S2$ is invention design, $S3$ is detailed design and testing, $S4$ is incubation platform, $S5$ is redesign and production, and $S6$ refer to distribute and market. Third, construct a matrix M based on multimodal data, where rows represent each subset D_i of the datasets and columns represent each stage of S. The element m_{ij}, in the matrix represents the amount or density of data related to the IEC stage S_j (or O_j, if O is being used to denote stages) in the dataset D_i. The multimodal data distribution matrix M is represented as:

$$M = \begin{bmatrix} m_{11} \, m_{12} \, m_{13} \cdots m_{18} \\ \vdots \qquad\qquad \vdots \\ m_{n1} \, m_{n2} \, m_{n3} \cdots m_{n8} \end{bmatrix} \tag{1}$$

Among them m_{ij}, represents the distribution of data related to the dataset D_i and the ecological chain stage O_j (where j represents the scientific stage, with $j = 1, 2$) or S_j (where j represents the technological stage, with $j = 3, 4 \cdots 8$). Finally, based on the 31 types of multimodal data, the study creates an existence matrix, which is a 31 × 8 matrix where the columns represent the data and the rows indicate the IEC. And produce an UpsetView graph based on data distribution to identify the richness or scarcity of data on the IEC. We can learn from the Fig. 3 that the data in $O1$ and $O2$ are the largest, the multimodal data, which consist of journal article, dissertation, conference paper, and academic monograph, have the widest distribution in the chain. Besides, production, sales, and other data with typical industrial and commercial characteristics are relatively scarce.

Step2, build the distance matrix of multimodal data. The distance between multi-modal data must be determined. The author divides multimodal data into five categories based on the depth of literature processing, with semantic distances ranging from 0 to 4, and a distance of 1 set between each adjacent type. Then, the semantic distance among the stages of the IEC needs to be defined. Since NASA's Technology Readiness Level (TRL) [41] aligns with the description and direction of the IEC, the author assesses the distance based on the description of technological maturity, establishes corresponding relationships, and assigns distances accordingly. (see Table 1.)

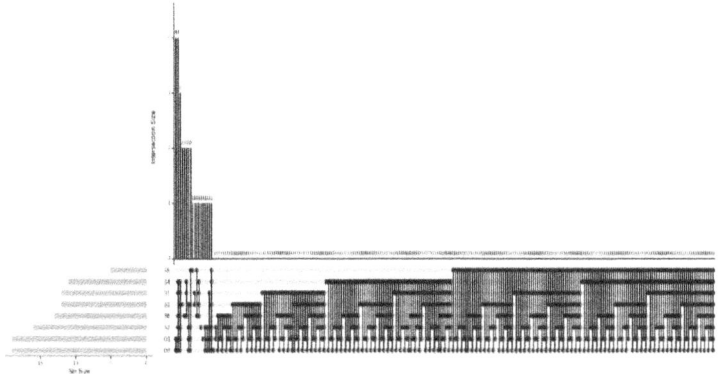

Fig. 3. Multi-Modal Data Existence Matrix UpsetView Graph

Step3, build a distance matrix construction. Establish a distance matrix with the multimodal dataset as the x-axis and the ecological chain as the y-axis. The distance between multimodal data pairs is 1, and the distance between ecological chains $O1$ to $S6$ is 9. Let A be the distance matrix of multimodal data, as not all data are correlated, let B be the mask matrix. There is a multimodal data distance formula:

$$C_{ji} = A_{ji}B_{ji} \qquad (2)$$

Among them, $0 < j \leq 8$, $0 < i \leq n$ and $n \neq 0$.

4.3 Spatial Topic Model Construction

The spatial topic model takes the ontology into the LDA to improve the knowledge discovery method. The goal of it is to build a spatial ontology to support multimodal data semantic distribution on IEC. The technical route involves topic distribution probability computing, Natural Language Processing (NLP) and ontology.

LDA infers the hidden topic distribution and the topic distribution of words by observing the word distribution in the documents [42, 43]. When inferring the topic distribution, LDA takes into account the co-occurrence of words and co-word within the documents, based on the assumptions of word correlation and semantic homogeneity.

Table 1. The Mapping of IEC and TRL

Ecological chain	Distance	Mapping to TRL	Description
Natural observation	1	T1	Formulate concepts or application directions
Experimental observation	2	T2	Develop concepts or application directions
Market finding	2.5	T2	Construct a conceptual model to determine the feasibility of a technology
Invent and/or analytic design	3.5	T3	Validate the conceptual model and achieve it in a laboratory setting
		T4	Component and/or experimental model validation in relevant environments
Detailed design and test	6	T5	System/subsystem model or prototype validation in relevant environments
		T6	System prototype validation in simulated environments
		T7	Marketization activities of achievements
Incubation platform	7.5	/	Experimental validation of the completed actual system
Redesign and produce	8	T8	Successful use of the actual system
Distribute and market	9	T9	Formulate concepts or application directions

But terminology may differ in different stages of IEC, and some word semantics are hard to capture. Additionally, it is hard to find the complex relationships among sentence components; therefore, researchers have introduced deep learning to solve this problem, for instance SeqLDA and BERT-LDA. Regards to self-attention mechanism in the transformer enables LLMs to automatically identify and assign different weights to the relationships between different words, thereby effectively capturing long-distance dependencies. [44] There for it can compensate for the shortcomings of LDA.

The purpose of construction the ontology in tokenization phase, as a dictionary to help the distinguish the spatial features of multimodal data. In the topic discovery stage, it will help LDA identified the concepts and relationships more close to the topic. The construction of ontology from top to bottom, and takes the IEC sectors as concepts. As to terms, the author build a questioning framework of LLM, Role + Objective + Concept + Output + Format + Reason + Corpus (ROCOFRC), to extract the topics from abstract of journal papers as the core terms by ERNIE Bot 4, while referring to the classification of Chinese library, AGROVOC and AGROIN [40]. In terms of evaluation methods, this study is based on data-driven evaluation, comparing the segmentation results of the ontology with relevant data sources, calculating precision, recall, and F1 score to evaluate its relevance to the corpus structure.

5 Empirical Research

5.1 Data Selection and Preprocessing

Highland barley was chosen as the empirical field for the study. It is also known as naked barley, is a small grain crop of the Poaceae family and Hordeum genus, characterized by its small range, scarcity, specificity, and diversity. It is primarily distributed in high-altitude regions such as Tibet, Qinghai, Sichuan of China, as well as in the northwestern Himalayas of India, Nepal, Ethiopia, Germany, Canada etc. [45] Highland barley industry is key industry in Tibet, with clear research community characteristics and comprehensive data coverage, and suitable for the multimodal data integration.

The research constructs the formulas to retrieve the data, from databases of CNKI, VIP, Incopat, Wind and open-access in Chinese. And TIAB = qingke OR highland barley OR Semen Avenae Nudae OR zanba OR Tsamba etc., finally, 13,466 pieces of valid data across 12 types were selected. The data included: germplasm, production data, enterprise annual report, enterprise name list, journal paper, conference paper, dissertation, invention, utility model, appearance design, standard literature and fund. The data formats included text, image-text mixed and numerical data.The data preprocessing included entities extraction from multimodal data, disambiguation of author and institution, removal of redundant and irrelevant data, and supplementation of relevant data. First, is recognition the entities of multimodal data. In this step, the paper use ERNIE BOT4.0 recognizing textual images in standard literature, which transfer into text to integrate with the metadata of standards [46]. Second, make the author and institution of journal paper as the data anchor to disambiguate the author and institution name of other data. Unique identifiers for authors and institutions were established based on these anchors, which were then matched with other data to extend the unique identifiers. Third is supplement the information of cross-modal data based on data anchors, such as extracting germplasm resources or funds.

5.2 Knowledge Discovery in Enterprise

American scholar D. E. Stokes [22] proposed the application-oriented basic research quadrant and used the example of French scientist Pasteur's basic research with a strong application orientation to illustrate the coexistence of understanding the world and knowledge application in the research process. As the main body of technological innovation, enterprises drive the development of scientific and technological research. Therefore, this study selects the landscape of enterprises demand driven scientific and technological development. The paper selects Qinghai Huzhu Tianyoude Qingke Liquor Co., Ltd. (Tianyoude), the largest Qingke liquor enterprise in China as an example to extracts relevant multimodal data to identify the scientific and technological correlation points closely related to application demand.

The Spatial Topics Distribution of Enterprise Annual Reports. Due to the enterprises are lack of willingness to express themselves in academic circles, along with fewer papers and patents, the author selects annual reports of the company that has been made public since 2011 as the research object to identify their activity features and purposes. Finally, 65 instances of science and technology activities from 2011 to 2022 were selected as the corpus, and LDA was used to analyze the spatial topic distribution on multimodal datasets. When score of the topic probability ≥ 0.5, the record will classified in it, and come by Fig. 4. Among them, 8 colors represent sectors of IEC, gray bars represent the total number of words, and curve height represents the total number of words in the spatial topic of the data. The less intersection between curves, the better the classification is. Figure 4 shows that the topics of 65 records are distributed across five sectors of the IEC: $O1$, $O2$, $S1$ and $S6$. The top 3 are $O2$, which accounts for 46% with microbiology and Daqu as the main topics; $S1$ accounts for 32%, with a focus on drinking comfort and product development; $S2$ accounts for 18% respectively, with research topics mainly focused on processes, raw materials, and brewing.

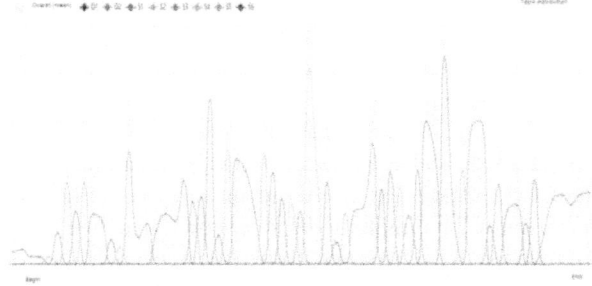

Fig. 4. Topic Distribution of Annual Report of Tianyoude(2011–2022)

Multimodal Data Discovery Based on Social Structure. Current research refers to authors who have both academic papers and invention patents as academic inventors, which is considered an important feature of identifying the linkage between science and technology. This concept originated from the recognition of dual identities among researchers. These researchers not only promote basic research in academia by publishing high-quality papers, but also drive technological innovation in industry by applying for patents, serving as a bridge between scientific research and technological innovation. However, due to the different willingness of researchers from research institutions and enterprises to participate, there are author ambiguities, regional differences, and the Matthew effect of cooperation in the data, in addition, due to the insufficient sample size of academic inventors, the accuracy of research results is limited [10, 11, 47].

This part aims to address this issue by extending the dual identity recognition of researchers to multiple identity recognition, identifying co-occurrence phenomena through multimodal data joint recognition, and further exploring themes to assist in the discovery of scientific and technological correlations. Step 1: Extract the topic of Qingqing Liquor and Huzhu Qingke Liquor from journal articles, yielding 88 records out of 3,148 papers based on titles, abstracts, institutions and keywords. And extract entities, serving as a data anchor for studying relevant topics distribution. Step 2: Identify the author names from journal articles, and find their co-occurrences in 4 other types of data: dissertation, patent (Invention, utility modal, appearance designs), standard literature and fund. Step 3: Using statistical methods to compare the co-occurrence of authors and identified 17 authors with appeared over 3 types of data. And we find the outputs of corporate personnel are manifested in the co-occurrence of papers, patents, and standards, while researchers are represented as dissertation authors, academic supervisors, and funds leader in national level. A distinction between these two roles emerges in the fund data, where the principals are researchers. Step 4:

Identified the topics distribution on the IEC. The topic distribution among the top 10 authors, with 251 (94%) effectively categorized, reveals their focus across four stages: $O1$, $S1$, $S2$, and $S3$. The topics exhibit the characteristics of space vectors. For example, the top three themes of $O1$ are content, activity, and variety. Research on content is associated with activity, variety, function, and daqu; activity related topics include content, cultivation, and metabolism; and variety related involve content, photosynthetic characteristics, and screening. The author believes that effective features of barley in natural observation, such as variety and photosynthesis, can be identified from the theme and its high-frequency coupling words.

The Space Distance Recognition Based on LDA. Integrate enterprise annual reports and author co-occurrence multimodal data to analysis the distribution on IEC. There are a total of 332 pieces of data from 6 types, with 315 valid topic classifications identified. The data is distributed across 6 links in the ecological chain, mainly in $O1$, $S1$ and $S2$. According to Formula (3), obtain the mask matrix b and spatial distance distribution map. (see Fig. 5). It can be seen that multimodal data can be effectively integrated into

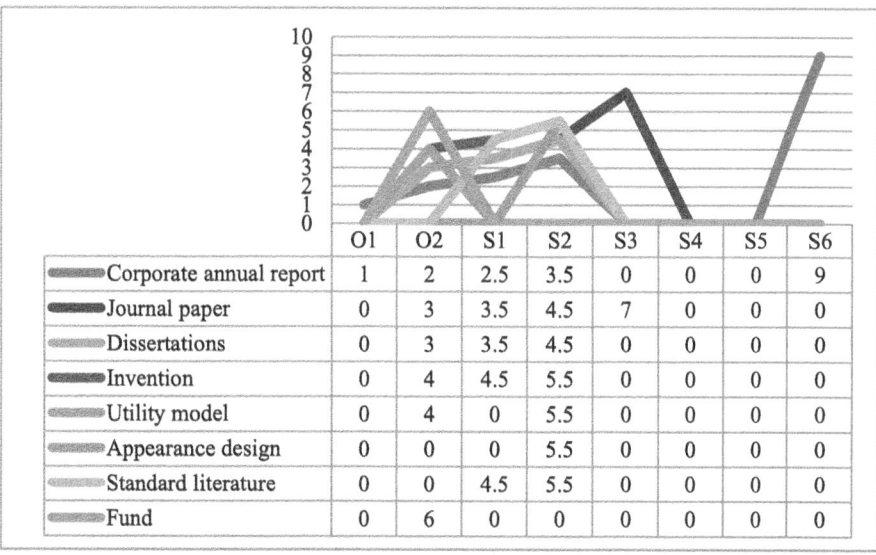

	O1	O2	S1	S2	S3	S4	S5	S6
Corporate annual report	1	2	2.5	3.5	0	0	0	9
Journal paper	0	3	3.5	4.5	7	0	0	0
Dissertations	0	3	3.5	4.5	0	0	0	0
Invention	0	4	4.5	5.5	0	0	0	0
Utility model	0	4	0	5.5	0	0	0	0
Appearance design	0	0	0	5.5	0	0	0	0
Standard literature	0	0	4.5	5.5	0	0	0	0
Fund	0	6	0	0	0	0	0	0

Fig. 5. The Distribution of 6 Multimodal Data in the Vector Spaces

the six sectors of the ecological chain. The use of data beyond journal articles and patents can enrich the spatial scope of research topics and support further research on scientific and technological correlations.

6 Conclusion and Future Work

In order to improve the research of linkage relationships in agricultural science and technology, this paper proposes a vector spaces model to integrate knowledge. This method considers text, numerical, and image text data from the entire watershed to address shortcomings of paper and patent-based recognition. Use the Vector Spaces modal is a better way to integrate the multimodal data in semantics.

Multimodal data reduces conformity and disperses protective research interference. Driven by different evaluation mechanisms, there is insufficient coupling between authors and inventors, and behavior motivations are not fully reflected. Therefore, using multi-modal data to identify co-occurrences of responsible persons can reduce the conformity and protective behavior in papers and patents, laying the foundation for further discovery of science and technology activities centered on responsible persons and analyzing linkage relationships on the IEC.

Furthermore, metadata and ontology are beneficial for constructing spatial topic models, particularly when utilizing terms from Chinese Library Classification, AGROVOC, and AGROIN, which provide criteria for categorization. Based on the metadata of journal paper, more information can be supplemented, which is beneficial for enhancing the accuracy, interpretability, and robustness of the multimodal data.

In the future, the Vector Spaces Model will be utilized in the landscape of digital infrastructure of highland barley to integrate multimodal data and facilitate knowledge discovery.

Acknowledgments. This research was funded by the Key Research and Development Project of Science and Technology Plan of Xizang Autonomous Region. (grant number XZ202301ZY0004N) and Chinese National Social Science Foundation Project. (grant number 18BTQ067). I would like to thank Zhu Jiang (National Science Library Chengdu branch, CAS) for data download help, Chen Jing and Pan Zhifen (Chengdu Institute of Biology, CAS) for ecological chain construction and Lin Jingli (Xihua University) for his help in spatial distance matrix construction.

References

1. Dong Kun, X., Haiyun, L.R., et al.: Review of the research on relationship between science and technology (in Chinese). J. China Soc. Sci. Tech. Inf. **37**(06), 642–652 (2018)
2. Verbeek, A., Debackere, K., Luwe, M., et al.: Linking science to technology: using bibliographic references in patents to build linkage schemes. Scientometrics **54**(3), 399–420 (2002)
3. Xu, H.Y., Winnink, J., Yue, Z., Liu, Z., Yuan, G.: Topic-linked innovation paths in science and technology. Journal of Inform. **14**(2), Article 101014 (2020)

4. Bhattacharya, S., Kretschmer, H., Meyer, M.: Characterizing intellectual spaces between science and technology. Scientometrics **58**(2), 369–390 (2003)

5. Narin, F., Noma, E.: Is technology becoming science? Scientometrics **73–6**, 369–381 (1985)

6. Wang, G., Guan, J.: Measuring science–technology interactions using patent citations and author-inventor links: an exploration analysis from Chinese nanotechnology. J. Nanopart. Res. **13**, 6245–6262 (2011)

7. Guan, J.C., He, Y.: Patent-bibliometric analysis on the Chinese science–technology linkages. Scientometrics **72**(3), 403–425 (2007)

8. Gardner, P.: Representations of the relationship between science and technology in the curriculum. Stud. Sci. Educ. **24**(1), 1–28 (1994)

9. Boyack, K.W., Klavans, R.: Measuring science–technology interaction using rare inventor–author names. J. Informet. **2**(3), 173–182 (2008)

10. Winnink, J.J., Tijssen, Robert, J.W.: Dynamics and scientific breakthroughs in HIV/AIDS drugs development: the case of integrase inhibitors. Scientometrics **101**, 1–16 (2014)

11. Zhao, H., Leng, F.: Relationship between science and technology research frontiers from the perspective of academic inventors (in Chinese). China Inven. Patent **18**(01), 3–12 (2021)

12. Jaffe, A.B.: The real effects of academic research. Am. Econ. Rev. **79**(5), 957–970 (1989)

13. Jaffe, A.B., Henderson, T R.: Geographic localization of knowledge Spillovers as evidenced by patent citations. Q. J. Econ. **108**(3), 577–598 (1992)

14. Fischer, M.M., Scherngell, T., Patents, J.E.: Patent citations and the geography of knowledge spillovers in Europe (2009)

15. Liu, Z., Xu, H., Luo, R., et al.: Research on scientific and technological interaction patterns based on topic relevance analysis (in Chinese). J. China Soc. Sci. Tech. Inform. **38**(10), 997–1011 (2019)

16. Hucheng, Z., Leixiao, L., Dongjiang, L.: A survey of multimodal data fusion research (in Chinese). J. Front. Comput. Sci. Technol. 1–22, 23 July 2024. http://kns.cnki.net/kcms/det ail/11.5602.tp.20240620.1752.002.html

17. Cheng, J.C., Dai, Y.L., Yuan, Y., Zhu, H.L.: A simple analysis of multimodal data fusion. In: 2020 IEEE 19th International Conference on Trust, Security and Privacy in Computing and Communications (TRUSTCOM 2020), pp. 1472–1475 (2020)

18. Bush, V., Holt, R.D.: Science, the Endless Frontier (in Chinese). CITIC Press, Beijing (2021)

19. De. Solla Price, D.J.: Is technology historically independent of science? a study in statistical historiography. Technol. Cult. **6**(4), 553–568 (1965)

20. HuiQin, Z., Xin, W., Xu, W., Changpu, S.: Beyond pasteur's quadrant model: a new dynamic model of basic research and its implementation (in Chinese). Strategic Study CAE, **23**(04),145–152 (2021)

21. Kline, S.J.: Innovation is not a linear process. Res. Manag. **28**(2), 36–45 (1985)

22. Donald, E.S.: Basic Science and Technological Innovation (in Chinese). Science Press, Beijing (1999)

23. Elliott, C., Colvin, A., Pearson, D., et al.: Current status of the DARPA quantum network. In: Conference on Quantum Information and Computation III; 20050329-30, Orlando, FL (US). BBN Technologies, 10 Moulton Street, Cambridge MA 02138 (2005)

24. Thrun, S., et al.: Stanley: the robot that won the DARPA grand challenge. J. Field Robot. **23**(9), 661–692 (2006)

25. Dugan, R.E., Gabriel, K.J.: Changing the business of breakthroughs. Issues Sci. Technol. (2022)

26. Pan, Q., Fan, Q., Tang, S.: The Pasteur model of development: science, technology and innovation at the Institut Pasteur in France (in Chinese). World Sci-tech R&D, **40**(05), 528–532 (2018)

27. Shouhua, Z.: Research on technology innovation model of china based on Pasteur's quadrant (in Chinese). Sci. Technol. Prog. Policy, **34**(20),15–19 (2017)

28. Grant, R.M.: Toward a knowledge-based theory of the firm. Strateg. Manag. J. **17**(S2), 109–122 (1996)
29. Cowan, R.S.: A Social History of American Technology. Oxford University Press (1997)
30. Wright, G.: Can a Nation Learn? American Technology as a Network Phenomenon. NBER Chapters, pp. 295–332 (1999)
31. Lander, B., Atkinson-Grosjean, J.: Translational science and the hidden research system in universities and academic hospitals: a case study. Soc Sci Med **72**(4), 537–544 (2011)
32. Zhimin, Z., Bingyan, Z., Maochang, C.: Construction of scientific research institutions classification model: based on the perspective of Pasteur quadrant mode (in Chinese). Sci. Manag. Res. **41**(04), 48–55 (2023)
33. Mayr, P., Tudhope, D., Clarke, S.D., et al.: Recent applications of Knowledge organization systems: introduction to a special issue. Int. J. Digit. Libr. **17**, 1–4 (2016)
34. Palavitsinis, N., Manouselis, N.: Agricultural knowledge organization systems: an analysis of an indicative sample. In: Handbook of Metadata, Semantics and Ontologies, pp. 279–296 (2013)
35. Rosenfeld, L., Morville, P.: Information architecture for the World Wide Web, 2nd Edition. Libr. Q. Inf. Commun. Policy **14**(11), 498–500 (2002)
36. Wu, Q., Kuang, Y., Hong, Q., et al.: Frontier knowledge discovery and visualization in cancer field based on KOS and LDA. Scientometrics **118**, 979–1010 (2019)
37. Goldstein, A., Fink, L., Ravid, G.: A framework for evaluating agricultural ontologies. Sustainability **13**(11), 6387:6387 (2021)
38. Diamantopoulos, N., Sgouropoulou, C., Kastrantas, K., Manouselis, N.: Developing a metadata application profile for sharing agricultural scientific and scholarly research resources. In: García-Barriocanal, E., Cebeci, Z., Okur, M.C., Öztürk, A. (eds.) Metadata and Semantic Research. MTSR 2011. Communications in Computer and Information Science, vol. 240. Springer, Heidelberg (2011). https://doi.org/10.1007/978-3-642-24731-6_45
39. Miaoling, C., Lin, H., Renyunyue.: A review of construction of major agricultural open scientific data resources (in Chinese). J. Libr. Inform. Sci. Agricult. **32**(10), 25–34 (2020)
40. Miaoling, C., Jiang, Z., Yi, Z., et al.: Research on the method of linking scientific data and literature data through metadata fusion and ontology construction - from the perspective of agricultural science and technology management in China. In: Proceedings of the International Conference on Dublin Core and Metadata Applications, DCMI, Korea, 1939–1358 (2023). https://doi.org/10.23106/dcmi.953357797
41. Technology Readiness Level, 24 Feb 2023. https://www.nasa.gov/directorates/heo/scan/engineering/technology/technology_readiness_level
42. Hu, J., Chen, G.: Mining and evolution of content topics based on dynamic LDA (in Chinese). Libr. Inform. Serv. **58**(02), 138–142 (2014)
43. Xiuhong, W., Min, G.: The key technology identification method based on BERT-LDA and its empirical research: a case study of agricultural robots (in Chinese). Libr. Inform. Serv. **65**(22), 114–125 (2021)
44. Cheng, N., Yan, Z., Wang, Z., et al.: Potential and limitations of LLMs in capturing structured semantics: a case study on SRL. In: International Conference on Intelligent Computing. Springer, Singapore (2024)
45. Yan, C., Bai-li, F.: Present situation and developing strategies of minor grain crops in China (in Chinese). Agricult. Res. Arid Areas (03), 145–151 (2003)

46. Miaoling, C., Xian, Z., Yi, Z., et al.: The method and evaluation of use of LLMs to build science-technology relationships ontology in agriculture domain -- taking the hull-less barley as an example. In: Eighteenth International Society for Knowledge Organization Conference (ISKO 2024), Wuhan, China (2024)

47. Meyer, M.: Are patenting scientists the better scholars? an exploratory comparison of inventor–authors with their non-inventing peers in nanoscience and technology. Res. Policy **35**, 1646–1662 (2006)

Track on Digital Humanities and Digital Curation

Ontological Approaches to Morphological Semantics in Modern Greek Derivation

Nikos Vasilogamvrakis[1]([✉]) [iD], Michalis Sfakakis[1] [iD], Maria Koliopoulou[2],
and Giannoula Giannoulopoulou[3]

[1] Department of Archives, Library Science and Museology, Ionian University, Corfu, Greece
{120vasi,sfakakis}@ionio.gr
[2] Department of German Language and Literature, National and Kapodistrian University of
Athens, Athens, Greece
mkoliopoulou@gs.uoa.gr
[3] Department of Italian Language and Literature, National and Kapodistrian University of
Athens, Athens, Greece
giannoulop@ill.uoa.gr

Abstract. In the present article, we explore the morphological semantics of Modern Greek (MG) and how these are expressed in ontological terms in the MMoOn ontology. First, we define the two core aspects of meaning, grammatical and lexical, pointing out that there are also other more abstract types of meaning such as derivational that pertain to affixes or confixes. Most prominently, we explore the transition of features of morphemic components to the output derivational structures, a process most commonly known as *percolation theory*. In order to ensure the consistency of the process, we specify an automated way of this transfer as well as the types of the transmitted features for each different case. To this end, we leverage OWL expressive language, defining appropriate classes, object properties and chain properties in the Protégé ontology editor. Afterwards, we confirm that the syntax works well by checking out the generated inferences. In the research to come, more investigation on morphemic semantics of MG is to be done touching upon other aspects of it.

Keywords: Linguistic Linked Data · Modern Greek derivation · Morphological semantics · Ontological morphology

1 Introduction

Language morphology studies two major aspects of words: structure and meaning. By structure we refer to the decomposition of morphological units practiced in concatenative processes [15, 16] while meaning constitutes semantic properties of morphs[1], ranging from pure grammatical or functional to more extra-linguistic lexical meanings. That means that words, which are the constructions of a series of morphs, conclusively appear

---

[1] The terms *morph* and *morpheme* are used interchangeably. Morph is the actual representation of a morpheme.

© The Author(s), under exclusive license to Springer Nature Switzerland AG 2025
M. Sfakakis et al. (Eds.): MTSR 2024, CCIS 2331, pp. 337–348, 2025.
https://doi.org/10.1007/978-3-031-81974-2_28

to be the amalgams of micro-meanings. However, words are not just the literal sum of those micro-meanings but many times the result of how these are infiltrated within the extra-linguistic framework and language use. *Meaning* is therefore related to *form* and in synthetic languages, like Modern Greek (MG), they do not comprise an one-to-one relation, as various meanings may reside in one morph (portmanteau morphemes) or multiple morphs may bear the same or nearly the same meaning [7, 8, 10].

In ontological terms or NLP language representational models, morphological semantics has not been dealt with sufficiently yet, since most of the models are limited to describe the morpho-syntactic aspect of morphs (Ontolex, OLiA, Unimorph, Universal Dependencies etc.) and not the whole range of their meaning. If we, therefore, assume that a word's meaning is, in principle, the sum of its constituent morphs' meanings, either as they are or infiltrated, then a model, except for the representation of those meanings, shall also be able to deal with their transfer into the final structures. This transfer of features or characteristics is widely known as *percolation theory* and, to the best of our knowledge, has not been represented ontologically so far.

In this article, we therefore deal with the aspects of meaning of morphs and how this meaning is processed within word structures. More specifically, in Sect. 2, we analyze the different meanings of morphs and their percolation into the final structures as features while, in Sect. 3, we ontologically represent this theory in the MMoOn model. Finally, in Sect. 4, we briefly summarize and conclude on the topic.

2 Morphological Framework

Often, the distinction between lexical and functional [3, 11, 13] intersects with that of open vs. closed class entities [3, 5, 6, 11]. A lexical concept pertains to something specific and extra-linguistic whereas functional to something more abstract and intra-linguistic that bears a relational significance between a syntagmatic alignment of items [11]. However, in order that lexical concepts function within the language system, they are expressed through POS categorizers (parts of speech) (nouns, verbs, adjectives etc.). For example, in the verb τρέχ-ω *(trex-o)* 'to run', the base τρεχ- *(trex-)* is a bound lexical morpheme, expressing at the same time a verbal grammatical meaning.

The divide between lexical and grammatical is sufficiently justified by *Grammatical-ization theory* and the related *Reanalysis* processes [1, 2, 5, 6] to which morphological units are subsumed. In Fig. 1, morphemes are characterized as more lexical if they reside towards the far left of the continuum and more grammatical towards the far right. We could assume that words initially enter the language system as roots that have a pure conceptual aspect before they are gradually subsumed to categorizers (Noun, Verb, Adjective etc.), integrating grammatical meanings as stems [11]. Derivational affixes, i.e. prefixes and derivational suffixes are put towards the grammatical side but we should note that they are not sheer grammatical morphemes, as they preserve an abstract refer-ence to a concept (e.g. profession, instrument, location, proximity, repetition etc.). This concept, which in derivational suffixes is accompanied by a POS category, contributes significantly to the structures it is attached, giving them a derivational meaning. As we also notice, confixes [17] gain semi-lexical or semi-grammatical properties, since they are put exactly between those two points in the continuum [5]. This gradual processing

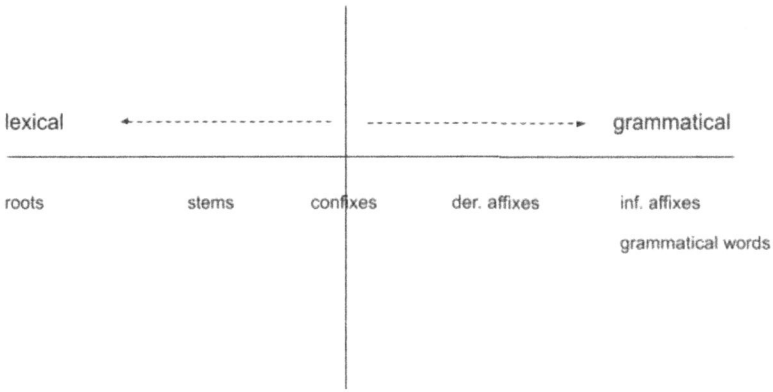

Fig. 1. The lexico-grammatical continuum with morphemic types placed appropriately

of morphemes over the derivational process ends up to the sheer grammatical side, which enable words to get into the syntactic system [10].

2.1 Percolation Theory

In a complex morphological structure, that is a structure which may consist of a stem (simplex or complex) and a derivational affix for derivation or of two stems, two words or a stem and a word for composition etc., we consider as *Head* the component that converts the grammatical category (i.e. POS) of the structure. In MG, it has been attested that a derivational suffix operates as *head* in the structure composed of a stem and that suffix [10]. Since derivational suffixes are always situated in the right position of a structure, we speak of the *right-hand head rule,* as we see in the example of γράφ-ω 'to write' (γráf-o) > γραφ-ικ-ός/-ή/-ó (γraf-ik-ós/-í/-ó) 'graphic' (Fig. 2)[2]. Conversely, derivational prefixes cannot affect the category of a complex structure γράφ-ω 'to write' > περι-γράφ-ω 'to describe' *(γráf-o > peri-γráf-o)* (Fig. 2) and thus are considered non-heads while, according to the right-hand head rule, the stem takes the head position in this case. This rule, however, does not apply to inflection, where the stem takes the head position, since an inflectional suffix cannot change the structure's category.

Next to the transposition of the category, there are also other features that come along either from the head or the non-head parts such as morpho-syntactic and semantic features. This feature-transferring has been largely known as *percolation theory* [4, 9, 12] according to which the resulting structure is a merger of the features of the parts it consists of. In our example, γραφ-ικ-, the head -ικ- is responsible for the Adj category and this Adj semantically extends the action of the non-head γράφ-, which makes its own semantic contribution to the structure.

With respect to the meaning of a word, and assuming that a word's pragmatic meaning comes from its stem, it has to be noted that the merger of meanings of a complex stem's components is many times not their literal sum but is related to pragmatics or symbolic

---

[2] The stems περι-γραφ- and γραφ-ικ-, in Fig. 2, transmit their lexical meanings of 'to describe' and 'graphic' to the resulting lexemes περι-γράφ-ω and γραφ-ικ-ός/-ή/-ó respectively.

transformations. In the case of γραφ-, for example, which means 'to write' and περι- which means 'around' the resulting meaning of their combination is not far from 'to write around something' i.e. 'to describe', although the act of describing may also have an oral sense. More characteristically, as Ralli [10] exemplifies, the word εκ-πομπή (ek-pombi), which literally means 'transmission' *from (ek-)* a medium, has also come to mean 'radio or tv programme' out of its connotations.

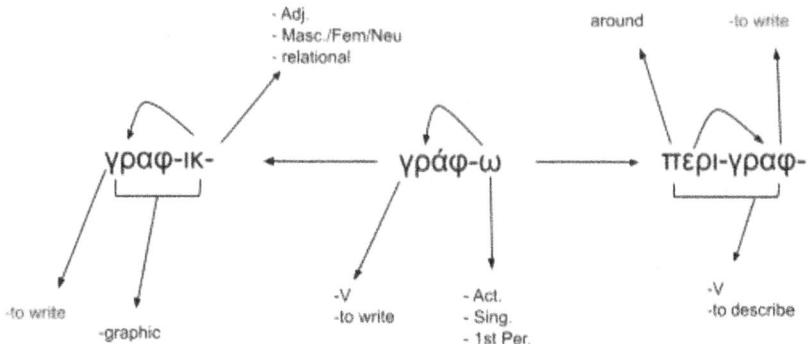

Fig. 2. The percolation of features between γραφ-ικ- < γράφ-ω > περι-γραφ- (Color figure online)

In our paradigm, we will model the input stem (i.e. γραφ-) not to transmit its pragmatic meaning (red letters in Fig. 2) to a resulting complex stem (i.e. περι-γραφ- or γραφ-ικ), because this is infiltrated each time by the new context it is put into. On the contrary, we will allow the derivational meaning of affixes to take place in the resulting structure (i.e. περι- or -ικ-) to show their contribution to the reformation of lexical sense.

Table 1. The features of each component assigned to each grammatical category (POS)

		POS category		
		Verb	Noun	Adjective
Component + Features	**Stem**	Sense POS	Sense POS Gender	Sense POS Gender
	DerSuf	Derivational meaning POS	Derivational meaning Gender POS	Derivational meaning Gender POS
	Prefix	Derivational meaning	Derivational meaning	Derivational meaning
	InfSuf	Number Person Voice	Case Number	Case Number

To set the framework of rules of the aforementioned process, in Table 1, we assign the features of each component of a structure to the appropriate grammatical category and in Table 2, we depict which features each 1st component transmits when combined with the 2nd.

Table 2. The features transmitted for each combination of 1st and 2nd component

		2nd component					
		Base	Prefixed stem	Suffixed stem	DerSuf	Pref	InfSuf
1st component + Features transmitted	**DerSuf**	POS, Gender, Derivational meaning					
	Prefix	Derivational meaning					
	InfSuf	Person, Number, Voice, Case					
	Stem				Sense	Sense, POS, Gender	Sense, POS, Gender

3   Ontological Analysis

In this section, we ontologically represent aspects of meaning based on the morphological analysis of Sect. 2. The ontology we use, as in previous research, is the MMoOn[3], a specialized model for the representation of language morphology. However, here, we have taken a different approach than before: we extend the core model only where a specific-language class is missing. In previous modeling [14, 15, 17], we had extended every class of the MMoOn core model as an ell_schema class, following the German or Hebrew schemas modeling with the expectation that MMoOn develops to a modular, syncretic, multi-lingual ontology. We have seen that this approach makes the ontology too heavy, hardening significantly tasks of querying and reasoning. On the other hand, just by extending the ontology only where the language has a specific difference would be sufficient for comparing multilingual schemas, provided that our *extended schema instance* is used by the community as a basis for other languages as well.

As we have seen in the previous section, morphological structures carry the characteristics of their constituents, which have had in previous stages, a process known as *percolation*. The process basically operates at two levels: at the stem and the lexeme level. In order to capture the behaviour of the different characteristics over this transferring process at different levels, we will analyze here three cases:

1. from a simplex stem (base) to a simple lexeme ($\gamma\rho\alpha\varphi$- > $\gamma\rho\acute{\alpha}\varphi$-$\omega$)

---

[3] The ttl file of the MMoOn model can be reached here: https://github.com/MMoOn-Project/MMoOn/blob/master/core.ttl.

2. from a simplex stem to a complex (prefixed) stem (γραφ- > περι-γραφ-)
3. from a simplex stem to a complex (suffixed) stem (γραφ- > γραφ-ικ-)

In what follows, is the analysis of the percolation theory in all three cases, according to the rules defined in Tables 1 and 2 of Sect. 2. All cases are represented ontologically in Figs. (3, 4, and 5 respectively). In all Figures, the dashed arrows represent the desired automation of feature-transferring throughout the procedure.

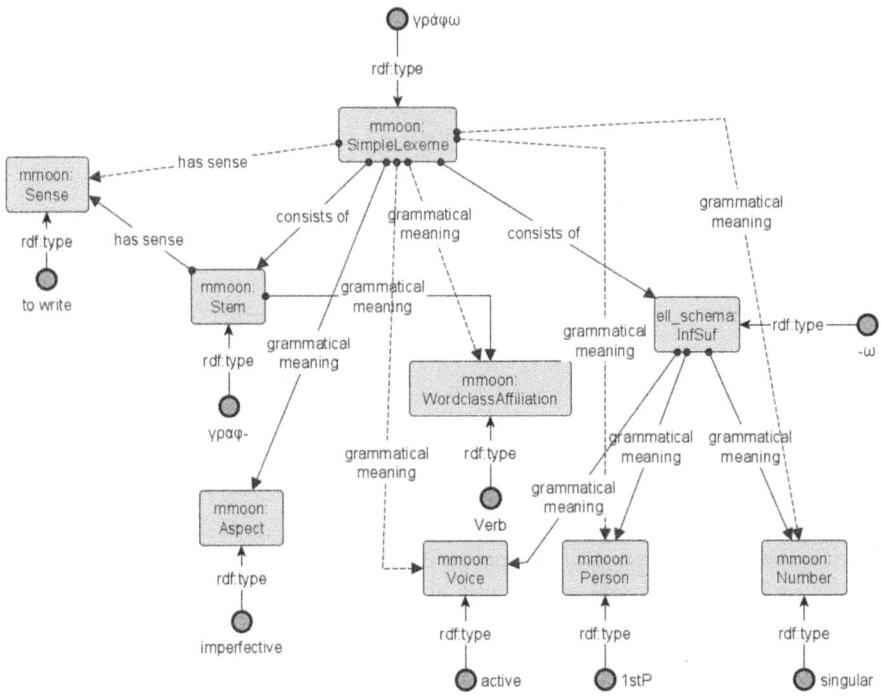

Fig. 3. The percolation process of γραφ- > γράφ-ω

In Fig. 3 (case 1), the simplex stem (base) γραφ- is the head of the structure, since the lack of a derivational suffix excludes the right-head principle. The stem transmits its grammatical category (Verb) along with its lexical sense 'to write' to the final structure γράφ-ω. On the other hand, the inflectional suffix -ω transmits all its features (Person, Number, Voice) to the final verbal lexeme. It is worth noting that the value *imperfective* stresses the underspecified *Aspect* feature of the word γράφω, as this cannot be associated with a particular morph in γράφω.

In Fig. 4 (case 2), we proceed from the simplex stem (base) γραφ- to a prefixed stem περι-γραφ-. All features of the stem γραφ- (POS category) are transmitted along with the derivational meaning of the prefix περι- to the prefixed stem περιγραφ-, excluding the transfer of the input stem's sense as it is (γραφ- 'to write'), because this is infiltrated and reformed to a new verbal concept (περιγραφ- 'to describe'). Here, we should also note that according to previous analysis [14], it would be more economical to attach a prefix to the simple lexeme γράφω i.e. γράφω > περι-γράφω, because this would require two levels rather than decomposing it into stems i.e. γραφ- > περι-γράφ- > περιγράφ-ω, which would require three levels.

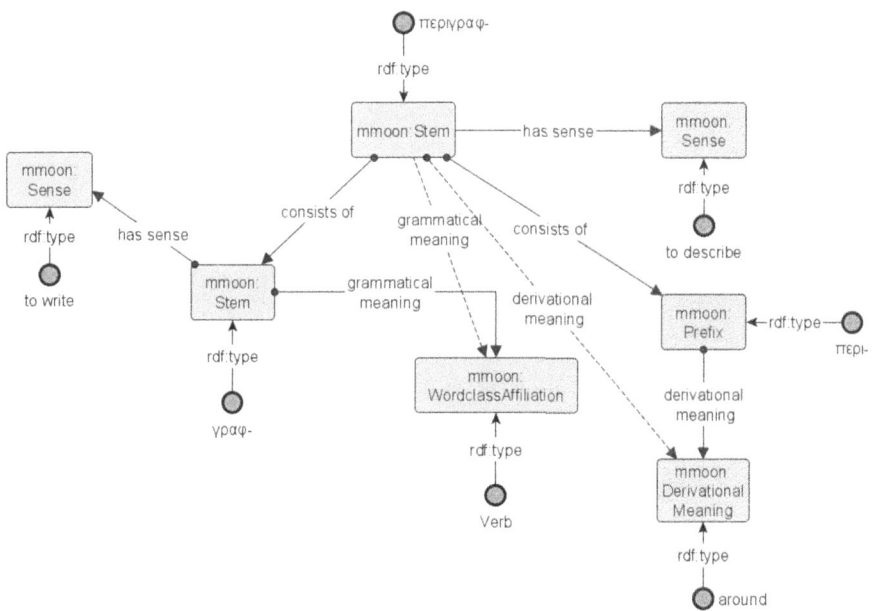

Fig. 4. The percolation process of γραφ- > περι-γραφ-

However, it seems that the stem-based approach is more consistent in terms of a generic derivational theory of word formation than a theory that has to alternate between stem-based and word-based derived words. We also think that a consistent and less complex approach would be more useful and functional in automatic word formation pipelines for analyzing already imported lexical data in the ontology morphologically.

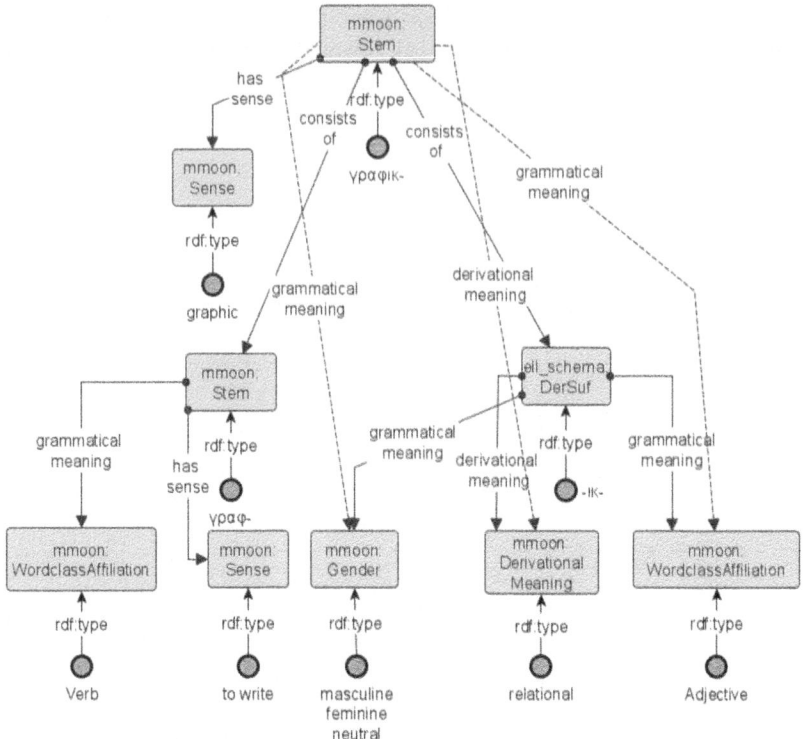

Fig. 5. The percolation process of *γραφ- > γραφ-ικ-*

In Fig. 5 (case 3), we proceed from a simplex stem to a suffixed stem (i.e. *γραφ- > γραφ-ικ*). Here, a derivational suffix applies the right-head principle, transmitting POS, Gender and derivational meaning to the resulting structure. On the other hand, the transfer of the sense of the stem *γραφ-* 'to write' is actually reformed in terms of lexical sense by *-ικ-* to the adjectival entity *γραφ-ικ-* 'graphic' and thus it is excluded here again.

In all three cases, we showed that the transportation of characteristics (i.e. features) is ideally made automatically (resp. Dashed arrows), applying the percolation theory into the ontology. To make this happen, we use OWL syntax to guarantee consistency in the ontological statements. More specifically, we create specific object properties (OPs) to define special affix and stem statements. That is, three subproperties of the *consists of affix* OP (*consistsOfDerSuf, consistsOfDerPref, consistsOfInfSuf*) and other three subproperties of the *consists of stem* OP (*consistsOfStemOfASufStem, consistsOf-StemOfAPrefStem* and *consistsOfStemOfAWord*) (Table 3). These three subproperties have as ranges three new stem entities, *StemOfASufStem, StemOfAPrefStem* and *Ste-mOfAWord* respectively. Each of these new Stem entities marks its respective function ("headness") in the percolation process: a *StemOfASufStem* takes part in the creation of a new suffixed stem (*γραφ- > γραφ-ικ-*) as non-head, a *StemOfAPrefStem* takes part in the creation of a prefixed stem (*γράφ- > περι-γράφ-*) as head and a *StemOfAWord* takes part in the creation of a word (*γραφ- > γράφ-ω*) also as head. In order to automate the percolation of features from one entity to the other, we subsume these OPs to the subproperties of the *has meaning* OP (*grammatical meaning, derivational meaning* and *has sense*) by creating appropriate *chain object property axioms* (Table 4).

Table 3. ell_schema subproperties of consists of affix and consists of stem OPs.

ell-schema object property	Domain	Range	Subproperty of
consistsOfDerSuf	Stem	ell_schema:DerSuf	consists of affix
consistsOfDerPref	Stem	ell_schema:DerPref	consists of affix
consistsOfInfSuf	Word	ell_schema:InfSuf	consists of affix
consistsOfStemOfASufStem	Stem	ell_schema:StemOfASufStem	consists of stem
consistsOfStemOfAPrefStem	Stem	ell_schema:StemOfAPrefStem	consists of stem
consistsOfStemOfAWord	Word	ell_schema:StemOfAWord	consists of stem

Table 4. Chain property axioms of the subproperties of meaning OP

Object property	SuperProperty Of (Chain)
grammatical meaning	consistsOfInfSuf o 'grammatical meaning' SubPropertyOf: 'grammatical meaning' consistsOfDerSuf o 'grammatical meaning' SubPropertyOf: 'grammatical meaning' consistsOfStemOfAWord o 'grammatical meaning' SubPropertyOf: 'grammatical meaning' consistsOfStemOfAPrefStem o 'grammatical meaning' SubPropertyOf: 'grammatical meaning'
has sense	consistsOfStemOfAWord o 'has sense' SubPropertyOf: 'has sense'
derivational meaning	consistsOfDerSuf o 'derivational meaning' SubPropertyOf: 'derivational meaning' consistsOfDerPref o 'derivational meaning' SubPropertyOf: 'derivational meaning'

Following are the statements either asserted or inferred (inf.) for each of the three cases[4]:

1. **ell_schema:γραφ- a ell_schema:stemOfAWord;**
   mmoon:has sense mmoon:to write;
   mmoon:grammatical meaning mmoon:Verb.
   ell_schema:-ω a ell_schema:InfSuf;
   mmoon:grammatical meaning mmoon:singular, mmoon:active, mmoon:1stP.
   mmoon:γράφω a mmoon:SimpleLexeme;

---

[4] The version of the ttl file of the MG schema and inventory can be reached here: https://github.com/nvasilogamvrakis/mmoon_project/blob/main/inventory/ell_inventory_04.owl.

ell_schema:consistsOfStemOfAWord ell_schema:γραφ-;
ell_schema:consistsOfInfSuf ell_schema:-ω;
mmoon:has sense mmoon:to write; (inf.)
mmoon:grammatical meaning mmoon:Verb; (inf.)
mmoon:grammatical meaning mmoon:singular, mmoon:active, mmoon:1stP. (inf.)

2. **ell_schema:γραφ- a ell_schema:stemOfAPrefStem**;
   mmoon:has sense mmoon:to write;
   mmoon:grammatical meaning mmoon:Verb.
   mmoon:περί- a mmoon:Prefix;
   mmoon:derivational meaning mmoon:around.
   mmoon:περιγράφ- a mmoon:Stem;
   ell_schema:consistsOfStemOfAPrefStem ell_schema:γραφ-;
   ell_schema:consistsOfDerPref mmoon:περι-;
   mmoon:has sense mmoon:to describe;
   mmoon:grammatical meaning mmoon:Verb; (inf.)
   mmoon:derivational meaning mmoon:around. (inf.)

3. **ell_schema:γραφ- a ell_schema:stemOfASufStem;**
   mmoon:has sense mmoon:to write;
   mmoon:grammatical meaning mmoon:Verb.
   ell_schema:-ικ- a ell_schema:DerSuf;
   mmoon: derivational meaning mmoon:relational;
   mmoon:grammatical   meaning   mmoon:masculine/feminine/neutral[5]   ,
   mmoon:Adjective.
   mmoon:γραφικ- a mmoon:Stem;
   ell_schema:consistsOfStemOfASufStem ell_schema:γραφ-;
   ell_schema:consistsOfDerSuf ell_schema:-ικ-;
   mmoon:has sense mmoon:graphic;
   mmoon:grammatical   meaning   mmoon:masculine/feminine/neutral,
   mmoon:Adjective; (inf.)
   mmoon: derivational meaning mmoon:relational. (inf.)

If we notice the three statements in bold of cases 1, 2 and 3, we can understand the necessity and the usage of the three functions of a Stem as *StemOfAWord*, *StemfOAPrefStem* and *StemOfASufStem*, the form of which takes the stem *γραφ-* each time. Indeed, the latter should behave differently when combined with *-ω*, *περι-* and *-ικ-*. In both *γράφ-ω* and *περι-γραφ-*, the original stem predominates over the inflectional suffix *-ω* and the prefix *περι-* and hence it should transmit, next to others, its verbal category to the resulting structure *γράφω* and *περιγραφ-* respectively. On the other hand, in the case of *γραφ-ικ*, the stem *γραφ-* subsumes to the prevalence of the derivational suffix *-ικ-*, which gives its adjectival category to the final structure *γραφικ-*.

---

[5] Here, the three gender values are used excessively because all three are possible.

4 Conclusion and Future Research

In the previous analysis, we have dealt with aspects of semantics of morph atoms and how these can be transformed and integrated into the resulting morphological structures. Initially, we divided the two basic aspects of meaning lexical and grammatical, defining the former as more conceptual and extra-linguistic and the latter pertaining to syntactic frames and intra-linguistic processes. At the same time, based on the cases of affixes and confixes, we pointed out that there are also more abstract types of meaning, i.e. derivational, which stands between the lexical and the grammatical. Afterwards, we focused on the transfer of features that takes place over the combination of two morphological components, known as *percolation theory*, which was explored on three different derivational cases. All cases were described and graphically represented to gain a clear view of how they would best fit into the ontology. Then, we extended the MMoOn ontology with appropriate owl axioms so that the percolation process is performed consistently and in an automated way at all levels and according to the rules we specified. In the research to come, more aspects of morphological semantics are to be explored and tested in the ontology.

References

1. Bybee, J., et al.: The Evolution of Grammar: Tense, Aspect, and Modality in the Languages of the World. University of Chicago Press, Chicago (1994)
2. Bybee, J.L.: Semantic substance vs. contrast in the development of grammatical meaning. Annu. Meet. Berkeley Linguist. Soc. **14**, 247–264 (1988). https://doi.org/10.3765/bls.v14i0.1785
3. Carnie, A.: Syntax: A Generative Introduction. Wiley-Blackwell (2012)
4. Di Sciullo, A.M., Williams, E.: On the Definition of the Word. MIT Press, Cambridge (1987)
5. Giannoulopoulou, G.: Morphosemantic comparison between affixes and confixes in Modern Greek and Italian (in Greek). Aristotle University of Thessaloniki (AUTH), School of Italian Language and Literature (1999)
6. Heine, B. et al.: Grammaticalization: A Conceptual Framework (1991)
7. Kroeger, P.R.: Analyzing Grammar: An Introduction. Cambridge University Press (2005). https://doi.org/10.1017/CBO9780511801679
8. Lieber, R.: Morphology and Lexical Semantics. Cambridge University Press, Cambridge (2004). https://doi.org/10.1017/CBO9780511486296
9. Lieber, R.: On the Organization of the Lexicon. MIT (1980)
10. Ralli, A.: Morfologia (in Greek). Patakis, Athens (2005)
11. Ramchand, G.: Grammatical vs. lexical formatives. In: Hornstein, N. et al. (eds.) Syntactic Structures after 60 Years, p. 18. Mouton de Gruyter (2018)
12. Selkirk, E.: The Syntax of Words. MIT Press, Cambridge (1982)
13. Svenonius, P.: Generalized applicatives: Reassessing the lexical–functional divide. Theor. Linguist. **40**, 3–4 (2014). https://doi.org/10.1515/tl-2014-0023
14. Vasilogamvrakis, N., Koliopoulou, M., Sfakakis, M., Giannoulopoulou, G.: Testing the word-based model in the ontological analysis of modern Greek derivational morphology. In: Chiusano, S., et al. New Trends in Database and Information Systems. ADBIS 2022. Communications in Computer and Information Science, vol. 1652, pp. 572–584. Springer, Cham (2022). https://doi.org/10.1007/978-3-031-15743-1_52

15. Vasilogamvrakis, N., Sfakakis, M.: A morpheme-based paradigm for the ontological analysis of Modern Greek derivational morphology. In: MTSR 2021. Communications in Computer and Information Science (2021)
16. Vasilogamvrakis, N., Sfakakis, M.: Ontological modeling of lists for modern Greek derivation. In: Garoufallou, E., Sartori, F. (eds.) Metadata and Semantic Research. MTSR 2023. Communications in Computer and Information Science, vol. 2048, pp. 181–192. Springer, Cham (2024). https://doi.org/10.1007/978-3-031-65990-4_16
17. Vasilogamvrakis, N., et al.: Ontological modeling of morphological entities, allomorphy and representation in Modern Greek derivation. Presented at the DeriMo 2023, Dubrovnik, Croatia, 5 October 2023

The Semantics of Emotion: Exploring Synonym Rings to Evaluate Emotive Contexts in Translations Across Sinhala and English

Malithi Alahapperuma$^{(\boxtimes)}$ and Andreas Vlachidis

University College London, London, UK
{malithi.alahapperuma.20,a.vlachidis}@ucl.ac.uk

Abstract. Each language has its own body of emotion vocabulary. It is also possible to map emotion terms of one language to similar terms in another language. However, the mere existence of similar terms across languages does not guarantee that emotion concepts being translated are identical. Emotion terms can evoke different feelings in different individuals and often embody the societal and cultural norms of a linguistic community. Hence, conveying emotions across languages poses a unique challenge in translation. This paper explores the role of knowledge organisation systems and synonym rings for enabling better understanding and encoding of emotionally weighted material in translations. The study uses synonym rings to present emotion vocabulary across Sinhala and English and employs contextual evidence and literary text translations to analyse and evaluate the findings. The research identifies and utilises three pillars of inquiry: (1) Cognition, (2) linguistics, and (3) socio-cultural factors to explore the ways in which individuals perceive and express emotions across Sinhala and English.

Keywords: Emotion Semantics · Knowledge Organisation System (KOS) · Synonym Ring (SR) · Sinhala language · Low-resource Languages

1 Introduction

In everyday settings, 'emotions' are peacefully conveyed through our vocabulary, typically, without causing much cognitive effort or overhead. However, unpacking the layers of meaning that underlie the concept 'emotions' may prove to be more challenging. To begin with, what is an 'emotion'? Is it purely a mental phenomenon? Where does one draw the boundary between mental and physical reactions to emotions? These questions are only the beginning of a set of ideas that complicate the notion of emotions. The concept becomes much more complex as we begin to factor in language, since, despite being a mental phenomenon, emotions are only identified with language 'labels'.

© The Author(s), under exclusive license to Springer Nature Switzerland AG 2025
M. Sfakakis et al. (Eds.): MTSR 2024, CCIS 2331, pp. 349–362, 2025.
https://doi.org/10.1007/978-3-031-81974-2_29

Understanding emotion perception and expression across languages is even more challenging. Often, it is possible to find equivalent terms in two languages that correspond to the same emotion. However, there is no guarantee that the emotion a person feels when they hear the word for that emotion in a given language, is the same emotion felt by a speaker of another language when they hear the name for the same emotion. Jackson et al. [10] elaborate on this idea:"Translation dictionaries, for example, suggest that the English word *love* can be equated with the Turkish word *sevgi* and the Hungarian word *szerelem*. But does this mean that the concept of "love" is the same in English, Turkish, and Hungarian?". Jackson et al. make it clear that translating emotion concepts across languages transcends beyond surface-level sense-making and can often lead to a change of meaning during the translation process. Based on readings by Jackson et.al., as well as others who stressed the importance of exploring emotion perception in multilingual settings [13,14], understanding where and how emotions get lost in translation proves to be a valuable area of research.

This study looks at the role of Knowledge Organisation Systems (KOSs), focusing on the contributions of Synonym Rings (SRs) as a language representation tool, for organising emotion concepts and enhancing contextual understanding across translations in Sinhala[1] and English. By an examination of synonym arrangements for the emotions 'happy', 'love' and 'desire', the study suggests that SRs can be used to better understand and encode the gain/loss of emotional contexts across translation, specifically within the Sinhala-English linguistic setting. The remainder of the paper elaborates on our approach and findings, and is organised as follows; the second section discusses the background to the study and key research, the third section discusses the methodological approaches, sections four and five present the findings and analysis, and the sixth section gives concluding remarks.

2   Literature Review

The current body of literature on emotions spans a wide field of disciplines. From philosophy and psychology to computer science, each subject area has attempted to understand the phenomenon of emotions that is core to human existence [12]. However, despite the many efforts made, Fox [6] writes that there may not exist a "scientific consensus on the fundamental nature of emotions".

2.1   Emotions, Language, and Multilingualism

Edward Sapir and Benjamin Whorf in the Sapir-Whorf hypothesis, put forward the idea that the language people speak can affect the way they think [7,15]. While this hypothesis itself has gone through debate, the existing body of scholarly work agree on the pivotal role that language plays on thought and

---

[1] Sinhala is an official language of Sri Lanka. For more information, see https://www.britannica.com/topic/Sinhalese-language.

emotion. The discussion on language and emotion becomes far more thought-provoking when looked at through the lens of multilingualism. Early publications by Wierzbicka [17] and Goddard [8] lay an ideal theoretical foundation to concepts underlying emotions and multilingualism. Wierzbicka asks, "Why should human psychology be interpreted through the prism of English rather than through that of other languages?".

Jackson et al. [10] note that languages may have unique terms for emotions which may not have translations in other languages. Their study notes that "the German word *Sehnsucht* refers to a strong desire for an alternative life and has no direct translation in English". This raises some important questions. Does the lack of a term simply imply that the emotion concept *Sehnsucht* will have no meaning for English speakers? If a translation for *Sehnsucht* does not exist in English, is there no way in which this idea can be conveyed to English speakers? In a discussion of emotion words and concepts, Pavlenko [14] writes,

> At present, no consensus exists in emotion research on the relationship between bodily experiences, words, and concepts, on the structure and nature of emotion concepts, on the structure of the emotion lexicon, and on methods of selection and analysis of emotion terms.

Based on these preliminary readings by Jackson et al. [10], Ng et al. [12], Wierzbicka [17], and others, three distinct pillars of inquiry begin to emerge in the study of the semantics of emotion in a cross-linguistic setting: (1) Cognition, (2) linguistics, and (3) socio-cultural factors. Looking at cognition is important to understand if there are psychological features that enable individuals to process emotions differently with each language they interact. A language-based inquiry allows to see whether there are features specific to languages that facilitate emotions to be perceived in a specific manner. An inquiry of socio-cultural factors retrieves the way in which factors unique to a given linguistic community may shape the way emotions are processed and perceived. Hence, in order to allow a thorough yet systematic investigation, these three pillars of inquiry will be utilised throughout this study.

2.2   Different Methodological Approaches to Evaluating the Semantics of Emotions

Research in the field of emotion semantics takes different approaches to selecting, analysing, and synthesising emotion concepts and terms. In a study that matches semantic values between languages, Ploux and Ji [16] take a spatial mapping approach to map semantic similarities between English and French. While the study is not particularly focused in the semantics of emotion, the spatial mapping approach is worth exploring, considering its relevance to our work. The researchers describe their model as "a construction process designed to reproduce cognitive functions and their extensions". The study employs three databases for constructing a model of 'cliques': a French synonym database, an English synonym database, and a translation database. 'Cliques' are a set of terms related to each other by synonymy, which are derived by a spatial mapping of the words in the synonym databases. Similar terms that cluster together for a given word form a 'clique'. The authors note that 'cliques' are different to 'synsets' in that synsets are only a group of synonyms for a given label for a concept. Ji at al. [11] further elaborate on cliques as follows:

A clique is a mathematical term in graph theory meaning a maximum, complete subgraph. If *w1* has *w2* and *w3* as its members and vice versa for *w2* and *w3*, then *w1*, *w2* and *w3* form a clique. Otherwise, if say *w3* has only *w1* as its member, they fail to form a clique. If *w1*, *w2*, *w3*, and *w4* form another clique, it 'absorbs' the clique *w1*, *w2*, *w3*, resulting in only one clique.

In order to evaluate a suitable KOS for this study, we looked at various tools and representations used in the field of information studies. Information studies identifies "controlled vocabularies" as a "standardized and organized" way of arranging words and phrases that allow to see the relationship between words contained in the vocabularies [4]. Zeng [18] discusses KOSs whose functions include "controlling synonyms" and "establishing explicit semantic relationships". According to Zeng, KOSs include "lists, authority files, gazetteers, synonym rings, taxonomies and classification schemes, thesauri, and ontologies". These different systems denote the different levels of relationships among words.

KOSs cover a variety of needs and tasks in the storage and retrieval of semantics, depending on the complexity and functionality of the KOS. A system with complex structure provides greater functionality, while more simplistic systems serve specific purposes. For instance, a glossary or a dictionary is able to eliminate ambiguity in representing semantic information, while however, being constrained in representing relationships between terms. A taxonomy is able to provide hierarchical relationships between terms, while being constrained in terms of the information that can be provided about the associative relationships between terms [18]. When representing cross-linguistic semantics of emotion, the KOS needs to be able to convey the complex and often ambiguous relationship between synonymous emotion terms within a language, as well as across languages. However, the semantics of emotion do not entail encoding any hierarchical information. As such SRs appear to be a clear choice in mapping emotion terms, specifically as SRs allow working with ambiguity that emotions present. Zeng particularly note that "sometimes the rings also contain terms that are more general or specific than other terms on the ring". Since emotion words and their synonyms are ideally a set of "equivalent yet different" collection of terms, SRs are a fitting choice for this study.

Based on the above readings and evaluations, we decided to use SRs as the most appropriate KOS for managing the conceptual arrangements and semantic variability of emotions. Given the multilingual objectives of this study, SRs offered the most suitable support for mapping equivalent terms between Sinhala and English, helping us mitigate vocabulary variability. More complex knowledge organisation systems were deemed less suitable due to their potential to increase vocabulary sparsity via broader and narrower term relationships.

2.3   Researching the Semantics of Emotions Within the Constraints Presented by a Low-Resource Language

Sinhala is a low-resource language with sparse digitised resources for text analysis, and limited compatibility with digital tools. As a result, it is useful to have a sense of what it is like to work with a low-resource language.

In a study that experiments with Arabic to create language resources for low-resource languages, El-Haj et al. [5] emphasise the importance of language resources to execute computational methods to study languages. Looking at the Arabic language, El-Haj et al. note the absence of capitalisation in Arabic as an intrinsic feature of the language which makes the creation of resources challenging. They also note that Arabic corpora have shown "a bias towards religious terminology". Arabic makes a good comparator language for this study, since similar to Arabic, Sinhala has a script of its own that does not include capitalisation. Further, the Sinhala language is also influenced by Buddhist concepts and terminology [1]. Uncovering these influences contributes to better understanding of the third pillar of inquiry, socio-cultural influences on emotion perception. Especially in a backdrop where the state-of-the-art in language research is driven by languages such as English, it is necessary to explore more ways to bring insights from under-represented languages. This allows to diversify the way emotion perception is understood within language research.

3   Method

This study was conducted in five steps. Step 1 is the selection of text corpora, step 2 is the selection of emotion terms, and step 3 includes the creations of SRs. In step 4, for each of the emotion terms selected in step 2, we extract the Key Words in Context (KWICs). Step 5 includes comparing the text data with the SRs to derive analyses and conclusions.

Step 1: Selection of Text Corpora
Despite the need to use large text corpora, due to challenges in collating and analysing Sinhala language material, this study utilised one English text and its Sinhala translation. Careful consideration was placed on seeking a text corpus that is heavy with emotional content. A literary text seemed most suitable for this purpose, and the English text of The Alchemist by Paulo Coelho was selected as the key text for analysis. A published Sinhala translation of The Alchemist is available, which made the text much fitting for this study. Particular attention was paid to selecting a text that had a published Sinhala version, since this implied that the Sinhala text used for analysis would have gone through a reliable editing process.

Step 2: Selection of Key Emotion Terms and Synonyms
Deriving from the semantic atlas and cliques-based approach of Ploux and Ji [16], this research also takes a word mapping-based method to analysing emotion concepts. By using Voyant Tools[2], an online text analysis tool, key emotion terms

---

[2] To access Voyant Tools, please see: https://voyant-tools.org/.

from The Alchemist were extracted. Voyant Tools was specifically selected given that its functionalities supported Sinhala at the same level as they did English. The terms were selected based on the frequency of occurrence and the emotional gravity of the term. Once key words were decided, a set of Sinhala and English synonyms was developed for each key word. For each key word, synonyms for English were be obtained from WordNet[3] and Sinhala synonyms were taken from the Madura Online dictionary[4].

Step 3: Creation of SRs
As reasoned in Sect. 2.1, SRs are the most fitting choice to represent emotion terms and synonyms for this study. For each emotion term selected, one SR each was created for English and Sinhala. In order to map the synonyms across the two languages, a numbering system is used, where the set of synonyms within the same semantic field across the two languages is represented by the same number.

Step 4: Extracting the Context of Key Words for English and Sinhala
For each of the selected emotion key words in English, their contexts were extracted using the Voyant Tools' KWIC panel. The Sinhala translations of the phrases were manually retrieved from the print text. KWICs are used to derive contextual information about how each word appears in the text, in an attempt to understand how for each of English and Sinhala, the selected emotion key word might convey similar or different emotive concepts.

Step 5: Comparison and Analysis
Lastly, the KWICs were analysed against the SRs to derive meaningful insights regarding the semantics of emotion in translation. The analysis is specifically tied to the three pillars of inquiry established in Sect. 2.1 of this study.

4   Analysis and Findings

As outlined in step 2 of the methodology, based on the frequency of occurrence, 'happy', 'love' and 'desire' were selected as the three key emotion terms for the analysis. Only the root form of the terms were considered, terms such as 'happily' or 'loved' were not considered.

4.1   Happy

Synonym Rings
The Sinhala and English SRs for 'happy' are given in Fig. 1. The same SRs can be alternatively represented in tabular format, as shown in Table 1.

In Fig. 1, WordNet synset included four synonyms for 'happy', denoting four different meaning fields. In the English SR, these terms have been numbered 1 to 4 to denote the four different meanings. For the Sinhala SR, the term 'සතුටු'

---

[3] To access WordNet, please see: http://wordnetweb.princeton.edu/perl/webwn.
[4] To access Madura Online, please see: https://www.maduraonline.com/.

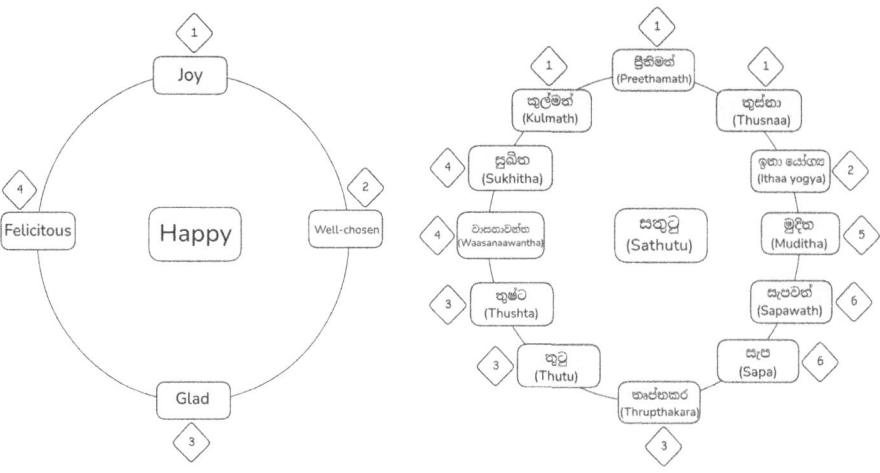

Fig. 1. Synonym Rings (SRs) for 'happy'

Table 1. Tabular rendering of the Synonym Rings (SRs) for 'happy'

English	Sinhala
Joy	ප්‍රීතිමත් (*Preethimath*), කුල්මත් (*Kulmath*), තුස්නා (*Thusnaa*)
Glad	තෘප්තකර (*Thrupthakara*), තුටු (*Thutu*), තුෂ්ට (*Thushta*)
Well-chosen	ඉතා යෝග්‍ය (*Ithaa yogya*)
Felicitous	වාසනාවන්ත (*Waasanaawantha*), සුඛිත (*Sukhitha*)
No equivalent English entry. Both of these terms overlap with the English term 'luxurious'.	සැපවත් (*Sapawath*), සැප (*Sapa*)
No equivalent English entry. This term overlaps with the English term 'delight'.	මුදිත (*Muditha*)

(*Sathutu*) was used as the headword, as it is the most common word to identify the emotion concept 'happy'. Sinhala terms that fall within the same semantic fields as English have been numbered accordingly. The Sinhala SR included three terms (numbered 5 and 6) which did not have a corresponding semantic field in the English SR.

Two of these terms '**සැප**' (*Sapa*) and '**සැපවත්**' (*Sapawath*), loosely translate to 'luxurious'. The Sinhala SR for 'happy' includes the term '**මුදිත**' (*Muditha*) which has Buddhist religious connotations of 'delight' (entry number 5 in the SR).

KWICs Analysis

The term 'happy' appeared in 20 instances in the English text. The Sinhala headword for 'happy' (including terms with different word forms of the headword) has been used in 14 occasions. There were 6 instances where substitute terms from within and outside the Sinhala SR were used by the translator. In two of the instances, the terms have been substituted by synonyms within the semantic fields 'joy' and 'glad'. By KWICs analysis it was noted that both these instances referred to a sense of being 'satisfied' or 'glad'. The translator's choice of substitution here is justifiable and can be considered a more fitting decision than choosing the generic term for 'happy'. Additional Sinhala word substitutions also included 'උද්දාමය' (*Uddaamaya*), which indicates a sense of extreme joy, and 'සන්තෘෂ්ටිය' (*Santhrushtiya*), which is a more formal term of the headword 'සතුටු' (*Sathutu*). Neither of these terms have been included in the Madura Online dictionary for 'happy', and hence, are not captured in the Sinhala SR. The word 'උද්දාමය' (*Uddaamaya*) could be stretching the sense of the meaning 'happy', but 'සන්තෘෂ්ටිය' (*Santhrushtiya*) is a word commonly used in formal settings. This word choice adds a formal sense of meaning to the narrative, and is considered fitting.

In the examples above, the Sinhala translator's use of the terms that are not captured in the SRs can be a result of a few factors. In terms of lexicography and information representation, this could be the result of the Madura Online dictionary not capturing the full breadth of Sinhala terms available for 'happy'. This is most likely the case for 'සන්තෘෂ්ටිය' (*Santhrushtiya*), which is a commonly used formal synonym for 'happy'. However, in the case of 'උද්දාමය' (*Uddaamaya*) it could be the case that the translator used his discretion to opt for a word that is not directly within the semantic field of 'happy' or its synonyms.

4.2   Love

Synonym Rings

Table 2 provides the entries of the SRs for 'love' in tabular format.[5]

The English SR uses 'love' as its headword. For the Sinhala SR, 'ආදරය' (*Aadaraya*) was selected as the headword, since this is the most direct and generic Sinhala term used to refer to the emotion identified as 'love' in English. WordNet's synset included 10 synonyms for 'love' (as given in the top 9 cells of the left column). Observing the synset, it was noted that these 10 synonyms fell into 9 semantic fields, with the synonym "sexual activities" having an overlap. The Sinhala SR showed more entries than the English one. However, most Sinhala terms fell within the same semantic fields as those in the English SR.

There were some unique entries noted in both English and Sinhala SRs. WordNet noted that 'love' in English could mean 'a score of zero in tennis or

---

[5] In this case, we have only provided the tabular format in order to optimise the space available.

Table 2. Tabular rendering of the Synonym Rings (SRs) for 'love'

English	Sinhala
Be in love	පෙම (*Pema*), ප්‍රේමය (*Premaya*), ආලය (*Aalaya*)
Enjoy	ඇල්ම (*Alma*), ඇලුම් කරනවා (*Alum karanawaa*), ප්‍රිය කරනවා (*Priya karanawaa*)
Have affection for	ආදරය දක්වනවා (*Aadaraya dakwanawaa*), ආදරය කරනවා (*Aadaraya karanawaa*)
Regard or affection	ස්නේහය (*Snehaya*), සාදරය (*Saadaraya*), සෙනෙහස (*Senehasa*), දයාව (*Dayaawa*)
Any object of affection or devotion	ආලය කරන වස්තුව (*Aalaya karana wasthuwa*)
Sexual desire	නුරා (*Nuraa*), රති (*rathi*), ශෘංගාර (*Shrungaara*)
Beloved person	පෙම්වතිය (*Pemwathiya*)
Make love, sexual activities	*No equivalent Sinhala term*
Score of zero in tennis or squash	*No equivalent Sinhala term*
No equivalent English entry	මෛත්‍රිය (*Maithriya*)
No equivalent English entries. These terms are not in common use.	ප්‍රාණය (*Praanaya*), සනා (*Sanaa*)

squash', which made a unique entry in the English SR. This Sinhala SR includes the term 'මෛත්‍රිය' (*Maithriya*), which is a concept that occurs in Buddhism which connotes 'compassion' or 'benevolence'. Sinhala entries also included terms that are not in popular use, which were difficult to place in a semantic field. However, they have still been included in the SR to capture all entries available in the Madura Online dictionary. It was also noted that while the Sinhala SR included terms in the semantic field of 'sexual desire', there were no terms to correspond to the English meaning of 'sexual activities' or the verb form.

KWICs Analysis

KWICs analysis showed that the term 'love' was used in 51 instances in the English text. The Sinhala KWICs revealed significant variation in the words used to denote 'love' across these 51 instances. The headword 'ආදරය' (*Aadaraya*) has been used only in 19 out of the 51 instances where the English term 'love' appeared. Some of the alternative terms used by the translator can be mapped back to the Sinhala SR. Word choices outside of the SR were also noted.

Synonyms 'ආලය' (*Aalaya*) and 'ප්‍රේමය' (*Premaya*), which have romantic connotations, most commonly replaced the headword 'love' in the Sinhala text. These substitutions were particularly found when the narrative was about the protagonist and his expression of feelings for his partner. As such, these lexical choices are much more suitable than the direct translation. The Sinhala KWICs also include a significant number of instances where 'ආදරේ' (*Aadare*), the low variety form of 'love', was used. Interestingly, all instances of the low variety term occur in conversations. Here, the translator's choice of the low variety term is a realistic reflection of the everyday language usage of Sinhala. Given that this term is not used in formal Sinhala, it was not available in the Madura Online dictionary, and hence has not been captured in the Sinhala SR.

4.3   Desire

Synonym Rings

Table 3 provides the entries of the SRs for 'desire', in tabular format.[6]

Table 3. Tabular rendering of the Synonym Rings (SRs) for 'desire'.

English	Sinhala
Want	රුසි (*Rusi*), රිසි (*Risi*), අභිරුචිය (*Abhiruchiya*), කැමැත්ත (*Kamaththa*), අභිලාෂය (*Abhilaashaya*), ආසාව (*Aasaawa*), පිරිය (*Piriya*), කැමති වෙනවා (*Kamathi wenawaa*), අභිමානය (*Abhimaanaya*), මනෝරථය (*Manorathaya*)
An inclination to want things	තණ්හාව (*Thanhaawa*), තෘෂ්ණාව (*Thrushnaawa*), ලෝභ (*Lobha*), ලොබ (*Loba*), ඇලියාව (*Aaliyaawa*)
Hope	අටිය (*Atiya*), අපේක්ෂාව (*Apekshaawa*), අභිප්‍රාය (*Abhipraaya*), පතනවා (*Pathanawaa*)
Express a desire for	ආසා කරනවා (*Aasaa karanawaa*), ඉල්ලා සිටිනවා (*Illaa sitinawaa*)
The feeling that accompanies an unsatisfied state	දොළ (*Dola*), දොළනවා (*Dolanawaa*), මනදොළ (*Manadola*)
Something that is desired	*No equivalent Sinhala term*
A term for 'sexual desire'. No equivalent English entry.	කාමය (*Kaamaya*)
No equivalent English entries. These terms are not in common use.	පුලනවා (*Pulanawaa*), තුස (*Thusa*), කලිමලි (*Kalimali*), ඉච්චාව (*Ichchaawa*)

The Sinhala SR for 'desire' had several entries compared to the English SR, where multiple entries were found for the concept 'want'. The Sinhala SR also included a unique entry, the term 'කාමය' (*Kaamaya*), which indicates the sense 'sexual desire'. Further, similar to the Sinhala SR for 'love', the Sinhala SR for 'desire' also includes a few terms that are not in common use, which could not be placed into a semantic field. As with the other SRs, the Sinhala SR for 'desire' also included terms such as 'ලෝභ' (*Lobha*) and 'තණ්හාව' (*Thanhaawa*) which are predominantly Buddhist religious terms used to address concepts of 'attachment'.

---

[6] In this case, we have only provided the tabular format in order to optimise the space available.

KWICs Analysis

There were seven instances where the term 'desire' was used in the English text. Repeating the trends seen in 'happy' and 'love', the headword for 'desire' has been used four times in the Sinhala text and is replaced by three different synonyms in the other three instances. All three substituted terms are available in the Sinhala SR.

In one of the substitutions, the original text reads, "when you really want something, it's because that desire originated in the soul of the universe" [3], where the author explicitly uses the phrase 'want something'. Here, the Sinhala translator continues with the sense of 'want' as opposed to using the term that indicates 'desire'.

5   Evaluating Findings: Perceiving Happy, Love, and Desire in Two Different Languages

This section collates the findings and analyses, staying in line with the initial three pillars of inquiry.

In our first pillar of inquiry, cognition, relevant literature brought to light how the language fluency of the speakers and their knowledge of the world shaped the way emotions were perceived. In going through the KWICs and the English text of The Alchemist, it was noted that the text contains a fairly 'heavy' style of writing. For example, consider this extract: 'The desert was full of men who earned their living based on the ease with which they could penetrate to the Soul of the World' [3]. This 'heavy' style of writing is resonated in the Sinhala translation. Further, the text makes references to concepts and terminology related to alchemy, omens, and life in the desert. Therefore, in order to truly understand the subtext of the narrative and grasp the emotional concepts, the reader requires a fairly strong understanding of the ideas in discussion and the language. In the context of Sinhala, the reader may also require the ability to understand the world and life outside the Sinhala-speaking world. These findings coincide with the body of research suggesting that the 'bilingual self maybe contextual', implying that the meanings gained/lost in translation could be due to each individual reader's level of comfort with the ideas being presented [2,9,13].

The key findings also exposed some of the ways in which language-based factors impact emotion perception, particularly when 'translating emotions'. Sections 4.1, 4.2, and 4.3 showed how the use of different lexical items in the Sinhala translation gave a more refined sense of meaning to certain references of the emotion concepts being translated. We infer that this may allow the Sinhala reader to perceive emotions with greater gravity and specificity than the English reader.

The KWICs and SRs also showed that Sinhala had a far greater number of synonyms available for each key word. This enabled the translator to draw from a diverse set of lexical choices, which further adds to the way in which readers perceive the written word. Pavlenko [14] notes that 'Cross- linguistic studies show that languages differ widely in the size of their emotion lexicons'. A reason for the considerable difference in the size of SR could be due to Sinhala having a richer emotion vocabulary. For example, the SR and KWICs for 'love' showed how English used the generic term 'love' to express romantic love, whereas Sinhala used a variety of terms that specifically denoted romantic love. These findings highlight the importance of lexical items available in a language to perceiving emotion.

Adding to linguistics factors, we also noted how in Sinhala, the low variety form of 'love' was used in conversational settings. Having a high variety and a low variety language form is a feature that is present in Sinhala but not in English. Using the low variety form of the word 'love' in selected instances better captured the context, thereby exposing the Sinhala reader to an aspect of the emotion concept that was not available to the English reader. Therefore, we infer that the speakers of diglossic languages may have access to more 'facets' of an emotion.

Along the socio-cultural pillar, a striking feature that was noted consistently across the Sinhala SRs was the existence of terms that give Buddhist religious connotations. These findings overlap with observations for Arabic, where El-Haj et al. [5] note that Arabic corpora may show 'a bias towards religious terminology'. The existence of terms with religious connotations across the three key words show a clear and strong impact of religion on Sinhalese emotion vocabulary, which can thereby impact the way in which these emotion concepts are perceived by language users.

For instance, the SRs for 'love' showed that the Sinhala term for 'love' has 'මෛත්‍රිය' (Maithriya), a term with Buddhist connotations of benevolence, as one of its synonyms. By virtue of the logic used by Ploux and Ji [16] to create cliques for their semantic atlas, it is possible to infer that if a Sinhala speaker associates the term for 'love' closely with a term that connotes 'benevolence' then this may lead the Sinhala speaker to associate 'love' with the concept that an 'English' speaker may identify as 'benevolence'. We then see a clear impact of socio-cultural (including religious) factors on perceiving emotions across Sinhala and English.

6   Conclusions and Limitations of the Study

Through a combination of information representation methods and readings of literary texts, we explored the use of SRs for evaluating emotive contexts across English-Sinhala translation. The study established three pillars of inquiry, (1) cognition, (2) linguistics, and (3) socio-cultural factors as pivotal in the way emotions are expressed and perceived. The findings suggest that SR arrangements can help better understand and encode emotional context changes across English-Sinhala translations.

Language-based factors significantly impact emotion perception in translation, as seen in how Sinhala uses various specific and contextually appropriate terms, in comparison with the use of the same terms in English. We also noted the impact of religion on how speakers of Sinhala may perceive the emotions that were discussed.

Two key limitations were noted in this study.

The Subjective Decisions That Went Into Developing the SRs: Given that the SRs were built entirely based on our understanding of English and Sinhala, the SRs face the risk of being skewed by subjective knowledge. However, since the conclusions derived in the study do not rely solely on the SRs, we decided to work with them, while acknowledging this limitation.

The Use of a Single Text for Analysis: This study uses a single text to make cross-linguistic comparisons, which has the ability to shift the analysis based on the quality of the text and its translation. In order to minimise the impact of this challenge on the research, we particularly worked with a text that had a published Sinhala translation. A larger range of literary texts and multiple translations could have led to more convincing results.

This study can be used as a basis to evaluate the semantics of emotions across a wider range of texts in Sinhala, or applied to different languages, particularly other low-resource languages. We believe that replicating the study across different languages and language families may uncover features specific to the translation of emotionally weighted material in different linguistic contexts.

Disclosure of Interests. The authors have no competing interests to declare that are relevant to the content of this article.

References

1. Ariyawansa, M.: The influence of Buddhist religion on sinhalese language. Bull. Deccan Coll. Res. Inst. **74**, 209–216 (2014), http://www.jstor.org/stable/26264699
2. Chen, P., Lin, J., Chen, B., Lu, C., Guo, T.: Processing emotional words in two languages with one brain: ERP and fMRI evidence from Chinese-English bilinguals. Cortex **71**, 34–48 (2015)
3. Coelho, P.: The Alchemist. HarperCollins (1992)
4. Cofield, M.: LibGuides: metadata basics: controlled vocabularies (2020). https://guides.lib.utexas.edu/metadata-basics/controlled-vocabs. Accessed 21 Aug 2020
5. El-Haj, M., Kruschwitz, U., Fox, C.: Creating language resources for under-resourced languages: methodologies, and experiments with Arabic. Lang. Resour. Eval. **49**(3), 549–580 (2015)
6. Fox, E.: Perspectives from affective science on understanding the nature of emotion. Brain Neurosci. Adv. **2**, 2398212818812628 (2018)
7. Gerrig, R.J., Banaji, M.R.: Chapter 8 - Language and Thought. In: Sternberg, R.J. (ed.) Thinking and Problem Solving, Handbook of Perception and Cognition, vol. 2, pp. 233–261. Academic Press, San Diego (1994). https://doi.org/10.1016/B978-0-08-057299-4.50014-1, https://www.sciencedirect.com/science/article/pii/B9780080572994500141
8. Goddard, C.: Anger in the western desert: a case study in the cross-cultural semantics of emotion. Man **26**(2), 265–279 (1991). http://www.jstor.org/stable/2803832
9. Hsu, C.T., Jacobs, A.M., Conrad, M.: Can Harry Potter still put a spell on us in a second language? An fMRI study on reading emotion-laden literature in late bilinguals. Cortex **63**, 282–295 (2015)

10. Jackson, J.C., et al.: Emotion semantics show both cultural variation and universal structure. Science **366**(6472), 1517–1522 (2019)
11. Ji, H., Ploux, S., Wehrli, E.: Lexical Knowledge Representation with Contexonyms. In: Proceedings of the 9th MT Summit (2003)
12. Ng, B.C., Susanto, Y., Cambria, E.: MICE: A crosslinguistic emotion corpus in Malay, Indonesian, Chinese and English (2021). https://api.semanticscholar.org/CorpusID:235377153
13. Panayiotou, A.: Switching codes, switching code: bilinguals' emotional responses in English and Greek. J. Multiling. Multicult. Dev. **25**(2–3), 124–139 (2004)
14. Pavlenko, A.: Emotions and Multilingualism. Cambridge Univeristy Press (2005)
15. Perlovsky, L.: Language and emotions: emotional sapir-whorf hypothesis. Neural Netw. **22**(5), 518–526 (2009)
16. Ploux, S., Ji, H.: A model for matching semantic maps between languages (French/English, English/French). Comput. Linguist. **29**(2), 155–178 (2003). https://doi.org/10.1162/089120103322145298
17. Wierzbicka, A.: The relevance of language to the study of emotions. Psychol. Inq. **6**(3), 248–252 (1995)
18. Zeng, M.: Knowledge organization systems (KOS) (2008)

Author Index

M. Sfakakis et al. (Eds.): MTSR 2024, CCIS 2331, pp. 363–365, 2025.
https://doi.org/10.1007/978-3-031-81974-2

The manufacturer's authorised representative in the EU is Springer
Nature Customer Service Centre GmbH, Europaplatz 3, 69115 Heidelberg,
Germany. If you have any concerns regarding our products, please
contact ProductSafety@springernature.com

Printed and bound by CPI Group (UK) Ltd, Croydon, CR0 4YY
06/05/2026
02104369-0002